INTERNATIONAL TRADE LAW

* Notes from Glob. class

↗ Poli Sci → int'l trade / Globalization
- Commerce
- Soci

Other books in *Essentials of Canadian Law* Series

Criminal Law
The Law of Evidence
Statutory Interpretation
Media Law
The Law of Trusts
Intellectual Property Law
Income Tax Law
The Law of Partnerships and Corporations
Constitutional Law
Immigration Law
Environmental Law
Young Offenders Law

ESSENTIALS OF
CANADIAN LAW

INTERNATIONAL TRADE LAW

JON R. JOHNSON

INTERNATIONAL TRADE LAW
© Publications for Professionals, 1998

All rights reserved. No part of this publication may be reproduced, stored in a retrieval system, or transmitted, in any form or by any means, without the prior written permission of the publisher or, in the case of photocopying or other reprographic copying, a licence from CANCOPY (Canadian Copyright Licensing Agency), 6 Adelaide Street East, Suite 900, Toronto, Ontario, M5C 1H6.

Published in 1998 by
Irwin Law
1800 Steeles Avenue West
Concord, Ontario
L4K 2P3

ISBN: 1-55221-027-8

Canadian Cataloguing in Publication Data

Johnson, Jon R. (Jon Ragnar), 1942-
   International trade law

(Essentials of Canadian law)
Includes bibliographical references and index.
ISBN 1-55221-027-8

1. Foreign trade regulation – Canada.
2. Canada – Commercial treaties. I. Title. II. Series.

KE1940.J63 1997   343.71'087   C97-932645-1
KF1976.J63 1997

Printed and bound in Canada.

1   2   3   4   5   01   00   99   98

SUMMARY TABLE OF CONTENTS

FOREWORD BY GORDON RITCHIE   xxvii

OVERVIEW: INTERNATIONAL TRADE LAW   1

CHAPTER 1: International Legal Structure   21

CHAPTER 2: Trade in Goods: Non-Discrimination and General Exceptions   52

CHAPTER 3: Tariffs and Related Border Measures   75

CHAPTER 4: Import and Export Restrictions and Related Border Measures   100

CHAPTER 5: The Origin of Goods   124

CHAPTER 6: Antidumping and Countervailing Duties, Subsidies, and Safeguards   146

CHAPTER 7: Undesigned Parallelism   170

CHAPTER 8: Investment, Services, and Other Matters   215

CHAPTER 9: Further Exceptions   261

CHAPTER 10: Institutional Structure, Dispute Resolution, and Conclusion   277

GLOSSARY OF TERMS   307

TABLE OF CASES   315

INDEX   319

DETAILED TABLE OF CONTENTS

FOREWORD BY GORDON RITCHIE   xxvii

OVERVIEW:
INTERNATIONAL TRADE LAW   1

A. **GATT: From Inception to the Tokyo Round**   2
B. **Beyond Trade in Goods: The Uruguay Round and the Free Trade Agreements**   3
C. **Extending the Disciplines of the International Trading System**   4
   1) Services   4
   2) Investment   5
   3) Movement of People   5
   4) Intellectual Property   5
   5) Environmental Issues   6
   6) Labour Issues   6
   7) Competition/Antitrust Laws   7
D. **Policy Instruments Subject to Discipline**   7
   1) Tariffs   8
   2) Quantitative Restrictions   8
   3) "Voluntary" Export Restraints   9
   4) Subsidies   9
   5) Special Trade Remedies   9
   6) Qualitative Restrictions   10
   7) Right of Establishment   10
   8) Performance Requirements   10

E. Rules-Based System versus Managed Trade   11
F. World Trade Organization: Institutional Structure for the World Trading System   12
G. Common Themes   13
   1) Non-Discrimination   13
   2) Reduction of Barriers   13
   3) Creation of Norms and Use of International Standards and Conventions   14
   4) Transparency and Procedural Fairness   14
   5) Exceptions and Reservations   15
      a) Exceptions   15
      b) Reservations: NAFTA and CCFTA   15
   6) Dispute Resolution   16
H. Effect of Trade Agreements on Canadian Law   17
   1) Treaties Not Self-Executing in Canada   17
   2) Effect on Provincial Laws   18
   3) Framework for Domestic Lawmakers   18
I. Purpose of the Book   19
J. Organization of the Book   20

CHAPTER 1:
INTERNATIONAL LEGAL STRUCTURE   21

A. The *WTO Agreement*   21
   1) Annex 1A: Multilateral Agreements on Trade in Goods   22
      a) GATT 1994   22
         i) Contents   22
         ii) Highlights   23
      b) Other Agreements in Annex 1A   24
         i) *Agreement on Agriculture*   24
         ii) *Agreement on Textiles and Clothing*   24
         iii) *Agreement on the Application of Sanitary and Phytosanitary Measures* and the *Agreement on Technical Barriers to Trade*   25
         iv) *Agreement on Trade-Related Investment Measures*   25
         v) *Agreement on Implementation of Article VI of the General Agreement on Tariffs and Trade 1994*   25
         vi) *Agreement on Implementation of Article VII of the General Agreement on Tariffs and Trade 1994*   25
         vii) *Agreement on Preshipment Inspection*   25

viii) *Agreement on Rules of Origin* 26
ix) *Agreement on Import Licensing Procedures* 26
x) *Agreement on Subsidies and Countervailing Measures* 26
xi) *Agreement on Safeguards* 26
c) Annex 1B: *General Agreement on Trade in Services* 26
d) Annex 1C: *Agreement on Trade-Related Aspects of Intellectual Property Rights* 27
e) Annex 2: *Understanding on Rules and Procedures Governing the Settlement of Disputes* 27
f) Annex 3: *Trade Policy Review Mechanism* 27
g) Annex 4: Plurilateral Agreements 27

B. **Permitted Preferential Arrangements: Customs Unions and Free Trade Areas** 28
1) Customs Unions and Free Trade Areas 28
   a) Customs Unions 28
   b) Free Trade Areas 29
2) Generalized System of Preferences and Other Permitted Preferential Arrangements 30

C. **NAFTA** 31
1) NAFTA Antecedents 31
2) Structure of NAFTA 32
3) GATT 1994 Plus: The NAFTA Trade-in-Goods Provisions 33
4) Undesigned Parallelism: Sanitary and Phytosanitary Measures, Technical Barriers, Government Procurement, and Intellectual Property 35
5) Beyond the WTO: Investment, Services, Financial Services 36
6) Further Exceptions 37
7) Transparency and Procedural Fairness 37
8) Dispute Resolution 37
   a) General Dispute Settlement Procedures: State to State 37
   b) Investor-State Dispute Settlement Procedures: Investor versus State 38

D. **Other Bilateral Trading Arrangements** 38
1) The *Canada–Israel Free Trade Agreement* (CIFTA) 38
2) The *Canada–Chile Free Trade Agreement* (CCFTA) 39

E. **Interpretation Issues** 40
1) Guides to Interpretation 40
   a) *Vienna Convention on the Law of Treaties* 41
   b) Panel and Appellate Body Reports 42
   c) Public International Law 43

2) Textual Analysis 44
   a) Scope and Coverage Provisions 44
   b) Preamble 44
   c) Tautological Provisions and the Principle of Effectiveness 44
   d) Provisions Incorporated by Reference 45
3) Inconsistencies within an Agreement: Which Provision Prevails? 46
4) Inconsistencies between Agreements: Which Agreement Prevails? 48
   a) Express Rules of Prevalence 48
   b) The *Vienna Convention* 48
   c) NAFTA Rules versus WTO Rules 50
5) International Agreements and Subregional Levels of Government: Are Provinces and States Bound? 50

CHAPTER 2:
TRADE IN GOODS: NON-DISCRIMINATION AND GENERAL EXCEPTIONS 52

A. **MFN Principle** 52

1) GATT 1994 52
   a) Article I of GATT 1994 52
   b) Significance of MFN Principle for Government Policy and Sectoral Arrangements 53
2) NAFTA, CIFTA, and CCFTA 54

B. **National Treatment** 54

1) Article III of GATT 1994 54
   a) Article III:1: No Protection to Domestic Production 55
   b) Article III:2: Internal Taxes and Charges 55
      i) First Sentence and "like products" 55
      ii) Second Sentence and "directly competitive or substitutable products" 57
   c) Article III:4: No Less Favourable Treatment 59
   d) Article III:8: Exceptions 60
2) NAFTA Rules 61
   a) NAFTA Article 301 61
   b) Goods of a Party 62
3) CIFTA and CCFTA Rules 62
4) Significance of National Treatment Obligations for Government Policy 63
5) Special Rules: Alcoholic Beverages 63
   a) CUFTA Chapter Eight: Trade in Wine and Distilled Spirits with the United States 64

  b) *EC Alcoholic Beverages Agreement*: Trade in Beer, Wine, and Distilled Spirits with the European Union 64
  c) *Beer Agreement*: Trade in Beer with the United States 65
  d) NAFTA Annex 312.2: Trade in Wine and Distilled Spirits with Mexico 65
  e) CIFTA and CCFTA 65

C. **General Exceptions** 65

 1) Article XX of GATT 1994 66
  a) Approach to Interpretation of Article XX Exceptions 66
   i) First Element: Policy Objective Falls within the Exception 68
   ii) Second Element: Inconsistent Measure Satisfies Qualifying Language of the Exception 69
   iii) Third Element: Inconsistent Measure Satisfies Introductory Clause of Article XX 71
  b) Scope of Exceptions in Article XX 73
 2) Incorporation of Article XX Exceptions into NAFTA, CIFTA, and CCFTA 73
 3) Use of Exceptions 74

CHAPTER 3:
TARIFFS AND RELATED BORDER MEASURES 75

A. **Harmonized System and Tariff Classification** 76

 1) The Harmonized System 76
 2) Tariff Classification 77

B. **Canadian Customs Laws** 78

 1) *Customs Tariff* 78
 2) *Customs Act* 79

C. **Tariff Treatments under Canadian Customs Law** 80

 1) MFN Tariff 80
 2) General Preferential Tariff and Least Developed Developing Country Tariff 80
 3) British Preferential Tariff and Goods of New Zealand and Australia 81
 4) Commonwealth Caribbean Countries Tariff 81
 5) NAFTA Tariffs 81
  a) United States Tariff 82
  b) Mexico Tariff 82
  c) Mexico–United States Tariff 82
 6) *Israel Tariff* 82

7) Chile Tariff   82
8) General Tariff   82

D. **Tariff Bindings and Tariff Reduction under GATT 1994**   83
   1) Article II of GATT 1994   83
   2) Tariff Reduction Resulting from the Uruguay Round   84

E. **Tariff Elimination under NAFTA, CIFTA, and CCFTA**   85
   1) Tariff Elimination under NAFTA   85
   2) Tariff Elimination under CIFTA   86
   3) Tariff Elimination under CCFTA   86

F. **Valuation**   87
   1) Transaction Value as the Customs Value   87
   2) The Other Methods of Calculating Customs Value   88

G. **Duty Relief Programs**   89
   1) Duty Relief and the WTO Agreements   90
   2) Duty Drawback, Duty Deferral, and NAFTA Rules   90
      a) Duty Drawback and Duty Deferral   90
      b) NAFTA Restrictions and Prohibitions   91
      c) NAFTA Exceptions   92
   3) NAFTA Rules Respecting Duty Waivers   93
      a) Duty Waivers Based on Performance Requirements   93
      b) Other Duty Waivers   93
   4) Canadian Programs: General   93
      a) *Customs Tariff*   93
      b) Company-Specific Duty Remission   94
   5) Canadian Programs: Specific Sectors   94
      a) Automotive Duty Remission   94
         i) The *Auto Pact* and *Auto Pact* Remission Orders   94
         ii) Other Automotive Duty Remission Programs   96
         iii) Other CUFTA/NAFTA Provisions Respecting Automotive Goods   97
      b) Textiles   97
         i) Textile Duty Remission Program   97
         ii) Textile Reference Guidelines   98

H. **Other NAFTA Provisions Respecting Tariffs and Related Border Measures**   98

I. **CIFTA and CCFTA Rules Respecting Duty Relief and Other Border Measures**   99

CHAPTER 4:
IMPORT AND EXPORT RESTRICTIONS AND RELATED BORDER MEASURES   100

A. Article XI of GATT 1994   101

B. Incorporation of Article XI of GATT 1994 into NAFTA, CIFTA, and CCFTA   102

C. Minimum Import and Export Prices under NAFTA, CIFTA, and CCFTA   102

D. Import and Export Restrictions under NAFTA, CIFTA, and CCFTA   102

E. Exceptions under NAFTA, CIFTA, and CCFTA   103

F. Prohibition of Export Taxes under NAFTA, CIFTA, and CCFTA   104

G. NAFTA and CCFTA Disciplines Respecting Export Restrictions   104

   1) The Disciplines   105
      a) Proportionality   105
      b) Pricing   106
      c) Normal Channels of Supply   106
   2) Application to Energy Goods: NAFTA   106

H. Special Cases: Agriculture and Textiles and Apparel   107

   1) Agricultural Goods   107
      a) Supply Management Programs   107
      b) The *Agriculture Agreement*: Tariffication and Safeguards   108
      c) Provisions of NAFTA Respecting Import and Export Restrictions   110
         i) Canada and the United States   110
         ii) Canada and the United States: The Supply Management Decision   111
         iii) The United States and Mexico   114
         iv) Canada and Mexico   114
         v) Special Safeguards   114
   2) Textile and Apparel Goods   115
      a) The *Multifibre Arrangement* and Bilateral Restraint Agreements   115
      b) The *Textile Agreement*   116
      c) Provisions of NAFTA and CCFTA   117
         i) Import and Export Restrictions: NAFTA   117
         ii) Tariff Preference Levels: NAFTA   117
         iii) Tariff Preference Levels: CCFTA   119

I. Canadian Law on Import and Export Restrictions   119
   1) The *Export and Import Permits Act*   120
      a) Export Controls   120
         i) General Rules   120
         ii) Softwood Lumber   120
      b) Import Controls   121
   2) Prohibited Goods   122
   3) Other Import Prohibitions   123

CHAPTER 5:
THE ORIGIN OF GOODS   124

A. Preferential Rules of Origin   126
   1) NAFTA, CIFTA, and CCFTA Rules of Origin   126
      a) Why Rules of Origin Are Necessary in a Free Trade Area   126
      b) Member Countries Interchangeable   127
      c) Basic Terminology   127
      d) Establishing that Goods Are Originating under NAFTA, CIFTA, and CCFTA   128
      e) Wholly Originating Goods   129
      f) Specific Rules of Origin   129
      g) Change in Tariff Classification or Tariff Shift   130
      h) When a Change in Tariff Classification Cannot Occur   131
      i) The *De Minimis* Rule   132
      j) The NAFTA and CCFTA Value-Content Requirement   133
         i) Transaction Value Method and Net Cost Method   133
         ii) Use of the Valuation Agreement   134
         iii) Transaction Value   134
         iv) Net Cost   134
         v) Value of Non-Originating Materials (VNM)   135
         vi) Value of Non-Originating Materials (VNM): Automotive Goods under NAFTA   136
         vii) Averaging   137
      k) Fungible Goods and Materials   137
      l) Accumulation   137
      m) CIFTA Rules and Free Trade Arrangements with the United States   137
         i) Certain Originating Goods   137
         ii) Special Transshipment Rule   138
      n) CCFTA Rules and Chilean Accession to NAFTA   138

2) Rules of Origin for Canada's Autonomous Trade Regimes   138
3) *Rules of Origin Agreement*   138
4) Establishing Originating Status   139
   a) NAFTA, CIFTA, and CCFTA   139
   b) General Preferential Tariff and Least Developed Developing Country Tariff   139
5) Observations   139

B. **Non-Preferential Rules of Origin**   140

1) GATT 1994 and *Rules of Origin Agreement*   140
   a) GATT 1994 and Country-of-Origin Marking   140
   b) The *Rules of Origin Agreement*   141
2) Non-Preferential Rules of Origin under NAFTA   142
   a) The Marking Rules   142
      i) Negotiation of the Marking Rules   142
      ii) Hierarchy of Rules and NAFTA Override   142
   b) Country-of-Origin Marking   143
      i) NAFTA Rules   143
      ii) Canadian Marking Requirements   144
   c) Country of Origin for NAFTA Tariff Preference Purposes   144
   d) Qualifying Goods   145
   e) Other Country-of-Origin Issues under NAFTA   145

CHAPTER 6:
ANTIDUMPING AND COUNTERVAILING DUTIES, SUBSIDIES, AND SAFEGUARDS   146

A. **Antidumping and Countervailing Duties, Subsidies Disciplines**   147

1) Article VI of GATT 1994   148
   a) Antidumping Duties   148
   b) Countervailing Duties   148
   c) Material Injury Requirement   148
2) Antidumping Duties and the *Antidumping Agreement*   148
3) The *Subsidies Agreement*   149
   a) Subsidies Disciplines   150
      i) Definition of Subsidy and "Specific" Subsidies   150
      ii) Prohibited Subsidies   150
      iii) Actionable and Non-Actionable Subsidies   151
   b) Countervailing Duty Actions   151
      i) Subsidies to Which Part V Applies   151
      ii) Procedural Requirements   152

4) Subsidies Disciplines and Agricultural Goods   *152*
   a) GATT Article XVI and Primary Products   *152*
   b) The *Agriculture Agreement*   *153*
      i) Export Subsidies   *153*
      ii) Domestic Support Programs   *153*
   c) NAFTA: Subsidy Disciplines on Agricultural Goods   *154*
      i) General NAFTA Obligations   *154*
      ii) Canada and the United States   *154*
   d) CCFTA: Export Subsidies on Agricultural Goods   *155*
5) Provisions of NAFTA Respecting Antidumping and Countervailing Duty Matters   *155*
   a) Antidumping and Countervailing Duty Procedures in NAFTA Countries   *155*
      i) Canada and the United States   *155*
      ii) Mexico   *156*
   b) Retention of Laws   *156*
      i) Minimal Norms   *157*
      ii) Panel Review   *157*
   c) Panel Review of Final Determinations   *158*
      i) Final Determinations Subject to Panel Review   *158*
      ii) Formation of Panels   *160*
      iii) Panel Review   *160*
      iv) Extraordinary Challenge   *162*
   d) Safeguarding the Panel Process   *162*
   e) Concluding Remarks   *163*
6) Provisions of CIFTA Respecting Antidumping and Countervailing Duty Matters   *163*
7) Provisions of CCFTA Respecting Antidumping and Countervailing Duty Matters   *163*

B. Safeguard (Emergency) Actions   *164*
   1) Article XIX of GATT 1994   *164*
   2) The *Safeguards Agreement*   *165*
   3) NAFTA and CCFTA Safeguard Provisions   *166*
      a) Global Actions   *166*
      b) Bilateral Actions: Goods Other Than Textile and Apparel Goods   *166*
      c) Bilateral Actions: Textile and Apparel Goods   *168*
         i) Tariff Actions   *168*
         ii) Quantitative Restrictions   *169*
      d) Procedural Requirements   *169*
   4) Provisions of CIFTA   *169*

CHAPTER 7:
UNDESIGNED PARALLELISM *170*

A. **Sanitary and Phytosanitary Measures and Technical Barriers to Trade** *171*
  1) Definition of a Sanitary and Phytosanitary Measure *172*
  2) Definitions of Technical Regulation, Standard, and Conformity Assessment Procedure *173*
     a) Technical Regulation *174*
     b) Standard *174*
     c) Conformity Assessment Procedure *174*
  3) Common Themes *174*
  4) Scope and Coverage *175*
     a) Sanitary and Phytosanitary Measures *175*
     b) Technical Barriers to Trade *176*
  5) Application to Provincial and State Laws and to Non-Governmental Organizations *176*
     a) Sanitary and Phytosanitary Measures *176*
     b) Technical Barriers to Trade *177*
  6) Right to Adopt *177*
     a) Sanitary and Phytosanitary Measures *177*
     b) Technical Barriers to Trade *177*
  7) Risk Assessment *178*
     a) Sanitary and Phytosanitary Measures *178*
     b) Technical Barriers to Trade *178*
  8) Level of Protection and Use of International Standards *178*
     a) Sanitary and Phytosanitary Measures *178*
     b) Technical Barriers to Trade *179*
  9) Non-Discrimination *180*
     a) Sanitary and Phytosanitary Measures *180*
     b) Technical Barriers to Trade *181*
  10) No Obstacles to Trade *181*
     a) Sanitary and Phytosanitary Measures *181*
     b) Technical Barriers to Trade *181*
  11) Procedural Fairness: Conformity Assessment *182*
     a) Sanitary and Phytosanitary Measures *182*
     b) Technical Barriers to Trade *182*
  12) Transparency *183*
     a) Sanitary and Phytosanitary Measures *183*
     b) Technical Barriers to Trade *183*
  13) Application of Exceptions in Article XX of GATT 1994 *184*

xviii   INTERNATIONAL TRADE LAW

    14) Environmental Issues   *184*
    15) Labour Issues   *185*

B. **Intellectual Property**   *186*
    1) Scope and Coverage   *187*
    2) Use of International Conventions   *187*
        a) *Paris Convention*   *188*
        b) *Berne Convention*   *189*
        c) *Geneva Convention* and the *Rome Convention*   *189*
        d) *UPOV Convention 1978* and *UPOV Convention 1991*   *190*
        e) *Integrated Circuits Treaty*   *190*
    3) Extension of Protection to "Nationals"   *190*
    4) Establishment of Norms: General Provisions   *191*
        a) Principles of Non-Discrimination   *191*
            i) National Treatment   *191*
            ii) Most-Favoured-Nation Treatment   *192*
        b) Control of Abusive or Anticompetitive Practices   *192*
    5) Establishment of Norms: Requirements Respecting Specific Categories of Intellectual Property   *192*
        a) Copyright   *192*
        b) Sound Recordings   *193*
        c) Trademarks   *194*
        d) Geographical Indications   *195*
        e) Industrial Designs   *195*
        f) Patents   *195*
        g) Layout Designs of Integrated Circuits   *197*
        h) Protection of Undisclosed Information (*TRIPS Agreement*) or Trade Secrets (NAFTA)   *197*
        i) Encrypted Program-Carrying Satellite Signals   *198*
    6) Exceptions to the Norms   *198*
        a) General Exceptions   *198*
            i) *TRIPS Agreement*   *198*
            ii) NAFTA   *199*
        b) Limited Exceptions in the *TRIPS Agreement* and NAFTA for Trademarks, Patents, and Industrial Designs   *199*
    7) Procedural Fairness: Enforcement of Intellectual Property Rights   *200*
    8) Dispute Resolution   *201*
    9) Transitional Provisions   *201*

C. **Government Procurement** 202
   1) Common Themes 203
   2) Scope and Coverage 204
      a) Specified Government Departments and Enterprises 204
         i) Central (Federal) Government Entities 204
         ii) Subcentral (Provincial and State) Government Entities 205
         iii) Other Enterprises 205
      b) Specified Goods 206
         i) Government Procurement Agreement 206
         ii) NAFTA 206
      c) Specified Services 206
         i) Government Procurement Agreement 206
         ii) NAFTA 207
      d) Specified Construction Services 207
         i) Government Procurement Agreement 207
         ii) NAFTA 207
      e) General Notes (Exclusions) 208
         i) Government Procurement Agreement 208
         ii) NAFTA 208
      f) Above Specified Monetary Thresholds 208
         i) Government Procurement Agreement 208
         ii) NAFTA 209
         iii) Valuation of Contracts 209
      g) Denial of Benefits under NAFTA 209
   3) Non-Discrimination 210
      a) Non-Discrimination Obligations 210
      b) Rules of Origin 210
   4) Creation of Norms 211
      a) Technical Specifications 211
      b) Tendering Procedures 211
      c) Prohibition of Offsets 212
   5) Transparency and Procedural Fairness 212
      a) Transparency 212
      b) Procedural Fairness: Bid Challenge Procedures 213
   6) Other Provisions 213
      a) Exceptions 213
      b) NAFTA and Privatization 214

CHAPTER 8:
INVESTMENT, SERVICES, AND OTHER MATTERS 215

A. Common Themes 215
  1) Non-Discrimination 215
  2) Creation of Norms 216
  3) Transparency 216
  4) Limitation of Scope through Exceptions and Reservations 216
B. Investment 216
  1) Scope and Coverage: NAFTA and CCFTA 216
     a) Investor of a Party 217
     b) Investment 218
     c) Exclusion of Financial Institutions 218
     d) Application to Provinces and States 219
  2) Non-Discrimination: NAFTA and CCFTA 219
     a) National Treatment 219
     b) MFN Treatment 219
  3) Creation of Norms: NAFTA, CCFTA, and TRIMs 220
     a) Minimum Standard of Treatment 220
     b) Performance Requirements 220
        i) NAFTA and CCFTA 220
        ii) TRIMs Agreement 222
     c) Senior Management and Boards of Directors 223
     d) Transfers 223
     e) Expropriation and Compensation 223
     f) Environmental Matters 225
  4) Exceptions: NAFTA and CCFTA 225
C. Services Provisions: NAFTA and CCFTA 226
  1) Scope and Coverage 226
     a) Services Covered 226
     b) Cross-Border Provision of a Service 226
     c) Service Provider of a Party 227
     d) Application to Provinces and States 227
  2) Non-Discrimination 227
     a) National Treatment 227
     b) MFN Treatment 227
  3) Local Presence 228
  4) Licensing and Certification Procedures 228
  5) Quantitative Restrictions and Liberalization Commitments 228
  6) Exceptions 228

D. Reservations Respecting NAFTA and CCFTA Investment
   and Services Obligations   229
   1) Reservations Respecting Existing Non-Conforming Measures
      at the Federal (National) Level   229
      a) Annex I Reservations: NAFTA and CCFTA   230
         i)   Schedule of Canada (NAFTA and CCFTA)   230
         ii) Schedule of Mexico (NAFTA)   231
         iii) Schedule of the United States (NAFTA)   232
         iv) Schedule of Chile (CCFTA)   232
      b) Annex III Reservations: NAFTA   233
   2) Reservations Respecting Existing Non-Conforming Measures
      at the Provincial, State, and Local Level   233
   3) Sectoral Reservations under NAFTA and CCFTA Annex II   234
      a) Social Services   234
      b) Other Annex II Reservations   235
   4) Reservations Respecting MFN Treatment: NAFTA Annex IV
      and CCFTA Annex III   235

E. Services: *General Agreement on Trade in Services*   236
   1) Scope and Coverage   236
      a) Service Supplier and Related Definitions   236
      b) Trade in Services   236
      c) Application to Regional and Local Governments   237
   2) General Obligations   237
      a) Non-Discrimination: MFN Obligation   237
      b) Transparency and Procedural Fairness   237
      c) Recognition of Education, Experience   238
      d) Subsidies   238
   3) Reduction of Barriers: Specific Commitments   238
   4) Exceptions and Qualifications   239
      a) General Exceptions   239
      b) National Security and Balance of Payments   239
      c) Government Procurement   240
      d) Economic Integration   240
   5) Sectoral Annexes   240
      a) Annex on Air Transport Services   240
      b) Annex on Negotiations on Maritime Transport Services   241

F. Telecommunications   241
   1) NAFTA and CCFTA   241
      a) NAFTA Chapter Thirteen and CCFTA Chapter I   241

xxii INTERNATIONAL TRADE LAW

    b) NAFTA Chapters Eleven and Twelve and CCFTA Chapters G and H 242
  2) GATS Annex on Telecommunications 243
G. **Financial Services** 244
  1) NAFTA Chapter Fourteen 244
    a) Scope and Coverage 244
      i) Financial Institutions 244
      ii) Financial Services 245
      iii) Denial of Benefits 246
      iv) Provinces and States 246
    b) Non-Discrimination 246
      i) National Treatment: Financial Institutions 246
      ii) Prospective Rules Respecting Establishment of Financial Institutions 246
      iii) National Treatment: Cross-Border Trade in Financial Services 247
      iv) Application to Provinces and States 248
      v) Equal Competitive Opportunities 248
      vi) Most-Favoured-Nation Treatment 248
    c) Creation of Norms 249
      i) Provisions Incorporated from Other NAFTA Chapters 249
      ii) Preservation of Concessions under CUFTA 249
      iii) New Financial Services and Data Processing 250
      iv) Senior Management and Boards of Directors 250
    d) Transparency 250
    e) Exceptions 250
    f) Reservations and Specific Commitments 250
      i) Section A Reservations 251
      ii) Section B Reservations and Section C Commitments 251
  2) GATS Annexes on Financial Services 252
H. **Temporary Entry** 253
  1) NAFTA Chapter Sixteen and CCFTA Chapter K: Creation of Norms 253
  2) GATS Natural Persons Annex 254
I. **Monopolies and State Enterprises** 254
  1) Common Themes 255
    a) Right to Designate 255
    b) Non-Discrimination 255

c) Commercial Considerations   255
d) Anticompetitive Practices   255
e) Regulatory Authority   255
2) WTO Agreements   256
 a) Provisions of GATT 1994   256
 b) GATS Article VIII   256
3) NAFTA, CIFTA, and CCFTA   257
 a) Monopolies   257
  i) Right to Designate   257
  ii) Requirements   257
 b) State Enterprises   259
  i) Right to Designate   259
  ii) Requirements   259

J. **Competition Law**   260

1) WTO Agreements   260
2) NAFTA, CIFTA, and CCFTA   260

CHAPTER 9:
FURTHER EXCEPTIONS   261

A. **National Security**   261

B. **Balance of Payments**   263

1) Common Themes   263
2) *IMF Agreement*   264
3) Article XII of GATT 1994   264
4) GATS   265
5) NAFTA and CCFTA   265

C. **Cultural Industries**   266

1) Canadian Cultural Policies   266
2) WTO Agreements   268
3) NAFTA, CIFTA, and CCFTA   269
 a) Cultural Industries Defined   269
 b) CIFTA and CCFTA   270
 c) NAFTA   270
  i) CUFTA Article 2005   271
  ii) Exceptions to CUFTA Article 2005   273
  iii) Concluding Remarks   273

D. Taxation Measures   273
  1) GATS Exception for Taxation Measures   274
  2) NAFTA, CIFTA, and CCFTA Exceptions for Taxation Measures   274
E. Disclosure of Information   276

CHAPTER 10:
INSTITUTIONAL STRUCTURE, DISPUTE RESOLUTION, AND CONCLUSION   277

A. Institutional Structure   277
  1) *WTO Agreement*   277
     a) Structure   278
     b) Decisions   279
     c) Amendments   279
     d) Accession   280
  2) NAFTA, CIFTA, and CCFTA   281
     a) Commission   281
     b) Secretariat: NAFTA and CCFTA   281
     c) Committees and Working Groups   282
     d) Amendments   282
     e) Accession   282
        i) NAFTA   282
        ii) CIFTA and CCFTA   282
B. General Dispute Resolution Procedures   283
  1) Common Themes   283
  2) Dispute Resolution under the WTO Agreements   284
     a) Articles XXII and XXIII of GATT 1994   284
        i) Application of Articles XXII and XXIII of GATT 1994 to Other WTO Agreements   285
        ii) Non-Violation Nullification and Impairment under Article XXIII of GATT 1994   286
     b) The *Dispute Settlement Understanding*   287
        i)   Consultations   287
        ii) The Panel Process   288
        iii) Appeals   288
        iv) Implementation of Recommendations, Compensation, and Suspension of Concessions   288
     c) The *Government Procurement Agreement*   289

3) Dispute Resolution under NAFTA, CIFTA, and CCFTA   *289*
   a) Scope of Procedures   *290*
   b) Non-Violation Nullification and Impairment   *290*
   c) Dispute Resolution Process   *291*
      i) Consultations   *291*
      ii) Request for Meeting of the Commission   *291*
      iii) Panels   *292*
      iv) Panel Proceedings   *293*
      v) Implementation and Suspension of Benefits   *293*
      vi) Special Situations   *294*
4) Which Procedures Apply?   *294*
   a) NAFTA and CCFTA   *295*
   b) CIFTA   *296*
5) Concluding Remarks   *296*

C. **Investor-State Dispute Settlement Procedures: NAFTA and CCFTA**   *296*
   1) Provisions That Could Give Rise to Claims   *297*
   2) Standing to Submit a Claim   *298*
   3) Invoking the Procedures   *299*
   4) Submitting the Claim to Arbitration   *300*
      a) The Choices   *300*
      b) Constraints on Choice   *300*
      c) The Arbitration Procedures   *300*
      d) Conditions to Submitting a Claim   *301*
      e) Arbitral Tribunals and Consolidation   *302*
      f) Procedure   *302*
      g) Awards   *303*
   5) Concluding Remarks   *304*

D. **Conclusion**   *305*

GLOSSARY OF TERMS   *307*

TABLE OF CASES   *315*

INDEX   *319*

To Ragnar, Jón, and Patrick

FOREWORD

Over the past half century, Canadians have played a crucial role in the construction of a rules-based trading system. The basic foundation was established by the original *General Agreement on Tariffs and Trade* concluded in Geneva in 1947. A series of GATT negotiations followed over the next forty years, culminating in the Tokyo Round. Then, on Canada's initiative, the important next step was taken to create the World Trade Organization — the central institution of the international trading system today.

Meanwhile, Canadians had found we could move further and faster in certain matters on a bilateral basis with our neighbour, the world's most dynamic and open economy, the United States. Agreements on defence products, petroleum, and farm machinery were succeeded, in 1965, by the *Canada–U.S. Auto Pact*, the most substantial sectoral agreement ever negotiated. After a number of abortive attempts to negotiate further sectoral arrangements, Canada reached a comprehensive free trade agreement with the United States in 1987. This was extended to Mexico under the *North American Free Trade Agreement*, which entered into force in 1994. Bilateral free trade agreements were also reached with Israel and with Chile.

A handful of Canadians played a central role in the great enterprise of putting these agreements in place, including Simon Reisman, whose career spanned membership on the Canadian delegation at the founding meeting of the GATT in 1947 through to service as Canada's chief negotiator for the *Canada–U.S. Free Trade Agreement* in 1987; A. Edgar Ritchie, who attended the 1947 meetings as an officer of the United Nations secretariat, worked on the Auto Pact, and then served as Canada's ambassador to the United States; and Jake H. Warren, Canada's deputy minister of trade for many years, ambassador to the United States, and chief Canadian negotiator for the Tokyo Round. There is perhaps no other field in which Canadians have been so influential in shaping global institutions as in the building of the postwar trading system.

Lacking the sheer power of the United States, Europe, or Japan, Canada must rely on greater skill based on a more informed awareness of the rules of the international trade game. Having invested half a century in constructing a rules-based system in which a medium-sized economy stands a fighting chance against the economic superpowers, Canadians must show equal genius in using those rules to advantage.

Each of these agreements would merit its own detailed analysis. Indeed, Jon Johnson collaborated with Joel Schachter in writing *The Free Trade Agreement: A Comprehensive Guide* to do just that for the original *Canada–U.S. Free Trade Agreement*. Too often, attempts to understand individual elements of this complex system founder on the failure to grasp the intricate interconnections among the components of the various agreements; therein lies the strength of Johnson's *International Trade Law* for he maps precisely these linkages to provide a much clearer understanding of the context within which international trade law must operate.

Jon Johnson is well equipped for this ambitious task. He has played the game in many different roles: as a member of the Canadian negotiating team for the *Canada–U.S. Free Trade Agreement*, as co-author of the authoritative work on the FTA, and as a practising trade lawyer. I believe he succeeds in pulling the strands together to weave a complete account of the rules that govern our trade. *International Trade Law* should prove a valuable weapon in the arsenal of Canada's international trade warriors as they do battle in the arena of global commerce.

Gordon Ritchie
Chief Executive, Strategico Inc.
Former ambassador for trade negotiations
and deputy chief trade negotiator for Canada

OVERVIEW: INTERNATIONAL TRADE LAW

International trade law is the body of law that has evolved under the postwar international trading system first established by the *General Agreement on Tariffs and Trade* (GATT) that came into effect on 1 January 1948. The purpose of the GATT was to prevent a recurrence of the collapse of international trade that occurred during the period between the First and Second World Wars. This period was characterized by high tariffs and retaliatory trade measures unilaterally imposed by trading countries that devastated world trade and contributed significantly to the Great Depression of the 1930s. When the consequences of the tariffs imposed by the disastrous U.S. *Tariff Act of 1930* became apparent, the United States endeavoured to reduce trade barriers with its trading partners, including Canada, through bilateral trade agreements. Following the Second World War, trading nations recognized that the only effective means of creating a stable and predictable international trading system was through a multilateral structure of rules. Each participant submitted to a common set of disciplines that restricted its ability to act unilaterally to the detriment of its trading partners.

The GATT established fundamental principles of non-discrimination recognized by all member countries, and it prohibited unilateral tariff action by binding all member countries to maximum tariff levels on most goods. The GATT provided the means for the progressive reduction of tariff barriers through periodic multilateral negotiations. Subject to exceptions, the GATT prohibited import and export restrictions. The GATT also introduced disciplines on the unilateral application of extraordinary trade remedies such as antidumping and countervailing duties as well as emergency actions taken against import surges.

A. GATT: FROM INCEPTION TO THE TOKYO ROUND

The GATT entered into effect on a provisional basis on 1 January 1948 with twenty-three signatories including Canada. The GATT was in effect provisionally pending the establishment of the International Trade Organization, a supranational body that was to have been the third pillar of the postwar world order along with the International Monetary Fund and the World Bank. Negotiations for the creation of the International Trade Organization were completed in Havana in 1952, but the U.S. Congress refused to approve the implementing legislation and the International Trade Organization was never established. The GATT continued in effect without a formal institutional structure until the establishment of the World Trade Organization (WTO) under the *Agreement Creating the World Trade Organization* (*WTO Agreement*) in 1995.

The GATT member countries engaged in successive rounds of negotiations throughout the 1950s and 1960s.[1] The objective of these negotiating rounds was the reduction of tariffs, and the result was a dramatic reduction in tariffs among the GATT member countries during this period. For example, the 1964/67 Kennedy Round, which involved seventy-two countries and the European Economic Community (now the European Union), resulted in a 35 percent average tariff cut for 60,000 industrial products.[2] As tariffs fell, non-tariff barriers to trade became of more concern than previously. These included discriminatory application of product standards, discriminatory government procurement practices, and increasingly aggressive use of trade remedies such as antidumping and countervailing duties. As a result, the Tokyo Round, which began in 1974 and ended in 1979, was the first serious attempt by the GATT contracting parties to address the question of non-tariff barriers,[3] and the result was the establishment of codes (Tokyo

---

1   1947 Geneva Round, 1949 Annecy Round, 1950/51 Torquay Round, 1955/56 Geneva Round, 1960/61 Dillon Round, 1964/67 Kennedy Round.
2   E.-U. Petersmann, "The Transformation of the World Trading System through the 1994 Agreement Establishing the World Trade Organization" (1995) 6 E.J.I.L. 161 at 181. The chart presented on this page sets out a useful summary of all the *General Agreement on Tariffs and Trade*, 30 October 1947, Can. T.S. 1947 No. 29 negotiating rounds.
3   The 1964/67 Kennedy Round had resulted in an Antidumping Code.

Round codes) covering such matters as technical barriers to trade, valuation of goods for duty purposes, government procurement, anti-dumping duties, and subsidies.[4]

During this period of time, GATT membership grew dramatically. From the original twenty-three countries in 1948, GATT membership had grown to eighty-five countries by the time that the Tokyo Round concluded.

B. BEYOND TRADE IN GOODS: THE URUGUAY ROUND AND THE FREE TRADE AGREEMENTS

GATT disciplines covered trade in goods only and did not extend into other areas. The Uruguay Round of GATT negotiations was initiated in 1986 with an ambitious agenda that included not only the resolution of some major unresolved trade-in-goods issues (particularly those relating to the trade in agricultural goods and textiles and apparel) but also the extension of GATT disciplines to services, investment, and intellectual property. The Uruguay Round negotiations were substantially completed by 1991 but final resolution was delayed for another two years while negotiators endeavoured to resolve intractable agricultural issues.

While the Uruguay Round negotiations were continuing, Canada concluded the *Canada–U.S. Free Trade Agreement* (CUFTA) with the United States on 1 January 1989. CUFTA was in part a trade-in-goods arrangement that created a free trade area,[5] tightened up GATT disciplines, elaborated upon Tokyo Round codes respecting standards and government procurement, and established new procedures for anti-dumping and countervailing duty actions. However, CUFTA provisions extended beyond trade in goods into investment, services, and the temporary movement of business persons. The successor agreement to CUFTA, the *North American Free Trade Agreement* (NAFTA), became effective on 1 January 1994 and created a free trade area composed of Canada, the United States, and Mexico. NAFTA expanded upon the CUFTA goods, investment, and services obligations, trilateralized the rules respecting the temporary entry of business persons and, based on Uruguay Round precedents available during the time of its negotiation, included an entirely new chapter on intellectual property. NAFTA also set out tentative provisions respecting competition law, and two

---

4   There were also codes covering civil aircraft, bovine meat, and dairy products. The codes were not automatically binding on GATT contracting parties.
5   Free trade areas and customs unions are discussed in chapter 1.

NAFTA side agreements, the *North American Agreement on Environmental Cooperation* (*Environmental Cooperation Agreement*) and the *North American Agreement on Labour Cooperation* (*Labour Cooperation Agreement*) create obligations affecting environmental law and labour law.

The Uruguay Round negotiations concluded in 1994 and the resulting *WTO Agreement*, which was adopted by 124 countries,[6] became effective on 1 January 1995. The original GATT (GATT 1947) was carried forward, with some additions and modifications, in Annex 1A to the *WTO Agreement* as the *General Agreement on Tariffs and Trade 1994* (GATT 1994). The annexes to the *WTO Agreement* also contain other agreements respecting various aspects of trade in goods, standards, and government procurement, some of which are based on Tokyo Round predecessors and some of which are new. Annexes 1B and 1C of the *WTO Agreement* set out entirely new agreements on services, investment, and intellectual property.

Since the *WTO Agreement* came into effect, Canada has entered into the *Canada–Israel Free Trade Agreement* (CIFTA) with Israel and the *Canada–Chile Free Trade Agreement* (CCFTA) with Chile, each of which creates a new free trade area. CIFTA covers trade in goods only, while CCFTA includes chapters on services, investment, and temporary entry that are based on their NAFTA counterparts.

C. EXTENDING THE DISCIPLINES OF THE INTERNATIONAL TRADING SYSTEM

There are a variety of reasons why the disciplines of the international trading system have extended beyond the trade in goods.

1) Services

Services can be traded just as goods can be traded, and the services sectors of developed countries have expanded exponentially since the original GATT was negotiated in 1947. The same economic arguments for removing trade barriers to trade in goods apply to services. The *General Agreement on Trade in Services* (GATS) that resulted from the Uruguay Round of negotiations, as well as NAFTA and CCFTA, set out comprehensive rules covering trade in services.

---

6   Petersmann, above note 2 at 189.

2) Investment

While not involving "trade" as such, direct foreign investment does involve the movement of capital from one country to another and has a powerful indirect effect on the trade in both goods and services. The NAFTA and CCFTA investment chapters set out comprehensive bodies of rules governing direct foreign investment. The Uruguay Round negotiators made tentative steps into the area of investment by concluding the *Agreement Respecting Trade-Related Investment Measures,* which imposes disciplines respecting performance requirements.

3) Movement of People

The free movement of business people is a necessary corollary to disciplines respecting services and investment. A supplier of cross-border services cannot provide these services if its service providers cannot cross borders. Investors cannot invest in foreign countries unless they or their employees can cross borders to supervise their foreign investments. NAFTA and CCFTA each set out comprehensive requirements respecting the temporary entry of business persons. One of the GATS' annexes contemplates the negotiation of specific commitments among member countries respecting the movement of natural persons who are service suppliers.

4) Intellectual Property

Intellectual property is unique among the areas into which trade agreements have expanded. Unlike the other areas mentioned above, for many years there have been multilateral conventions that set out international obligations respecting intellectual property rights. Since 1970 the World Intellectual Property Organization (WIPO) has supervised the administration of various intellectual property conventions. Nonetheless, the negotiation of an intellectual property agreement was high on the Uruguay Round agenda, and the result was the inclusion in the annexes of the *WTO Agreement* of the *Agreement on Trade-Related Aspects of Intellectual Property Rights (TRIPS Agreement).* NAFTA also contains a chapter on intellectual property rights that parallels the *TRIPS Agreement.* There are some clear linkages between trade in goods and services and direct foreign investment on the one hand and the protection of intellectual property rights on the other. It is reasonable to expect that intellectual property rights such as trademarks associated with goods and services to which market access obligations apply be protected in importing countries. The value of direct foreign investment should not be undermined by failure of host countries to protect intellectual property rights such as patents that are licensed to or developed by the investment. However, the principal impetus behind including the protection of intellectual property rights in both the *TRIPS Agreement* and NAFTA was the perception among developed countries (including Canada) that enforcement mechanisms in the existing intellectual property conventions were ineffectual; bringing the protection of intellectual property rights within the ambit of these trade agreements would afford more effective enforcement.

5) Environmental Issues

Environmental issues are also becoming increasingly intertwined with trade matters. The linkages between trade disciplines and measures necessary to protect the environment are obvious. Protection of the environment necessitates prohibiting or rigorously controlling the trade in hazardous products or products made from endangered species. Measures to protect the environment frequently take the form of product standards that are subject to disciplines in trade agreements. Lax enforcement of environmental laws can create an unfair trade advantage by allowing products to be produced through the use of cheaper but environmentally unacceptable processes. Concerns with Mexico raised by U.S. environmentalists during the NAFTA approval process resulted in the three NAFTA countries entering into the *Environmental Cooperation Agreement*. While WTO obligations affect environmental measures, none of the agreements resulting from the Uruguay Round is specifically directed at environmental issues. However the *Decision on Trade and Environment* made at Marrakesh at the time of the signing of the *WTO Agreement* established a Committee on Trade and Environment that is to address various issues relating to trade and environmental measures.

6) Labour Issues

Social activists have also raised concerns about the effect of the disciplines imposed by trade agreements (which impose limitations on what governments can do) on the ability of governments to pursue social policy. Free or freer trade have been anathema to the trade union movement because employers have the option of shifting their production to jurisdictions that are part of the preferential trading area and that have lower wages and weak employment laws. The *Labour Cooperation Agreement* was a direct result of these concerns raised by the U.S. labour movement during the NAFTA approval process.

7) Competition/Antitrust Laws

There are also linkages between trade issues and competition or antitrust laws. International trade policy and competition policy are both directed at anticompetitive conduct; the former against that resulting from protectionist trade measures adopted by government and the latter against anticompetitive practices pursued by individual companies. Although freer trade makes it more difficult for companies to restrict competition within a single country, cross-border problems are compounded. NAFTA, CIFTA, and CCFTA set out a few tentative provisions that address competition issues in the context of a trade agreement.

D. POLICY INSTRUMENTS SUBJECT TO DISCIPLINE

The international trading system as embodied in the *WTO Agreement* and as reflected in each of NAFTA, CIFTA, and CCFTA is based on the proposition that liberal trade policy (whether in respect of goods, services, or direct foreign investment) is the most conducive to overall welfare. Experience under the GATT, which created predictable rules and institutionalized the dismantling of barriers to trade, when contrasted with the unilateralism and beggar-thy-neighbour policies of the 1920s and 1930s, certainly suggests that this is true. However, it must be remembered that the GATT was the product of a great depression followed by an immensely destructive world war, both of which had a sobering effect on the political leaders of the immediate postwar era who were driven not to repeat past mistakes. Under normal circumstances, when short-term political considerations have considerable influence on policy, trade liberalization is a difficult option for governments. The benefits that result from liberalized trade are spread widely and thinly, whereas the burdens created by trade liberalization are concentrated and felt acutely by those affected. A trade agreement that eliminates or reduces trade barriers will likely make goods and services slightly less expensive for many consumers and will probably result in a somewhat more efficient allocation of resources within a country. These benefits are measurable by economists but are barely perceived by those who benefit from them. However, some inefficient businesses will be forced to close down or drastically restructure, with resulting lost jobs and diminished value of investments. Owners of those businesses and the unemployed workers are keenly aware of the negative effects of the trade agreement.

Trade barriers are much easier for governments to erect than to dismantle. Special interest groups organized by producer interests can bring a great deal of pressure to bear on politicians and bureaucrats, while those who benefit most from the dismantling of trade barriers are seldom as vocal. At the very least, if politicians agree to dismantle a trade barrier they must be seen to have received something in return in the form of improved market access elsewhere, even if the unilateral removal of the trade barrier may produce the optimal result in terms of overall welfare.

The reduction and removal of trade barriers is complicated by the fact that market economies do not always produce equitable or socially desirable results. Free market economies do not guarantee a fair distribution of wealth or job security or the availability of essentials, such as housing or medical care to all citizens. Unrestrained industrial growth can undermine legitimate objectives such as sustainable development and a clean environment. Governments are forced by both political pressure and genuine public policy concerns to intervene to rectify market failures. However, the intervention frequently creates trade barriers of some sort. For example, to ensure universal access to medicare Canadian governments have excluded non-Canadian service providers from most sectors of the Canadian health care system. Environmental regulations often make trade more difficult and can be used as effective barriers to trade with other countries.

The disciplines established by the *WTO Agreement* and by NAFTA, CIFTA, and CCFTA are largely concerned with regulating and, in some instances, curtailing the use of the various policy instruments that governments employ when they intervene. Some of the policy instruments subject to disciplines clearly have no other purpose than to give domestic producers or service providers or investors an edge over their foreign counterparts. Other policy instruments are used in conjunction with more broadly based programs of intervention designed to rectify what are perceived to be market failures.

1) Tariffs

Tariffs are taxes on imports that are not levied on domestic goods. As such they are discriminatory and cause distortions in consumer choices by creating artificial advantages in favour of domestic goods. However, tariffs raise revenue for public purposes, are transparent (i.e., not disguised) and, unless fixed at prohibitive levels, do not restrict the quantities of goods that foreign producers can sell and domestic consumers can buy.

2) Quantitative Restrictions

A quantitative restriction restricts the volume of imports that can enter a country. Quantitative restrictions are effective means of protecting local production but they create distortions by creating artificial scarcity and higher domestic prices. Rather than raising revenue, quantitative restrictions confer windfall profits (or economic rents) on those entitled to import. Import quotas must be established and allocated. Quota allocation is difficult to administer equitably because it involves the allotment of entitlements to economic rents. One variation of the quantitative restriction is the tariff rate quota, under which a prescribed annual quantity of imports may enter at a normal tariff rate; imports over that volume are subject to very high rates. Quantitative restrictions can also be applied to cross-border service providers by restricting the volume of services to be provided.

3) "Voluntary" Export Restraints

The "voluntary" export restraint is a form of quantitative restriction under which the task of administering quotas is transferred from the importing country to the exporting country. Customs officials do not enter the goods affected unless they are accompanied by an export permit issued by the exporting country in accordance with the manner it chooses to allocate its export quota. The expression "voluntary" is used because these arrangements result from negotiations between importing and exporting countries, but usually in circumstances in which the exporting countries have little option but to agree. A voluntary export restraint has all the unattractive characteristics of an import restriction with the added disadvantage that the economic rents are transferred from domestic holders of import quotas to foreign holders of export quotas.

4) Subsidies

Domestic production subsidies are, in some respects, the least intrusive of the policy instruments addressed by the trade agreements to which Canada is a party. However, subsidies become a trade problem when they enable domestic producers to compete unfairly in foreign markets, and export subsidies have caused serious distortions in the world trade in agricultural goods. All the trade agreements to which Canada is a party address subsidies in some manner.

5) Special Trade Remedies

Special trade remedies are remedies used to respond to dumping, subsidization, and import surges and result in the application of temporary trade measures. Antidumping duties are applied to offset the effect of dumping. Goods are "dumped" when they are sold at a price in the importing country that is lower than the price at which they are sold in the country in which they are produced, or at a price that is insufficient to recover costs. Countervailing duties are applied against imports to offset the effect of subsidization by the government of the exporting country. Safeguard or emergency actions are taken against import surges when domestic producers are threatened. Although dumping, subsidized imports, and import surges can create hardships for domestic producers, exploitation of these special trade remedies by interest groups can result in unwarranted protection, excess burdens on consumers, and an unpredictable trading environment.

6) Qualitative Restrictions

A qualitative restriction is a restriction that is directed at the quality of the good or service being traded. With goods, qualitative restrictions are directed at the characteristics of the good itself, while with services, qualitative restrictions usually relate to the qualifications of the persons providing the services. Qualitative restrictions are clearly necessary to protect consumers but can result in significant impediments to trade if they are applied in a discriminatory manner. For example, if qualifications to provide a service include a citizenship or local residency requirement, cross-border provision of that service is virtually eliminated.

7) Right of Establishment

Most governments regulate direct foreign investment to some extent. Regulation of direct foreign investment involves placing limitations on the right of foreign investors to establish new businesses or to acquire existing businesses. Some countries such as Canada and Mexico have investment screening legislation that requires at least some investors to receive approval before investing. Most countries identify certain sectors such as telecommunications, financial services, or broadcasting as "sensitive" and limit foreign ownership of businesses carrying on in these sectors.

8) Performance Requirements

Performance requirements can be attached to any government benefit, ranging from a subsidy or duty remission order to an investment approval. Performance requirements have formed the backbone of some very successful industrial strategies, such as Canada's automotive duty remission program under the *Canada–U.S. Auto Pact*. However, performance requirements that require export performance or that favour the use of domestic rather than imported inputs can create distortions in production decisions and increased prices for domestic consumers.

E. RULES-BASED SYSTEM VERSUS MANAGED TRADE

The objective of the *WTO Agreement* and of the free trade agreements to which Canada is a party is to establish rules-based systems to which measures adopted by member countries must conform. Market forces operating within a stable and predictable normative structure dictate economic outcomes, whether they be trade balances, volumes of cross-border trade in services, or flows of direct foreign investment. This objective was succinctly expressed by the WTO Appellate Body in *Japan — Taxes on Alcoholic Beverages* in a case involving the application of the non-discrimination requirements of Article III of GATT 1994: "Article III protects expectations not of any particular trade volume but rather of the equal competitive relationship between imported and domestic products."[7]

Despite this objective, for a variety of historical reasons the international trading system permits "managed" or "results-based" trade in several significant sectors of the economy. With managed or results-based trade, economic outcomes such as trade volumes, permitted numbers of service providers or levels of direct foreign investment are established through negotiation rather than by being left to the operation of market forces. For example:

- *Textile and apparel goods:* Until the *WTO Agreement* became effective, the entire textile and apparel sector was governed by agreements negotiated outside the GATT which permitted countries to negotiate annual volumes of trade in specified categories of textile and apparel goods. Invariably the importing countries were developed countries and the exporting countries were developing countries. Canada has entered into many such "voluntary" restraint agreements with developing countries. These agreements continue in effect but will be phased out by the year 2005 under the WTO *Agreement on Textiles and Clothing.*
- *Dairy and poultry products:* The Canadian government restricts imports of dairy and poultry products as part of a comprehensive scheme of supply management with production quotas for domestic production. The import restrictions, which now take the form of

---

7 WT/DS8/AB/R, WT/DS10/AB/R, WT/DS11/AB/R. See Appellate Body Report (AB-1996-2) at 19.

tariff rate quotas with prohibitive over-quota tariff rates, are sanctioned under the WTO *Agreement on Agriculture*[8] and have been upheld under NAFTA.[9] The U.S. government maintains similar programs respecting such products as sugar and peanuts. Unlike in the textile and apparel sector, managed trade is a permanent institution in this sector unless the participating governments choose to dismantle it.

Managed trade, with its reliance on quantitative restrictions, can be very unattractive, both in the administrative difficulties it creates and in the economic results it produces. For example, dairy and poultry products, which are basic necessities in any country, are much more expensive for consumers in Canada than they would be if market forces were permitted to govern. The high prices amount to a subsidy paid to the producers of these products by consumers. However, the Canadian government and the governments of its trading partners have been pressured into managed trade in certain sectors by producer groups. Once created, such regimes are difficult to dismantle because of the vested interests they create in the form of quota allocations and economic rent entitlements.

F. WORLD TRADE ORGANIZATION: INSTITUTIONAL STRUCTURE FOR THE WORLD TRADING SYSTEM

The creation of the WTO completes the unfinished business of establishing an institutional structure for the international trading system, and its significance cannot be overestimated. The GATT contracting parties managed to create an *ad hoc* system for resolving disputes through a panel process but it operated on a consensual basis and could always be blocked by the contracting party against which action was taken. The *WTO Agreement* removes the right of a contracting party to block the adoption of a panel report. The *WTO Agreement* has created an effective panel process for resolving disputes that is being actively used not only by traditional GATT litigants such as the United States, Canada, and the European Union but also by developing countries. The Appellate Body created by the *WTO Agreement* is producing a growing body of jurisprudence that

---

8   Set out in Annex 1A of the *Agreement Creating the World Trade Organization*, 15 April 1994 (Dobbs Ferry, N.Y.: Oceana Publications, 1997). This WTO agreement requires some reduction in the level of these over-quota tariff rates but they will still be prohibitive.
9   See *In the Matter of Tariffs Applied by Canada to Certain U.S.-Origin Agricultural Products*, 2 December 1996, CDA-95-2008-01 (Ch. 20 Panel).

will greatly clarify the meaning of the rules that govern the international trading system. The WTO is an international body that supervises the application by member countries of WTO rules and the implementation by affected member countries of panel and Appellate Body decisions. The WTO also provides a permanent vehicle for continuing negotiations of reductions in barriers. Most countries in the world are members of the WTO and if the countries (which include China and Russia) currently negotiating accession become members, the WTO and the rules that it administers will cover virtually all world trade.

G. COMMON THEMES

The disciplines imposed by the trade agreements to which Canada is a party are based on common themes that comprise the principal focus of this book.

1) Non-Discrimination

The two principles of non-discrimination that form the basis for the international trading system are the most-favoured-nation (MFN) principle and the principle of national treatment. The MFN principle requires that if a member country extends an advantage to another member, the same advantage must be extended to all members. The national treatment principle requires that non-nationals be treated no less favourably than nationals. When applied to goods, national treatment requires that once goods enter a member country from another member country, those goods must be treated no less favourably than domestic goods. When applied to services or investment, national treatment requires that investors or service providers of other member countries be treated no less favourably than domestic investors or service providers.

2) Reduction of Barriers

All the trade agreements to which Canada is a party address trade barriers in some manner. GATT 1994 binds contracting parties to maximum tariff rates on most goods, and NAFTA, CIFTA, and CCFTA all provide for the staged elimination of tariffs on most goods. The schedules to the GATS set out each member country's specific market access commitments in service sectors. Parties to all these agreements have made commitments to reduce or eliminate other specified barriers to trade in goods or services or to direct foreign investment.

3) Creation of Norms and Use of International Standards and Conventions

The principles of non-discrimination (MFN treatment and national treatment) upon which the original GATT was based function well for trade in goods. An exporter is usually sufficiently protected if it has the assurance that its goods will be treated no less favourably than competing locally produced goods under the laws of the importing country. However, a system of rules based solely on principles of non-discrimination will not afford adequate protection in some of the areas now covered by trade agreements.

For example, a country may nationalize an industry and decree that all companies, whether locally or foreign-owned, receive less than full compensation. If the only obligation imposed on the nationalizing country is to accord national treatment, the direct foreign investor will have no remedy because domestically owned companies are being treated no more favourably. To adequately protect direct foreign investment against expropriation, an investment treaty must oblige each member country to provide full compensation in the event of an expropriation regardless of how it treats domestically owned companies. A country's laws may be wholly inadequate in protecting intellectual property rights but nonetheless may be perfectly consistent with national treatment by treating non-nationals no less favourably than nationals. An effective intellectual property convention must oblige each member country to provide minimum levels of protection and means of enforcement.

The *WTO Agreement*, NAFTA, CCFTA, and CIFTA all establish minimum norms to which the laws of each member country or Party must conform that extend well beyond the basic non-discrimination principles of MFN treatment and national treatment. Norms are easier for exporters or service providers or investors to satisfy if they are substantially uniform from country to country. For this reason the WTO agreements and NAFTA encourage and, in a number of instances, require that norms be based upon international standards, where they exist, or that the norms established by international conventions be adopted.

4) Transparency and Procedural Fairness

A rule is "transparent" if its requirements are capable of being readily determined. The trade agreements to which Canada is a party all contain transparency requirements because the movement of goods, services, capital, and people can be frustrated if exporters, cross-border service providers, investors, and business persons cannot readily determine the applicable rules and regulations of the importing or host country. Transparency requires that rules be published and that changes in rules be made known well in advance of their taking effect.

Trade agreements also address issues of procedural fairness. NAFTA, CIFTA, and CCFTA all set out requirements that must be followed in the administration of customs laws. Agreements annexed to the *WTO Agreement* establish procedural requirements that must be followed in antidumping and countervailing duty cases. CUFTA required that Canada and the United States create entirely new binational panel procedures as an alternative to the normal appeal procedures that existed in each country for decisions in antidumping and countervailing duty matters. NAFTA has carried these requirements forward and extended them to Mexico. The *TRIPS Agreement* and NAFTA set out procedural requirements that must be observed in the enforcement of intellectual property rights.

5) Exceptions and Reservations

a) Exceptions

The trade agreements to which Canada is a party all contain exceptions. Many exceptions are subject to qualifying language that must be considered carefully in determining the scope of the exception. For example, a requirement that a measure adopted under the cover of an exception must be "necessary" means that the member country adopting the measure must establish that the policy objective of the measure falls within the exception and that there is not a less trade-restrictive means of achieving the policy objective. Exceptions relating to national security are particularly troublesome because of the lack of jurisprudence and fundamental disagreement, particularly between the United States and other countries, as to the extent to which these exceptions are "self-judging."

NAFTA sets out sectoral exceptions that apply to individual NAFTA countries. For example, cultural industries are largely exempt from NAFTA disciplines as between Canada and the other two NAFTA countries, and the energy sector is largely exempt from NAFTA obligations as between Mexico and the other two NAFTA countries. CIFTA and CCFTA also contain cultural exceptions.

b) Reservations: NAFTA and CCFTA

NAFTA and CCFTA contain annexes setting out exceptions for specific measures, sectors, subsectors, and activities that are called "reservations."[10] Unlike CUFTA, which grandfathered[11] most existing measures that did not conform with the requirements of the services and investment chapters, NAFTA and CCFTA adopted a "list-it-or-lose-it" approach that required each Party to identify the non-conforming measures that it wished to retain in "reservations" annexed to the agreement.[12] Provision is also made in each of these agreements for reservations that cover specified sectors, subsectors, and activities. The reservations set out in the NAFTA and CCFTA annexes must be carefully considered because they limit the scope of the non-discrimination and other normative requirements of each of these agreements.

6) Dispute Resolution

Disputes inevitably arise under international agreements but not every international agreement has procedures for resolving disputes. An international agreement is much more effective if it has a creditable means of resolving disputes and providing for the enforcement of the decisions that result from the process. However, the more effective and binding the process, the greater the surrender of sovereignty that is required of each member country. The negotiation of dispute settlement procedures in international agreements entails balancing the need for effectiveness against the preservation of sovereignty.

As discussed above, the *WTO Agreement* has established an effective process for adjudicating disputes between WTO member countries and an institutional structure to supervise the implementation of decisions. NAFTA, CIFTA, and CCFTA also establish procedures for adjudicating disputes before panels, but these agreements do not create institutional structures comparable to the WTO that monitor implementation. None of the trade agreements to which Canada is a party provides that adjudicated decisions are binding in the sense of changing the domestic law of the mem-

---

10 The expression "reservation" has another meaning in the law of treaties which is not relevant here.
11 Grandfathering a measure means permitting it to continue even though it fails to conform with new rules that have come into effect.
12 Canadian federal government measures are listed, as are those of the federal governments of the United States and Mexico under the *North American Free Trade Agreement*, 17 December 1992, Can. T.S. 1994 No. 2, and the Chilean government under the *Canada–Chile Free Trade Agreement*, see http://www.dfait-maeci.gc.ca/english/trade/agrement.htm [CCFTA]. The same approach was intended to be applied to non-conforming measures of provinces and states but, in the end, these measures were grandfathered, as were those of local governments. CCFTA grandfathers existing non-conforming provincial and state measures.

ber country against which they are made. It is up to that member country to implement the decision in its own law and if this is not done within prescribed time limits, other member countries can withdraw benefits.

The dispute settlement procedures established by the *WTO Agreement* and the general dispute settlement procedures of each of NAFTA, CIFTA, and CCFTA can only be pursued by the governments of the affected member countries and do not provide for the involvement of non-government entities. However, NAFTA and CCFTA establish special procedures that apply to investment disputes that can only be invoked by non-government entities. These procedures are additional to and not in lieu of the NAFTA and CCFTA general dispute resolution procedures. Under these procedures, an investor who has incurred damages resulting from the actions of the government of another NAFTA or CCFTA country that breach NAFTA or CCFTA investment requirements may initiate a proceeding against that government and, if successful, will be awarded a judgment for damages that is legally enforceable.[13]

H. EFFECT OF TRADE AGREEMENTS ON CANADIAN LAW

The international obligations undertaken by the Canadian government under trade agreements to which Canada is a party have far-reaching effects on Canadian law, both at the federal and provincial levels.

1) Treaties Not Self-Executing in Canada

In some countries, like Mexico, international treaties are self-executing in that, upon being entered into in accordance with legal or constitutional requirements, they automatically become the law of the land. This is not the case in Canada. The Canadian government can assume international obligations but those obligations do not become Canadian law unless and until implemented by laws or regulations enacted by the competent level of government. If the law required to implement the obligation falls within the exclusive area of provincial competence, the obligation does not become law in Canada until enacted by the provincial legislatures.

---

13 If the government is a provincial or state government, the proceeding is initiated against the federal government of the country in question.

2) Effect on Provincial Laws

Under the Canadian constitution, laws affecting the international trade in goods, as well as laws affecting intellectual property, fall within the exclusive competence of the federal government. However, many areas covered by the trade agreements to which Canada is a party touch on areas of provincial competence. The regulation of the distribution of goods within a province is within the province's sphere of jurisdiction. Provincial laws that treat imported goods less favourably than domestic goods will be inconsistent with national treatment obligations. Norms established by trade agreements respecting the trade in services, direct foreign investment, financial services and standards also affect laws falling within exclusive provincial jurisdiction.

The federal government is the only party to the *WTO Agreement* and to NAFTA, CIFTA, and CCFTA. However, a number of the WTO agreements and each of NAFTA, CIFTA, and CCFTA require the federal government to take measures to ensure observance by regional governments.

While provincial governments are not bound by international agreements and, within their areas of exclusive competence, cannot be forced by the federal government to enact measures or refrain from enacting measures, provincial governments usually make efforts to ensure that provincial laws and regulations conform to Canada's international obligations.[14]

3) Framework for Domestic Lawmakers

The *WTO Agreement*, NAFTA, CIFTA, and CCFTA, as well as other international agreements to which Canada is a party, establish norms to which Canadian laws must conform. The implementation of the *WTO Agreement*, NAFTA, CIFTA, and CCFTA each required extensive changes to federal laws and regulations.

The structure of federal laws and regulations respecting tariffs, customs procedures, import and export restrictions, and the administration of trade remedies such as antidumping and countervailing duties is largely dictated by the requirements of the trade agreements to which Canada is a party. Implementation of CUFTA and NAFTA required significant modifications to Canada's laws respecting investment screening. Both NAFTA and the *TRIPS Agreement* required changes to Canadian intellectual property laws. The legislation implementing NAFTA

---

14 As discussed in chapter 2 under "Special Rules: Alcoholic Beverages," there have been some notable instances where this has not been the case.

and the *WTO Agreement* in each case amended more than twenty different federal statutes and required extensive changes to federal regulations. The legislation implementing CIFTA and CCFTA has also required extensive amendments to Canadian laws.

The trade agreements to which Canada is a party also affect laws in Canada by placing limits on the measures that may be enacted and the policies that may be pursued by both levels of governments. National treatment obligations preclude measures that discriminate in favour of Canadian goods, service providers, or investors. Measures taken for the protection of health that affect intellectual property rights, such as packaging requirements for cigarettes, must be consistent with WTO and NAFTA intellectual property requirements. Canadian lawmakers must consider whether a proposed course of action might amount to an expropriation and expose the government to compensation requirements under the NAFTA or CCFTA investment chapter.

The constraints imposed on law making by the trade agreements to which Canada is a party have practical consequences for industry groups and others who lobby for statutory or regulatory changes. Potential non-compliance with a trade agreement is a ready excuse for governmental non-action. Those advocating any measure are well advised to be prepared to convince the federal or provincial bureaucrats with whom they are dealing that the proposed measure is consistent with Canada's obligations under these agreements.

I. PURPOSE OF THE BOOK

This book is intended as a comprehensive introduction to the field of international trade law. The book describes the principles that underpin the international trading system of which Canada is a part and the evolving jurisprudence under the WTO that is providing ever-increasing definition to the international rules with which Canadian laws must conform. The book also describes each of the trade agreements to which Canada is a party, how they interrelate with each other and to other international agreements, and how they affect Canadian domestic law. Although the book describes various Canadian laws affecting international trade, particularly in the customs area, the descriptions are intended to demonstrate how the requirements of the international trading system are translated into domestic laws. While the book makes a number of observations respecting the practical application of customs law, it is not intended as a practitioner's guide in this area.

J. ORGANIZATION OF THE BOOK

Chapter 1 of this book sets out an overview of the *WTO Agreement* and NAFTA and contains brief descriptions of CIFTA and CCFTA. Chapter 1 also discusses interpretation issues that arise when analysing each of these agreements.

Chapters 2 through 6 cover various topics related to the trade in goods. Chapter 2 describes the basic principles of non-discrimination as applied to trade in goods and the general exceptions. Chapter 3 covers tariffs, tariff reduction under the *WTO Agreement*, and tariff elimination under NAFTA, CIFTA, CCFTA, as well as related matters such as valuation of goods for duty purposes, duty drawback and duty deferral programs, duty waivers, and temporary entry of goods. Chapter 4 covers rules respecting import and export restrictions and export taxes, with particular emphasis on agricultural goods and textile and apparel goods. Chapter 5 covers rules respecting the origin of goods, both for preferential and non-preferential purposes. Chapter 6 concludes the discussion on trade in goods by describing antidumping and countervailing duties and safeguard actions, as well as disciplines respecting subsidies.

Chapter 7 covers sanitary and phytosanitary measures, technical barriers to trade, intellectual property, and government procurement. These areas are discussed together because the *WTO Agreement* and NAFTA create parallel but somewhat differing sets of obligations covering each area. This chapter also discusses the *Environmental Cooperation Agreement* and the *Labour Cooperation Agreement*.

Chapter 8 covers investment, services, financial services, and temporary entry. These topics are covered in one chapter here because, under NAFTA and CCFTA, the investment and services chapters of those documents are linked by common reservations. Also, the NAFTA financial services chapter, while self-contained, incorporates by reference several of the critical provisions of the investment chapter. Temporary entry is discussed with these other topics because the temporary entry of business persons may be seen as ensuring the integrity of the services and investment obligations. Chapter 8 also covers monopolies, state enterprises, and competition law.

Chapter 9 describes further exceptions (additional to the general exceptions discussed in chapter 2) respecting national security, balance of payments for cultural industries, taxation measures, and disclosure of information.

Chapter 10 describes the general dispute settlement procedures in all the trade agreements to which Canada is a party, as well as the special investor-state dispute settlement provisions in the NAFTA and CCFTA investment chapters. It also sets out some concluding remarks.

CHAPTER 1

INTERNATIONAL LEGAL STRUCTURE

The purpose of this chapter is to describe in general terms the two major trade agreements by which Canada is bound, namely the *WTO Agreement* and NAFTA. CIFTA and CCFTA will also be briefly described. The chapter will then set out guidelines to be followed in interpreting international agreements and will discuss how the *WTO Agreement*, NAFTA, CIFTA, and CCFTA relate to each other and to other international agreements.

A. THE *WTO AGREEMENT*

The *WTO Agreement* is an umbrella agreement that establishes the World Trade Organization (WTO) and sets out, in four annexes, a series of agreements and understandings that contain the substantive obligations of the member countries respecting trade in goods, trade in services, and intellectual property rights.[1] The fifteen agreements set out in Annexes 1A, 1B, and 1C are referred to as "Multilateral Agreements." Unlike the Tokyo Round codes that bound only GATT members that accepted them, each

---

1   As discussed below, the annexes to the *Agreement Creating the World Trade Organization*, 15 April 1994 (Dobbs Ferry, N.Y.: Oceana Publications, 1997) [*WTO Agreement*] set out agreements and understandings covering a variety of matters. In this book, the expression "*WTO Agreement*" means the *Agreement Creating the World Trade Organization* while the expression "WTO agreements" means the agreements and understandings set out in the four annexes to the *WTO Agreement*.

21

Multilateral Agreement binds all WTO members.² Annex 2 sets out a dispute settlement process and institutional structure in the *Understanding on Rules and Procedures Governing the Settlement of Disputes*. Annex 3 sets out a *Trade Policy Review Mechanism* providing for periodic review of the trade policies and practices by a Trade Policy Review Body. Annex 4 contains four additional agreements referred to as "Plurilateral Agreements," which bind only member countries that accept them. These agreements and understandings are amplified by decisions and declarations included in the Final Act that was adopted by the WTO member countries in Marrakesh, Morocco, on 15 April 1994. Members are obliged to ensure that their laws, regulations, and administrative procedures conform with the obligations set out in the agreements in the annexes.³

The *WTO Agreement* itself covers various institutional matters respecting the WTO and sets out procedures for amendment, accession by new members, and withdrawal.

1) Annex 1A: Multilateral Agreements on Trade in Goods

Annex 1A of the *WTO Agreement* sets out thirteen agreements that deal with various aspects of trade in goods. The first Multilateral Agreement in Annex 1A is the *General Agreement on Tariffs and Trade 1994* (GATT 1994), which carries forward, with some modifications, the principles established by GATT 1947. The remaining twelve agreements in Annex 1A elaborate on various aspects of GATT 1994. Two of these agreements cover particular sectors, namely agriculture and textile and apparel goods, while the remaining ten agreements cover particular topics.

a) GATT 1994

i) Contents

GATT 1994 consists of GATT 1947, as amended and modified since that time and as further modified by understandings set out in GATT 1994.⁴ GATT 1994 also includes protocols and certifications that contain the

---

2 Art. XIII of the *WTO Agreement, ibid.*, provides for the non-application of the *WTO Agreement* and the Multilateral Agreements between particular members under some circumstances. Canada has not made use of this provision.
3 *WTO Agreement, ibid.*, art. XVI:4.
4 See the understandings respecting arts. II:1(b) (relating to tariff concessions), XVII (state enterprises), XII and XVIII:B (balance of payments), and XXVIII (modification or withdrawal of concessions) of the *General Agreement on Tariffs and Trade*, 30 October 1947, Can. T.S. 1947 No. 27, 55 U.N.T.S. 187 [GATT 1947]. There is also an understanding respecting waivers.

tariff concessions made by member countries in the successive rounds of GATT negotiations as well as the protocols of accession of member countries that were not original signatories to GATT 1947. Each new country joined the GATT on terms set out in a protocol of accession. For example, Mexico became a GATT member in 1985 under the terms of a protocol of accession that permitted the continuance of certain Mexican laws even though they were not consistent with GATT provisions. All these protocols are part of GATT 1994. GATT 1994 also includes all waivers that have been granted to member countries from time to time. For example, the U.S. government applied for and received a waiver to permit it to allow duty-free treatment to automotive goods imported from Canada under the *Auto Pact*. Without the waiver, this action would have violated the MFN requirement of GATT Article I.[5] Finally, GATT 1994 incorporates "other decisions" of the member countries.

ii) Highlights

GATT 1994 establishes a rules-based international trading system that covers the trade in goods among the member countries of the *WTO Agreement*.

- *Non-discrimination*: Articles I and III of GATT 1994 provide respectively for MFN and national treatment (see chapter 2).
- *Tariff reduction*: Article II sets out member countries' obligations respecting tariffs (see chapter 3) and Article XXVIII*bis* establishes procedures for successive rounds of tariff negotiations.[6]
- *Prohibition of import and export restrictions*: Subject to several significant exceptions, Article XI prohibits import and export restrictions (see chapter 4). Where import restrictions are permitted, they must conform to the non-discrimination requirements set out in Article XIII.
- *Special trade remedies*: Article VI establishes basic disciplines respecting the application of antidumping and countervailing duties, and Article XIX sets out rules for emergency actions (see chapter 6). Each of these provisions is amplified by other agreements in Annex 1A.
- *Subsidies*: Article XVI sets out disciplines respecting export subsidies (see chapter 6).

---

5   The waiver is set out in *U.S. — Imports of Automotive Products*, 20 December 1965, 14th supp. B.I.S.D. (1966) 37.
6   *General Agreements on Tariffs and Trade 1994*, set out in Annex 1A of the *WTO Agreement*, above note 1 [GATT 1994], art. XXVIII, sets out circumstances in which tariff concessions can be renegotiated and, in certain circumstances, unilaterally withdrawn.

- *Transparency and procedural fairness*: Article X requires that member countries publish laws, regulations, judicial decisions, and administrative rulings affecting various aspects of the trade in goods and establish tribunals for the purpose of reviewing and correcting administrative action relating to customs matters.
- *Other norms*: Article IV sets out rules respecting screen quotas for cinematographic films. Article V provides for freedom of transit when goods are being transported through territories of member countries. Article VII covers the valuation of goods for customs purposes (see chapter 3). Article VIII sets out rules respecting fees and formalities connected with importation and exportation. Article IX sets out basic rules respecting marks of origin (see chapter 5). Article XVII sets out rules respecting state trading enterprises (see chapter 8).
- *Exceptions*: Article XII permits certain restrictions to safeguard balance of payments, and Articles XIII and XIV establish rules for applying such restrictions (see chapter 9). Article XX provides general exceptions for measures necessary for matters including the protection of public morals, the protection of human, animal and plant life or health, and the conservation of exhaustible natural resources (see chapter 2). Article XXI sets out a national security exception (see chapter 9).
- *Dispute resolution*: Article XXII provides for consultations and Article XXIII sets out a course of action to be followed if a member country considers that benefits that it expected to receive are being "nullified or impaired" as the result of actions of another member country or for other reasons. The process begins with consultations and can end with the withdrawal of concessions. The manner in which this process functioned evolved over the years on an *ad hoc* basis and was not formalized until the conclusion of the *WTO Agreement* and the *Understanding on Rules and Procedures Governing the Settlement of Disputes*.

b) Other Agreements in Annex 1A

i) Agreement on Agriculture
The *Agreement on Agriculture* (*Agriculture Agreement*) is a sectoral agreement affecting only agricultural goods. The *Agriculture Agreement* requires that member countries convert into customs duties all border measures affecting agricultural goods other than customs duties (see chapter 4). The *Agriculture Agreement* also imposes disciplines on both domestic support programs and export subsidies (see chapter 6).

ii) Agreement on Textiles and Clothing
The *Agreement on Textiles and Clothing* (*Textile Agreement*) is the other sectoral agreement in Annex 1A and affects only textile and apparel

goods. The *Textile Agreement* phases out the system of bilateral restraint agreements that have governed this sector since the early 1960s and brings this sector back under normal GATT disciplines (see chapter 4).

iii) *Agreement on the Application of Sanitary and Phytosanitary Measures and the Agreement on Technical Barriers to Trade*
The *Agreement on the Application of Sanitary and Phytosanitary Measures (SPS Agreement)* and the *Agreement on Technical Barriers to Trade (TBT Agreement)* impose disciplines on two different types of standards (see chapter 7). Each of these agreements is based on principles of non-discrimination and each establishes norms in respect of the standards it covers. Each agreement also sets out transparency requirements.

iv) *Agreement on Trade-Related Investment Measures*
The *Agreement on Trade-Related Investment Measures (TRIMs Agreement)* prohibits the application of certain types of performance requirements (see chapter 8).

v) *Agreement on Implementation of Article VI of the General Agreement on Tariffs and Trade 1994*
The *Agreement on Implementation of Article VI of the General Agreement on Tariffs and Trade 1994 (Antidumping Agreement)* elaborates upon the basic rules respecting the application of antidumping duties set out in Article VI of GATT 1994 (see chapter 6).

vi) *Agreement on Implementation of Article VII of the General Agreement on Tariffs and Trade 1994*
The *Agreement on Implementation of Article VII of the General Agreement on Tariffs and Trade 1994 (Valuation Agreement)* expands upon the rules in Article VII of GATT 1994 for valuing goods for duty purposes (see chapter 3).

vii) *Agreement on Preshipment Inspection*
The *Agreement on Preshipment Inspection (Preshipment Inspection Agreement)* sets out disciplines respecting preshipment inspection. Preshipment inspection is required by a number of developing WTO member countries and entails verification of the quantity, quality, and price of exported goods before their exportation. The *Preshipment Inspection Agreement* requires that inspections be carried out in a non-discriminatory manner in the territory of the exporting member country or, in some circumstances, the country of manufacture. This agreement also sets out transparency and procedural requirements respecting grievances raised by exporters.

viii) Agreement on Rules of Origin

The *Agreement on Rules of Origin* (*Rules of Origin Agreement*) sets out basic disciplines respecting the application of both preferential and non-preferential rules of origin and provides for the creation of a Committee on Rules of Origin to work towards harmonization of non-preferential rules of origin (see chapter 5).

ix) Agreement on Import Licensing Procedures

The *Agreement on Import Licensing Procedures* (*Import Licensing Agreement*) sets out disciplines respecting the application of import licensing procedures. The *Import Licensing Agreement* requires that import licensing procedures be neutral in application and be administered in a fair and equitable manner. The agreement covers both automatic import licensing and non-automatic import licensing. The rules respecting non-automatic import licensing include requirements respecting the administration of quotas through import licensing. The agreement sets out various transparency requirements, such as Article 5 that requires notification of new procedures or changes to existing procedures.

x) Agreement on Subsidies and Countervailing Measures

The *Agreement on Subsidies and Countervailing Measures* (*Subsidies Agreement*) expands upon and clarifies the obligations of member countries respecting subsidies under Article XVI of GATT 1994 (see chapter 6). The *Subsidies Agreement* also elaborates upon Article VI of GATT 1994 by setting out a comprehensive code respecting the application of countervailing duties (see chapter 6).

xi) Agreement on Safeguards

The *Agreement on Safeguards* (*Safeguards Agreement*) clarifies and reinforces the provisions of Article XIX of GATT 1994 as well as prohibiting certain practices such as voluntary export restraints (see chapter 6).

c) Annex 1B: *General Agreement on Trade in Services*

Annex 1B consists of the *General Agreement on Trade in Services* (GATS) that sets general MFN non-discrimination and transparency requirements respecting the trade in services, as well as specific commitments of member countries respecting market access and national treatment (see chapter 8). The GATS also sets out provisions respecting monopolies and exclusive service providers (see chapter 8). The GATS contains exceptions (general exceptions, a security exception, and balance of payment exceptions) and safeguard provisions that are based on their counterparts in GATT 1994.

d) Annex 1C: *Agreement on Trade-Related Aspects of Intellectual Property Rights*

Annex 1C consists of the *Agreement on Trade-Related Aspects of Intellectual Property Rights (TRIPS Agreement)* that incorporates basic non-discrimination requirements, requires member countries to comply with specified provisions of the major intellectual property conventions, and sets out substantive obligations respecting copyright, trademarks, geographic indications, industrial designs, patents, layout designs of integrated circuits, the protection of undisclosed information, and the control of anticompetitive practices in contractual licences (see chapter 7). The *TRIPS Agreement* also sets out norms for domestic laws respecting the enforcement of intellectual property rights.

e) Annex 2: *Understanding on Rules and Procedures Governing the Settlement of Disputes*

Annex 2 consists of the *Understanding on Rules and Procedures Governing the Settlement of Disputes (Dispute Settlement Understanding)*. The *Dispute Settlement Understanding* establishes procedures for the settlement of disputes arising under the WTO agreements (see chapter 10). Several WTO agreements set out dispute settlement procedures that must be read together with the procedures set out in the *Dispute Settlement Understanding*.

f) Annex 3: *Trade Policy Review Mechanism*

The *Trade Policy Review Mechanism* set out in Annex 3 provides for periodic review by a body known as the Trade Policy Review Policy of the trade policies and practices of member countries. The frequency of reviews depends upon the share of world trade of each member country (counting the European Union as a single country).[7]

g) Annex 4: Plurilateral Agreements

Annex 4 sets out four plurilateral agreements to which some but not all WTO members are party. The only plurilateral agreement to which Canada is a party is the *Agreement on Government Procurement (Government Procurement Agreement)*.[8]

---

[7] The policies and practices of the top four countries will be reviewed every two years. Those of the next sixteen members will be reviewed every four years, and those of other members every six years.

[8] See chapter 7 under "Government Procurement." The other three plurilateral agreements are the *Agreement on Trade in Civil Aircraft*, the *International Dairy Agreement*, and the *International Bovine Meat Agreement*, all set out in Annex 4 of the *WTO Agreement*, above note 1.

B. PERMITTED PREFERENTIAL ARRANGEMENTS: CUSTOMS UNIONS AND FREE TRADE AREAS

Notwithstanding the most-favoured-nation principle of Article I of GATT 1994, which requires that an advantage extended to one country be extended to all, several arrangements are permitted under GATT 1994 that permit preferential treatment to be accorded to some WTO member countries and not to others.

1) Customs Unions and Free Trade Areas

Article XXIV of GATT 1994 permits the creation by groups of contracting parties of customs unions and free trade areas under which the participating contracting parties grant preferential treatment to other participating contracting parties but not to non-participating contracting parties. Both arrangements result in tariff-free trade among participating countries but for somewhat different reasons. The distinction is important to understanding the structure of NAFTA, CIFTA, and CCFTA and the limitations of these arrangements.

a) Customs Unions

Article XXIV:8(a) of GATT 1994 defines a customs union as the substitution of a single customs territory for two or more customs territories so that duties and other restrictive regulations of commerce are eliminated with respect to substantially all trade among the members and each member maintains substantially the same duties and regulations of commerce to trade with non-members.[9] Member countries of a customs union must maintain common border policies vis à vis non-member countries. This involves much more than simply maintaining common tariff rates. For example, policies respecting the imposition of special trade remedies such as antidumping or countervailing duties must be coordinated. The free movement of goods (i.e., the movement of goods between countries without the imposition of border measures) is possible within a customs union because (theoretically at least) once the good enters one member country of a customs union from a non-member

---

9   Above note 6, art. XXIV:8(a)(i) permits contracting parties that are members of a customs union to maintain restrictions against each other that are sanctioned under art. XI (import and export restrictions), or art. XX (general exceptions), or imposed for balance of payments reasons under arts. XII to XV.

country and the commonly agreed border measure (whether a tariff, a quantitative restriction, an import permit requirement, or an antidumping duty) is applied, the good is free to move to other member countries without the further application of border measures. However, because of the requirement that policies be coordinated, countries entering into a customs union must be prepared to surrender a substantial measure of sovereignty.

The European Union is, *inter alia*, a customs union, with a supranational institutional structure that establishes border measures and policies touching many other areas that are binding on all member countries. The Treaties of Rome and the subsequent agreements among the member countries of the European Union are based on the "four freedoms," namely, the free movement of goods (which, as indicated above, is possible within a customs union), together with the free movement of services, investment, and people. Each member country of the European Union is a signatory of the *WTO Agreement*. The European Union is also a signatory to the *WTO Agreement* with standing in its own right as a member of the WTO. This is necessary because many activities within the European Union are conducted at the supranational level rather than at the national level.

MERCOSUR, composed of Brazil, Argentina, Uruguay, and Paraguay, is the other major customs union among WTO member countries. MERCOSUR is a more basic customs union along the lines described in Article XXIV:8(a), without the comprehensive supranational structure of the European Union.

b) Free Trade Areas

Article XXIV:8(b) of GATT 1994 defines a free trade area as a group of two or more customs territories in which duties and other restrictive regulations of commerce are eliminated with respect to substantially all trade among the members.[10] However, unlike under a customs union, each country that is a member of a free trade area is free to establish its own tariffs and other border policies *vis à vis* non-member countries. A free trade area is a much less intrusive arrangement than a customs union and requires a minimal institutional structure because border measures *vis à vis* non-member countries need not be coordinated. However, because of the absence of coordinated border policies, the

---

10 Art. XXIV:8(b), *ibid.*, permits these contracting parties to maintain restrictions against each other that are sanctioned under art. XI (import and export restrictions), or art. XX (general exceptions), or imposed for balance of payments reasons under arts. XII to XV.

creation of a free trade area results in more complex rather than simplified border measures because of the need for rules of origin to determine whether goods entering from other member countries qualify for preferential tariff treatment.

NAFTA, CIFTA, and CCFTA all create free trade areas.[11] Each member country maintains its own policies vis à vis non-member countries and retains the ability to apply certain restrictive measures against other member countries. Each arrangement sets out complex rules of origin for establishing the eligibility for preferential tariff treatment of goods imported from other member countries and, typical of free trade areas, the institutional structure of each arrangement is minimal.

2) Generalized System of Preferences and Other Permitted Preferential Arrangements

The Generalized System of Preferences was established in 1971 by a waiver of the GATT contracting parties that permits developed countries to accord non-discriminatory and non-reciprocal preferences to developing countries.[12] Programs such as Canada's General Preferential Tariff and Least Developed Developing Country Tariff, pursuant to which preferential tariff treatment is unilaterally accorded by Canada to goods of prescribed developing countries, depend for their justification under GATT 1994 on the waiver of the Generalized System of Preferences.

Article I:2 of GATT 1994 permits the continuation of certain preferential arrangements that pre-existed the GATT, most notably preferences among Commonwealth countries.[13]

---

11 Other free trade areas include the *Israel–United States Free Trade Area Agreement*, 22 April 1985, (1985), 24 I.L.M. 653; the European Free Trade Association (EFTA), the remaining members of which are Iceland, Norway, and Switzerland; the *Australia–New Zealand Closer Economic Relations Trade Agreement*, 28 March 1983, (1983), 22 I.L.M. 945; and the *G-3 Agreement* (*Grupo de los tres*), 13 June 1994, (1994), 197 Integracion Latinamericana 41, among Mexico, Colombia, and Venezuela. Mexico has also entered into a free trade agreement with Chile.

12 *Generalized System of Preferences*, (1971), GATT Doc. L/3545, 18th supp. B.I.S.D. (1970–1971) 24. See also the decision of 28 November 1979 on *Differential and More Favourable Treatment, Reciprocity and Fuller Participation of Developing Countries* (1979), GATT Doc. L/4903, 26th supp. B.I.S.D. (1978–1979) 203.

13 As reflected in Canada's British Preferential Tariff, discussed below. Ironically, GATT 1994, above note 6, art. I:2, makes a specific exception for preferences between the United States and the Republic of Cuba. Cuba was one of the original GATT member countries and is a member of the WTO.

C. NAFTA

From the end of the Second World War until the mid-1980s, Canadian trade policy was based on the multilateral trading system that was established by the GATT. The only regional trade agreement entered into by Canada during this time was the *Auto Pact*, a free trade arrangement with the United States covering the automotive sector. However, in 1986 the Canadian government initiated negotiations with the U.S. government that resulted in CUFTA, which entered into effect on 1 January 1989. CUFTA created a free trade area consisting of Canada and the United States and imposed obligations respecting standards, government procurement, services (including financial services), investment, and the application of special trade remedies. The CUFTA trade-in-goods provisions were largely based on GATT obligations, while the investment provisions had their antecedents in the U.S. *Model Bilateral Investment Treaty* (*Model BIT*).

In 1991, the government of Mexico initiated free trade negotiations with the government of the United States. To avoid the creation of a disadvantageous hub-and-spoke trading model (with the United States as the hub and Canada and Mexico each as spokes), the government of Canada asked to be included in the negotiations. The result of the negotiations was NAFTA, which became effective on 1 January 1994.[14]

1) NAFTA Antecedents

NAFTA is based largely on CUFTA. The national treatment provisions and the provisions respecting import and export restrictions are virtually the same as those of CUFTA. The NAFTA investment chapter is largely based on its CUFTA counterpart, with additional concepts drawn from the U.S. *Model BIT*. As between Canada and the United States, large portions of CUFTA, such as the tariff elimination schedules, the rules respecting duty waivers, and the agricultural provisions have been incorporated by reference into NAFTA. The NAFTA negotiators also made extensive use of the draft Uruguay Round agreements that had then recently been made public as precedents.

---

14   See the *North American Free Trade Agreement Implementation Act*, S.C. 1993, c. 44.

2) Structure of NAFTA

NAFTA consists of a single agreement divided into eight parts. Each part is divided into chapters, which in turn are divided into articles. Many chapters have annexes. The general idea behind the drafting was that the main body of each chapter contain general provisions while country-specific provisions, exceptions, and reservations were to be set out in the annexes.

Part One sets out overall objectives, rules respecting the relationship of NAFTA to other agreements, a general provision respecting observance by provinces and states, and definitions of general application. Part Two, consisting of Chapters Three through Eight, covers trade in goods. Part Three, consisting of Chapter Nine, covers technical barriers to trade. Part Four, consisting of Chapter Ten, covers government procurement.

Part Five, entitled "Investment, Services and Related Matters," comprises Chapters Eleven through Sixteen. Chapter Eleven sets out the NAFTA rules respecting investment, and Chapter Twelve sets out rules respecting the cross-border trade in services. Chapter Thirteen contains special provisions respecting telecommunications. Chapter Fourteen sets out rules respecting financial services. Chapter Fifteen contains general provisions respecting competition laws, designating monopolies and maintaining state enterprises. Chapter Sixteen sets out rules respecting the temporary entry of business persons. Part Six, consisting of Chapter Seventeen, covers intellectual property.

Part Seven, entitled "Administrative and Institutional Provisions," comprises Chapters Eighteen through Twenty. Chapter Eighteen sets out provisions respecting the publication of laws and regulations, provision of information, and administrative procedures. These provisions of general application, which are directed at achieving transparency and procedural fairness, are supplemented by specific transparency and procedural rules in individual NAFTA chapters. Chapter Nineteen sets out the binational panel procedures respecting antidumping and countervailing duty matters. Chapter Twenty creates the Free Trade Commission and the Secretariat and sets out the dispute settlement procedures of general application.

Part Eight comprises Chapters Twenty-One and Twenty-Two. Chapter Twenty-One sets out exceptions to NAFTA obligations, most notably respecting national security, taxation measures, and cultural industries, as well as the exceptions set out in Article XX of GATT 1994. Chapter Twenty-Two covers amendments, entry into force, accession, and withdrawal.

Three supplemental agreements to the NAFTA were negotiated after the original NAFTA text had been signed by the three NAFTA countries. These agreements are the *Environmental Cooperation Agreement* and the *Labour Cooperation Agreement* referred to in the "Overview," together with the *Understanding Between the Parties to the North American Free Trade Agreement Concerning Chapter Eight – Emergency Action.*

3) GATT 1994 Plus: The NAFTA Trade-in-Goods Provisions

In addition to creating a free trade area consisting of Canada, the United States, and Mexico (Article 101), the NAFTA trade-in-goods provisions incorporate GATT norms and build upon them by adding further clarifications and disciplines. NAFTA clarifications codify positions that have evolved through GATT jurisprudence and in a number of respects NAFTA expands upon GATT norms to create a tighter, more disciplined regime. In a few instances, NAFTA derogates from the disciplines of the GATT regime, the most obvious of which is the qualified NAFTA exception for "cultural industries," which has no counterpart in GATT 1994 or any of the other WTO agreements.[15]

- *Non-discrimination*: Article 301 incorporates by reference the national treatment obligations in GATT Article III (see chapter 2). However, the NAFTA trade-in-goods provisions do not contain an MFN rule.[16]
- *Tariff elimination and related border measures*: Chapter Three provides for the phased elimination of tariffs on "originating" goods and addresses other tariff-related border measures such as duty drawback and duty deferral programs, duty waivers based on performance requirements, the temporary entry of goods, and the imposition of customs user fees (see chapter 3). Chapter Four sets out the rules of origin for determining whether goods are "originating" and eligible for NAFTA preferential duty treatment (see chapter 5).
- *Prohibition of import and export restrictions*: Chapter Three incorporates by reference the rules respecting import and export restrictions set out in GATT Article XI, prohibits export taxes, and imposes

---

15 Discussed in chapter 9 under "Cultural Industries."
16 Except for para. 1 of the *North American Free Trade Agreement*, 17 December 1992, Can. T.S. 1994 No. 2 [NAFTA], Annex 300-A, respecting producers of motor vehicles.

disciplines on certain export measures additional to those required under GATT rules (see chapter 4). Annex 300-B sets out special rules respecting textile and apparel goods that include provision for tariff preference levels (see chapter 4).

- *Special trade remedies*: Chapter Nineteen provides for the establishment of binational panels as an alternative to appeal procedures available under the domestic law of each NAFTA country in antidumping and countervailing duty actions (see chapter 6). However, subject only to complying with WTO disciplines, each NAFTA country retains its antidumping and countervailing duty laws. Chapter Eight sets out binational emergency procedures that may be invoked during the period that tariffs are being phased out, and it imposes disciplines on the application of GATT/WTO safeguard actions among NAFTA countries (see chapter 6). Annex 300-B establishes special safeguard procedures that apply to textile and apparel goods.
- *Subsidies*: NAFTA Chapter Seven carries forward the CUFTA prohibition of export subsidies on agricultural goods as between Canada and the United States and contains somewhat less stringent trilateral rules respecting export subsidies.
- *Transparency and procedural fairness*: Chapter Five sets out procedural requirements respecting customs procedures (see chapter 5). Annex 803.3 establishes procedures to be followed in emergency actions (see chapter 6).
- *Special sectoral provisions*: In addition to rules for textile and apparel goods, NAFTA contains provisions specifically relating to automotive goods (Annex 300-A), energy and basic petrochemicals (Chapter Six), agricultural goods (Section A of Chapter Seven), and wine and distilled spirits. The provisions respecting automotive goods relate primarily to Canadian duty waivers under the *Auto Pact* and certain other programs (see chapter 3), and to the dismantling of the Mexican Automotive Decree.[17] The provisions respecting energy and basic petrochemicals for the most part repeat the general provisions in NAFTA Chapter Three respecting import and export restrictions, export taxes, and other export measures (see chapter 4). The provisions respecting agricultural goods are directed primarily at export subsidies (see chapter 6) and import restrictions (see chapter 4). The provisions respecting wine and distilled spirits relate primarily to

---

17 Annex 300-A, *ibid.*, also sets out provisions respecting Canadian and Mexican restrictions on the importation of used cars (see chapter 3 under "Other CUFTA/NAFTA Provisions Respecting Automotive Goods") and imposes requirements respecting the U.S. Corporate Average Fuel Economy rules.

practices followed by the Canadian provinces respecting the internal sale and distribution of these products (see chapter 2).
- *Exceptions*: Article 2101 incorporates the general exceptions set out in GATT Article XX (see chapter 2). Unlike the GATT Article XX exceptions, which apply only to matters covered by GATT 1994, the application of the NAFTA Article 2101 exceptions extends to the NAFTA provisions respecting technical barriers to trade. There are also specific exceptions involving individual NAFTA countries. For example, the disciplines respecting export measures do not apply as between Mexico and the other two NAFTA countries.

4) Undesigned Parallelism: Sanitary and Phytosanitary Measures, Technical Barriers, Government Procurement, and Intellectual Property

The NAFTA provisions respecting sanitary and phytosanitary measures (Section B of Chapter Seven), technical barriers to trade (Chapter Nine), government procurement (Chapter Ten), and intellectual property (Chapter Seventeen) are largely based on the 1991 draft Uruguay Round agreements that ultimately became, respectively, the *SPS Agreement*, the *TBT Agreement*, the *Government Procurement Agreement*, and the *TRIPS Agreement*. However, the wording of the NAFTA provisions covering each of these areas differs in many respects from the wording in the corresponding WTO agreement. The NAFTA negotiators were negotiating their own arrangements in each of these areas and did not choose to follow consistently the wording of the Uruguay Round precedents. In some instances, the wording evidences a truly different arrangement while other differences seem to be in mode of expression. In some cases, it is difficult to tell whether the wording was intended as a difference in substance or of style. Also, the 1991 drafts of each of these agreements changed somewhat in the final two years of the Uruguay Round negotiations.

The result is that Canada is bound by parallel sets of somewhat different obligations in each of these areas. The same may be said for a number of trade-in-goods provisions. However, while the parallels as between GATT 1994 and NAFTA were by design, the existence of parallel obligations in each of these areas is simply the result of the manner in which the timing of the NAFTA and Uruguay Round negotiations happened to work out. The result is awkward, but the NAFTA negotiators had little choice but to follow this approach. There was no assurance at the time that NAFTA was being negotiated that the Uruguay Round would proceed to a successful conclusion.

5) Beyond the WTO: Investment, Services, Financial Services

The NAFTA provisions respecting investment, services, and financial services are much more extensive than those of the *WTO Agreement*. NAFTA Chapter Eleven, "Investment," is a comprehensive investment treaty without any parallel in the WTO agreements. NAFTA Chapter Twelve, "Services," which is directed primarily at the cross-border provision of services from one NAFTA country into another, imposes more extensive obligations than the GATS. NAFTA Chapter Fourteen, "Financial Services," which covers both investments in financial institutions and the cross-border provision of financial services, is a principles-based code that goes well beyond its GATS counterpart.

- *Non-discrimination*: The NAFTA investment and services chapters each contain MFN and national treatment requirements. The financial services chapter also sets out MFN and national treatment requirements in somewhat modified form.
- *Creation of norms*: The investment chapter establishes norms respecting minimum equity requirements, minimum standard of treatment, the imposition of performance requirements, the composition of senior management and boards of directors, the repatriation of earnings, compensation in the event of expropriation, and special formalities. The services chapter contains rules respecting local presence and licensing and certification. The financial services chapter incorporates the investment chapter norms respecting the repatriation of earnings, compensation in the event of expropriation and special formalities, and establishes norms respecting new financial services, data processing, and senior management and boards of directors.
- *Subsidies*: The performance requirement norms in the investment chapter extend to the granting of subsidies. However, subsidies are generally excepted from the application of the provisions of these chapters.
- *Transparency and procedural fairness*: The financial services chapter sets out special rules respecting the notification of measures by regulatory authorities and administrative decisions by such authorities.
- *Exceptions and reservations*: Each of the investment, services, and financial services chapters set out general exceptions. For example, the investment and services provisions do not apply to government procurement. The services provisions do not apply to certain air services. The financial services chapter contains prudential exceptions. There are also reservations set out in Annexes I, II, III, IV, and VII that cover both specific non-conforming measures and entire sectors.

6) Further Exceptions

Besides incorporating the GATT Article XX exceptions, NAFTA Chapter Twenty-One sets out further exceptions of general application. Article 2102 contains an exception for national security measures. Article 2103 provides that certain taxation measures are exempt from NAFTA coverage. Article 2104 sets out an exception for balance of payments provisions. Article 2105 ensures that NAFTA countries will not be required to disclose information under certain circumstances. Article 2106 and Annex 2106 set out the exemption for cultural industries that applies as between Canada and each of the other two NAFTA countries.

7) Transparency and Procedural Fairness

In addition to the procedural requirements applying specifically to customs procedures and emergency actions referred to above, NAFTA establishes procedural requirements respecting sanitary and phytosanitary measures (Section B of Chapter Seven), technical barriers to trade (Chapter Nine), government procurement (Chapter Ten), and the enforcement of intellectual property rights (Chapter Seventeen). NAFTA Chapter Eighteen also sets out general requirements respecting the publication of laws and regulations by the governments of NAFTA countries and procedural fairness (right to notice, right to be heard, and right to judicial review) in this application.

8) Dispute Resolution

a) General Dispute Settlement Procedures: State to State

NAFTA Chapter Twenty establishes general dispute settlement procedures that may be initiated by the government of one NAFTA country against the government of another NAFTA country. The procedures commence with a request for consultations and proceed from there to mediation by the Free Trade Commission (composed of the cabinet level representatives of NAFTA countries, or their designees) and, failing resolution through mediation, to a hearing before a panel. If the government against which the complaint has been brought does not comply with a positive panel finding against it, the government of the complaining NAFTA country can withdraw NAFTA benefits. The application of these procedures is modified by some specific provisions in the NAFTA text.[18]

---

18 For example, NAFTA, *ibid.*, art. 1414 sets out special rules respecting the composition of panels in disputes involving the financial services chapter.

b) Investor-State Dispute Settlement Procedures: Investor versus State

The investment chapter establishes special procedures that permit individual investors of NAFTA countries to initiate arbitration proceedings against governments of other NAFTA countries that do not comply with the requirements of the NAFTA investment chapter. The investor must have suffered damage as the result of the non-compliance. These procedures have been incorporated into the financial services chapter in respect of provisions incorporated into that chapter from the investment chapter.

D. OTHER BILATERAL TRADING ARRANGEMENTS

Canada has entered into a free trade agreement with Israel that became effective on 1 January 1997[19] and a free trade agreement with Chile that became effective on 5 July 1997.[20]

1) The *Canada–Israel Free Trade Agreement* (CIFTA)

The provisions of CIFTA apply almost exclusively to trade in goods. CIFTA Article 1.1 establishes a free trade area consisting of Canada and Israel. Chapter Two provides for the elimination of tariffs, and Chapter Three sets out the rules of origin for determining eligibility for preferential tariff treatment. CIFTA Article 4.1 incorporates the national treatment provisions of GATT Article III but does not contain an MFN obligation. CIFTA deals with import and export restrictions in much the same way as NAFTA and prohibits export taxes but, unlike NAFTA and CCFTA, does not impose additional requirements respecting export restrictions. CIFTA Articles 4.5 and 4.6 set out bilateral emergency procedures and discipline global actions in much the same manner as the corresponding NAFTA provisions. CIFTA contains requirements respecting customs procedures.

---

19 See *Canada–Israel Free Trade Agreement Implementation Act*, S.C. 1996, c. 33, and *Order Fixing January 1, 1997 as the Date of Coming into Force of the Act*, SI/97-9, C. Gaz. 1997.II.448.

20 See *Canada–Chile Free Trade Agreement Implementation Act*, S.C. 1997, c. 14 and *Order Fixing July 5, 1997 as the Date of Coming into Force of the Act*, SI/97-86, C. Gaz. 1997.II.2288.

CIFTA Chapter Seven sets out rules respecting competition policy, monopolies, and state enterprises similar to those in NAFTA Chapter Fifteen. CIFTA provides that rights and obligations of the parties respecting standards-related measures, sanitary and phytosanitary measures, government procurement, temporary entry, intellectual property rights, and antidumping and countervailing duties are to be governed by the relevant WTO agreements.

CIFTA Chapter Eight sets out dispute settlement procedures that are modelled on those in NAFTA Chapter Twenty, and CIFTA Chapter Ten contains exceptions analogous to those in NAFTA Chapter Twenty-One.

2) The *Canada–Chile Free Trade Agreement* (CCFTA)

CCFTA is, with some notable exceptions, a clone of NAFTA. CCFTA Article A-01 establishes a free trade area consisting of Canada and Chile. CCFTA Chapter C closely follows the provisions of NAFTA Chapter Three respecting trade in goods. CCFTA Chapter D sets out rules of origin that are largely based on their counterparts in NAFTA Chapter Four. CCFTA Chapter E sets out customs procedures based on those set out in NAFTA Chapter Five. CCFTA Chapter F (Emergency Action) is based on NAFTA Chapter Eight.

CCFTA Chapters G (Investment), H (Cross-Border Trade in Services), I (Telecommunications), J (Competition Policy, Monopolies and State Enterprises), K (Temporary Entry), and L (Administrative and Institutional Provisions) closely follow their NAFTA counterparts in NAFTA Chapters Eleven, Twelve, Thirteen, Fifteen, and Sixteen, respectively.

The institutional arrangements and dispute settlement procedures set out in CCFTA Chapter N are modelled after those in NAFTA Chapter Twenty and the exceptions in CCFTA Chapter O are similar to those in NAFTA Chapter Twenty-One.

Unlike NAFTA, CCFTA does not contain separate chapters covering agricultural goods or energy goods. There are no provisions covering sanitary and phytosanitary measures, technical barriers, government procurement, financial services, or intellectual property. Matters between Canada and Chile involving sanitary and phytosanitary measures, technical barriers, and intellectual property are governed by the applicable WTO agreement. Matters involving government procurement are not covered by any agreement because Chile is not a party to the *Government Procurement Agreement*. CCFTA Chapter M covers antidumping and countervailing duty matters but in a manner quite different from the approach taken in NAFTA Chapter Nineteen.

E. INTERPRETATION ISSUES

The *WTO Agreement*, NAFTA, CIFTA, and CCFTA establish sets of norms with which Canadian laws must comply. Canadian governments (both federal and provincial) must consider Canada's international obligations when initiating any significant policy initiative. Prior to the mid-1980s, this was not difficult because the international agreements by which Canada was bound covered discrete areas and did not overlap. Canada was party to the multilateral GATT and most of the Tokyo Round codes, the scope of which was confined to issues relating to trade in goods. Other than the *Auto Pact*, which affected only the automotive sector, Canada was not bound by bilateral arrangements. Other international conventions binding Canada, such as intellectual property conventions, covered discrete areas separate from GATT obligations. Although there were interpretative problems within the GATT and these other international arrangements, there was virtually no overlap among agreements.

This began to change once CUFTA became effective. CUFTA and the GATT overlapped with inconsistent obligations affecting the same areas. In the CUFTA/GATT context, these inconsistencies were relatively easy to sort out because the GATT became effective long before CUFTA, and CUFTA set out relatively clear rules as to which agreement applied in any given circumstance. The advent of NAFTA and the WTO agreements has compounded interpretive difficulties. There is significant overlap between the two. Parts of NAFTA are based on drafts of agreements that pre-existed NAFTA but evolved into WTO agreements that became effective a full year after NAFTA's effective date. The scope of the WTO agreements and NAFTA extend to areas, such as intellectual property, that are already covered by long-standing international conventions.

The objective of the remainder of this chapter is to identify interpretative problems and to suggest approaches to resolving them.

1) Guides to Interpretation

For international law purposes, the WTO agreements and NAFTA, as well as CIFTA and CCFTA, are treaties and are subject to the rules of interpretation that apply to treaties.[21]

---

21 U.S. law distinguishes between treaties and trade agreements in that it sets out different approval procedures for each. The *WTO Agreement*, above note 1, and NAFTA, above note 16, are trade agreements that required approval by a simple majority of both Houses of Congress, while a treaty requires approval by two-thirds of the Senate. For international law purposes, both types of agreements are treaties.

a) Vienna Convention on the Law of Treaties

The most useful single authoritative guide to the interpretation of treaties[22] is the *Vienna Convention on the Law of Treaties* (*Vienna Convention*), which is a codification of principles of treaty interpretation.[23] The Appellate Body has held in several decisions that Articles 31 and 32 of the *Vienna Convention* have attained the status of customary international law.[24] Article 31 of the *Vienna Convention* requires that a "treaty shall be interpreted in good faith in accordance with the ordinary meaning to be given to the terms of the treaty in their context and in the light of its object and purpose." Besides the text and the annexes of the treaty, the "context" includes agreements made by the parties to the treaty in connection with its conclusion and instruments made by one or more parties that are accepted by all parties as related to the treaty. Besides the context, subsequent agreements on interpretation and subsequent practice establishing agreement on interpretation will be taken into account. Special meaning will be given to terms if the parties so intend. Article 32 of the *Vienna Convention* permits recourse to supplementary means of interpretation, such as the preparatory work of the treaty, if following the application of Article 31 the meaning is ambiguous or obscure or if the result is manifestly absurd or unreasonable.

Articles 31 and 32 of the *Vienna Convention* have been applied in the interpretation of NAFTA provisions. The panel convened under NAFTA Chapter Twenty in *In the Matter of Tariffs Applied by Canada to Certain U.S.-Origin Agricultural Products*[25] referred to NAFTA Article 102(2) that requires, *inter alia*, that NAFTA be interpreted "in accordance with applicable rules of international law" and stated that these include Articles 31 and 32 of the *Vienna Convention*. This panel decision is a textbook case of the practical application of the Articles 31 and 32

---

22   23 May 1969, 8 I.L.M. 679 [*Vienna Convention*]. The United States is not a signatory to this convention but follows its principles.
23   The principles set out in the *Vienna Convention*, *ibid.*, are not dissimilar to principles of statutory interpretation, but one cannot assume that a rule of interpretation that applies to a statute also applies to the interpretation of a treaty.
24   See *U.S. — Standards for Reformulated and Conventional Gasoline*, WT/DS2/R, Panel Report, and *Japan — Taxes on Alcoholic Beverages*, WT/DS8/AB/R, WT/DS10/AB/R, WT/DS11/AB/R, Appellate Body Report (AB-1996-2) at 11 [*Japan — Taxes Appellate Body*]. As the Appellate Body in *Japan — Taxes on Alcoholic Beverages* observes, art. 3:2 of the *Dispute Settlement Understanding* (*Understanding on Rules and Procedures Governing the Settlement of Disputes*, set out in Annex 2 of the *WTO Agreement*, above note 1) requires that provisions of GATT 1994, above note 6, and other "covered agreements" be clarified in accordance with customary rules of interpretation of international law.
25   2 Dècember 1996, CDA-95-2008-01 (Ch. 20 Panel) [*U.S.-Origin*].

of the *Vienna Convention* because of the opaqueness of the provisions requiring interpretation.[26] The NAFTA provision in question incorporates a CUFTA provision that retains certain rights and obligations under the GATT and agreements negotiated under the GATT.[27] The panel observed that "[T]he terminology used in the drafting of various provisions, both within and across these agreements, is not marked by uniformity or consistency."[28] The panel had to apply the "object and purpose" rule in Article 31 and the "supplementary means of interpretation rule" in Article 32 to derive meaning out of the provisions that it was called upon to consider. This panel decision is discussed in chapter 4 under "Canada and the United States: The Supply Management Decision."

b) Panel and Appellate Body Reports

While jurisprudence under GATT 1947 is not vast, most of the key provisions of GATT 1947 were considered at one time or other by panels, and many panel reports were adopted by the GATT contracting parties. The dispute resolution procedures established by the *Dispute Settlement Understanding* are being actively pursued by WTO member countries, and an increasing body of jurisprudence is being generated by WTO panels and the Appellate Body. The reports of the Appellate Body to date provide particularly valuable insight into the meaning of specific provisions of the WTO agreements (particularly GATT 1994) and the approach to interpretation that should be followed. Relevant Appellate Body and WTO or GATT panel reports are essential guides to interpretation.

The status of adopted panel reports was considered by the Appellate Body in *Japan — Taxes on Alcoholic Beverages*. The panel in that case held that panel reports adopted by the GATT contracting parties constituted "subsequent practice,"[29] which, as noted above, is one of the guides to interpretation referred to in Article 31 of the *Vienna Convention*. The Appellate Body rejected this conclusion, stating that: "Adopted panel reports are an important part of the GATT *acquis*. . . . They create legitimate expectations among WTO Members, and, therefore, should be taken into account where they are relevant to any dispute. However, they are not binding, except with respect to resolving the particular dispute between

---

26 *Ibid.*, paras. 118 & 119.
27 NAFTA, above note 16, Annex 702.1 incorporates, *inter alia*, *Canada–United States Free Trade Agreement*, 22 December 1987, Can. T.S. 1989 No. 3, 27 I.L.M. 281 [CUFTA], art. 710.
28 *U.S.-Origin*, above note 25, para. 123.
29 *Japan — Taxes on Alcoholic Beverages*, WT/DS8/R, WT/DS10/R, WTDS11/R, Panel Report, para. 6.10. [*Japan — Taxes Panel*].

the parties to that dispute."³⁰ The Appellate Body concurred with the panel that, while unadopted reports have no legal status in the GATT or WTO system, "a panel could nevertheless find useful guidance in the reasoning of an unadopted panel report that it considered to be relevant."³¹

CUFTA Chapter Eighteen generated little jurisprudence³² and NAFTA Chapter Twenty is proving to be equally unfruitful.³³ Therefore, there are few panel reports to provide guidance to the meaning of NAFTA provisions. GATT and WTO panel reports and those of the Appellate Body, while clearly not binding, are useful guides to the interpretation of NAFTA provisions that incorporate GATT terms by reference and to NAFTA provisions that are closely analogous to provisions in WTO agreements. The methodology of interpretation that has been and is being prescribed in the evolving Appellate Body jurisprudence should be carefully considered in interpreting NAFTA provisions. GATT and WTO jurisprudence will also be useful in interpreting the meaning of CIFTA and CCFTA provisions.

c) Public International Law
There is an extensive body of public international law that must be consulted to determine the meaning of certain provisions of the trade agreements to which Canada is a party. For example, NAFTA Article 1105 and CCFTA Article G-05 require "treatment in accordance with international law," in respect of investors of other Parties, which has the effect of incorporating public international law into these agreements as a standard. NAFTA Article 1110 and CCFTA Article G-10 each require that full compensation be paid if a Party nationalizes or expropriates an investment of an investor of another Party or takes action tantamount to nationalization or expropriation. Neither the NAFTA nor the CCFTA text defines "nationalization" or "expropriation." The only way to determine if NAFTA Article 1110 or CCFTA Article G-10 applies to any given

---

30 *Japan — Taxes Appellate Body*, above note 24 at 16.
31 *Ibid.* at 17, quoting from the *Japan — Taxes Panel*, above note 29, para. 6.10.
32 There were only five panel reports under CUFTA, above note 27, Chapter Eighteen. These were: *In the Matter of Canada's Landing Requirement for Pacific Coast Salmon and Herring* (1989), 2 T.C.T. 7162 (Ch. 18 Panel); *In the Matter of Lobsters from Canada* (1990), 3 T.C.T. 8182 (Ch. 18 Panel); *In the Matter of Article 304 and the Definition of Direct Cost of Processing or Direct Cost of Assembling* (1992) 5 T.C.T. 8118 (Ch. 18 Panel); *Interpretation of and Canada's Compliance with Article 701.3 with Respect to Durum Wheat Sales*, [1993] F.T.A.D. No. 2 (Ch. 18 Panel) (QL); and *In the Matter of Puerto Rico Regulations on the Import, Distribution and Sale of U.H.T. Milk from Quebec*, [1993] F.T.A.D. No. 7 (Ch. 18 Panel) (QL).
33 To date, the only panel report is *U.S.-Origin*, above note 25.

fact situation is by reference to the body of international jurisprudence that establishes principles for distinguishing between government actions that amount to compensable taking (i.e., nationalization or expropriation) as opposed to those that are non-compensable regulation.

2) Textual Analysis

The Appellate Body in *Japan — Taxes on Alcoholic Beverages* stressed that the principal guide to treaty interpretation is the text of the treaty itself.[34] If a clear meaning can be derived from the text that is not manifestly absurd or unreasonable, supplementary means of interpretation are irrelevant.

a) Scope and Coverage Provisions

Most NAFTA, CIFTA, and CCFTA chapters are introduced by an article entitled "Scope and Coverage" that describes what the chapter is intended to cover and not to cover. The scope and coverage provision is the starting point in the textual analysis of any chapter that contains one because it sets out a road map for the chapter.

b) Preamble

The preamble of a treaty gives guidance as to its "object and purpose" and will be considered by a panel or the Appellate Body in interpreting a substantive provision of a treaty if its meaning is what might be referred to as "elastic."[35] As to whether a panel or the Appellate Body stretches a treaty provision to cover a particular measure or adopts a narrower view can depend on the object and purpose of the treaty set out in the preamble.

c) Tautological Provisions and the Principle of Effectiveness

Trade negotiators sometimes insert tautological provisions into trade agreements to make them saleable to particular constituencies. For example, a provision of an agreement may permit a member country to adopt any measure to protect public health or the environment, as long as the measure is consistent with the agreement.[36] Such a provision may

---

34 *Japan — Taxes Appellate Body*, above note 24 at 13.
35 See the "accordion" metaphor in relation to "likeness" from the Appellate Body decision in *Japan — Taxes Appellate Body, ibid.*, described in chapter 2 under "First Sentence and 'like products.'"
36 Examples include art. 8:1 of the *Agreement on Trade-Related Aspects of Intellectual Property*, set out in Annex 1C of the *WTO Agreement*, above note 1 [*TRIPS Agreement*] and NAFTA, above note 16, art. 904(1).

appear to be "tautological" or "superfluous" because a member country can adopt any measure for whatever purpose it chooses as long as it is consistent with the agreement.

The Appellate Body in *Japan — Taxes on Alcoholic Beverages* enunciated the principle of effectiveness (*ut res magis valeat quam pereat*). Interpretation must give meaning and effect to all terms of the treaty and no clause or paragraph may be reduced to "redundancy or inutility."[37] Thus, while a tautological provision may appear to be without meaning, it is unlikely that a panel or the Appellate Body will readily accept this position. This can make textual analysis challenging because it is difficult to predict how a panel or the Appellate Body might choose to give meaning to a seemingly meaningless provision. However, the principle of effectiveness broadens the scope for creative analysis of provisions that might otherwise seem unhelpful.[38]

d) Provisions Incorporated by Reference

Provisions incorporated by reference from one trade agreement into another trade agreement can make textual analysis difficult. NAFTA is a case in point. NAFTA makes extensive use of incorporation by reference, both in respect of GATT provisions and CUFTA provisions. The technique of incorporating by reference makes for easy drafting but can give rise to interpretative problems.

The terminology of the incorporated provision may not be the same as that of the rest of the agreement into which it is incorporated. For example, NAFTA Annex 702.1 incorporates into NAFTA most of the CUFTA obligations between Canada and the United States respecting agricultural goods. These provisions make reference to "originating" goods, which in the context of CUFTA means qualifying under CUFTA rules of origin. It is not clear that the expression "originating" as incorporated into NAFTA means qualifying under NAFTA rules of origin. However, this is the only interpretation that makes any sense and, based on the rule in Article 32 of the *Vienna Convention* respecting absurd results, the interpretation that makes sense is the one to be applied.

There is also a question as to whether the incorporated provision is static and remains fixed in its form as at the time of its incorporation, or dynamic and evolves as the agreement from which it is incorporated evolves or is superseded by subsequent agreements. The incorporating language in NAFTA with respect to a number of incorporated GATT

---

37 *Japan — Taxes on Appellate Body*, above note 24 at 14.
38 For an example, see chapter 7 under "Limited Exceptions in the *TRIPS Agreement* and NAFTA for Trademarks, Patents, and Industrial Designs."

provisions makes it clear that equivalent provisions of successor agreements are included and that the incorporated provisions evolve as underlying agreements evolve. However, real interpretative problems can result where, as in the situation considered by the NAFTA panel in *In the Matter of Tariffs Applied by Canada to Certain U.S.-Origin Agricultural Products*, the incorporating language does not make any clear reference to subsequent agreements but does not preclude their inclusion.[39] The decision of the panel is discussed in chapter 4 under "Canada and the United States: The Supply Management Decision."

3) Inconsistencies within an Agreement: Which Provision Prevails?

Comprehensive agreements such as the *WTO Agreement*, NAFTA, CIFTA, and CCFTA inevitably contain inconsistencies. These agreements are negotiated by individual teams of negotiators, each of which has a discrete area of responsibility and does not necessarily know what other teams are doing. Teams of lawyers "scrub" the legal texts before finalization, but this process does not always result in a clear text. Provisions affecting politically sensitive areas are sometimes purposely ambiguous, so as to be saleable to opposing constituencies.

Both the *WTO Agreement* and NAFTA contain rules of interpretation that assist in resolving at least some of these interpretative problems. For example, if there is a conflict between a provision of the *WTO Agreement* and a provision of any of the Multilateral Agreements, the *WTO Agreement* prevails to the extent of the conflict.[40] The introductory note to Annex 1A of the *WTO Agreement* provides that if there is a conflict between GATT 1994 and a provision of another agreement in Annex 1A, the provision of the other agreement prevails to the extent of the conflict. NAFTA Article 1112(1) provides that if there is an inconsistency between Chapter Eleven (Investment) and another chapter, the other chapter prevails, while NAFTA Article 1307 provides that if there is an inconsistency between Chapter Thirteen (Telecommunications) and another chapter, Chapter Thirteen prevails. As discussed in chapter 4, the NAFTA panel in *In the Matter of Tariffs Applied by Canada to Certain U.S.-Origin Agricultural Products* applied the rule in NAFTA Article 701(2) that Section A of NAFTA Chapter Seven prevails over other NAFTA provisions.[41] Therefore, the first place to look when trying to resolve an inconsistency is to

---

39 Above note 25.
40 *WTO Agreement*, above note 1, art. XVI:3.
41 Above note 25, paras. 202–207.

the text itself. If an inconsistency or ambiguity cannot be resolved in this way, one must fall back on the general rules of interpretation set out in Articles 31 to 33 of the *Vienna Convention*.

The approach taken by the Appellate Body in *Canada — Certain Measures Concerning Periodicals* to apparent inconsistencies between the agreements included in the *WTO Agreement* is instructive.[42] While the *WTO Agreement* sets out the rule described above respecting the relationship among the agreements within Annex 1A, there is no rule describing the relationship between agreements in different annexes. In this case, Canada argued that its 80 percent tax on advertising revenues derived from split-run editions of periodicals was a measure regulating access to the magazine advertising market and, as such, was covered by the GATS. As Canada had not undertaken any commitments under the GATS with respect to the provision of advertising services, Canada was not obliged to accord national treatment to WTO members.[43] Canada maintained that the GATS and GATT 1994 should be interpreted so as to avoid overlaps.[44] Both the panel and the Appellate Body rejected these arguments. The panel concluded that the "ordinary meaning of the texts of GATT 1994 and GATS as well as Article II:2 of the *WTO Agreement*, taken together, indicates that obligations under GATT 1994 and GATS can co-exist and that one does not override the other."[45] The Appellate Body upheld this decision.[46]

A WTO panel and the Appellate Body would doubtless adopt a similar approach respecting a measure covered by both GATT 1994 or another Annex 1A agreement and the *TRIPS Agreement*, or a measure covered by both the GATS and the *TRIPS Agreement*. Measures must conform to each agreement. Judging from the approach taken in *Canada — Certain Measures Concerning Periodicals*, a WTO panel and the Appellate Body would reject an argument that if the subject matter of a measure is primarily covered by one of these agreements, the other agreements do not apply.[47]

---

42 WT/DS31/R, Panel Report [*Periodicals Panel*]; WT/DS31/AB/R, Appellate Body Report (AB-1997-2) [*Periodicals Appellate Body*].
43 See *Periodicals Appellate Body, ibid.* at 5–6.
44 *Periodicals Panel*, above note 42 at 19, para. 3.38.
45 *Ibid.*, at 73–74, para. 5.17.
46 *Periodicals Appellate Body*, above note 42 at 17. The Appellate Body in *EEC — Regime for the Importation, Sale and Distribution of Bananas*, WT/DS27/AB/R, adopted the same approach. See para. 221 of this Appellate Body Report (AB-1997-3).
47 An example of such an argument would be that a regulation encumbering the use of cigarette trademarks in contravention of the *TRIPS Agreement*, above note 36, is primarily a measure related to the trade in goods and thus covered by GATT 1994, above note 6, and the exception for human, animal, or plant life or health in art. XX(b) of GATT 1994, which has no counterpart in the *TRIPS Agreement*.

4) Inconsistencies between Agreements: Which Agreement Prevails?

The *WTO Agreement* on the one hand and NAFTA, CIFTA, and CCFTA on the other cover much the same ground. Canada is also party to other international agreements, some of which address subject matter covered by the *WTO Agreement*, NAFTA, CIFTA, and CCFTA. If two or more international agreements cover the same subject matter, which applies?

a) Express Rules of Prevalence

The place to start in determining which of two or more international agreements applies is with express rules of prevalence in each of the agreements. For example, NAFTA Article 103 states that, except where otherwise provided, NAFTA prevails over other agreements that *existed* at the time that NAFTA became effective. However, NAFTA Article 104(1) provides that certain international agreements affecting endangered species, hazardous waste, and other environmental matters that pre-date NAFTA nonetheless prevail over NAFTA. Also, NAFTA Annex 608.2 provides that the *Agreement on an International Energy Program (IEP Agreement)*, which became effective in 1974 and to which Canada and the United States (but not Mexico) are party, prevails over NAFTA.

It should be kept in mind that just because two agreements set out different provisions in respect of the same subject matter does not necessarily mean that they are inconsistent and that one must prevail over the other. For example, NAFTA Article 1710(8) prohibits encumbering trademarks with special requirements, whereas the corresponding rule in Article 20 of the *TRIPS Agreement* qualifies the word "encumber" with the word "unjustifiably." The two provisions are clearly not the same but it does not follow that the later *TRIPS Agreement* provision prevails over the earlier NAFTA provision. The more reasonable conclusion is that the more exacting NAFTA provision is intended to apply among the three NAFTA countries, while the less exacting *TRIPS Agreement* provision is intended to apply as between each of the NAFTA countries and the other WTO member countries.

b) The *Vienna Convention*

Article 30 of the *Vienna Convention* provides that, absent an express rule to the contrary, later treaties covering the same subject matter and including the same parties prevail over earlier treaties. It is questionable how useful this provision is in sorting out the apparent inconsistencies between the trade agreements to which Canada is a party.[48] There are timing issues between NAFTA on the one hand and the WTO agreements on the other. For example, GATT 1947 clearly came into effect before NAFTA so, according to the rule in Article 30 of the *Vienna Convention* (and to the rule in NAFTA Article 103), NAFTA prevailed over GATT 1947. However, GATT 1947 has been superseded by GATT 1994, which is part of the *WTO Agreement* that came into effect after NAFTA. GATT 1994 contains the same provisions as GATT 1947 but also includes protocols, certifications, waivers, and understandings that are not part of GATT 1947 and, as stated in Article II:4 of the *WTO Agreement*, is legally distinct from GATT 1947. It is unlikely that Article 30 of the *Vienna Convention* will be of much use in resolving inconsistencies between NAFTA and GATT 1994.

Sometimes the relationship between apparently inconsistent agreements can be resolved through an analysis of the context. For example, as well as establishing certain norms, the *TRIPS Agreement* requires that member countries comply with the provisions of certain intellectual property conventions that clearly came into effect many years before the *TRIPS Agreement*. However, the norms set out in the *TRIPS Agreement* are not uniformly consistent with the provisions of the intellectual property conventions with which compliance is required. According to Article 30 of the *Vienna Convention*, the *TRIPS Agreement* would prevail. However, the same conclusion can be derived from applying Article 31 of the *Vienna Convention*, which requires that a treaty be interpreted "with the ordinary meaning to be given to the terms of the treaty in their context." The *TRIPS Agreement* requires compliance with the provisions of earlier conventions in the context of establishing new norms intended to bind the WTO members. Reading the earlier conventions and the *TRIPS Agreement* together, it is reasonable to conclude that among WTO members, the provisions of the earlier conventions with which compliance is required be interpreted in a manner that is consistent with the new norms that the *TRIPS Agreement* establishes.[49]

---

48 For a discussion of some of the difficulties in applying art. 30 of the *Vienna Convention*, above note 22, see E.W. Vierdag, "The Time of the 'Conclusion' of a Multilateral Treaty: Article 30 of the Vienna Convention on the Law of Treaties and Related Provisions," (1988) British Y.B. Int'l L. 75.

49 Similar arguments could be made in respect of a similar provision in NAFTA, above note 16, Chapter Seventeen, which requires that effect be given to the provisions of certain intellectual property conventions, all of which pre-date NAFTA. However, the rule in NAFTA, art. 103 would also apply with the result that NAFTA Chapter Seventeen would prevail over these existing agreements.

c) NAFTA Rules versus WTO Rules

The question as to which of WTO or NAFTA rules applies is for the most part resolved by NAFTA Article 2005, which provides that if a dispute arises under both NAFTA and WTO rules,[50] the complaining party may choose either NAFTA or WTO dispute settlement procedures, but having chosen one cannot switch to the other.[51] If NAFTA procedures are chosen, NAFTA rules will apply, and if WTO procedures are chosen, WTO procedures will apply. Accordingly, which of NAFTA or WTO rules apply will depend on the dispute resolution forum chosen by the complaining member country, and it will choose the set of rules most favourable to its case. For example, in challenging Canada's rules respecting split-run periodicals in *Canada — Certain Measures Concerning Periodicals*, the United States chose the WTO dispute settlement procedures as opposed to NAFTA procedures because, unlike NAFTA, there is no cultural exemption under WTO rules.[52]

Similar considerations apply between the *WTO Agreement* on the one hand and CCFTA and CIFTA on the other.

5) International Agreements and Subregional Levels of Government: Are Provinces and States Bound?

Subregional governments, such as provincial governments, are not party to either the *WTO Agreement* or to NAFTA and are not bound as contracting parties by either agreement. However, each agreement imposes obligations on the federal government in respect of measures adopted by provincial governments.

Article XXIV:12 of GATT 1994 requires that member countries take measures reasonably available to them to ensure compliance by subregional governments. Canada has been involved in a number of GATT cases involving provincial laws and practices and has never been successful in persuading a GATT panel that all reasonably available measures have been taken to ensure provincial compliance. Other WTO agreements have their own rules respecting compliance by subregional governments. For example, Article 3 of the *Agreement on Technical Barriers to Trade (TBT Agreement)* contains a "reasonably available measures" requirement, with an exception affecting publication. Some WTO agree-

---

50 Art. 2005, *ibid.*, refers to GATT 1947, above note 4, but includes successor agreements.
51 As discussed in chapter 10 under "Which Procedures Apply?" there are some exceptions to this.
52 *Periodicals Panel*, above note 42; *Periodicals Appellate Body*, above note 42.

ments, such as the *Antidumping Agreement* or the *Valuation Agreement*, clearly have no relevance to provincial laws because of their subject matter. Others, such as the *Government Procurement Agreement*, do not apply to the provinces. However, if a WTO agreement affects provincial areas of jurisdiction, the agreement must be reviewed to determine how it deals with measures of subregional or local governments.

The obligation in NAFTA Article 105 is even stronger than that in Article XXIV:12 of GATT 1994. NAFTA countries must take all measures necessary to ensure provincial or state compliance. There are several exceptions to this requirement. The federal government has what amounts to a best efforts obligation in respect of provincial compliance with NAFTA requirements respecting technical barriers to trade, and the NAFTA government procurement requirements do not apply to provincial governments. CCFTA Article A-04 is similar to NAFTA Article 105 but, because Chile is a unitary state, is applicable only to Canada. CIFTA Article 1.4, on the other hand, provides that observance of CIFTA obligations by regional and local governments will be governed by Article XXIV:12 of GATT 1994.

CHAPTER 2

TRADE IN GOODS: NON-DISCRIMINATION AND GENERAL EXCEPTIONS

The core discipline of the rules-based international trading system of which Canada is a part is non-discrimination. Market access is most frequently denied through the application of measures that discriminate against goods from certain countries in favour of those from others or that treat domestic goods more favourably than imported goods. This chapter describes the principles of non-discrimination of the trade-in-goods provisions of the trade agreements to which Canada is party.

Article XX of GATT 1994 sets out general exceptions that apply to all provisions of GATT 1994. These exceptions are frequently invoked to justify discriminatory and other GATT-inconsistent measures. Evolving jurisprudence through WTO panels and the Appellate Body is defining the limits of these exceptions with increasing precision. This chapter describes these GATT 1994 exceptions and their incorporation into and refinement by each of NAFTA, CIFTA, and CCFTA.

A. MFN PRINCIPLE

1) GATT 1994

a) Article I of GATT 1994
The most-favoured-nation or MFN principle described in the "Overview" to the effect that an advantage granted to one be extended to all is applied to trade in goods by Article I of GATT 1994. Article I requires

that any advantage, favour, privilege, or immunity granted by a contracting party to any product originating in or destined for another country (whether or not a contracting party) be granted to like products originating in or destined for all contracting parties.[1] The rule applies to duties or any other charges in connection with importation or exportation, border formalities, internal taxes (such as GST and PST), and regulations respecting internal sale and distribution.

The Appellate Body in *EEC — Regime for the Importation, Sale and Distribution of Bananas*[2] considered the application of import rules applied by the European Union in respect of bananas that were more onerous with respect to importing bananas from some countries than with others. The Appellate Body observed that the term "advantage" had been given a broad definition by earlier GATT panels and found that the requirements were inconsistent with Article I:1 of GATT 1994.[3]

b) Significance of MFN Principle for Government Policy and Sectoral Arrangements

The MFN obligation of GATT 1994 requires the Canadian government and the governments of its trading partners to be even-handed in the application of measures to other countries. The MFN obligation has the effect of preventing trade measures from becoming a morass of special arrangements with individual trading partners.[4] The MFN obligation also requires that the government carefully consider the impact of changing its trade policies because alterations must apply to all trading partners that are WTO members.

Sectoral free trade is raised from time to time as a policy that should be pursued by the Canadian government. The difficulty with sectoral arrangements is that the MFN obligation of GATT 1994 prevents Canada and other WTO member countries from entering into preferential arrangements covering specific sectors. Since the GATT first became effective in

---

1 The scope of art. I of the *General Agreement on Tariffs and Trade 1994*, set out in Annex 1A of the *Agreement Creating the World Trade Organization*, 15 April 1994 (Dobbs Ferry, N.Y.: Oceana Publications, 1997) [GATT 1994] depends on the meaning of the expression "like products." The meaning of this expression in the context of GATT art. III has been considered in recent WTO jurisprudence described below under "First Sentence and "like products.""
2 WT/DS27/AB/R, Appellate Body Report (AB-1997-3) [*Bananas Appellate Body*].
3 See *ibid.*, paras. 205–207. This case involves a complex scheme for regulating the importation of bananas into the European Union that was found to be inconsistent with a number of provisions of GATT 1994, *ibid.* There had been several earlier GATT panel decisions on the banana importation issue.
4 As will be seen in following chapters, the permitted exceptions (free trade areas, Generalized System of Preferences) have resulted in a substantial variation in the manner in which Canada treats goods imported from its trading partners.

1948, Canada has been party to only one preferential sectoral arrangement, namely the *Auto Pact*. The *Auto Pact* was GATT-consistent because the U.S. government obtained a waiver under GATT Article XXV and because the benefits conferred by the Canadian government under the *Auto Pact* apply to imported automotive goods from any country entitled to the benefit of Canada's MFN Tariff Rate. Preferential free trade arrangements must be pursued within the parameters of Article XXIV of GATT 1994 or not at all.

2) NAFTA, CIFTA, and CCFTA

None of NAFTA, CIFTA, or CCFTA contains a general MFN requirement respecting the trade in goods.[5] However, all the parties to these agreements are WTO member countries and are bound by the MFN requirements of GATT 1994.

B. NATIONAL TREATMENT

1) Article III of GATT 1994

The MFN principle just described requires non-discriminatory treatment among products imported from different countries. Article III of GATT 1994 requires non-discriminatory treatment between imported products and domestic products under internal (as opposed to border) measures such as internal taxes and regulations respecting various aspects of internal distribution. Article III has been considered by a number of GATT panels and jurisprudence respecting the interpretation of the various provisions of Article III is continuing to evolve through the WTO dispute settlement process. Articles III:1, III:2, and III:4 are the most significant provisions of Article III, and these are subject to exceptions set out in Article III:8.[6]

---

5 Paragraph 1 of the *North American Free Trade Agreement*, 17 December 1992, Can. T.S. 1994 No. 2 [NAFTA], Annex 300-A (Trade and Investment in the Automotive Sector) requires that NAFTA countries accord to existing automotive producers treatment that is no less favourable than to new producers. While this is an MFN requirement and Annex 300-A is included within NAFTA Part Two (Trade in Goods), this MFN requirement does not apply to automotive goods themselves but, rather, to the producers of them.

6 GATT 1994, above note 1, arts. III:3 & III:6 are transitional provisions. Articles III:5 & III:7 prohibit regulations relating to the mixture, processing or use of products that require that a specified amount or proportion of any product be supplied from domestic sources or be allocated among external sources. Article III:9 requires that contracting parties take into account the interests of exporting contracting parties when applying internal maximum price control measures.

a) Article III:1: No Protection to Domestic Production

Article III:1 provides that the contracting parties recognize that internal taxes and various other internal measures should not be applied to imported or domestic production to protect domestic production. In *Japan — Taxes on Alcoholic Beverages*, a case involving Japanese taxes on spirits applied at a higher rate against imported than domestic products, the Appellate Body held that Article III articulates a general principle that internal measures should not be applied so as to afford protection to domestic production and that this general principle "informs the rest of Article III" and forms part of the context of each other provision in Article III.[7] As noted below, the Appellate Body has applied this principle on several occasions.[8]

b) Article III:2: Internal Taxes and Charges

Article III:2 covers internal taxes and other internal charges.[9] The first sentence of Article III:2 requires that products imported from a contracting party imported into another contracting party not be subject to internal taxes or other internal charges in excess of those applied to like domestic products. The second sentence requires that no contracting party shall apply internal taxes or other internal charges in a manner contrary to the principles in Article III:1. *Ad Article III:2* clarifies the meaning of the second sentence by providing that a tax consistent with the first sentence would be considered inconsistent with the second sentence only where competition was involved between the taxed product and a directly competitive or substitutable product that was not similarly taxed.

i) First Sentence and "like products"

The scope of the first sentence of Article III:2 depends upon the meaning of the expression "like products." This expression, which appears in other provisions of GATT 1994, most notably Article III:4 and Article I:1, was considered both by a WTO panel and the Appellate Body in

---

7   WT/DS8/AB/R, WT/DS10/AB/R, WT/DS11/AB/R, Appellate Body Report (AB-1996-2) at 21 [*Japan — Taxes Appellate Body*].
8   In *U.S. — Standards for Reformulated and Conventional Gasoline*, WT/DS2/R, Panel Report [*Gasoline Panel*], the United States had argued that GATT 1994, above note 1, art. III:1 was only hortatory and could not form the basis of a violation. The WTO panel did not rule on this position because it had already found inconsistency under GATT 1994, above note 1, art. III:4. See *Gasoline Panel*, para. 6.17. Judging from the decision in *Japan — Taxes Appellate Body, ibid.*, the Appellate Body clearly does not view art. III:1 as "hortatory."
9   Even though GST is collected at the border on imported goods, it is still an internal tax because it applies to domestic goods. See GATT 1994, *ibid.*, *Ad Article III*.

Japan — Taxes on Alcoholic Beverages. The Appellate Body cited the general approach for interpreting "like or similar" products set out in the Report of the Working Party on Border Tax Adjustments where it is stated that interpretation must be examined on a case-by-case basis and suggested some criteria as being "the product's end-uses in a given market; consumers' tastes and habits, which change from country to country; the product's properties, nature and quality."[10]

The WTO panel in *Japan — Taxes on Alcoholic Beverages* adopted this approach in comparing the domestic Japanese product, shochu, with the imported products, namely vodka, liqueurs, gin and genever, rum, whisky, and brandy. The panel concluded that shochu and vodka were like products because of similar physical characteristics. However, none of the other products was a "like product" because the use of additives disqualified liqueurs, gin and genever, the use of ingredients disqualified rum, and appearance disqualified brandy and whisky.[11] The panel considered that like products constitute a subset of "directly competitive or substitutable products" and that, for the purposes of Article III:2, the expression "like products" was to be narrowly construed. The WTO panel found that Japanese taxes on vodka were higher than on shochu and were inconsistent with the first sentence of Article III:2, and rejected arguments made by Japan that as shochu and vodka received "roughly" the same treatment, the tax measures were consistent with Article III:2.[12]

The Appellate Body did not reverse these findings. The Appellate Body commented that sufficiently detailed tariff classification could be a factor in determining likeness but emphasized that there was no single approach to determining likeness.[13] In commenting on the narrow meaning of like products in Article III:2, the Appellate Body drew the following analogy:

---

10 GATT, Working Party on Border Tax Adjustments, *Report Adopted by the Council on 2 December 1970*, GATT Doc. L/3464, para. 18., 18th supp. B.I.S.D. (1970–1971) 97 at 102.
11 *Japan — Taxes on Alcoholic Beverages*, WT/DS8/R, WT/DS10/R, WT/DS11/R, Panel Report, para. 6.22 [*Japan — Taxes Panel*].
12 *Ibid.*, para. 6.25.
13 The Harmonized Commodity and Coding System (Harmonized System) is now used by WTO countries and provides for a common system for classifying goods. There are permitted variations between countries under the Harmonized System (see chapter 3). Before the wide acceptance of the Harmonized System, tariff classification would not have been a factor in determining "likeness" because each country had its own tariff classification system.

The concept of "likeness" is a relative one that evokes the image of an accordion. The accordion of "likeness" stretches and squeezes in different places as different provisions of the *WTO Agreement* are applied. The width of the accordion in any one of those places must be determined by the particular provision in which the term "like" is encountered as well as by the context and the circumstances that prevail in any given case to which that provision may apply. We believe that, in Article III:2, first sentence of the GATT 1994, the accordion of likeness is meant to be narrowly squeezed.[14]

ii) Second Sentence and "directly competitive or substitutable products"
As none of the imported spirits except vodka were like products to shochu, both the WTO panel and the Appellate Body in *Japan — Taxes on Alcoholic Beverages* had to consider whether the taxation measures in question were consistent with the second sentence of Article III:2. The Appellate Body noted that the second sentence made specific reference to Article III:1 which affected its meaning and concluded that determining whether a measure was inconsistent with the second sentence of Article III:2 involved three separate issues,[15] namely, whether the imported and domestic products are "directly competitive or substitutable products" in competition with each other,[16] and if so, whether these products are not similarly taxed,[17] and if such is the case, whether the dissimilar taxation is (quoting from Article III:1) applied so as to "afford protection to domestic production."[18]

The Appellate Body noted (as had the WTO panel), that "directly competitive or substitutable products" constituted a broader category than "like products," but how much broader depended on the particular case. The Appellate Body concurred with the WTO panel's view that "the decisive criterion in order to determine whether two products are directly competitive or substitutable is whether they have common end-uses, *inter alia*, as shown by elasticity of substitution"[19] and supported the panel's finding that all the products in question were directly

---

14 *Japan — Taxes Appellate Body*, above note 7 at 25.
15 *Ibid.* at 29.
16 GATT 1994, above note 1, *Ad Article III:2*.
17 *Ibid., Ad Article III:2*.
18 The words "afford protection to domestic production" come from *ibid.*, art. III:1.
19 *Japan — Taxes Appellate Body*, above note 7 at 31, quoting from *Japan — Taxes Panel*, above note 11, para. 6.22. The panel observed that establishing commonality of end-uses is necessary to establish "likeness" but not, by itself, sufficient.

competitive or substitutable. The Appellate Body then considered whether the imported and domestic products were not similarly taxed and concurred with the panel that for this criterion to apply, the differential taxation must be more than *de minimis* and the tax burden on the imported products must be heavier than on the "directly competitive or substitutable" domestic products. With respect to the "so as to afford protection" inquiry, the Appellate Body observed that the issue was not one of the intent behind the measure but how it is applied.[20] The Appellate Body concurred with the panel's finding that the taxation was dissimilar and was applied so as to afford protection. The end result was that the taxation measures in question were found to be inconsistent with the second sentence of Article III:2, even though they were consistent with the first sentence (except insofar as they applied to vodka).

The methodology applied by the Appellate Body in analysing the second sentence of Article III:2 in *Japan — Alcoholic Beverages* was followed by the Appellate Body in *Canada — Certain Measures Concerning Periodicals*.[21] The Appellate Body, which was considering the consistency with Article III:2 of an 80 percent tax that applied only to "split-run" periodicals, examined various statements that had been made in Canadian studies concerning the effect of U.S. split-run periodicals on the Canadian magazine industry and quoted a passage from the Task Force *Report*[22] to the effect that the majority of the magazines are from the United States and are a close substitute.[23] The Appellate Body concluded that imported split-run periodicals and domestic non-split run periodicals are directly competitive or substitutable products,[24] that

---

20 *Japan — Taxes Appellate Body*, ibid. at 33.
21 WT/DS31/R, Panel Report [*Periodicals Panel*] and WT/DS31/AB/R, Appellate Body Report (AB-1997-2) [*Periodicals Appellate Body*]. In this case, the WTO panel had found that imported "split-run" periodicals and domestic "non-split run" periodicals were "like products" and the 80 percent excise tax under consideration was inconsistent with the first sentence in GATT 1994, above note 1, art. III:2. See *Periodicals Panel*, paras. 5.20 to 5.30. The conclusion was based on a hypothetical example because the importation of "split-run periodicals" was prohibited under Tariff Code Item 9958. The Appellate Body rejected the panel's conclusion because the panel failed to take into account the relevant factors enumerated in *Japan — Taxes Appellate Body* and because the hypothetical example was incorrect. As a result of its conclusion on "like products," the Appellate Body could not find that the measure was inconsistent with the first sentence of art. III:1 and had to consider the second sentence.
22 *A Question of Balance: Report of the Task Force on the Canadian Magazine Industry* (Ottawa: Supply and Services, 1994).
23 *Periodicals Appellate Body*, above note 21 at 31.
24 Ibid. at 32.

they were dissimilarly taxed, and that the dissimilar taxation was applied so as to afford protection. As a result of these findings, the 80 percent tax was held to be inconsistent with the second sentence of Article III:2.

c) Article III:4: No Less Favourable Treatment

Article III:4 requires that imported products be accorded treatment no less favourable than like products of national origin in respect of all laws, regulations and requirements affecting their internal sale, offering for sale, purchase, transportation, or use. Article III:4 has been considered by a number of GATT panels and continues to be the subject of evolving jurisprudence under the WTO. In *United States — Section 337 of the Tariff Act of 1930*, a GATT panel held that the words "treatment no less favourable" call for "effective equality of opportunities" in respect of the laws, regulations, and requirements referred to in Article III:4.[25] This standard has been applied in a number of subsequent decisions. In *Canada — Import, Distribution and Sale of Certain Alcoholic Drinks by Provincial Marketing Agencies (Beer Case)*, a GATT panel found that "by allowing the access of domestic beer to points of sale not available to imported beer, Canada accorded domestic beer competitive opportunities denied to imported beer."[26] No less favourable treatment does not necessarily mean the same treatment. The GATT panel in the *Beer Case*, in reviewing the delivery systems that applied to imported and domestic beer, observed that the mere fact that imported and domestic beer were subject to different delivery systems was not, in itself, conclusive in establishing an inconsistency with Article III:4. However, it was up to Canada to demonstrate that the application of different systems did not result in less favourable treatment of imported beer.[27]

Article III:4 was considered by a WTO panel in *U.S. — Standards for Reformulated and Conventional Gasoline* in respect of differing baseline establishment requirements applicable to imported and domestic gasoline. The panel applied the "effective equality of opportunities" test described above and concluded that imported gasoline was treated less favourably.[28] The panel rejected a U.S. argument that the requirements of Article III:4 were satisfied because imported gasoline was being

---

25 *U.S. — Section 337 of the Tariff Act of 1930 (EEC v. U.S.)* (1988), GATT Doc. L/6439, para. 5.11, 36th supp. B.I.S.D. (1988–1989) 345 at 386 [*Section 337 Case*].
26 (*U.S. v. Canada*) (1991), GATT Doc. DS17/R, para. 5.6, 39th supp. B.I.S.D. (1991–1992) 27 at 76 [*Beer Case*].
27 *Ibid.*, para. 5.12 (at 78–79). The panel found that the differing delivery systems were inconsistent with art. III:4.
28 *Gasoline Panel*, above note 8, para. 6.10.

treated similarly to gasoline from similarly situated domestic parties. The panel stated that Article III:4 deals with the treatment of like products and noted that its wording did not permit less favourable treatment on the basis of the characteristics of the producer.[29] The panel also considered a U.S. argument that the treatment of imported gasoline under the statutory baseline was, on the whole, no less favourable than that accorded to domestic gasoline under the individual baseline and rejected the notion that less favourable treatment of some imported products could be offset by more favourable treatment of other imported products.[30]

The panel in *U.S. — Standards for Reformulated and Conventional Gasoline* also considered the question as to whether imported gasoline and domestic gasoline were like products for the purposes of Article III:4. The panel considered much the same criteria that had been considered by the WTO panel and the Appellate Body in *Japan — Alcoholic Beverages* respecting the first sentence of Article III:2 and found that the imported and domestic gasoline were like products because they had exactly the same physical characteristics, end-uses, and tariff classification, and were perfectly substitutable.[31]

d) Article III:8: Exceptions

Article III:8(a) of GATT 1994 provides that the obligations of Article III of GATT 1994 do not apply to government procurement. However, the plurilateral *Government Procurement Agreement* sets out national treatment obligations that apply to the measures covered by that agreement.

Article III:8(b) of GATT 1994 provides that the obligations of Article III of GATT 1994 do not apply to the payment of subsidies exclusively to domestic producers.[32] In *Canada — Certain Measures Concerning Periodicals*, the Appellate Body adopted a strict interpretation of this exception.[33] The Canadian government has assisted the Canadian magazine industry through reduced postal rates. Periodic payments are made by the Department of Canadian Heritage to Canada Post (a Crown corporation) to support the special postal rates for the Canadian magazines. The United States challenged this practice and the WTO panel hearing the case concluded that the policy, while inconsistent with Article III:4 of

---

29 *Ibid.*, para. 6.11.
30 *Ibid.*, para. 6.14.
31 *Ibid.*, paras. 6.8 & 6.9.
32 However, as discussed in chapter 6, there are other international obligations that affect the ability of governments to grant subsidies.
33 *Periodicals Panel*, above note 21; *Periodicals Appellate Body*, above note 21.

GATT 1994,[34] fell within the exception.[35] The Appellate Body reversed the panel's decision on the grounds that the policy of reducing postal rates was indistinguishable from a tax reduction or exemption and that permissible producer subsidies covered by the exception were limited to payments after taxes were collected.[36] Accordingly, benefits to producers conferred as reductions in payments such as taxes or postal rates, rather than by government expenditure, are excluded from the exception.

2) NAFTA Rules

a) NAFTA Article 301

NAFTA Article 301(1) incorporates GATT Article III in its entirety.[37] The incorporating language includes "any equivalent provision of a successor agreement" which means that Article III of GATT 1994 is incorporated into NAFTA.[38]

NAFTA Article 301(2) requires that a province or a state provide treatment to goods of other NAFTA countries at least as favourable as the most favourable treatment that it provides to "like, directly competitive or substitutable goods" of the NAFTA country of which it is a part. As noted above, the expression "directly competitive or substitutable" goods covers a broader range of goods than the expression "like" goods. The jurisprudence described above under "Second Sentence and 'directly competitive or substitutable products'" would be relevant to determining the scope of NAFTA Article 301(2). If a Canadian province treats its own goods more favourably than goods of other provinces, it must treat goods of the United States and Mexico no less favourably than its own goods, even though the treatment is more favourable than that of goods of other provinces.

---

34 *Periodicals Panel, ibid.*, para. 5.39.
35 *Periodicals Panel, ibid.*, para. 5.44.
36 *Periodicals Appellate Body*, above note 21 at 38. See the quote from *U.S. — Measures Affecting Alcoholic and Malt Beverages (Canada v. U.S.)* (1992), GATT Doc. DS23/R, para. 5.10, 39th supp. B.I.S.D. (1991–1992) 206 at 272, with which the Appellate Body concurred.
37 Including the exceptions for government procurement and subsidies paid to domestic producers in GATT 1994, above note 1, art. III:8.
38 *Canada — United States Free Trade Agreement*, 22 December 1987, Can. T.S. 1989 No. 3, 27 I.L.M. 281 [CUFTA] followed a similar approach but the incorporating language in CUFTA art. 501 differed in that it referred to the "existing provisions of Article III," meaning those that were in effect on 1 January 1989. This language froze GATT, *ibid.*, art. III obligations as of a point in time. The NAFTA, above note 5, incorporating language is dynamic, and incorporates the evolving art. III.

NAFTA Annex 301.3 lists exceptions to Articles 301 (National Treatment) and 309 (Import and Export Restrictions). The matters listed relate almost entirely to import and export restrictions rather than to national treatment and are discussed in chapter 4.

b) Goods of a Party

The national treatment requirement of NAFTA Article 301 must be applied to "the goods of another Party." The expression "goods of a Party" is defined in NAFTA Article 201 as "domestic products" as these are understood under the GATT.[39] While the expression "domestic products" is not defined in GATT 1994, it appears in several articles, most notably in Article III.[40] For example, Article III:2 prohibits the application of internal taxes on imported products unless they also apply to like *domestic products*. If a good is a *domestic product* of Canada for the purposes of applying the obligations in Article III:2 to the Canadian government, that same good is a "good of Canada" when entering the United States or Mexico for the purposes of applying the national treatment obligation in NAFTA Article 301 to the U.S. or Mexican government.

The definition of "good of a Party" and its use in conjunction with the national treatment obligation in NAFTA Article 301 is to incorporate an imprecise but nonetheless objective standard as to which goods entering one NAFTA country from another are entitled to protection. In this one respect, the NAFTA rule differs from the GATT rule. GATT Article III applies to "products of the territory of any contracting party" and, until the *Rules of Origin Agreement* came into effect (see chapter 4), each member country was free to make its own rules for determining the country of origin of goods.

3) CIFTA and CCFTA Rules

Like NAFTA Article 301, CIFTA Article 4.1 and CCFTA Article C-01 incorporate Article III of GATT 1994 by reference. The scope of the obligation extends to "goods of the other Party." The CIFTA and CCFTA definitions of "goods of a Party" are the same as the NAFTA definition, and the same considerations described above under NAFTA Article 301 apply. CIFTA Annex 4.1 and CCFTA Annex C-01.3 set out substantially

---

39 NAFTA, *ibid*. The definition also includes "originating" goods of a NAFTA country (i.e., goods satisfying the rules required for preferential tariff treatment) and "such goods as the Parties may agree."
40 GATT 1994, above note 1, art. XI:2(c).

the same items for Canada[41] as NAFTA Annex 301.3. CCFTA Article C-01(2), to which there is no CIFTA counterpart, sets out a rule respecting provinces similar to that in NAFTA Article 301(2) described above.

4) Significance of National Treatment Obligations for Government Policy

Just as Article I of GATT 1994 requires that the Canadian and provincial governments be even-handed in their treatment of goods imported from various trading partners, Article III of GATT 1994 requires that government policy be even-handed in its treatment of imported goods and domestic goods. Provincial governments have had particular difficulty in meeting the requirements of Article III in the treatment of alcoholic beverages. While discriminatory rules are currently being phased out, alcoholic beverages form a special case to which special rules apply.

5) Special Rules: Alcoholic Beverages

For many years, Canada's provincial liquor monopolies followed practices that were inconsistent with Canada's national treatment under GATT Article III.[42] Mark-ups on imported products were much higher than on domestic products. Foreign producers had difficulty in obtaining listings for their products in provincial liquor stores. Domestic products were available at more points of sale than imported products.

The CUFTA provisions respecting wine and distilled spirits eliminated most of these practices as between Canada and the United States. CUFTA grandfathered discriminatory practices respecting beer but GATT rights were preserved. Just after CUFTA became effective, the European Community received a favourable decision in a challenge to the practices of the provincial liquor monopolies.[43] The report of the panel was adopted and Canada and the European Union negotiated the *Agreement between Canada and the European Economic Community concerning Trade and Commerce in Alcoholic Beverages* (*EC Alcoholic Beverage Agreement*). The United States commenced its own GATT challenge

---

41 Except for item 4 in NAFTA Annex 301.3, which applies to certain categories of ships traded between Canada and the United States. There are a few other differences.
42 Provincial practices have also been found to be inconsistent with GATT 1994, above note 1, arts. II and XI.
43 See *Canada — Import, Distribution and Sale of Alcoholic Drinks by Canadian Provincial Marketing Agencies* (*EEC v. Canada*) (1987), GATT Doc. L/6304, 35th supp. B.I.S.D. (1987–1988) 37.

to provincial practices respecting beer and received a favourable decision,[44] the result of which was the negotiation of the *Memorandum of Understanding on Provincial Beer Marketing Practices of 5 August 1993* (*Beer Agreement*).[45] NAFTA incorporates CUFTA Chapter Eight to apply between Canada and the United States and sets out separate provisions to apply between Canada and Mexico.[46]

a) CUFTA Chapter Eight: Trade in Wine and Distilled Spirits with the United States

CUFTA Chapter Eight exempts wine and distilled spirits from national treatment provisions except as specifically required in Chapter Eight. Non-conforming measures cannot be made more non-conforming. National treatment is required in respect of listing with the exception of certain automatic listing practices in British Columbia respecting estate wineries existing on 4 October 1987. Price differentials between the products of the two countries maintained by public entities were phased out, with complete elimination of differentials taking place in 1995. National treatment is required respecting points of sale except that on-premises sales of domestic products by domestic wineries and distilleries is permitted and private wine outlets in Ontario and British Columbia existing on 4 October 1987 are allowed to discriminate in favour of wine of those provinces. Quebec may continue to require that wine sold in grocery stores be bottled in Quebec provided that there are alternative outlets in Quebec for the sale of U.S. wine, whether or not such wine is bottled in Quebec.

b) *EC Alcoholic Beverages Agreement:* Trade in Beer, Wine, and Distilled Spirits with the European Union

The *EC Alcoholic Beverages Agreement* requires that discriminatory mark-ups on wine be phased out. Ontario, British Columbia, and Nova Scotia have until 1998 to phase out price differentials between 100 percent Canadian wine and imported wine. Differentials in other provinces

---

44 *Beer Case*, above note 26.
45 See Foreign Affairs and International Trade Canada, News Release No. 152 (5 August 1993). See also Foreign Affairs and International Trade Canada, News release No. 89 (5 May 1994).
46 NAFTA, above note 5, Annex 313 also sets out requirements respecting distinctive products, being "Bourbon" or "Tennessee Whiskey" in the case of the United States, "Canadian Whisky" in the case of Canada and "Tequila" or "Mezcal" in the case of Mexico. Other than these requirements, there are no special rules in NAFTA respecting the trade in wine and distilled spirits between the United States and Mexico.

were eliminated in 1995. Discriminatory mark-ups on beer were frozen. The agreement requires national treatment in the marketing of wine except for the private outlets operated by wineries in Ontario and British Columbia.

c) *Beer Agreement:* **Trade in Beer with the United States**

The *Beer Agreement* required that the province of Ontario discontinue its minimum price requirements and lower fees, and permit U.S. beer to be sold in the Brewer's Retail Outlets. This agreement also accelerated the elimination of tariffs on beer, which would otherwise not have been eliminated until 1 January 1998. However, Ontario's controversial levy on beer cans, which arguably treats U.S. beer less favourably than domestic beer (which is packaged primarily in bottles), was not affected by the *Beer Agreement*.

d) **NAFTA Annex 312.2: Trade in Wine and Distilled Spirits with Mexico**

NAFTA Annex 312.2 contains provisions similar to those in CUFTA Chapter Eight. The only significant difference is in elimination of price differentials. While differentials on distilled spirits had to be eliminated upon NAFTA becoming effective, Annex 312.2 adopts the timetable in the *EC Alcoholic Beverages Agreement* for the elimination of price differentials on wine. There is no special rule for beer, meaning that the national treatment requirement of NAFTA Article 301 applies.

e) **CIFTA and CCFTA**

CIFTA does not contain any special provisions respecting alcoholic beverages. CCFTA Article C-10 prohibits requirements that imported distilled spirits be blended with domestic distilled spirits and CCFTA Annex C-10.2 sets out requirements respecting wine and distilled spirits that are identical to those in NAFTA Annex 312.2.

C. GENERAL EXCEPTIONS

This section covers the general exceptions in Article XX of GATT 1994 and their incorporation into NAFTA, CIFTA, and CCFTA. Chapter 9 describes further exceptions that affect Canada's obligations in respect of trade in goods and other areas covered by the *WTO Agreement*, NAFTA, CIFTA, and CCFTA.

1) Article XX of GATT 1994

Article XX permits member countries to adopt certain measures notwithstanding GATT obligations. These are measures:

(a) necessary to protect public morals;

(b) necessary to protect human, animal or plant life or health;

(c) relating to the importations or exportations of gold or silver;

(d) necessary to secure compliance with laws or regulations which are not inconsistent . . . with [the GATT], including those relating to customs enforcement, the enforcement of monopolies . . . , the protection of patents, trade marks and copyrights, and the prevention of deceptive practices;

(e) relating to the products of prison labour;

(f) imposed for the protection of national treasures of artistic, historical or archaeological value;

(g) relating to the conservation of exhaustible natural resources if such measures are made effective in conjunction with restrictions on domestic production or consumption;

(h) undertaken in pursuance of obligations under any intergovernmental commodity agreement . . . ;

(i) involving restrictions on exports of domestic materials necessary to assure essential quantities of such materials to a domestic processing industry during periods when the domestic price of such materials is held below the world price as part of a government stabilization plan; *Provided* that such restrictions shall not operate to increase the exports of or the protection afforded to such domestic industry, and shall not depart from . . . [GATT non-discrimination principles; and]

(j) essential to the acquisition . . . of products in general or local short supply . . . [subject to the principle of international sharing among contracting parties and provided] that any such measures, which are otherwise inconsistent with the . . . [GATT] shall be discontinued as soon as the conditions giving rise to them have ceased. . . .

a) Approach to Interpretation of Article XX Exceptions

A member country invoking an exception in Article XX bears the burden of demonstrating that its inconsistent measure falls within the scope of the exception.⁴⁷ The member country invoking an exception must establish three elements:⁴⁸

(1) that the policy objective in respect of the measure for which the exception is invoked falls within the range of policies covered by the exception;

(2) that, depending on the language of the exception, the measure is "necessary"⁴⁹ or "essential"⁵⁰ or "relating to"⁵¹ or "involving"⁵² or is "for the protection of"⁵³ or "in pursuance of"⁵⁴ the policy objective in question, and satisfies other qualifying language of the exception; and

(3) that the measure is applied in conformity with the introductory clause of Article XX.

The application of these requirements is best demonstrated by describing the approach taken by GATT and WTO panels and the Appellate Body in several situations in which GATT/WTO member countries invoked exceptions to justify inconsistent measures. The exceptions considered in these cases include those that have been most frequently invoked in GATT and WTO jurisprudence to justify GATT-inconsistent measures, namely the exceptions in Article XX(b) (protection of human, animal, or plant life or health), XX(d) (necessary to secure compliance with laws), and XX(g) (preservation of exhaustible natural resources).

In *Thailand — Restrictions on Importation of and Internal Taxes on Cigarettes*⁵⁵ (*Cigarette Case*), a GATT panel considered the applicability of the exception in Article XX(b) (human, animal and plant life or health) to restrictions on imports of cigarettes imposed by Thailand. In

---

47 *Gasoline Panel*, above note 8, para. 6.20.
48 These elements are set out in *ibid.*, in respect of the exception for human, animal or plant life or health in GATT 1994, above note 1, art. XX(b). See also *U.S. — Restrictions on Imports of Tuna (EEC & Netherlands v. U.S.)* (1994), 33 I.L.M. 839 [*U.S. — Tuna*], para. 5.12, where these elements are described in respect of the exception for exhaustible natural resources in Article XX(g).
49 Exceptions in GATT 1994, *ibid.*, are arts. XX(a) (public morals), (b) (human, animal or plant life or health), & (d) (compliance with laws).
50 *Ibid.*, art. XX(j) (short supply).
51 *Ibid.*, arts. XX(c) (gold and silver), (e) (prison labour), & (g) (exhaustible natural resources).
52 *Ibid.*, art. XX(i) (assuring essential quantities).
53 *Ibid.*, art. XX(f) (national treasures).
54 *Ibid.*, art. XX(h) (international commodity agreements).
55 (*U.S. v. Thailand*) (1990), GATT Doc. DS10/R, 37th supp. B.I.S.D. (1989–1990) 200 [*Cigarette Case*].

U. S. — Restrictions on Imports of Tuna[56] (*Tuna Case*), a GATT panel considered the applicability of the exceptions in Articles XX(b) and XX(g) (exhaustible natural resources) to U.S. import restrictions on fish or fish products harvested by a method resulting in an incidental kill of marine mammals in excess of U.S. standards. The restriction was aimed at tuna caught in the eastern tropical Pacific Ocean where schools of tuna are accompanied by dolphins. In *U.S. — Standards for Reformulated and Conventional Gasoline* (*Gasoline Case*), the Appellate Body considered the applicability of the exception in Article XX(g) to regulations under which certain "baseline establishment rules" for establishing that imported gasoline satisfied standards aimed at reducing air pollution was less favourable than those that applied to domestic gasoline. In *Canada — Certain Measures Concerning Periodicals*[57] (*Periodicals Case*), a WTO panel considered, *inter alia*, the applicability of the exception in Article XX(d) (securing compliance with laws) to an import restriction (Tariff Code 9958) on the importation of split-run periodicals.

In each of these four cases, the country invoking the exception failed to establish all three elements. In the *Periodicals Case*, the invoking country, Canada, failed to establish the first element and the other two elements were not considered. In the *Cigarette* and *Tuna Cases*, Thailand and the United States established the first element but failed to establish the second element. In the *Gasoline Case*, the United States established the first and second elements but failed to establish the third element.

i) First Element: Policy Objective Falls within the Exception

In the *Cigarette Case*, the panel accepted that smoking constituted a serious risk to health and that measures designed to reduce cigarette consumption fell within the scope of Article XX(b).[58] In the *Tuna Case*, the panel held that dolphins were an exhaustible natural resource covered by Article XX(g)[59] and that the protection of dolphin life or health fell within Article XX(b).[60] The panel observed that neither Articles XX(g) or (b) placed any limits on the location of the exhaustible natural resources or the living things to be protected[61] and the fact that the dol-

---

56 Above note 48. There is an earlier panel report, *U.S. — Restrictions on Imports of Tuna (Mexico v. U.S.)* (1991), GATT Doc. DS21/R, 39th supp. B.I.S.D. (1991–1992) 155, respecting U.S. restrictions on tuna imports.
57 *Periodicals Panel*, above note 21.
58 Above note 55, para. 73.
59 Above note 48, para. 5.13.
60 *Ibid.*, para. 5.30.
61 *Ibid.*, paras. 5.15 & 5.31.

phins in question were not in U.S. territory was not a valid objection in respect of this particular element. In the *Gasoline Case*, the WTO panel found that clean air was an exhaustible natural resource that could be depleted, and the fact that it was renewable was not a valid objection to the applicability of the exception in Article XX(g).[62] The Appellate Body did not take issue with this finding.

In the *Periodicals Case*, Canada argued that the import restriction on split-run periodicals was intended to secure the objectives of Section 19 of the *Income Tax Act* which allows a deduction of expenses for advertising directed to the Canadian market on the condition that the advertisements appear in Canadian editions of Canadian periodicals.[63] The panel found that Tariff Code 9958 was a measure separate from Section 19, which was designed to give an incentive for placing advertisements in Canadian as opposed to foreign periodicals and that Tariff Code 9958 did not secure compliance with Section 19.[64] As the first element was not satisfied, the panel did not consider the application of the other elements to the exception.[65]

ii) Second Element: Inconsistent Measure Satisfies Qualifying Language of the Exception

The exceptions in Articles XX(b) and XX(d) are qualified by the word "necessary," meaning that the measure must be "necessary" for the protection of human, animal, or plant life or health, or to secure compliance with laws. In the *Cigarette Case*, the panel adopted with respect to Article XX(b) the view of an earlier panel in considering the applicability of Article XX(d). In *U.S. — Section 337 of the Tariff Act of 1930*[66] (*Section 337 Case*), the GATT panel held that a contracting party cannot justify a measure as being necessary if there is an alternative measure available to it that is not inconsistent with other GATT provisions, and if the only measures that are reasonably available are inconsistent with GATT requirements, the contracting party must employ the measure

---

62 *Gasoline Panel*, above note 8, para. 6.37. Respecting renewability, the panel cited *Canada — Measures Affecting Exports of Unprocessed Herring and Salmon* (U.S. v. Canada) (1987), GATT Doc. L/6368, para. 4.4, 35th supp. (1987–1988) 98 at 113.
63 *Periodicals Panel*, above note 21, para. 5.8.
64 *Ibid.*, para. 5.10.
65 *Ibid.* While Canada appealed various findings of the panel to the Appellate Body, the finding on Tariff Code 9958 was not appealed.
66 Above note 25, para. 5.26. In this case, the panel was considering the meaning of the word "necessary" in the exception in GATT 1994, above note 1, art. XX(d). The panel in the *Cigarette Case*, above note 55, was of the view that the reasoning applied equally to the exception in art. XX(b).

that is least inconsistent with GATT provisions. The panel in the *Cigarette Case* concluded that Thailand could achieve its public health restrictions through measures that were consistent with GATT provisions (such as non-discriminatory bans on cigarette advertisements) and that import restrictions were not necessary to achieve the policy objective. Thus, although Thailand had established the first element, it failed on the second. On the basis of these cases, an exception based on the requirement that a measure be necessary will not justify a measure inconsistent with GATT 1994 if a consistent or less inconsistent measure is available to achieve the policy objective.

The exception in Article XX(g) is qualified by the words "relating to," meaning that the measure must relate to the conservation of exhaustible natural resources. This exception is further qualified by the requirement that the measure be made effective in conjunction with restrictions on domestic production or consumption. In the *Gasoline Case*, the United States invoked Article XX(g) to justify the baseline establishment rules.[67] The Appellate Body analysed the wording of Article XX(g) and adopted the reasoning of the GATT panel in *Canada — Measures Affecting Exports of Unprocessed Herring and Salmon*,[68] where the panel concluded that while trade measure did not have to be necessary or essential to the conservation of exhaustible natural resources, it had to be *primarily aimed* at the conservation of an exhaustible natural resource to fall within the exception.[69] The Appellate Body concluded that the "baseline establishment rules" under consideration were not "merely incidental or inadvertently aimed at" the conservation of clean air in the United States and, therefore, fell within Article XX(g). The Appellate Body also considered the requirement in Article XX(g) that the measure must be made effective in conjunction with domestic restrictions and concluded that because there were baseline establish-

---

67 In addition to invoking GATT 1994, *ibid.*, art. XX(g), the United States invoked art. XX(b) to justify the inconsistent measures under consideration. The WTO panel in the *Gasoline Case*, above note 8, applied the reasoning in the *Cigarette Case*, above note 55, and in the *Section 337 Case*, above note 25, and concluded that the inconsistent measures were not necessary to protect human, animal, or plant life and health and that the exception in art. XX(b) did not apply. See *Gasoline Panel*, above note 8, paras. 6.24 to 6.29. The United States did not dispute this finding on appeal.

68 Above note 62, adopted on 22 March 1988.

69 *Ibid.*, para. 4.6. The panel in that case concluded that because Canada maintained statistics on other fish species without imposing an export prohibition, the export prohibition in respect of unprocessed salmon and herring was not primarily aimed at conservation and did not fall within the exception. See para. 4.7.

ment rules for domestic U.S. gasoline as well as for imported gasoline, the requirement was fulfilled. The Appellate Body concluded that there was no textual requirement for requiring identical treatment of domestic and imported products.[70] Accordingly, the Appellate Body considered that the United States had established that the second element was satisfied in respect of the "baseline establishment rules."

In the *Tuna Case*, the panel held that the United States had failed to establish the second element in respect of the exceptions in both Articles XX(b) and XX(g). The panel observed that the objective of the embargoes on tuna products being imposed by the United States was to change policies in other countries towards protection of the life and health of dolphins and concluded that these U.S. measures did not fall within either Article XX(b) or XX(g). The panel made reference to the interpretation of the word "necessary" in Article XX(b) adopted in the *Cigarette Case* but did not base its conclusion respecting the second element on that analysis. Instead, the conclusion that neither exception applied was based on the panel's observation that Article XX exceptions must be narrowly construed and that to interpret the exceptions in Articles XX(b) and (g) so broadly as to permit measures designed to change the policies of other countries within their own jurisdictions would seriously impair the objectives of the GATT.[71]

iii) *Third Element: Inconsistent Measure Satisfies Introductory Clause of Article XX*

The introductory clause, or "chapeau,"[72] of Article XX requires that a measure justified under Article XX must not "constitute a means of arbitrary or unjustifiable discrimination" between countries, or a "disguised restriction on international trade." Having concluded in the *Gasoline*

---

70 *U.S. — Standards for Reformulated and Conventional Gasoline*, WT/DS2/AB/R, Appellate Body Report (AB-1996-1) at 78 [*Gasoline Appellate Body*]. As discussed in chapter 4, NAFTA, above note 5, art. 315, and *Canada–Chile Free Trade Agreement*, in force 5 July 1997, see http://www.dfait-maeci.gc.ca/english/trade/agrement.htm, art. C-13, impose additional requirements in respect of the exception in GATT 1994, above note 1, art. XX(g), as well as several other art. XX exceptions.

71 *U.S. — Tuna*, above note 48, para. 5.26, in respect of GATT 1994, *ibid.*, art. XX(g) and para. 5.38 in respect of art. XX(b).

72 This is the expression used in the *Gasoline Appellate Body* report, above note 70, to refer to the introductory clause of GATT 1994, *ibid.*, art. XX. The expression is commonly used by officials of the Canadian Department of Foreign Affairs and International Trade and the Department of Justice to refer to the introductory language in a treaty provision.

Case that the baseline establishment rules satisfied the first two elements, the Appellate Body proceeded to consider whether these measures satisfied these requirements. The Appellate Body observed that the requirements of the chapeau of Article XX were directed not so much at the contents of a measure but in the manner of its application.[73] While the Appellate Body observed that the text of the chapeau was not without ambiguity,[74] the fundamental theme of the chapeau is "to be found in the purpose and object of avoiding abuse or illegitimate use of the exceptions to the substantive rules available in Article XX."[75] The Appellate Body observed that the expressions "arbitrary discrimination," "unjustifiable discrimination," and "disguised restriction" gave meaning to each other and that a "concealed" or "unannounced" restriction did not exhaust the meaning of "disguised restriction."[76] The Appellate Body observed that while the United States permitted domestic refiners to apply individual as opposed to statutory baselines in order to save domestic refiners the physical and financial costs and burdens of immediate compliance, they disregarded such considerations in respect of foreign refiners.[77] The Appellate Body also found that the U.S. government had not explored means of overcoming the administrative problems involved in permitting foreign refiners to establish individual baselines. The Appellate Body held that these omissions went well beyond the degree of discrimination that was necessary for the panel to find that the measures violated the non-discrimination requirements of Article III:4 and, accordingly, constituted "unjustifiable discrimination" and a "disguised restriction on international trade." Thus the United States failed to establish the third element in respect of its measures, and, while falling within Article XX(g), the measures were "not entitled to the justifying protection afforded by Article XX as a whole."[78]

The analysis of the meaning of the chapeau of Article XX in the *Gasoline Case* is relevant to the interpretation of any provision in the WTO agreements or in NAFTA, CIFTA, or CCFTA that contains the expressions "arbitrary discrimination," "unjustifiable discrimination," and "disguised restriction on international trade." Rather than applying a strict

---

73   *Gasoline Appellate Body*, ibid. at 79.
74   In his treatise, *World Trade and Law of GATT* (Indianapolis: Bobbs-Merrill, 1969), Professor J.H. Jackson characterized this language as "nebulous" at 744. As will be noted, the Appellate Body nonetheless managed to derive meaning from them.
75   *Gasoline Appellate Body*, ibid. at 80.
76   Ibid.
77   Ibid. at 82.
78   Ibid.

textual analysis, panels interpreting provisions containing these expressions may follow the approach of the Appellate Body in the *Gasoline Case* and apply provisions containing these expressions on the basis that the fundamental purpose and object of such provisions is to prevent abuse.

b) Scope of Exceptions in Article XX

While the cases discussed above involved measures that were inconsistent with Articles III and XI of GATT Article 1994, the Article XX exceptions apply to all provisions of GATT 1994. It should be kept in mind, however, that the exceptions in Article XX of GATT 1994 apply only to the obligations imposed by GATT 1994 and not to the obligations that are imposed by the other WTO agreements. Some of the WTO agreements do not contain general exceptions while in some others the excepting language is substantially different from that in Article XX. For example, Article 8:1 of the *TRIPS Agreement* permits member countries to adopt measures necessary to protect health and nutrition, provided that such measures are consistent with the *TRIPS Agreement*. Consider a regulation requiring generic cigarette packaging adopted for the purpose of protecting human health by reducing smoking. The measure affects the ability of cigarette manufacturers to use their trademarks and falls within the ambit of the *TRIPS Agreement*. The exception in Article XX(b) for measures necessary to protect human life or health would not apply because it is an exception only to obligations under GATT 1994 and not to obligations under the *TRIPS Agreement*. The only health provision relevant to the measure would be the significantly weaker "health and nutrition" provision of Article 8:1 of the *TRIPS Agreement*.

2) Incorporation of Article XX Exceptions into NAFTA, CIFTA, and CCFTA

NAFTA Article 2101 incorporates GATT Article XX into NAFTA, as well as any equivalent successor provision. Article XX of GATT 1994 is the successor provision and is unchanged from the original GATT Article XX. The incorporated GATT Article XX applies to Part Two of NAFTA (Trade in Goods), except to the extent that part applies to services or investment, and to Part Three of NAFTA (Technical Barriers to Trade), except to the extent that part applies to services.[79] The objective

---

79 There are provisions in NAFTA, above note 5, Part Two, such as some of those in NAFTA Annex 300-A (Trade and Investment in the Automotive Sector) that relate to investment as opposed to trade in goods, and NAFTA Part Three applies to land transportation and telecommunication services as well as goods.

of these clarifications is to point out that the scope of the incorporated GATT Article XX exceptions does not extend beyond their application to measures respecting the trade in goods.

NAFTA provides that the "human, animal, or plant life or health" exception in GATT Article XX(b) includes "environmental measures necessary to protect human, animal or plant life or health." NAFTA also provides that the exhaustible natural resources exception in GATT Article XX(g) applies to both living and non-living exhaustible natural resources. These clarifications codify positions determined through GATT jurisprudence. Statements made by the Panel in the *Gasoline Case* indicate that the exception in Article XX(b) covers environmental measures[80] and several GATT panels have held that Article XX(g) applies to exhaustible living natural resources.

CIFTA Article 10.1 and CCFTA Article 0-01 incorporate Article XX of GATT 1994 into CIFTA and CCFTA respectively, with similar clarifications to Articles XX(b) and XX(g) as made in the NAFTA text.

As discussed in chapter 4 under "NAFTA and CCFTA Disciplines Respecting Export Restrictions," NAFTA Article 315 and CCFTA Article C-13 impose additional qualifications that must be satisfied if certain Article XX exceptions are relied upon to justify GATT-inconsistent export restrictions.

3) Use of Exceptions

Many Canadian laws, particularly those imposing import restrictions, depend for their consistency with Canada's international obligations on being justified under one of the exceptions in GATT Article XX. For example, the *Customs Tariff* prohibits the entry of obscene books, drawings, paintings and the like. This prohibition depends for its consistency with GATT 1994 under the exception in Article XX(a) which provides an exception for measures "necessary to protect public morals." As is apparent from the discussion above of Article XX jurisprudence, GATT and WTO panels and the Appellate Body are strict in their approach to the applicability of these exceptions. Lawmakers cannot assume that an exception will be available to justify a measure inconsistent with GATT 1994 just because the measure appears to fall within the wording of an exception. This is particularly the case if there is an alternative GATT-consistent or less GATT-inconsistent means of achieving the desired policy objective.

---

80   *Gasoline Panel*, above note 8 at para. 6.21.

CHAPTER 3

TARIFFS AND RELATED BORDER MEASURES

Tariffs or customs duties are commodity taxes levied on imported goods. The application of tariffs results in different and less favourable treatment being accorded to imported goods than to domestic goods. However, discrimination through tariffs is permissible under GATT 1994 up to the tariff levels to which each member country is committed.

Tariffs are used both to raise revenue and to protect domestic producers. At the time of Confederation, tariffs were the most single important source of revenue for the new Canadian government. However, with the advent of income taxes and other forms of commodity taxes, tariffs now account for a relatively insignificant proportion of the revenues raised by the federal government. Only the federal government can impose tariffs.

Tariffs are also used as instruments of industrial policy to protect domestic producers. The National Policy of Sir John A. Macdonald's government included among its objectives the encouragement of domestic manufacturing through high tariffs. With the successive rounds of GATT negotiations, tariffs in all industrialized countries have dropped dramatically and for most products have ceased to afford much protection from foreign competition. However, some Canadian industries, such as the textile and apparel industry, continue to be protected through relatively high tariffs.

For trade theorists, tariffs are preferable to non-tariff measures of protection such as quantitative import restrictions, discretionary import licensing, non-tariff measures maintained through state trading enterprises, voluntary export restraints, and the like. Tariffs are transparent while other measures of protection frequently lack transparency. Tariffs do not involve the allocation problems that measures of protection such as quantitative restrictions entail.

Tariffs are levied either on a per unit or an *ad valorem* basis. A per unit tariff is expressed as a fixed sum per kilogram or litre or other unit of measurement. An *ad valorem* tariff is expressed as a percentage that is applied to the value of the good for duty purposes. As discussed under "Valuation," the *Valuation Agreement* sets out rules for valuing goods for duty purposes.

Tariffs are usually applied at a constant rate regardless of the annual volume of imports. However, tariff rate quotas are applied to some goods. Under a tariff rate quota, a prescribed annual quantity of goods enters at a lower rate of duty and imports over that quantity enter at a higher rate. Tariff rate quotas have replaced quantitative restrictions for agricultural goods under the *Agriculture Agreement* (see chapter 4 under "The Agriculture Agreement and Tariffication"), and the NAFTA textile and apparel provisions create "tariff preference levels" for certain textile and apparel goods (see chapter 4 under "Tariff Preference Levels").

A. HARMONIZED SYSTEM AND TARIFF CLASSIFICATION

1) The Harmonized System

The Harmonized Commodity Description and Coding System (Harmonized System or HS) is an international numerical system for classifying goods for customs and statistical purposes and is used by Canada, the United States, Mexico, Chile, Israel, and most other countries. The Harmonized System is used in the WTO agreements as well as in NAFTA, CIFTA, and CCFTA as the principal means of referring to goods.

The Harmonized System is divided into sections covering broad categories of goods. Each section is broken down into chapters, which are broken down into headings and subheadings. HS chapters are assigned two-digit numbers (01 through to 97). HS headings are assigned four-digit numbers, the first two being the number of the chapter within which the heading falls. HS subheadings are assigned six-digit numbers, the first four being the number of the heading within which the subheading falls. Each good is classified under a tariff item, which is a number with eight or more digits. The first two digits of a tariff item correspond to the chapter under which the good is classified. The first four digits correspond to the heading and the first six digits to the subheading under which the good is classified. The classification of goods by all countries that have adopted the Harmonized System is identical down to the six-digit subheading level. Harmonization ceases below the subheading level and each country develops its own tariff items.

For example, a bumper under Canadian tariff item 8708.10.11 is classified under:

Chapter 87	Vehicles other than Railway or Tramway Rolling Stock and Parts and Accessories Thereof
Heading 87.08	Parts and accessories of the motor vehicles of heading Nos. 87.01 to 87.05
Subheading 8708.10	Bumpers and parts thereof

Chapter 87, Heading 87.08, and Subheading 8708.10 are exactly the same in the U.S. and Mexican tariff schedules, as well as in the tariff schedules of all countries that have adopted the Harmonized System. However, the U.S. tariff item is 8708.10.00.A and the Mexican tariff item is 8708.10.01 or 02 or 03, depending on the type of bumper.

2) Tariff Classification

Unlike other commodity taxes, such as the Goods and Services Tax and provincial sales taxes, which are generally applied at flat rates that apply to all goods, tariff treatment varies from good to good. Determining the correct tariff treatment begins with correct classification of the good. The Harmonized System contains general rules of interpretation, as well as additional rules that appear at the beginning of sections and chapters. For example, General Rule of Interpretation (GRI) 2(a) provides that an unassembled or disassembled good (such as an item of furniture that one would buy at IKEA) is classified under the same tariff item as the assembled product. Individual countries supplement the HS rules with their own rules of interpretation. Further guidance to interpretation is provided by the *Explanatory Notes* that are published by the Customs Cooperation Council in Brussels.

Classification of goods under the Harmonized System progresses from primary products (the first twenty-four chapters) through to various types of manufactured goods. Each chapter includes headings and subheadings entitled "other" that capture goods that do not fall within a specific heading or subheading within a heading.

B. CANADIAN CUSTOMS LAWS

Customs law is the body of federal statutory law that provides for the levying and collection of customs duties. Canadian customs law is set out in two federal statutes, the *Customs Tariff*[1] and the *Customs Act*[2] and in the regulations enacted under each of these statutes. The *Customs Tariff* and the *Customs Act* collectively establish the rules respecting the customs duties that are routinely collected on imported goods. Antidumping and countervailing duties, which are extraordinary duties that may only be levied in certain circumstances (see chapter 6), are covered by the *Special Import Measures Act*.[3] The administration of tariff rate quotas on agricultural goods is provided for in the *Export and Import Permits Act*[4] although the applicable "within access commitment" and "over access commitment" rates for these goods are set out in Schedule I of the *Customs Tariff*.

The provisions of the *Customs Tariff* are primarily directed at the establishment of rates and applicable tariff treatments, while the *Customs Act* covers matters relating to collection and enforcement. The existence of two separate statutes reflects the historical division of responsibility for customs duties between the Department of Finance (establishing tariff treatment, rates of duty, and entitlement to tariff relief) and the Department of National Revenue (collection and enforcement).

1) *Customs Tariff*

The *Customs Tariff* contains the customs charging provision by imposing customs duties on all goods imported into Canada at the rates set out in Schedule I.[5] The *Customs Tariff* describes the different tariff treatments that apply under Canadian customs law and the rules by which

---

1   R.S.C. 1985, (3d Supp.), c. 41 [*CT*]. On 7 October 1997, the Canadian minister of finance introduced a Notice of Ways and Means Motion (Ways and Means Motion) setting out extensive amendments to the *Customs Tariff*, the *Customs Act* and related statutes. These amendments had not taken effect as of the time of writing but are scheduled to become effective on 1 January 1998. Section references of the *Customs Tariff* and the *Customs Act* given in this book for the period following 1 January 1998 are based on the Ways and Means Motion.
2   R.S.C. 1985, (2d Supp.), c. 1 [*CA*].
3   R.S.C. 1985, c. S-15.
4   R.S.C. 1985, c. E-19.
5   Section 19(1) until 31 December 1997 and Section 20(1) following 1 January 1998. Note also that excise tax under the *Excise Act*, R.S.C. 1985, c. E-14 and Goods and Services Tax under Part IX of the *Excise Tax Act*, R.S.C. 1985, c. E-15 are also collected on imported goods under the authority of the *CT*, above note 1.

the eligibility for each particular treatment is determined.[6] The *Customs Tariff* sets out the staging categories for the phased reduction of tariffs under GATT 1994 and the phased elimination of tariffs under NAFTA. The *Customs Tariff* also contains the various emergency provisions in Canadian customs law, sanctioned by the *Safeguards Agreement* and under NAFTA (see chapter 6). Part II of the *Customs Tariff* sets out various duty relief programs available under Canadian customs law. As discussed below, some of these programs are affected by NAFTA rules.

Following 1 January 1998, the seven schedules to the *Customs Tariff* will be combined into a single schedule that will list all goods by tariff item in accordance with the Harmonized System, identify the rate that applies for each type of tariff treatment, and set out in separate tariff items the various concessionary provisions that apply to certain goods in prescribed circumstances. The schedule also creates new tariff items under Chapters 98 and 99 to cover certain duty relief programs as well as prohibited importations.

2) *Customs Act*

The *Customs Act* establishes the procedures for the collection of duty and for enforcement of customs laws. Imported goods must be reported, and duties are assessed and paid. The *Customs Act* sets out rules respecting the movement and storage of goods before release by customs authorities, and for proving the origin of goods and marking of goods with the country of origin. The *Customs Act* establishes the procedures for calculating duty, including the rules for valuing goods for duty purposes. The *Customs Act* also sets out the rules for reassessment of duty, appeals from reassessments, origin determinations, and marking determinations. The *Customs Act* provides for the refund of duty in various circumstances. As one would expect in an enforcement statute, the *Customs Act* establishes the powers of customs authorities and penalties for non-compliance.

---

6 Schedule III of the *CT, ibid.* is a table with a list of most countries in the world. The table identifies the tariff treatment or treatments to which goods of each country are entitled. If more than one tariff treatment is identified, goods originating in that country are eligible for the most advantageous tariff treatment. See s. 21(2). If a country is not included on the list, the goods of that country are subject to the General Tariff, which is the most disadvantageous tariff treatment that Canada accords. Section 13(2) of the *CT* empowers the Governor in Council to make regulations setting out the rules (preferential rules of origin) by which it is determined whether goods originate in a country. As discussed in chapter 5, there are different rules of origin for each tariff treatment. Following 1 January 1998, see the List of Countries and Applicable Tariff Treatments set out in the schedule to the *CT*.

C. TARIFF TREATMENTS UNDER CANADIAN CUSTOMS LAW

There are multiple tariff treatments under Canadian customs law. The treatment for which an imported good is eligible depends on the country or countries from which the goods originate. The country or countries of origin are determined in accordance with the rules of origin discussed in chapter 5.

1) MFN Tariff

Goods originating in all WTO member countries are entitled to the most-favoured-nation or MFN Tariff. Canada has also unilaterally extended the application of the MFN Tariff to a number of non-WTO countries. MFN Tariff rates, which are based on the bound rates to which the Canadian government agreed in the Uruguay Round, are set out in the "MFN" column of the schedule to the *Customs Tariff*. The appellation "Most-Favoured-Nation" is a little misleading because MFN treatment is Canada's least favourable treatment except for the General Tariff described below that applies to very few countries.

2) General Preferential Tariff and Least Developed Developing Country Tariff

The General Preferential Tariff or GPT is granted pursuant to the GATT-sanctioned Generalized System of Preferences established to assist developing countries through preferential tariff treatment. GPT rates have been established for many goods, and the goods of most developing countries are eligible for GPT treatment. GPT rates, which are often although not invariably free, are identified with the letters "GPT" in the Preferential Tariff column of the schedule to the *Customs Tariff*. The benefit of the GPT can be extended to the goods of a developing country and can be withdrawn by Order in Council.[7] The least developed developing country tariff applies to goods of countries that are eligible for GPT treatment and that have been designated by Order

---

7   The *CT*, *ibid.*, s. 36 until 31 December 1997 and s. 34 following 1 January 1998. Note that following 1 January 1998, s. 36 of the *CT* will provide that ss. 33 to 35, which make provision for the general preferential tariff, will cease to apply after 30 June 2004 or such earlier date as may be fixed by Order in Council.

in Council as least developed developing countries.[8] The least developed developing country tariff, which is always free, applies only to goods entitled to GPT treatment identified with the letters "LDCT" in the Preferential Tariff column of the schedule to the *Customs Tariff*.

3) British Preferential Tariff and Goods of New Zealand and Australia

The British Preferential Tariff or BPT was a relic of the old Commonwealth system of preferential tariffs that predated the GATT and was sanctioned by Article I:2(a) and Annex A of GATT 1994. The BPT will cease to exist as a separate tariff treatment following 1 January 1998.[9] Some goods of New Zealand and Australia are eligible for special rates of duty that are identified with the letters "AUT" and "NZT" in the Preferential Tariff column of the schedule to the *Customs Tariff*.

4) Commonwealth Caribbean Countries Tariff

Goods of Commonwealth Caribbean countries are eligible for the Commonwealth Caribbean Countries Tariff. These rates are identified with the letters "CCCT" in the Preferential Tariff column of the schedule to the *Customs Tariff*.

5) NAFTA Tariffs

NAFTA provides for three different tariffs, depending on the country of origin of the goods. To be eligible for any of the NAFTA tariffs, a good must be "originating" under the NAFTA preferential rules of origin.[10] The rules for determining the country of origin of "originating goods" are described in chapter 5. All NAFTA tariffs will ultimately be free.

---

8 The *CT*, *ibid.*, s. 38. Note that following 1 January 1998, s. 40 of the *CT* will provide that ss. 37 to 39, which make provision for the least developed developing country tariff, cease to apply after 30 June 2004 or such earlier date as may be fixed by order in council.
9 A remission order will continue BPT rates until 2004 for about 200 tariff items. See Customs Notice N-126, 23 April 1997, para. 11.
10 Prescribed annual quantities of certain textile and apparel goods will be eligible for *North American Free Trade Agreement*, 17 December 1992, Can. T.S. 1994 No. 2 [NAFTA] tariff treatment under tariff preference levels even though they do not satisfy NAFTA preferential rules of origin. See chapter 4 under "Tariff Preference Levels."

a) United States Tariff

NAFTA originating goods that are goods of the United States are eligible for the United States Tariff, which is identified with the letters "UST" in the Preferential Tariff column of the schedule to the *Customs Tariff*. The UST will be free for all originating goods beginning 1 January 1998.

b) Mexico Tariff

NAFTA originating goods that are goods of Mexico are eligible for the Mexico Tariff, which is identified with the letters "MT" in the Preferential Tariff column of the schedule to the *Customs Tariff*.

c) Mexico–United States Tariff

NAFTA originating goods that are goods of neither the United States (because they have too much Mexican content) nor Mexico (because they have too much U.S. content) are eligible for the Mexico–United States Tariff, which is identified with the letters "MUST" in the Preferential Tariff column of the schedule to the *Customs Tariff*.

6) Israel Tariff

Goods imported from Israel that are originating goods under the CIFTA rules of origin are eligible for the Israel Tariff, which is identified with the letters "CIAT" in the Preferential Tariff column of the schedule to the *Customs Tariff*.

7) Chile Tariff

Goods imported from Chile that are originating goods under the CCFTA rules of origin are eligible for the Chile Tariff, which is identified with the letters "CT" in the Preferential Tariff column of the schedule to the *Customs Tariff*.

8) General Tariff

The General Tariff applies to the few countries that are not eligible for any of the tariff treatments described above. The General Tariff is 35 percent.

D. TARIFF BINDINGS AND TARIFF REDUCTION UNDER GATT 1994

GATT 1947 established two broad objectives respecting tariffs that have been carried over into GATT 1994. The first has been to secure commitments from member countries that tariffs on goods would not exceed specified levels. The second has been to progressively lower tariffs through successive rounds of negotiations.

1) Article II of GATT 1994

Article II:1(a) of GATT 1994 provides that the products of other member countries shall be exempt from ordinary customs duties in excess of those set out in each member country's schedule to the GATT. A member country is free to charge a lower duty so long as MFN requirements are met or the lower duty otherwise sanctioned (either under another provision of GATT 1994 or a waiver). The bound tariffs in each country's schedule do not apply to charges collected at the border that are equivalent to internal taxes,[11] or to antidumping or countervailing duties, or to fees or charges commensurate with cost of service.

Article II:1(a) was considered by a GATT panel in *EEC — Regime for the Importation, Sale and Distribution of Bananas*.[12] New EEC regulations that became effective on 1 July 1993 replaced the EEC bound tariff of 20 percent *ad valorem* on bananas with tariffs per ton of 100 ECUs, 750 ECUs, and 850 ECUs, depending on the origin of the bananas and whether they fell within or outside a tariff quota. The panel noted that the 100 ECUs per ton rate exceeded the 20 percent *ad valorem* rate on 1 July 1993 and the 750 and 850 ECUs per ton rates were clearly far in excess of the *ad valorem* rate. The panel commented in respect of changing the basis for calculating a tariff (in this case from *ad valorem* to ECUs per ton) that not only actual consequences on present imports but also the effect on possible future imports had to be taken into account because "the provisions of the General Agreement serve not only to

---

11 For example, Canadian excise taxes and goods and services taxes are collected on imported goods when they enter Canada. Each of these taxes apply equally to domestic goods and therefore are not affected by art. II of *General Agreement on Tariffs and Trade 1994*, set out in Annex 1A of the *Agreement Creating the World Trade Organization*, 15 April 1994 (Dobbs Ferry, N.Y.: Oceana Publications, 1997) [GATT 1994]. However, they are subject to the requirements of Article III:2 of GATT 1994.
12 GATT Doc. DS38/R [unadopted], Report of the Panel, 11 February 1994.

protect actual trade flows but also to create predictability for future trade."[13] The panel found that the new tariffs were inconsistent with the EEC's Schedule of Concessions and that the inconsistency was not justified by the fact that the EEC had removed previously existing quantitative import restrictions.[14]

2) Tariff Reduction Resulting from the Uruguay Round

The Uruguay Round of negotiations resulted in the elimination of tariffs in nine industrial sectors: pulp and paper; steel; pharmaceuticals; construction equipment; agricultural equipment; medical equipment; office equipment; toys; and whiskies, brandies, and beer. Tariffs will be reduced for other products. The Canadian government has estimated that the trade-weighted tariff reduction of its major non-NAFTA trading partners (Japan and the European Union) will be reduced by 60 percent and that Canadian tariffs will be reduced by an average of 50 percent.[15] For non-agricultural goods, tariff reductions will generally be phased in five equal annual rate reductions. There are a number of exceptions in the Canadian tariff schedule. For example, reductions for beer will be over eight stages and for steel over ten stages. The reductions for most agricultural products will be phased over six stages.[16]

The staging categories for tariff reduction resulting from the Uruguay Round are described in the *Customs Tariff*.[17] The staging categories describe the progression from an initial or base rate (the rate in effect just prior to 1 January 1995) to a final rate. The staging categories are E, F, G, H and I. Goods in staging categories E were reduced to their final rate on 1 January 1995. Goods in staging categories F, G, H, and I will be reduced to their final rates on 1 January 1999, 1 January 2000,

---

13 *Ibid.*, para. 135.
14 *Ibid.*, para. 136.
15 See the *Canadian Statement on Implementation of the Agreement Establishing the World Trade Organization*, C. Gaz. 1994.I.4847 at 4866.
16 *Ibid.* at 4869.
17 The description of the staging categories here is taken from the amendments to s. 22 of the *CT*, set out in Section 77 of the *World Trade Organization Agreement Implementation Act*, S.C. 1994, c. 47. The schedule to this legislation is useful because it sets out the staging categories for each good, as well as the base rate and the final rate. Following 1 January 1998, the MFN staging categories will be set out in s. 30(3) of the *CT*. The letter designations for each staging category have been changed in the new s. 30(3) and the descriptions of each staging category take into account the fact that by the time the new section becomes effective, several elimination stages will have already passed.

1 January 2002, and 1 January 2004, respectively. Goods in staging category J will be reduced to their final rate in accordance with the schedule set out in the MFN Tariff column. Rates on goods in staging category K will not be reduced.

E. TARIFF ELIMINATION UNDER NAFTA, CIFTA, AND CCFTA

As NAFTA, CIFTA, and CCFTA create free trade areas, customs duties are eliminated on most goods traded among the member countries that satisfy the applicable rules of origin. The customs duties eliminated are ordinary customs duties and do not include antidumping or countervailing duties or the very high "over access commitment" duties that have resulted from tariffication under the WTO *Agriculture Agreement* (see chapter 4 under "The Agriculture Agreement and Tariffication").[18]

1) Tariff Elimination under NAFTA

NAFTA provides for the elimination of tariffs on virtually all goods traded among the NAFTA countries.[19] Tariff elimination was immediate for some goods and is introduced over stages for other goods. Tariff elimination between Canada and the United States commenced on 1 January 1989 under CUFTA and continued under NAFTA in accordance with the CUFTA schedule. Tariff elimination is already complete for many goods and will be complete for all goods by 1 January 1998.

Tariff elimination between Mexico and each of Canada and the United States will be complete by 1 January 2003 or, in the case of a few goods traded between the United States and Mexico, 1 January 2005 or 1 January 2008. The staging categories for goods of Mexico describe how tariffs are progressively reduced from a base rate (the rate in effect at the end of 1993) to free. The categories are A, B, C, and D.[20] Duties on goods in staging category A were eliminated on 1 January 1994. Tariffs

---

18   See the definition of "customs duty" in NAFTA, above note 10, art. 318. There are several other exclusions.
19   Tariffs on dairy, poultry, and sugar-containing goods traded between Canada and Mexico will not be eliminated.
20   See para. 1 of NAFTA Annex 302.2, which also sets out staging category C+ that applies only between the United States and Mexico. Following 1 January 1998, the staging categories for the Mexico and Mexico–United States tariffs will be set out in Section 45 of the *Customs Tariff*.

on goods in staging categories B and C will be completely eliminated on 1 January 1998, 1 January 1999, 1 January 2001, and 1 January 2003, respectively. Tariffs on goods in staging category D were already free when NAFTA became effective. NAFTA Article 302(1) prohibits increases in tariffs on originating goods.

2) Tariff Elimination under CIFTA

With very few exceptions, customs duties on all originating goods in Chapters 25 through to 97 of the Harmonized System were eliminated on 1 January 1997.[21] Canadian tariffs on women's or girls' swimwear and Israeli tariffs on woven cotton fabric are eliminated in four stages, with complete elimination on 1 July 1999.[22] Customs duties will not be eliminated on goods of either country classified under HS headings 35.01 and 35.02 (casein or albumins and related products).[23]

Customs duties on originating goods in Chapters 1 through 24 (which for the most part include agricultural and fisheries products) of the Harmonized System are eliminated or reduced as described in CIFTA Annex 2.1.2. CIFTA Annex 2.1.2A lists specific Canadian tariff items with the duty (usually but not always free) that will apply on 1 January 1997, together with exceptions. CIFTA Annex 2.1.2B does the same with specific Israeli tariff items. If a tariff item falling within HS Chapters 1 through 24 is not listed in CIFTA Annex 2.1.2, customs duties on goods classified under that tariff item will not be eliminated.

3) Tariff Elimination under CCFTA

Tariffs on originating goods entering Canada from Chile will be eliminated in various stages. Certain goods became free when CCFTA became effective. Tariffs on other goods will be eliminated on 1 January 1999, 1 January 2000, 1 January 2001, 1 January 2002, or 1 January 2003, depending on the staging category.[24]

---

21 Following 1 January 1998, see s. 50 of the *CT*.
22 See *Canada–Israel Free Trade Agreement*, in force 1 January 1997, see http://www.dfait-maeci.gc.ca/english/trade/agrement.htm [CIFTA], Annex 2.1.1. The Canadian tariff items are 6112.41.00, 6112.49.00, and 6211.12.00. The Israeli tariff items are 5209.32.00, 5209.39.00, and 5209.42.00.
23 See CIFTA, *ibid.*, Annex 2.1.1.
24 The staging categories for goods eligible for the Chile Tariff are set out in s. 46 of the *CT*.

F. VALUATION

As mentioned above, *ad valorem* customs duties are calculated as a percentage of the value of imported goods. The *Valuation Agreement* sets out rules governing the valuation of goods for duty purposes.[25] The provisions of the *Valuation Agreement* are reflected in Sections 45 to 55 of the *Customs Act*.

1) Transaction Value as the Customs Value

The concept behind the rules in the *Valuation Agreement* is that the basis for value for duty (or "customs value") is the invoice price of the imported goods except when it is inappropriate to use this price. Accordingly, the calculation of value for duty purposes begins with the price paid or payable for the goods in the transaction in which they are sold for export to the country of importation.[26] The price paid or payable is adjusted to arrive at the "transaction value" of the imported goods. The *ad valorem* duty is applied to the transaction value.

To the extent not already included, the following are added to the price paid or payable:

- commissions and brokerage (other than buying commissions), the cost of containers or the cost of packing;[27]
- the value of "assists," which include such items as materials incorporated into the imported goods or tools or dies or moulds used in their production that are supplied by the buyer;[28]
- royalties and licence fees related to the goods paid by the buyer as a condition of sale are added to the price paid or payable;[29]
- the value of any part of the proceeds of the subsequent resale, disposition, or use of the goods that accrues to the seller.[30]

---

25 The provisions of the *Valuation Agreement* (*Agreement on Implementation of Article VII of the General Agreement on Tariffs and Trade 1994*, set out in Annex 1A of the *Agreement Creating the World Trade Organization*, 15 April 1994 (Dobbs Ferry, N.Y.: Oceana Publications, 1997) [VA] are virtually the same as those set out in its Tokyo Round predecessor.
26 Article 1 of the *VA*, *ibid*. *CA*, above note 2, s. 48.
27 Article 8:1(a) of the *VA*, *ibid*. *CA*, *ibid*., ss. 48(5)(a)(i) & (ii).
28 Article 8:1(b) of the *VA*, *ibid*. *CA*, *ibid*., s. 48(5)(a)(iii).
29 Article 8:1(c) of the *VA*, *ibid*. *CA*, *ibid*., s. 48(5)(a)(iv) uses the expression "in respect of the goods" rather than "relating to the goods."
30 Article 8:1(d) of the *VA*, *ibid*. *CA*, *ibid*., s. 48(5)(a)(v).

Under the *Customs Act*, the cost of transportation and insurance up to when the goods arrive at the point of their direct shipment to Canada must be added if not included in the price, but these costs, once the goods pass the point of direct shipment, are not included and may be deducted if included in the price.[31]

2) The Other Methods of Calculating Customs Value

With some importations, such as a consignment sale or a transfer of goods to a domestic branch operation by its foreign "parent," there is no "price paid or payable" so that a transaction value cannot be calculated. In other instances, such as when the seller and the buyer are related and that relationship influenced the price, or when there are certain restrictions on the disposition or use of the goods, or when the sale or price is subject to a consideration or condition that cannot be valued, value for duty cannot be based on the transaction value.[32] In these instances, value for duty is based on one of the following methods applied in the following order:

- *Identical goods*: Under this method, the customs value is based on the transaction value of identical goods that were exported at about the same time as the goods being imported to a purchaser at substantially the same trade level as the purchaser of the imported goods and in substantially the same quantities.[33]
- *Similar goods*: If the customs value cannot be determined under the identical goods method, the customs value is based on the transaction value of similar goods, applied on the same basis for identical goods.[34]
- *Deductive value or computed value*: If the customs value cannot be determined under either of the identical goods or similar goods methods, the customs value is based on deductive value or, if the importer wishes, computed value.

---

31 CA, *ibid.*, ss. 48(5)(a)(vi) & 48(5)(b)(i). Article 8:2 of the VA, *ibid.*, leaves it to the discretion of each member country as to whether to include or exclude these items.

32 See generally art. 1:1 of the VA, *ibid.*, and CA, *ibid.*, s. 48(1). Permitted restrictions are set out in art. 1:1(a) of the VA (s. 48(1)(a) of the CA). Related party transactions are covered in arts. 1:1(d) and 1:2 of the VA (ss. 48(1)(d), 48(2) & 48(3) of the CA). The restriction on a condition or consideration cannot be valued is in art. 1:1(b) of the VA (s. 48(1)(b) of the CA).

33 Article 2 of the VA, *ibid.* CA, *ibid.*, s. 49. See art. 15:2 of the VA and s. 45(1) of the CA for the definition of "identical goods."

34 Article 3 of the VA, *ibid.* CA, *ibid.*, s. 50. See art. 15:2 of the VA and s. 45(1) of the CA for the definition of "identical goods."

- *Deductive value*: The deductive value is based on the sale price within Canada of the imported goods or identical or similar goods, subject to deductions for commissions, profit and general expenses, transportation within Canada, and taxes and duties. The idea behind the deductions is to adjust the sale price by backing out those elements that reflect expenses incurred or profit generated within Canada.[35]
- *Computed value*: The computed value is based on the cost of producing the imported goods plus an amount for profit and general expenses.[36]
• *Residual method*: If the customs value of imported goods cannot be determined under any of the above methods, customs authorities may apply the residual method. This method permits customs authorities to adopt elements of the other methods and use the best information available.[37] The *Valuation Agreement* sets out limitations on the application of this method. For example, customs value cannot be based on the selling price within the importing country of domestically produced goods.[38]

The transaction value method is preferable over all the other methods because its result can be predicted by the exporter and the importer and its calculation is relatively straightforward. The most commonly applied method, if the transaction value method cannot be used, is the deductive method or some variation of it under the residual method.

G. DUTY RELIEF PROGRAMS

Canadian customs law provides for a variety of duty relief programs. Under a duty relief program, duty that would otherwise be payable on an imported good is reduced or eliminated on some basis. The basis can be the subsequent exportation of the imported good, or a good into which it is incorporated, or the use in Canada of the imported good, or the fulfilment of performance requirements by the importer. Duty relief can be general or company-specific. The objective of a duty relief program is to

---

35 Article 5 of the *VA, ibid. CA, ibid.*, s. 51. This description is a simplification. The application of the deductive method is quite complex, and the relevant provisions of the *VA* and the *CA* set out a number of permutations and combinations not discussed here.
36 Article 6 of the *VA, ibid. CA, ibid.*, s. 52.
37 Article 7 of the *VA, ibid. CA, ibid.*, s. 53.
38 See art. 7:2 of the *VA, ibid.*, for these restrictions.

stimulate a particular economic activity through granting selective relief from customs duties. Some duty relief programs, such as the *Auto Pact*, have been critical to the development of particular industries in Canada.

1) Duty Relief and the WTO Agreements

Several WTO agreements contain provisions that affect duty relief programs. Duty relief programs must conform to the MFN requirements of Article I of GATT 1994 and apply to goods of all WTO countries. Duty relief programs that are conditional on domestic purchases or that limit imports based on volume of exports are inconsistent with the *TRIMs Agreement*.[39] Remission of duty on exports that exceeds the duty paid on the imported inputs in the exported goods can constitute a prohibited subsidy under the *Subsidies Agreement*.[40] Company-specific duty remission can constitute a countervailable subsidy if the requirements for imposing countervailing duties are satisfied.

2) Duty Drawback, Duty Deferral, and NAFTA Rules

a) Duty Drawback and Duty Deferral

Duty drawback is the refund of duty paid on imported goods if the goods are subsequently exported, either in the same condition or after being used as materials in producing other goods that are exported. Drawback includes refunds of duty paid on imported goods when identical or similar goods are used in manufacturing goods that are subsequently exported. Canadian customs law provides for duty drawback, as do the customs laws of many other countries.

Duty deferral is the postponement of duty on imported goods until the good enters the commerce of the importing country. If the good never enters the commerce of the importing country but is exported, either in the same condition or as a material used in producing another exported good, the duty is never paid. Under Canada's inward processing rules, a manufacturer can apply in advance for duty relief on imported materials that will be used in goods that will subsequently be

---

39 See para. 1 of the Annex (Illustrative List) of the *Agreement Respecting Trade-Related Investment Measures*, set out in Annex 1A of the *Agreement Creating the World Trade Organization*, 15 April 1994 (Dobbs Ferry, N.Y.: Oceana Publications, 1997) [*WTO Agreement*].

40 See art. 3 and para. (i) of Annex I of the *Agreement on Subsidies and Countervailing Measures*, set out in Annex 1A of the *WTO Agreement, ibid.*

exported. U.S. law permits the establishment within the United States of "foreign trade zones" which are, in effect, outside of U.S. customs jurisdiction. Imported materials can enter a plant that is a foreign trade zone without the payment of duty. Duty is not paid until the finished goods enter U.S. commerce and if the finished goods are exported, duty is never paid.[41] The Mexican maquiladoras are in-bond manufacturing plants into which imported materials enter duty-free and duty is never paid so long as the finished goods are exported.

Duty drawback and duty deferral programs along the lines just described are readily justifiable. Customs duties are indirect taxes on domestic consumers. It makes no sense whatsoever to burden re-exported goods, particularly those used as inputs in the manufacture of domestic products for export, with customs duties. However, drawback and duty deferral programs create distortions within preferential trading blocs by creating an advantage in favour of goods imported duty-free from a member country of the bloc (which, absent restrictions, would benefit from duty drawback or deferral respecting third country inputs) over competing domestic goods (which would not benefit from duty drawback or deferral on comparable inputs).

b) NAFTA Restrictions and Prohibitions

NAFTA restricts refunding duty paid or waiving or reducing duty owed on imported goods exported to another NAFTA country, used as materials in goods exported to another NAFTA country, or substituted by identical or similar goods used as materials in goods exported to another NAFTA country.[42] A NAFTA country may refund, waive, or reduce duty in an amount equal to the lesser of:

- the duty paid or owed on the imported goods; and
- the duty paid when those goods or the goods into which the imported goods or substituted goods are incorporated enter the other NAFTA country.

On 1 January 1996, these restrictions commenced applying to goods traded between Canada and the United States and following 1 January 2001, these restrictions will apply to goods traded between Mexico and each of Canada and the United States.

In the case of a duty deferral program, an imported good exported to another NAFTA country or used as a material or substituted by an

---

41   If the rate of duty on the finished goods is lower than that on the imported materials, the lower finished goods rate applies.
42   NAFTA, above note 10, art. 303(1).

identical or similar good used as a material in a good exported to another NAFTA country, will be treated as if that good had been withdrawn for domestic consumption. Duties must be assessed to the extent that they exceed duties paid to the other NAFTA country on the exported good or the good into which it or the substituted good is incorporated.[43]

NAFTA prohibits any refund, waiver, or reduction of antidumping and countervailing duties, quota allocation premiums, and certain other fees. NAFTA also prohibits refunds, waivers, or reductions of customs duties on imported goods that are substituted by identical or similar goods that are exported in the same condition (as opposed to being used as a material in the production of another good).[44]

c) NAFTA Exceptions

The restrictions on duty drawback and duty deferral do not apply to goods entered under bond for transportation and exportation to another NAFTA country or to goods exported in the same condition as when imported.[45] There are exceptions for goods delivered to duty-free shops, or for supplies for ships or aircraft, or for use in certain joint undertakings.[46] The restrictions do not apply to refunds or waivers of duty on imports of goods that are "originating" under the NAFTA preferential rules of origin.[47] There are also exceptions for goods that fail to conform to specifications,[48] raw sugar cane,[49] citrus products,[50] and certain apparel and piece goods.[51]

---

43 *Ibid.*, art. 303(3).
44 *Ibid.*, art. 303(2)(d). This is called "same-condition substitution duty drawback." There are also special rules respecting colour cathode ray television picture tubes in NAFTA art. 303(8) and NAFTA Annex 303.8 that are not discussed here.
45 *Ibid.*, arts. 303(6)(a) & (b). Testing, cleaning, repacking, or inspecting a good or preserving it are not considered to change its condition.
46 *Ibid.*, art. 303(6)(c).
47 *Ibid.*, art. 303(6)(e). Note that this exception will cease to have practical significance once the duty elimination under NAFTA is complete unless the originating good in question happens to be subject to an antidumping or countervailing duty. The exception in NAFTA art. 303(6) is broad enough to cover the prohibition of refunds of antidumping and countervailing duties set out in NAFTA art. 303(2)(a).
48 *Ibid.*, art. 303(6)(d).
49 Exported from the United States to Canada or Mexico to make refined sugar. See *ibid.*, Annex 303.6, para. 1.
50 *Ibid.*, Annex 303.6, para. 2(a). This exception applies only between Canada and the United States.
51 *Ibid.*, Annex 303.6, paras. 2(b) (piece goods) & 2(c) (apparel goods). These exceptions apply only between Canada and the United States. The exception for apparel goods applies only in certain limited circumstances.

3) NAFTA Rules Respecting Duty Waivers

a) Duty Waivers Based on Performance Requirements
NAFTA Article 304 prohibits programs that waive or remit customs duties on imported goods on the condition that the recipient satisfy "performance requirements." These are defined as requirements that a given level of goods be exported, or domestic goods or services be substituted for imported goods or services, or the recipient purchase other goods or services or accord preference to domestic goods or services, or the recipient produce goods or provide services with given levels of domestic content. Canada may continue existing programs based on performance requirements until 1 January 1998 but must discontinue such programs after that date.[52] Such programs may not be expanded. As discussed below, there are special rules governing automotive duty remission programs.

b) Other Duty Waivers
A program that waives customs duties respecting goods for commercial use by a designated person must be discontinued or made generally available if it has an adverse impact on the commercial interests of a national or enterprise constituted under the laws of another NAFTA country, or a subsidiary of such an enterprise located within the NAFTA country granting the waiver. If the Canadian government grants a duty remission order to a company that adversely affects U.S. or Mexican companies or their Canadian subsidiaries, the government would have to choose between discontinuing the order or making the duty remission available to all importers.

4) Canadian Programs: General

a) Customs Tariff
At the time of writing, the duty relief provisions of the *Customs Tariff* were in a state of transition. Up to 31 December 1997, Schedule II of the *Customs Tariff* set out statutory and temporary concessionary rates that applied to specified goods if certain conditions prevailed, usually tied to

---

52 Between Canada and the United States, the cut-off date for existing programs was in 1988 (see *Canada–United States Free Trade Agreement*, 22 December 1987, Can. T.S. 1989 No. 3, 27 I.L.M. 281 [CUFTA] art. 405, which is incorporated into NAFTA, *ibid.*, by para. (b) of NAFTA Annex 304.2). Between Canada and Mexico, the cut-off date was 1 January 1989 (see para. (a) of NAFTA Annex 304.2).

end use. Schedules IV and V made provision for "home consumption" duty drawbacks for specified goods subject to specified conditions. The *Customs Tariff* also made provision for a "Machinery Program" under which machinery and equipment not available in Canada could be imported duty-free.

Following 1 January 1998, many of the concessions will be eliminated and the remaining concessions will be converted to individual tariff items set out in the schedule to the *Customs Tariff*. Concessions covering ranges of goods will have been converted to tariff items under Chapter 99 of the schedule to the *Customs Tariff*. Section 82(1) will authorize the amendment of tariffs in respect of goods that are used in the production of other goods or the provision of services. The Machinery Program will be eliminated and replaced with tariff items that will distinguish between dutiable items that are available in Canada and duty-free items for equipment that is not available in Canada.

b) Company-Specific Duty Remission

The minister of finance may reduce or remit any taxes, including customs duties, under the authority of Section 23 of the *Financial Administration Act*.[53] Orders granted under this authority must satisfy NAFTA requirements, meaning that the remission allowed cannot be contingent on fulfilling performance requirements.

5) Canadian Programs: Specific Sectors

The Canadian government has made extensive use of duty remission programs in the automotive and textile and apparel sectors.

a) Automotive Duty Remission

i) *The Auto Pact* and *Auto Pact Remission Orders*

In 1965, the Canadian and U.S. governments signed the *Agreement Concerning Automotive Products between the Government of Canada and the Government of the United States of America*, otherwise known as the *Auto Pact*.[54] Under the *Auto Pact*, automotive goods entering the United States from Canada were allowed duty-free treatment if they satisfied a 50 percent Canadian/U.S. content requirement. Canada also accorded duty-free treatment on automotive goods entering Canada; however, the basis for the duty-free treatment depended not on content but on

---

53 R.S.C. 1985, c. F-11.
54 The *Auto Pact* came into effect provisionally on 16 January 1965 and definitively on 16 September 1966.

whether the importer had been producing automobiles in Canada during the *Auto Pact* base year (1 August 1963 to 31 July 1964) and was satisfying safeguards consisting of meeting a production-to-sales ratio and maintaining a prescribed level of Canadian value added in its finished vehicles. An importer that was complying with the safeguards could import new finished vehicles and original equipment (OEM) parts from any country entitled to the benefit of the MFN Tariff.[55] The objective of the safeguards was to ensure that in the tariff-free, integrated North American market for automotive goods created by the *Auto Pact*, Canada maintained a certain level of automotive production.

The only companies eligible to import duty-free under the *Auto Pact* were those assembling vehicles in Canada during the *Auto Pact* base year, namely, the Big Three (General Motors, Ford, and Chrysler) and Volvo. However, the Canadian government began extending *Auto Pact* benefits by way of company-specific duty remission orders to any vehicle assembler in Canada that could meet a production-to-sales ratio and a Canadian value-added requirement similar to those in the *Auto Pact*. Most of the companies to which orders were granted were small specialty vehicle manufacturers.

CUFTA permitted the continuance of the *Auto Pact* and, notwithstanding the fact that the safeguards are performance requirements, Canada's duty remission program based on the safeguards was permitted to be continued indefinitely, despite the general rule that existing duty remission programs based on fulfilling performance requirements had to be phased out by 1 January 1998. However, the program could not be expanded. CAMI Automotive Inc., a joint venture of General Motors and Suzuki, was the last company to receive an *Auto Pact* remission order. Toyota and Honda, both of which had started manufacturing in Canada when CUFTA became effective, did not receive remission orders and, because of CUFTA, will never receive remission orders.[56] The effect of the CUFTA, the provisions of which have been carried forward into NAFTA,[57] was to create two classes of automotive assemblers in Canada: those (the Big Three, CAMI, and various specialty vehicle manufacturers)[58] entitled to the *Auto Pact* benefit of being able to import

---

55 Except tires and tubes.
56 The Korean automotive manufacturer, Hyundai, had also established a plant in Bromont, Quebec, which was subsequently closed.
57 See para. 1 of NAFTA, above note 10, Appendix 300-A.1. Paragraph 1 of the *Canada–Chile Free Trade Agreement*, in force 5 July 1997, see http://www.dfait-maeci.gc.ca/english/trade/agrement.htm, Annex C-00-A, contains a similar provision.
58 See CUFTA, above note 52, Annex 1002.1, Part I, for the complete list.

new vehicles and OEM parts duty-free and those (Toyota and Honda) not entitled to such benefits.

On the U.S. side, the duty-free treatment continued but the origin requirement was changed from the 50 percent *Auto Pact* requirement to the CUFTA and then to the NAFTA preferential rules of origin described in chapter 5.

Once tariff elimination is complete under NAFTA, *Auto Pact* assemblers such as the Big Three will be able to import originating automotive goods from the United States and Mexico without regard to the *Auto Pact* safeguards. The incentive to comply with the safeguards will be to earn duty remission on automotive goods imported from non-NAFTA countries. At the time that CUFTA became effective, the applicable MFN Tariff rate for automotive goods was generally 9.2 percent. In December 1993 the Canadian government reduced the rate to 2.5 percent, and in December 1995 the duty on all parts, except tires and tubes, was reduced to free.[59] The only remaining incentive to satisfy *Auto Pact* safeguards is to earn duty remission on the importation of finished vehicles. In the case of the Big Three, the amount of duty saved is insignificant. Accordingly, while the *Auto Pact* still exists in a technical sense, it has ceased to have any practical significance.

ii) Other Automotive Duty Remission Programs

Prior to the time that CUFTA became effective, the Canadian government had issued thirteen company-specific orders providing for duty remission based on the value of exports. Under CUFTA and NAFTA, exports to the United States must be excluded in computing the duty remission under these orders, and these orders must be discontinued by 1 January 1998.[60] The government had also issued duty remission orders to Toyota and Honda that allowed duty remission based on the Canadian value added in their production in Canada. Under CUFTA and NAFTA requirements, these orders were discontinued on 1 January 1996.[61]

---

59 See *Customs Duties Reduction or Removal Order, 1988, amendment,* SOR/94-18 for the 1993 order, and *Customs Duties Reduction or Removal Order, 1988, amendment,* SOR/96-4 for the 1995 order. Following 1 January 1998, the duty relief provided for by those orders will be carried forward as tariff item 9958.00.00 in the schedule to the *Customs Tariff.*
60 See CUFTA, above note 52, art. 1002(2), and Part Two of CUFTA, Annex 1002.1. See also para. 2, NAFTA, above note 10, Appendix 300-A.1
61 See CUFTA, *ibid.*, art. 1002(3), Part Three of CUFTA, Annex 1002.1, and para. 3 of NAFTA, *ibid.*, Appendix 300-A.1. Hyundai was also the recipient of a production-based duty remission order.

iii) Other CUFTA/NAFTA Provisions Respecting Automotive Goods
CUFTA Article 1005 required that Canada's embargo on used vehicles be phased out by 1993 for vehicles from the United States. NAFTA incorporates this provision and phases out the embargo for used vehicles from Mexico over a ten-year period commencing in 2009.[62] NAFTA makes certain modifications to the U.S. Corporate Average Fuel Economy (CAFE) rules and significantly improves access for Canadian and U.S. automotive products by dismantling the Mexican Automotive Decree over a ten-year period ending in 2004.

b) Textiles

i) Textile Duty Remission Program
Canada's textile and apparel duty remission program currently consists of six duty remission orders enacted in 1988. Some were new and others replaced earlier programs. The orders cover women's and girls' blouses and shirts, denim apparel fabrics, outerwear fabrics and outerwear,[63] outerwear greige[64] fabrics, shirting fabrics, and tailored shirt collars.[65] These orders employ various performance requirements. For example, the blouses and shirts order provides for duty remission for imported blouses and shirts based on the net factory value of shirts and blouses manufactured domestically by the importer. The shirting fabric order grants remission of duty on shirting fabrics imported by a shirting fabric producer and sold to a shirt manufacturer based on that producer's domestic production and sale of shirting fabric. None of these duty remission orders by its own terms extends beyond the end of 1997.[66]

---

62 See paras. 1 & 4 of NAFTA, *ibid.*, Appendix 300-A.1.
63 Outerwear consists of various coats, jackets, and snow and ski wear.
64 "Greige" is fabric directly from the loom before undergoing any process to convert it into a finished fabric.
65 See *Blouses and Shirts Remission Order*, SOR/88-332; *Denim Apparel Fabrics Remission Order*, SOR/88-333; *Outerwear Fabrics and Outerwear Remission Order*, SOR/88-334; *Outerwear Greige Fabrics for Converting Remission Order*, SOR/88-335; *Shirting Fabrics Remission Order, 1988*, SOR/88-331; and *Tailored Collar Shirts Remission Order, 1988*, SOR/88-330, all dated 23 June 1988. These orders were all retroactively amended by the *General Textile and Apparel Amendment Order (Customs Tariff), 1989*, SOR/89-83, dated 19 January 1989.
66 The denim order expired at the end of the 1993 calendar year. The other orders expire on 31 December 1997. These programs are being replaced by new remission programs not based on performance requirements.

ii) Textile Reference Guidelines

While requests for tariff relief are generally made on an informal basis to the Department of Finance, a formal procedure for tariff relief requests respecting textile and apparel products has been developed under the authority of Section 19 of the *Canadian International Trade Tribunal Act*.[67] Section 19 empowers the Canadian International Trade Tribunal (CITT) to enquire into and report to the minister of finance on any tariff-related matter. Pursuant to written terms of reference of the minister of finance addressed to the chairman of the CITT, the CITT developed a procedure for considering requests for tariff relief on imports of textile inputs by domestic producers which is set out in the *Textile Reference Guidelines*.[68] The procedure begins with a written request by the domestic producer. Once the CITT is satisfied that the request is properly documented, the CITT commences an investigation by publishing a notice in the *Canada Gazette*. Interested parties may file submissions and the requester has the opportunity to file a response. The CITT conducts its own investigation and makes recommendations to the minister that the relief be either granted or denied. While recommendations are usually made without a hearing, an interested party may request a hearing or the CITT may hold a hearing on its own initiative.[69]

The advantage of this formalized process is that requesters have the opportunity to respond to the submissions against their request. The disadvantage is that the formalization of the procedures makes a tariff relief request more expensive to pursue, particularly if the request is strenuously resisted.

H. OTHER NAFTA PROVISIONS RESPECTING TARIFFS AND RELATED BORDER MEASURES

There are a number of other NAFTA provisions that affect customs duties that should be mentioned but will not be discussed in detail. NAFTA Article 305 sets out rules respecting the temporary admission

---

67 R.S.C. 1985 (4th Supp.), c. 47.
68 Set out in Appendix 2 of the Tariff Reference Guide, October 1996, http://www.citt.gc.ca/...e/english/guide96e.htm.
69 At the time of writing, there had been only one hearing. See *Beco Industries Ltd.*, Request Nos. TR-95-035, TR-95-043, and TR-95-044. The requests involved certain poly-cotton and cotton fabrics used in the production of home furnishing products. The requests were denied.

of goods on a duty-free basis. NAFTA Article 306 provides for duty-free entry of certain commercial samples and printed advertising materials, and NAFTA Article 307 provides for duty-free entry of goods re-entered after repair or alteration, provided certain conditions are satisfied. NAFTA Article 310 and NAFTA Annex 301.1 continue the CUFTA prohibition as between Canada and the United States of customs user fees on originating goods provided for in CUFTA Article 403[70] and set out similar rules respecting originating goods from Mexico.

NAFTA Article 308 and NAFTA Annex 308.1 have the effect of creating a mini-customs union in respect of certain categories of computer goods. The MFN tariff rates of the three NAFTA countries will be harmonized by 1 January 2003. Once the commonly agreed tariff is in effect, there will be no need for these goods to comply with preferential rules of origin in order to receive the benefit of duty free treatment as they cross borders between NAFTA countries.

I. CIFTA AND CCFTA RULES RESPECTING DUTY RELIEF AND OTHER BORDER MEASURES

Unlike NAFTA, CIFTA does not contain any prohibitions or restrictions of duty drawback, duty deferral, or duty waivers based on performance requirements. CCFTA does not restrict duty drawback or duty deferral, but CCFTA Article C-03 contains restrictions on duty waivers based on performance requirements that are similar to those in NAFTA.

CIFTA Article 2.2 and CCFTA Article C-06 each prohibit applying customs duties to goods entering one of Canada or Israel after being exported to the other for repair or alteration, or to goods entering one country from the other for repair or alteration. Unlike NAFTA, CIFTA does not contain provisions relating to temporary admission of goods, commercial samples and advertising materials, or customs user fees. CCFTA Articles C-04 (Temporary Admission of Goods), C-05 (Commercial Samples and Printed Advertising Materials), and C-09 (Customs User Fees) are similar to their NAFTA counterparts. CCFTA Article C-07 requires the elimination of MFN tariffs on certain computer goods.

---

70 Under this CUFTA provision, the introduction of these fees was prohibited and existing U.S. fees were phased out by 1 January 1994.

CHAPTER 4

IMPORT AND EXPORT RESTRICTIONS AND RELATED BORDER MEASURES

This chapter covers the rules under the trade agreements to which Canada is a party respecting import and export restrictions and various other non-tariff measures that affect the trade in goods.

Import restrictions range from outright prohibitions to quantitative restrictions or quotas (under which only specified quantities of a good are admitted) to import licencing requirements (under which a licence must first be obtained before importing a good) to "voluntary" export agreements (under which imports are limited by having the exporting country control the volume of its exports). Import restrictions are less transparent than tariffs and are much more effective barriers to trade. Quantitative restrictions involve quota allocation issues that are difficult to resolve equitably. Allocation on a historical basis is unfair to new entrants, while ignoring pre-quota importing patterns can be grossly unfair to existing importing businesses. Allocation by auction and fees can result in breaches of tariff bindings. Quotas generate "economic rents" or windfall profits to those who hold them because of the scarcity that they artificially induce. Import restrictions must conform to the requirements of Article XIII of GATT 1994 which, *inter alia*, requires that import restrictions be applied in a non-discriminatory manner. Import restrictions of various sorts have been widely used in the sensitive agricultural and the textile and apparel sectors. Until the *Textile Agreement* came into effect, the trade in textile and apparel goods was governed by the *Arrangement Regarding International Trade in Textiles* (*Multifibre Arrangement* or MFA), which sanctioned bilateral restraint agreements with export quotas for various categories of textile and apparel goods.

Export restrictions can also take a variety of forms ranging from outright prohibitions to export licensing requirements to export quotas. Export restrictions are most likely to be applied in strategic sectors such as energy goods. Export restrictions are also sometimes implemented as an industrial policy to ensure further domestic processing of raw materials. Export quotas entail the same administrative nightmares as import quotas.

The basic rules governing import and export restrictions are set out in GATT 1994. NAFTA, CCFTA, and, to a lesser extent, CIFTA build upon the regime set out in GATT 1994. The *Agriculture Agreement* converts import restrictions on agricultural goods into tariff rate quotas and prohibits the imposition of new import restrictions, while the *Textile Agreement* dismantles the *Multifibre Arrangement* and, over a ten-year period, will bring the trade in textile and apparel goods back under GATT rules.

A. ARTICLE XI OF GATT 1994

Article XI:1 of GATT 1994 prohibits both import and export restrictions other than duties and other charges on imports and exports. The prohibition of import restrictions applies to products of territories of other contracting parties. Until the *Rules of Origin Agreement* became effective, the determination of the country of origin of goods was left to individual member countries. As discussed in chapter 5, the *Rules of Origin Agreement* requires that the WTO member countries develop objective rules for determining the country of origin of goods. The prohibition of export restrictions applies to any product destined for export to the territory of another contracting party.

Article XI sets out three exceptions to the general prohibition of import and export restrictions. Article XI:2(a) permits restricting exports in order to relieve critical shortages. Article XI:2(b) allows import or export restrictions necessary for the application of classification, grading, or marketing standards or regulations. Article XI:2(c) sanctions import restrictions of agricultural and fisheries products that are part of government schemes to restrict domestic supply. Before the *Agricultural Agreement* became effective, Article XI:2(c) was used by Canada to justify agricultural supply management programs in the dairy and poultry sectors. As discussed below, the application of the Article XI exceptions to agricultural goods has been substantially modified by the *Agriculture Agreement*. Import and export restrictions can also be justified under the general exceptions in Article XX of GATT 1994 (see chapter 2).

B. INCORPORATION OF ARTICLE XI OF GATT 1994 INTO NAFTA, CIFTA, AND CCFTA

NAFTA Article 309(1) incorporates Article XI of GATT 1994 and its interpretative notes into the NAFTA text. The prohibition of import restrictions in the incorporated Article XI of GATT 1994 applies only to "any good of another Party." As discussed in chapter 2 under "Goods of a Party," this definition provides an imprecise but objective standard for identifying the goods of a NAFTA country that are entitled to protection from import restrictions. The fact that the standard is objective means that a NAFTA country cannot escape its obligations under NAFTA Article 309(1) by unilaterally defining the country of origin of goods.

CIFTA Article 4.4(1) and CCFTA Article C-08(3) incorporate Article XI of GATT 1994 with virtually the same language as NAFTA Article 309(1). The comments made above respecting NAFTA 309(1) apply equally to CIFTA Article 4.4(1) and to CCFTA Article C-08(3).

C. MINIMUM IMPORT AND EXPORT PRICES UNDER NAFTA, CIFTA, AND CCFTA

NAFTA Article 309(2) confirms the NAFTA countries' understanding that the prohibition in GATT Article XI extends to minimum export price requirements and, except for antidumping and countervailing duties, minimum import price requirements. CIFTA Article 4.4(2) sets out the same understanding between Canada and Israel, as does CCFTA Article C-08(2) between Canada and Chile. A GATT panel has found minimum import prices to be inconsistent with GATT obligations.[1] The objection to a minimum import price requirement is that it can have the effect of nullifying the benefit of a tariff concession.

D. IMPORT AND EXPORT RESTRICTIONS UNDER NAFTA, CIFTA, AND CCFTA

NAFTA Article 309(3) provides that if a NAFTA country maintains a prohibition or restriction on imports from a non-NAFTA country, it may limit the importation of goods of that non-NAFTA country from a

---

1   EEC — *Programme of Minimum Import Prices, Licences and Surety Deposits for Certain Processed Fruits and Vegetables* (U.S. v. EEC) (1978), GATT Doc. L/4687, 25th supp. B.I.S.D. (1977–1978) 68.

NAFTA country. On the basis of this rule, the United States can prohibit the importation from Canada of goods that originate in Cuba. Similarly, if a NAFTA country prohibits or restricts exports of a good to a non-NAFTA country, it may require that if that good is exported to another NAFTA country, it must be further processed or manufactured so as to be substantially changed before being further exported to the non-NAFTA country. CIFTA Article 4.4(3) and CCFTA Article C-08(3) contain similar provisions.

E. EXCEPTIONS UNDER NAFTA, CIFTA, AND CCFTA

NAFTA Annex 301.3 contains exceptions to the obligations respecting import and export restrictions set out in Article 309.[2] Each NAFTA country retains the right to control the export of logs of all species. The four Atlantic provinces and Quebec may maintain controls on the export of unprocessed fish set out in the legislation listed in NAFTA Annex 301.3. Certain measures that were mandatory legislation at the time that Canada acceded to GATT 1947 are excepted. Canada may maintain import restrictions respecting certain ships and vessels originating in the United States so long as the United States continues to maintain quantitative restrictions under its maritime legislation on the importation of comparable Canadian goods. The exceptions apply to amendments to these measures so long as the measure is not made more non-conforming. NAFTA 301.3 also sets out exceptions that apply to certain U.S. and Mexican measures.

CIFTA Annex 4.1 and CCFTA Annex C-01.3, insofar as they apply to Canada, are both similar to NAFTA Annex 301.3.[3] Annex 4.1 also excepts certain Israeli import and export controls. CCFTA Annex C-01.3 permits Chile to prohibit imports of used vehicles. Chile has also taken a reservation in Annex C-08 that CCFTA Article C-08 not apply to copper and copper reserves.

---

2   All the exceptions in the *North American Free Trade Agreement*, 17 December 1992, Can. T.S. 1994 No. 2 [NAFTA], Annex 301.3, also apply to NAFTA art. 301. See chapter 2.
3   Except for the exception concerning vessels. There are a few other minor differences.

F. PROHIBITION OF EXPORT TAXES UNDER NAFTA, CIFTA, AND CCFTA

NAFTA Article 314 provides that a NAFTA country may not impose a tax on the export of a good to another NAFTA country unless the tax is imposed on the good both when destined for domestic consumption and when exported to all NAFTA countries. While export taxes are not prohibited, the requirement that a corresponding charge be imposed on goods destined for domestic consumption defeats their purpose. An export tax has the effect of favouring domestic buyers of a domestic good over foreign buyers. NAFTA Article 314 prohibits this discriminatory treatment. CIFTA Article 4.7 and CCFTA Article C-12 contain similar provisions.[4] Export taxes and other export charges are not prohibited by Article XI of GATT 1994.

Other than an export tax imposed on oil during the 1970s and 1980s as part of a price stabilization scheme and a tax on exports of softwood lumber in the late 1980s and early 1990s that resulted from the settlement of a U.S. countervailing duty action, the Canadian government has made little use of export taxes.

G. NAFTA AND CCFTA DISCIPLINES RESPECTING EXPORT RESTRICTIONS

NAFTA Article 315 and CCFTA Article C-13 impose disciplines on the use of certain exceptions of GATT 1994 to justify export restrictions.[5] The exceptions affected by the disciplines are the "critical shortages" exception in Article XI:2(a) of GATT 1994, the "exhaustible natural resources" exception in Article XX(g) of GATT 1994, the "governmen-

---

4   Certain Israeli charges are exempt under the *Canada–Israel Free Trade Agreement*, in force 1 January 1997, see http://www.dfait-maeci.gc.ca/english/trade/agrement.htm [CIFTA], Annex 4.1.

5   The "GATT" referred to in NAFTA, above note 2, art. 315, is the original *General Agreement on Tariffs and Trade*, 30 October 1947, Can. T.S. 1947 No. 27 [GATT] and not the *General Agreement on Tariffs and Trade 1994*, set out in Annex 1A of the *Agreement Creating the World Trade Organization*, 15 April 1994 (Dobbs Ferry, N.Y.: Oceana Publications, 1997) [*WTO Agreement*][GATT 1994] 1994. NAFTA art. 315, unlike NAFTA arts. 301 and 309(1), does not make reference to "successor agreements." However, the author believes it is reasonable to conclude that the GATT provisions referred to in NAFTA art. 315 include the corresponding provisions of GATT 1994, which are all unchanged from the original GATT provisions.

tal stabilization" exception in Article XX(i) of GATT 1994, and the "products in short supply" exception in Article XX(j) of GATT 1994.[6]

The disciplines apply to restrictions on exports of a "good of a Party" to the "territory of another Party."[7] For the disciplines to apply, an export restriction must be inconsistent with GATT obligations were it not for one of the exceptions named in NAFTA Article 315 or CCFTA Article C-13. If the restriction is consistent with GATT 1994 or can be justified under a GATT exception not referred to in NAFTA Article 315 or CCFTA Article C-13, such as the "human, animal and plant life or health" exception, the disciplines do not apply.

1) The Disciplines

The disciplines set out in NAFTA Article 315 and CCFTA Article C-13 are as follows.

a) Proportionality

If the export restriction justified under one of the identified GATT exceptions cuts back shipments of a good for export, shipments to domestic users must also be reduced so that the proportion of export shipments to total shipments that has prevailed over the preceding thirty-six months is maintained. This discipline is clearly more rigorous than the loose requirements which the GATT 1994 attaches to some of the exceptions. The "exhaustible natural resources" exception, as expressed in GATT 1994, may be used only if the restriction is made effective in conjunction with restrictions on domestic production or consumption, but no proportion is set. The use of the "products in short supply exception" under GATT 1994 is subject to "principles of international sharing," but GATT 1994 does not say what these are. The GATT "government stabilization plan" exception is subject only to a vague non-discrimination requirement. The "critical shortages" exception is not subject to any constraint under GATT 1994, although Article 12 of the Agriculture Agreement requires notification and that the country imposing the restriction give due consideration to the food security of importing member countries.

---

6   There is no counterpart to NAFTA, *ibid.*, art. 315, or the *Canada–Chile Free Trade Agreement,* in force 5 July 1997, see http://www.dfait-maeci.gc.ca/english/trade/agrement.htm[CCFTA], art. C-13 in CIFTA, above note 4.

7   NAFTA Annex 315 provides that NAFTA art. 315 does not apply between Mexico and the other two NAFTA countries. This means that Mexico is neither bound by NAFTA art. 315 nor entitled to its protections. Chile has reserved the right not to apply CCFTA, *ibid.*, art. C-13, to copper and copper reserves.

b) Pricing

A restriction justified under one of the specified GATT exceptions must not impose a higher price on exports of a good than the price charged when the good is consumed domestically. The operative word is "impose." The discipline does not apply to differences in prices for goods that may result from the operation of market forces. The discipline expressly does not apply to a higher price that results from a measure taken under the proportionality discipline that only restricts the volume of exports. In this situation, market forces can drive up prices so that there is a differential between the prices in the exporting and importing Parties.

c) Normal Channels of Supply

A restriction justified under one of the enumerated exceptions must not disrupt normal channels of supply or normal proportions among specific goods or categories of goods supplied to the other Party or to other Parties.

2) Application to Energy Goods: NAFTA

The obligations set out in NAFTA[8] Article 309 (import and export restrictions), Article 314 (export taxes), and Article 315 (export measures) are repeated for energy goods in Articles 603, 604, and 605,[9] respectively. This is peculiar drafting in that the provisions of Articles 309, 314, and 315 are sufficiently broad to cover energy goods without having to be repeated. The explanation for this curious approach is that the impetus for rules on export charges and export measures (which were in the CUFTA) originated in practices followed by the Canadian government between 1973 and 1985 respecting the oil industry. As a response to the oil crisis of 1973–74, the Canadian government imposed a Canadian regulated price that was below the world price. Exports of oil, however, were required by law to be priced at higher world prices. The difference was taxed away through an export charge and these funds, together with the proceeds of an excise tax on gasoline, were used to fund a subsidy to bring down the price of imports of oil into eastern Canada (which, because of limitations in the pipeline system, did not have access to domestic oil) to the Canadian regulated price. During the period from 1974 to 1980, oil exports to the United States were substantially cut back and exports of some grades of oil were all but eliminated by the National Energy Board.

---

8   Neither CIFTA, above note 4, nor CCFTA, above note 6, contains a chapter dealing specifically with energy goods.
9   As with art. 315 of NAFTA, above note 2, art. 605 of NAFTA does not apply between Mexico and each of Canada and the United States.

The purpose of the prohibition of export taxes and the imposition of the proportionality, pricing, and normal channels disciplines, was primarily to prevent a repetition of these policies.

The proportionality requirement imposed by NAFTA Articles 315 and 605 might be viewed as a type of sharing arrangement. In the event of a shortage, imposed cutbacks must be shared proportionately between exports and domestic shipments. It should be noted that Canada and the United States are parties to the *Agreement on an International Energy Program* (IEP), which provides for sharing in the event of an oil crisis. The requirements of the IEP differ from those in NAFTA Articles 315 and 605 and it is difficult to tell which are more onerous. However, NAFTA Annex 608.2 provides that the IEP prevails in the event of an inconsistency.

H. SPECIAL CASES: AGRICULTURE AND TEXTILES AND APPAREL

The agricultural and the textile and apparel sectors (food and clothing) are regarded as sensitive in most countries and Canada is no exception. Both the WTO agreements and NAFTA contain special rules to address the unique problems respecting the trade in these goods. CCFTA sets out special rules respecting textile and apparel goods that are modelled on those in NAFTA.

1) Agricultural Goods

The agricultural sector is particularly sensitive because its products are basic necessities. Production of primary agricultural goods is subject to the vagaries of weather, and dependence on imported food, while unavoidable for many countries, is perceived as being contrary to good public policy. Many societies identify their agriculture communities with values that transcend economics. Farming communities frequently have political influence that goes well beyond their numbers. Programs to protect an agricultural sector typically restrict domestic production so that higher prices are maintained and also limit imports through quantitative restrictions or import licensing requirements.

a) Supply Management Programs
Canadian supply management programs cover dairy and poultry products. Yearly production quotas are established by federal agencies. The quotas are allocated to the provinces and provincial agencies allocate the production quotas within each province. The restriction of domestic

supply is complemented by restrictions on imports. Until the *Agriculture Agreement* became effective, the restrictions took the form of quantitative restrictions under the cover of GATT Article XI:2(c).[10] As required under the *Agriculture Agreement*, the quantitative restrictions were converted into tariff rate quotas.

The Canada Wheat Board (CWB), which is maintained by the Canadian government, has a monopoly over the interprovincial and international trade in certain grains (most notably wheat) and their products. However, these products are not supply-managed like dairy and poultry goods.

Despite its endless criticism and its NAFTA Chapter Twenty challenge of Canadian supply management programs, the United States has established programs covering a variety of U.S. agricultural products, most notably sugar and sugar-containing products, dairy products, and peanuts, which have much the same effect. The principal statutory provision under which quantitative restrictions are imposed is Section 22 of the *Agricultural Adjustment Act* (AAA), which authorizes fees of up to 50 percent *ad valorem* or import quotas if imports "render or tend to render ineffective or materially interfere with" U.S. Department of Agriculture programs respecting agricultural commodities or their products.[11] On 5 March 1955, the United States was granted a waiver by the GATT in respect of these statutory powers.[12]

b) The *Agriculture Agreement*: Tariffication and Safeguards

Tariffication is the term of art adopted to denote the conversion of non-tariff barriers into customs duties. Part III of the *Agriculture Agreement* requires that all border measures other than customs duties be converted into customs duties. The products covered by this requirement are set out in Annex 1 to the *Agriculture Agreement* and include hides and skins and various fibres used for textiles as well as foodstuffs.[13] The

---

10 The applicability of GATT, above note 5, art. XI:2(c), was successfully challenged by the United States in the case of restrictions on the importation of ice cream and yoghurt, on the grounds that milk, the domestic product being restricted, was not a "like product" to ice cream and yoghurt because these latter products are processed. See *Canada — Import Restrictions on Ice Cream and Yoghurt* (U.S. v. Canada) (1989), GATT Doc. L/6568, 36th supp. B.I.S.D. (1988–1989) 68 [*Ice Cream Case*].
11 7 U.S.C. §624(a) & (b) (1988).
12 See *Waiver Granted to the United States in Connection with Import Restrictions Imposed under Section 22 of the United States Agricultural Amendment Act of 1933, as Amended* (1955), 3d supp. B.I.S.D. (1955) 32.
13 The product coverage is expressed in terms of Harmonized System chapters, headings, and subheadings. All products in Chapters 1 to 24 except fish and fish products are included, as well as certain other specified products.

border measures include quantitative import restrictions, variable import levies, minimum import prices, discretionary import licensing, non-tariff measures maintained through state trading enterprises and voluntary export restraints.[14] Article 4(2) of the *Agriculture Agreement* prohibits WTO countries from maintaining or reverting to any such border measures in the future. The effect of this provision is to preclude WTO member countries from introducing any new supply management programs under the cover of Article XI:2(c) of GATT 1994.

As required under the *Agriculture Agreement*, Canada converted all the quantitative restrictions that it maintained under GATT Article XI into tariff rate quotas.[15] A market access commitment in terms of quantity is established for each product. Imports during a year that are within the market access commitment are subject to a within-access rate, and imports in excess of the market access commitment are subject to an over-access rate. For example, the annual market access commitment for fluid milk is 64,500 tonnes.[16] Unlike with some products, this quantity does not increase. The within-access rate for fluid milk is 17.5 percent and the over-access rate for fluid milk is 283.8 percent.[17] The over-access rate will be reduced somewhat over time but will still remain prohibitively high. The allocation of quotas within the market access commitment is administered by the Department of Foreign Affairs and International Trade under the *Export and Import Permits Act*.

In *EEC — Regime for the Importation, Sale and Distribution of Bananas*,[18] the Appellate Body held that the rules set out in Article XIII of GATT 1994 requiring the non-discriminatory administration of

---

14 This list is taken from note 1 to art. 4(2) of the *Agreement on Agriculture*, set out in Annex 1A of the *WTO Agreement*, above note 5, [*Agriculture Agreement*].
15 This includes ice cream and yoghurt. Canada delayed implementing the decision in the *Ice Cream Case*, above note 10, pending the outcome of the Uruguay Round negotiations. Canada took the position that the obligation to tariffy applied to all quantitative restrictions, regardless of whether they were GATT-consistent or not. In effect, the *Agriculture Agreement*, ibid., provided for a one-time amnesty. The United States did not challenge this action directly but challenged all Canadian over-access rates on supply-managed products under NAFTA, above note 2. As discussed below, the NAFTA panel decided in Canada's favour.
16 For a summary of the Canadian market access commitments, see the *Canadian Statement of Implementation of the Agreement Establishing the World Trade Organization*, C. Gaz. 1994.I.4847 at 4884.
17 For a summary of all Canada's within-access and over-access rates, see ibid. at 4872–4873 (Table i).
18 WT/DS27/AB/R, Appellate Body Report (AB-1997-3).

quantitative restrictions applied to tariff quotas resulting from tariffication under the *Agriculture Agreement*.[19]

The *Agriculture Agreement* contains safeguards for products respecting which member countries have made concessions. The safeguards may be invoked upon volumes of imports exceeding a trigger level or prices of imports falling below a trigger price. Upon the occurrence of either of these events, a member country may impose additional duties calculated in accordance with a formula.

c) Provisions of NAFTA Respecting Import and Export Restrictions

Section A of NAFTA Chapter Seven sets out three separate bilateral arrangements respecting the trade in agricultural goods between each of Canada and the United States, the United States and Mexico, and Canada and Mexico.

i) Canada and the United States

NAFTA Annex 702.1 incorporates by reference virtually all of CUFTA Chapter Seven. Several provisions of CUFTA Chapter Seven address import and export restrictions respecting specific products. CUFTA Article 702(1) permits the application of temporary or "snapback" duties on fresh fruits and vegetables under limited circumstances.[20] The duty may be applied only once in a twelve-month period and must not exceed the lesser of MFN rate that applied on 1 January 1989 or the current MFN rate. The right to apply these temporary duties expires on 1 January 2009. CUFTA Article 704 eliminated quantitative import restrictions on originating meat goods other than restrictions necessary to preserve the integrity of quantitative import restrictions or voluntary agreements limiting meat imports from third countries. CUFTA Article 705(1) requires Canada to eliminate import permit requirements for wheat, oats, barley, or products made from them originating in the United States if the level of U.S. government support for any of these grains becomes equal to or less than the level of Canadian government support.[21] CUFTA Article 706 requires Canada to permit limited quantities of poultry and

---

19 *Ibid.*, para. 154.
20 The fruits and vegetables to which the temporary duty may be applied are listed in *Canada — United States Free Trade Agreement*, 22 December 1987, Can. T.S. 1989 No. 3, 27 I.L.M. 281 [CUFTA], art. 702(7).
21 The formulae are set out in CUFTA, *ibid.*, Annex 705.4. In 1991, the Canadian government eliminated import provisions respecting wheat. See SOR/91-302.9. In 1993, the Canadian government unilaterally eliminated CWB licensing requirements for barley and barley products imported from and exported to the United States.

egg products to be imported.²² CUFTA Article 707 requires that the United States not maintain any quantitative import restriction or import fee on any good originating in Canada which contains 10 percent or less sugar by dry weight for the purposes of restricting its sugar content. However, U.S. restrictions on sugar and sugar-containing products with higher percentages by dry weight of sugar are unaffected.

Under CUFTA Article 710, each of Canada and the United States retains their rights under the GATT and agreements negotiated under the GATT, which means, in effect, that subject to the concessions specifically agreed to, each country retains the right to maintain restrictions on imports of agricultural products under GATT Article XI:2(c) and, in the case of the United States, the GATT waiver in respect of Section 22 of the AAA.²³ However, between Canada and the United States, NAFTA does not take into account the tariffication requirements of the *Agriculture Agreement*, which existed in draft form at the time that NAFTA was negotiated. The U.S. government took the position that the Canadian over-access tariffs on dairy and poultry products resulting from tariffication under the *Agriculture Agreement* were new tariffs prohibited by NAFTA Article 302(1). Canada took the position that the *Agriculture Agreement* was an agreement "negotiated under the GATT" within the meaning of CUFTA Article 710 and that the effect of NAFTA Annex 702.1 was to incorporate into NAFTA the tariffication regime in the *Agriculture Agreement*. The United States commenced proceedings under NAFTA Chapter Twenty and the panel decided in Canada's favour.

ii) Canada and the United States: The Supply Management Decision
In its decision, the panel in *In the Matter of Tariffs Applied by Canada to Certain U.S.-Origin Agricultural Products*²⁴ cited the principles of interpretation in the *Vienna Convention*²⁵ and proceeded to examine whether CUFTA Article 710 was intended to refer to GATT rights and obligations

---

22 CUFTA, *ibid.* The limit for chicken and chicken products for a year is not less than 7.5 percent of the previous year's domestic production. The limit for turkey and turkey products for a year is not less than 3.5 percent of the domestic turkey quota for that year. The limits for shell eggs, frozen, liquid, and further processed eggs and powdered eggs for a year are 1.647 percent, 0.714 percent, and 0.627 percent, respectively, of the previous year's domestic production.
23 The incorporating language in para. 4 of CUFTA, *ibid.*, Annex 702.1, makes it clear that the rights and obligations incorporated in CUFTA art. 710 include GATT waivers as well as exemptions under para. 1(b) of the *Protocol of Provisional Application of the General Agreement on Tariffs and Trade*, 30 October 1947, B.I.S.D. vol. 4 (1969) 77.
24 2 December 1996, CDA-95-2008-01 (Ch. 20 Panel) [*U.S.-Origin*].
25 *Ibid.*, para. 122.

as they existed when NAFTA became effective or as they evolved over time. The panel rejected the U.S. contention that the Parties could not retain rights under future agreements by citing an example in the CUFTA where "retain" was used in connection with an evolving system.[26] The panel cited instances in CUFTA where it was clearly intended that incorporated rights be frozen in time and concluded that the terms of the incorporated CUFTA Article 710 were forward looking.[27]

The panel then proceeded to consider what rights and obligations were incorporated into NAFTA by CUFTA Article 710. Canada argued that the rights and obligations incorporated included those under the *Agriculture Agreement* that required Canada to replace agricultural quotas with tariff equivalents.[28] The United States took the position that the *Agriculture Agreement* required members to eliminate non-tariff barriers but their replacement by tariff equivalents was optional.[29] The *Agriculture Agreement* itself is unclear as to whether conversion of non-tariff barriers into tariff equivalents is mandatory. Article 4.2 of that agreement provides that members "shall not maintain, resort to, or revert to any measures of the kind *which have been required to be converted into ordinary customs duties*, except as otherwise provided for in Article 5 and Annex 5" [emphasis added]. The panel observed that these words did not themselves create an obligation to tariffy but that some meaning had to be attributed to the emphasized words.[30] The panel adopted the approach to interpretation prescribed by Article 32 of the *Vienna Convention* and examined the *travaux préparatoires* of the *Agriculture Agreement* and the general circumstances of its conclusion. The *travaux préparatoires* included an *Agreement on Modalities for the Establishment of Specific Binding Commitments under the Reform Programme* (*Modalities Agreement*) which did require that tariff equivalents be established.[31] The panel exam-

---

26 *Ibid.*, para. 134. The example given is CUFTA, above note 20, art. 1608(2), where Parties and their investors retain their rights and obligations under customary international law, which is evolving and not static.
27 *Ibid.*, para. 145. The panel considered the incorporating language in para. 4 of CUFTA Annex 702.1 and concluded that it did not alter the forward-looking character of CUFTA art. 710, notwithstanding the absence in such provision of a reference to tariffication. See *U.S.-Origin*, *ibid.*, para. 148. The panel also examined subsequent actions of Canada and the United States and concluded that none of these affected their interpretation. *U.S.-Origin*, *ibid.*, paras. 151–154.
28 *Ibid.*, para. 168.
29 *Ibid.*, para. 169.
30 *Ibid.*, paras. 171–172.
31 *The Dunkel Draft* (GATT Secretariat (Buffalo, N.Y.: William S. Hein & Co., Inc., 1992). The *Modalities Agreement* is set out at L.19 to L.28. The provision requiring the establishment of tariff equivalents is set out in para. 3 of Annex 3 of the *Agreement*. See page L.25.

ined the course of events that ultimately resulted in the filing by WTO member countries of the tariff schedules that included the tariff equivalents and concluded that tariffication was a "*right* arising from an agreement negotiated under the GATT."³² In essence, the panel viewed the process of the removal of agricultural non-tariff barriers and the *quid pro quo* of their replacement with tariff barrier equivalents as a package deal, with one being inexorably tied to the other. It would make no sense whatever to bring one part of the WTO agricultural package into NAFTA (namely the requirement that non-tariff barriers be eliminated) without the other (the *quid pro quo* of replacing non-tariff barriers with tariff equivalents).³³

Having concluded that the rights covered by CUFTA Article 710 included the right to tariffy, the panel then considered the effect of the incorporation of CUFTA Article 710 into NAFTA. The panel concluded that the effect of the incorporation of CUFTA Article 710 into NAFTA was to incorporate the entire tariffication package. However, the rights and obligations incorporated did not include the entire WTO agricultural package. Tariffs that were not part of the tariffication package (namely WTO in-quota rates) were not included, and the rights of Canada and the United States respecting these tariffs was governed by the NAFTA tariff elimination requirements.³⁴

The panel examined the relationship between NAFTA Chapters Three and Seven and concluded that, because of the rule of prevalence in NAFTA Article 701(2), Chapter Seven (and the tariffication package incorporated by CUFTA Article 710) prevailed over Chapter Three (and the tariff elimination requirements of NAFTA Article 301(2)).³⁵

The panel's logic in permitting Canadian supply management programs to continue under NAFTA applies equally to comparable U.S. programs. Therefore, the effect of this decision is that the trade in a

---

32 *U.S.-Origin, ibid.*, para. 182.
33 The notion of the tariffication "package" is expressed in a number of places in the Panel Report. See, for example, *ibid.*, para. 198.
34 *Ibid.*, para. 201. The panel does not give a reason for this conclusion. However, in para. 120 of the Panel Report, the panel cited the "object and purpose" rule in art. 31 of the *Vienna Convention on the Law of Treaties*, 23 May 1969, 8 I.L.M. 679, and in para. 122 of the Panel Report, the panel stated that it attached importance to the "trade liberalization background" against which the agreements under consideration must be considered. The "object and purpose" of "trade liberalization" would lead the panel to the conclusion that NAFTA tariff elimination would apply to agricultural tariffs other than those arising from tariffication.
35 *U.S.-Origin, ibid.*, paras. 202–207.

number of agricultural goods between Canada and the United States will continue to be highly restricted.

iii) *The United States and Mexico*
In marked contrast to the Canada–U.S. bilateral arrangement, the bilateral arrangement between the United States and Mexico builds upon the tariffication approach taken in the *Agriculture Agreement* and follows it through to its logical conclusion. U.S. quantitative restrictions on dairy products, peanuts and peanut products, and sugar and sugar-containing products, and Mexican quantitative restrictions on poultry products, powdered milk, potatoes, kidney beans, and maize (corn) are all converted to tariff rate quotas. The initial over-quota tariff rates are prohibitive but will be completely phased out over ten or fifteen years, depending on the product. The end result will be free trade in agricultural goods between the United States and Mexico.

iv) *Canada and Mexico*
Each of Canada and Mexico reserved their rights under GATT Article XI:2(c)(i) with respect to dairy, poultry, and egg goods specified for each country in NAFTA Appendix 703.2.B.7. The lists cover all of Canada's supply-managed goods. The effect of the reservation is that quantitative restrictions may be applied against these goods by each of Canada and Mexico against the other.[36] Canada and Mexico will not maintain quantitative restrictions against each other with respect to other agricultural goods, and Mexican import licensing requirements respecting goods from Canada will be converted to tariff rate quotas. As between Canada and Mexico, tariffs will not be eliminated on dairy products, poultry products, or sugar-containing products.

v) *Special Safeguards*
NAFTA Article 703 permits special safeguards in the form of tariff rate quotas to be maintained by each country in respect of agricultural goods listed in NAFTA Annex 703.3. The safeguards apply between Canada and Mexico and between Mexico and the United States, but not between Canada and the United States. The over-quota tariff rate cannot exceed the lower of the MFN rate in effect on 1 January 1991 or the MFN rate currently in effect. The list for Canada includes certain categories of cut

---

36 NAFTA, above note 2, Annex 703.2, Section B, para. 7(a). Canada does not maintain quantitative restrictions against these goods of Mexico. These goods are subject to the same over-access tariff rates as apply to these goods of all other countries.

flowers, fresh and chilled tomatoes, onions and shallots, cucumbers and gherkins, strawberries, and prepared or preserved tomatoes.

2) Textile and Apparel Goods

Since 1961, the trade in various categories of textile and apparel goods has been governed by rules that depart significantly from GATT rules. The objective of these rules has been to protect the textile and apparel sectors in developed countries from developing country competition. The first special arrangement affecting the textile and apparel sector was the Short Term Arrangement that covered cotton textiles. The Short Term Arrangement was replaced by the Long Term Arrangement which, in turn, was replaced in 1974 with the *Multifibre Arrangement*.

a) The *Multifibre Arrangement* and Bilateral Restraint Agreements

The *Multifibre Arrangement* covered "textiles," which are "tops, yarns, piece-goods, made-up articles, garments and other textile manufactured products" of cotton, wool, man-made fibres or combinations thereof. Like its predecessors, the *Multifibre Arrangement* permitted action to be taken by a party on the occurrence of "market disruption," which occurred with the "existence of serious damage to domestic producers or actual threat thereof." If the market of a participating importing country was being "disrupted" by imports of a textile product, it could seek consultations with the exporting country. The *Multifibre Arrangement* permitted participating countries to enter into bilateral agreements to eliminate the risk of market disruption, provided that the agreements adhered to certain principles. If consultations did not result in an agreement within a certain period of time, import restrictions could be unilaterally imposed by the participating importing country.

Canada, the United States, and other developed countries entered into a host of bilateral restraint agreements with developing countries under the umbrella of the *Multifibre Arrangement*. A restraint agreement typically set out maximum levels of exports from the exporting country for a base year of various categories of "textiles" and provided for a percentage annual increase in the restraint level for each product. A restraint agreement was administered by both the exporting and the importing country. An exporter in the exporting country would have to obtain an "export permit" or "export visa" from its government.[37] Each

---

37 The Canadian terminology is "export permit" while the U.S. terminology is "export visa."

time during a year that a permit or visa was issued, the exporter's export quota would be reduced by the number of items in the shipment and once the exporter's quota was used up, no further permits or visas would be issued until a new year commenced. The importing country's customs officials would not admit goods subject to the restraint agreement unless the shipment was accompanied by an export permit or visa.

b) The *Textile Agreement*

The *Textile Agreement* will eliminate the restrictive regime constructed under the cover of the *Multifibre Arrangement* and will return the textile and apparel sector to normal GATT disciplines over a ten-year transition period. When the *Textile Agreement* became effective, WTO member countries were required to notify a WTO body known as the Textiles Monitoring Body (TMB) of all quantitative restrictions maintained under bilateral agreements.[38] No new restrictions may be introduced except as authorized under the *Textile Agreement* transitional safeguard rules[39] or justified under some other provision of GATT 1994.[40] Products are to be "integrated into GATT 1994" in stages. Upon being integrated into GATT 1994, a product will be subject to the normal trade disciplines of GATT 1994 and will cease to be subject to export restraint levels. The first stage of integration took place on 1 January 1995 when the *Textile Agreement* came into effect. The second and third stages occur in 1998 and 2002, respectively, with complete "integration into GATT" occurring on 1 January 2005.[41] Each stage is expressed in terms of a percentage of the total volume of imports in 1990 of the products listed in the Annex to the *Textile Agreement*. The percentage that applied when the *Textile Agreement* became effective was 16 percent,[42] and the percentages for 1996 and 2002 are 17 percent and 18 percent, respectively. Importing countries will integrate their least sensitive products in the earlier stages and will defer integrating their more sensitive products until the last stage. Therefore, export restraint will continue to be a significant factor in the textile and apparel sector until the transition period is complete.

---

38 *Agreement on Textiles and Clothing*, set out in Annex 1A of the *WTO Agreement*, above note 5, [*Textile Agreement*], art. 2, para. 1.
39 *Ibid.*, art. 6.
40 *Ibid.*, art. 2, para. 4.
41 *Ibid.*, art. 2, para. 8. For the second and third stages, see paras. 8(a) and 8(b), respectively. For complete "integration into GATT," see para. 8(c).
42 *Textile Agreement, ibid.*, art. 2, para. 6.

Transitional safeguard rules permit member countries to request consultations in the event that increases in imports of a product cause or threaten serious damage. The consultations can result in a restraint agreement or unilaterally imposed restrictions. The restraints may be maintained for up to three years or until the product is integrated into GATT 1994, whichever occurs first.

c) Provisions of NAFTA and CCFTA

NAFTA Annex 300-B sets out rules governing import and export restrictions respecting the trade in textile and apparel goods among the NAFTA countries and expands upon the tariff rate quota system — renamed tariff preference levels or TPLs under NAFTA — established under CUFTA. CCFTA Annex C-00-B establishes a TPL system that is based on the one in NAFTA. NAFTA Annex 300-B and CCFTA Annex C-00-B also set out safeguard procedures (described in chapter 6) that apply to textile and apparel goods.

i) Import and Export Restrictions: NAFTA

At the time that NAFTA became effective, the only bilateral textile restraint agreement that existed among the NAFTA countries was between Mexico and the United States. Part B of Appendix 3.1 of NAFTA Annex 300-B supersedes this agreement and phases out textile restraints of exports of textile and apparel goods from Mexico to the United States over a period of time.[43]

Part A of Appendix 3.1 of NAFTA 300-B sets out general rules that apply between Mexico and the United States and that would apply between Canada and Mexico or the United States and Mexico if the transitional safeguards under the *Textile Agreement* were invoked. The rules set out certain criteria that must be applied to the application of restraint. Restraint cannot be applied to any good that is originating under the NAFTA rules of origin or to any good that has been integrated into GATT 1994.

ii) Tariff Preference Levels: NAFTA

Appendix 6 of NAFTA Annex 300-B establishes tariff preference levels (TPLs) for certain categories of textile and apparel goods. A TPL is an annual quantity of non-originating goods that may be imported into a NAFTA country under the NAFTA preferential tariff rate provided that certain

---

43   NAFTA, above note 2. Restrictions on certain goods remain until 1 January 2001 and 1 January 2004, respectively.

criteria are met. If imports during a year exceed the TPL, imports for the balance of the year are subject to the importing NAFTA country's MFN rate.

Take, for example, the TPLs that apply to apparel goods imported into the United States from Canada and Mexico. The TPLs are shown in table 4.1:[44]

TABLE 4.1 Tariff Preference Levels for Apparel Goods

Imports into United States	From Canada	From Mexico
Cotton or man-made fibre apparel:		
Total NAFTA TPL	80,000,000 SME	45,000,000 SME
Maximum from non-NAFTA country fabric	60,000,000 SME	45,000,000 SME
Wool apparel:		
NAFTA TPL	5,066,948 SME	1,500,000 SME

The rule of origin applicable to most apparel goods requires that the yarn, the fabric, and the finished apparel good must all be produced in NAFTA countries. The TPLs apply to apparel goods made from fabric or yarn produced or obtained from outside the NAFTA countries. To qualify for the NAFTA preferential tariff, these non-originating apparel goods must be cut and sewn or otherwise assembled in the NAFTA country from which they are exported. Consider the application of the TPL to wool apparel exported from Canada to the United States. The finished products must be cut and sewn and assembled in Canada but the wool fabric may be imported from a non-NAFTA country. During each year, the United States applies the NAFTA preferential tariff to imports of these non-originating products until the TPL of 5,066,948 SME is reached. Imports for the balance of the year are subject to the U.S. MFN rate of duty.

Similarly, TPLs have been established for imports of cotton or man-made fibre apparel and wool apparel into Canada from the United States and Mexico, and into Mexico from Canada and the United States. TPLs have also been established for certain non-originating fabric and made-up goods and for spun yarn. The TPL for fabric and made-up goods applies to cotton and man-made fibre fabric, and to made-up goods pro-

---

44 NAFTA, *ibid.*, Annex 300-B, Schedule 6.B.1. "SME" means "square metre equivalents."

duced from cotton and man-made fibre fabric that are woven or knit in the territory of a Party from yarn produced outside the free trade area (excluding goods containing 36 percent or more by weight of wool or fine animal hair). This TPL also covers bedding product classified under HS subheading 9409.90 produced from prescribed categories of fabric.[45] The TPL for spun yarn applies to prescribed categories of cotton or man-made fibre yarns spun from prescribed categories of fibre obtained from outside the free trade area.[46]

iii) Tariff Preference Levels: CCFTA
Appendix 5.1 of CCFTA Annex C-00-B establishes TPLs between Canada and Chile that are based on the same principles as those in NAFTA. As under NAFTA, TPLs have been established for apparel and made-up goods, fabric and made-up goods, and spun yarn. The wording of the TPL for apparel and made-up goods is virtually the same as that in NAFTA, with levels established for annual imports into each country of 2,000,000 SMEs for cotton and man-made apparel and 100,000 SMEs for wool apparel.[47] The TPL for fabric and made-up goods applies to the same goods as does its NAFTA counterpart but also establishes a TPL for wool fabric and wool made-up goods containing 36 percent or more by weight of wool or fine animal hair, to which there is not a NAFTA counterpart. The levels of annual imports into each country of cotton and man-made fibre fabrics and made-up goods is 1,000,000 SMEs and for wool fabrics and made-up goods is 250,000 SMEs.[48] The spun yarn TPL is similar to its NAFTA counterpart, with levels of annual imports into each country set at 500,000 kilograms.[49]

I. CANADIAN LAW ON IMPORT AND EXPORT RESTRICTIONS

Canadian law respecting export and import restrictions is, for the most part, set out in the *Export and Import Permits Act* and the *Customs Tariff.*

---

45 The levels of annual imports into each country are set out in Schedule 6.B.2 to NAFTA, *ibid.*, Annex 300-B.
46 The levels of annual imports into each country are set out in Schedule 6.B.3 to NAFTA, *ibid.*, Annex 300-B.
47 See the table in Schedule 5.B.1 of Appendix 5.1 to CCFTA, above note 6, Annex C-00-B. These quantities are subject to an annual increase of 2 percent for the six consecutive years beginning 1 January 1998.
48 See the table in Schedule 5.B.2 of Appendix 5.1 to CCFTA, *ibid.*, Annex C-00-B.
49 See the table in Schedule 5.B.3 of Appendix 5.1 to CCFTA, *ibid.*, Annex C-00-B.

1) The *Export and Import Permits Act*

The *Export and Import Permits Act*, which is administered by the Department of Foreign Affairs and International Trade, sets out a comprehensive regulatory regime for the application of both export and import controls.

a) Export Controls

i) General Rules

Goods subject to export controls are set out on the *Export Control List*. The inclusion of certain goods reflects Canadian treaty obligations. For example, Group 4 includes items the export of which Canada has agreed to control under the *Treaty on the Non-Proliferation of Nuclear Weapons*, and Group 5 includes species of wild flora or fauna covered by the *Convention on International Trade in Endangered Species of Wild Fauna and Flora*. The list includes certain wood products such as logs, pulpwood, and red cedar suitable for the manufacture of shakes and shingles. The list also includes items such as pancreas glands, human serum albumin, prohibited weapons, chemicals for the use of illicit drugs, and so on. The *Export and Import Permits Act* also contains area control lists that list countries to which exports are controlled. Goods on the *Export Control List* may be exported only under the authority of an export permit.[50]

ii) Softwood Lumber

Softwood lumber is subject to export controls as a result of negotiations between the Canadian and U.S. governments that arose out of a threatened U.S. countervailing duty action. U.S. softwood lumber producers have claimed for years that imports of Canadian softwood lumber are subsidized through a variety of provincial practices such as the setting of stumpage fees on timber cut on Crown land. The Canadian government settled an earlier U.S. countervailing duty action in 1987 by agreeing to impose a 15 percent export charge on softwood lumber. Subsequently, the Canadian government unilaterally revoked the 15 percent export tax and successfully resisted a new U.S. countervailing duty action through the CUFTA Chapter Nineteen binational panel and extraordinary challenge process. The U.S. government and U.S. lumber interests threatened yet a further countervailing duty action and, not-

---

50 The regulations set out some general permits. If none of these applies, the person wishing to export a good subject to control must apply to the Department of Foreign Affairs and International Trade for an export permit.

withstanding its earlier success, the Canadian government chose to settle rather than risk the imposition of countervailing duties.

The settlement resulted in the *Softwood Lumber Agreement between the Government of Canada and the Government of the United States of America* (*Softwood Lumber Agreement*), which came into force on 29 May 1996 with effect from 1 April 1996 for a term of five years. The United States agreed not to self-initiate any countervailing duty actions and to dismiss any such actions that were initiated by the industry.[51] In return, Canada agreed to place softwood lumber on the *Export Control List* and to require export permits for exportations to the United States of softwood lumber from Ontario, Quebec, British Columbia, and Alberta.[52] The agreement establishes a base of 14.7 billion board feet. Exports in a year above the established base up to 15.35 billion board feet are subject to a fee of US$50.00 per thousand board feet and over 15.35 billion board feet to a fee of US$100.00 per thousand board feet. The agreement sets out details as to how the fees are to be collected and circumstances under which fees may be remitted, as well as providing for information collection and cooperation and dispute resolution. As required under the agreement, the Canadian government added softwood lumber products to the *Export Control List* as Item 5104[53] and enacted regulations for the collection of fees[54] and issuing permits to exporters.[55]

As discussed in chapter 6, Article 11:1(b) of the *Safeguards Agreement* prohibits members from seeking, taking, or maintaining "voluntary export restraints." The arrangement provided for in the *Softwood Lumber Agreement* is a voluntary export restraint within the meaning of this prohibition.

b) **Import Controls**
Goods subject to import controls are set out on the *Import Control List*. The *Import Control List* includes all the supply-managed agricultural goods (dairy and poultry products) to which tariff rate quotas resulting from tariffication under the *Agriculture Agreement* apply and all textile and apparel goods subject to restraint under Canadian bilateral restraint agreements or unilaterally imposed restraints. The list also includes

---

51 *Softwood Lumber Agreement between the Government of Canada and the Government of the United States of America*, 29 May 1996, Can. T.S. 1996 No. 16, art. I:2.
52 *Ibid.*, art. II:1.
53 *Export Control List*, amendment, SOR/96-315.
54 *Softwood Lumber Products Export Permit Fees Regulations*, SOR/96-317.
55 *Export Permits Regulations (Softwood Lumber Products)*, SOR/96-319.

miscellaneous items such as various weapons and certain steel products.[56] Goods on the *Import Control List* may be imported only under the authority of an import permit.[57]

2) Prohibited Goods

The *Customs Tariff* lists certain goods for which entry into Canada is prohibited.[58] Unlike goods on the *Import Control List* under the *Export and Import Permits Act*, for which there is discretion to issue an import permit, the prohibitions in the *Customs Tariff* are absolute. The prohibitions cover goods such as obscene literature, child pornography, posters depicting violence and goods manufactured by prison labour, certain animal and bird species, offensive weapons, certain goods that infringe intellectual property rights, and base or counterfeit coin, used or second-hand goods such as cars, aircraft, and mattresses[59] The prohibition on the importation of used cars does not apply to used cars imported from the United States and will be phased out for used cars imported from Mexico over a ten-year period commencing in 2009.[60]

---

56 See, for example, items 70 & 71 (weapons) and 81 (specialty steel products) of the *Import Control List*, C.R.C., c. 604.
57 As with export permits, the regulations set out some general permits. If none of these applies, the person wishing to import a good subject to control must apply to the Department of Foreign Affairs and International Trade for an import permit. For supply-managed goods, permits to import under the within-access tariff rate are allocated in accordance with rules internally established by the department. Import permits for goods subject to textile restraint agreements that are not covered by a general import permit are issued only if the shipment of goods is accompanied by an export permit issued by the exporting country.
58 Schedule VII of the *Customs Tariff* until 31 December 1997 and, thereafter, (assuming that the amendments to the *Customs Tariff* set out in the Ways and Means Motion become effective on 1 January 1998) Part 5 of the *Customs Tariff* and tariff items 9897.00.00, 9898.00.00, and 9899.00.00 of the schedule to the *Customs Tariff*.
59 This list is not exhaustive. Also, some of the prohibitions are subject to exceptions.
60 The exceptions respecting used cars from the United States and Mexico implement obligations under CUFTA, above note 20, art. 1003, and para. 4 of NAFTA, above note 2, Appendix 300-A.1, respectively. There are other exceptions, such as the exception for cars left by bequest. For the prohibitions and exceptions respecting used cars, see Code 9963 of Schedule VII of the *Customs Tariff* up to 31 December 1997, and tariff item 9897.00.00 in the schedule to the *Customs Tariff* following 1 January 1998.

Some of the prohibitions (such as the prohibitions respecting obscene material and products of prison labour) are clearly governed by exceptions in Article XX of GATT 1994. With other exceptions the justification under Article XX is questionable. For example, there does not appear to be any basis under Article XX for prohibiting the importation of second-hand goods such as used cars.

Code item 9958, which prohibits the entry into Canada of split-run periodicals, is discussed in chapter 9 under "Canadian Cultural Policies."[61]

3) Other Import Prohibitions

The *Import Control List* in the *Export and Import Permits Act* and the prohibitions in the *Customs Tariff* do not constitute an exhaustive list of goods subject to Canadian import restrictions. Outright prohibitions are found in other statutes. For example, it is an offence under Section 202(1)(b) of the *Criminal Code* to import various gambling devices.[62] The *Narcotic Control Act* prohibits the importation of certain drugs. The conditions under which many goods may be imported are affected by statutes such as the *Hazardous Products Act* and the *Food and Drugs Act*. With many products, one must conduct a careful review of federal legislation before concluding that no import restrictions apply.

---

61 Following 1 January 1998, this prohibition is set out in tariff item 9897.00.00 in the schedule to the *Customs Tariff*.
62 R.S.C. 1985, c. C-46. There are exceptions set out in s. 207, most notably for lottery schemes operated by provincial governments.

CHAPTER 5

THE ORIGIN OF GOODS

Rules for establishing the origin of goods are necessary for the application of many provisions of international agreements respecting the trade in goods. Preferential trading arrangements require rules for determining eligibility for preferential tariff treatment. Some quantitative restrictions, such as those under textile restraint agreements, apply to goods of specific countries. Many countries require that at least some imported goods be marked with their country of origin. Antidumping and countervailing duties and the restrictions resulting from safeguard actions are country-specific in their application. The benefits of government procurement disciplines apply only to goods of countries covered by the applicable agreement.

There are two types of rules of origin: preferential and non-preferential. Preferential rules of origin are used to determine whether goods traded among members of a preferential trading area are eligible for preferential tariff treatment. Goods must be "wholly originating" or be sufficiently transformed and/or have sufficient value added within the preferential trading area to be considered as "originating" and entitled to preferential treatment. The preferential trading area can be a free trade area, such as those created by NAFTA, CIFTA, and CCFTA, or an "autonomous trade regime" in which a country unilaterally grants preferential tariff treatment to goods of other countries. For example, Canada unilaterally grants the General Preferential Tariff to goods of a number of developing countries.

Non-preferential rules of origin are rules for determining the origin of goods for reasons other than the granting of preferences. These reasons include the administration of country-of-origin marking requirements, the application of discriminatory quantitative restrictions or tariff rate quotas, the application of antidumping or countervailing duties or safeguard measures, the administration of government procurement rules and the accumulation of trade statistics.[1]

The distinction between preferential and non-preferential rules of origin is complicated under NAFTA by the fact that the determination of eligibility for tariff treatment is a two-step process. It must first be determined that a good satisfies the NAFTA Chapter Four rules of origin that apply for determining eligibility for preferential tariff treatment and that the good is "originating." However, because tariff elimination among the NAFTA countries proceeds in different stages, there are several different NAFTA preferential tariffs from which to choose, depending on the country of origin of the good. The rules of origin in NAFTA Chapter Four determine only whether a good is originating and not its country of origin. The country of origin determination is made in accordance with the non-preferential rules of origin used for country of origin purposes or, in the case of most goods entering Canada, in accordance with special country of origin rules set out in NAFTA Annex 302.2.

Under GATT 1947, each member country established its own rules for establishing the origin of goods. The difficulty with this approach was that negotiated benefits under trade agreements could be denied through manipulation of origin rules. The solution to the problem of rule manipulation is the creation of norms through the development of commonly agreed rules. The *Rules of Origin Agreement* lays the groundwork for developing commonly agreed non-preferential rules of origin and sets out minimum standards for the application of both preferential and non-preferential rules of origin. NAFTA, CIFTA, and CCFTA each contain commonly agreed rules of origin for determining eligibility for preferential tariff treatment. The NAFTA negotiators attempted to address the question of non-preferential rules of origin but failed even to develop common principles let alone a common set of rules. CIFTA and CCFTA do not contain provisions respecting non-preferential rules of origin.

---

1   The *Agreement on Rules of Origin*, set out in Annex 1A of the *Agreement Creating the World Trade Organization*, 15 April 1994 (Dobbs Ferry, N.Y.: Oceana Publications, 1997) [*Rules of Origin Agreement*], distinguishes between preferential and non-preferential rules of origin. These various purposes for non-preferential rules of origin are all referred to in para. 2 of art. 1.

A. PREFERENTIAL RULES OF ORIGIN

Eligibility for preferential tariff treatment under each of Canada's preferential tariffs is determined under rules of origin set out in regulations enacted under the *Customs Tariff*. The regulations for determining eligibility for preferential tariff treatment under NAFTA are the trilaterally agreed *Uniform Regulations* negotiated by the NAFTA countries under NAFTA Article 511 which, in turn, are based on the rules of origin set out in NAFTA Chapter Four.[2] References to the *Uniform Regulations* throughout this chapter are to the NAFTA *Uniform Regulations* unless otherwise indicated. As under NAFTA, the regulations for determining eligibility for preferential tariff treatment under CCFTA are bilaterally agreed uniform regulations based on the rules set out in CCFTA Chapter D.[3] Unlike NAFTA and CCFTA, CIFTA does not contain a requirement that the Parties establish uniform regulations. The Canadian government enacted its own regulations based on CIFTA Chapter Three for determining eligibility for preferential treatment under CIFTA.[4]

As the other Canadian preferential tariff rates are unilaterally applied, the applicable rules of origin are not based on rules set out in an international agreement. However, these rules and their application must conform to the requirements set out in the *Rules of Origin Agreement*.

1) NAFTA, CIFTA, and CCFTA Rules of Origin

a) Why Rules of Origin Are Necessary in a Free Trade Area

Rules of origin are necessary in a free trade area for determining which goods entering one member country from another are eligible for preferential tariff treatment because each member country applies its own border measures to goods of non-member countries. If all member countries applied commonly agreed border measures to goods of non-member countries, as in a customs union, rules of origin would not be necessary. A good can enter one member country of a customs union subject to the commonly agreed tariff or other border measure and then freely circulate within the customs union, either in the form in which it

---

2   See NAFTA *Rules of Origin Regulations*, SOR/94-14, as am. by NAFTA *Rules of Origin, amendment*, SOR/95-382. These regulations set out the Canadian version of the *Uniform Regulations* [UR]. The U.S. and Mexican forms are virtually the same.
3   *Canada–Chile Free Trade Agreement*, in force 5 July 1997, see http://www.dfait-maeci.gc.ca/english/trade/agrement.htm [CCFTA], art. E-11. See CCFTA *Rules of Origin Regulations*, SOR/97-340. These rules are similar to the UR, *ibid*.
4   See CIFTA *Rules of Origin Regulations*, SOR/97-63.

was imported or as incorporated into a good produced within the customs union. Within a free trade area such as NAFTA, a member country (e.g., Canada) is clearly committed to granting preferential tariff treatment to goods that are wholly the product of another NAFTA country (e.g., Mexico). It is equally clear that Canada is not committed to granting preferential tariff treatment to goods that are produced in non-NAFTA countries and are transshipped through a NAFTA country. For example, a good produced in China, which is transshipped through Mexico, is still a good of China as far as Canada is concerned, and subject to the border measures that Canada applies to goods of China. The question of origin arises when the good of China is an input used in Mexico with Mexican inputs to produce another good. Is the new good sufficiently "Mexican" so as to be eligible for preferential tariff treatment? Rules of origin are required to make this determination. A good that is originating under the rules of origin is eligible for preferential tariff treatment while a good that is non-originating under the rules is not eligible.[5]

b) Member Countries Interchangeable

The member countries of a free trade area are interchangeable under preferential rules of origin. Consider the good produced in Mexico with a Chinese input. The determination of eligibility for preferential treatment under the NAFTA rules of origin should be the same regardless of whether the Mexican producer combines the Chinese input with U.S. or Mexican inputs because Canada has agreed to allow the same treatment to U.S. goods as to Mexican goods.[6] The same determination should also follow if the Mexican producer combines the Chinese input with Canadian inputs. Accordingly, the NAFTA rules of origin do not distinguish between the territories of Canada, the United States, and Mexico. For similar reasons the CIFTA rules of origin do not distinguish between the territories of Israel and Canada, and the CCFTA rules of origin do not distinguish between the territories of Canada and Chile.

c) Basic Terminology

Rules of origin refer to "goods" and "materials." A good is what a producer produces and materials are the inputs that the producer uses to

---

5   As discussed in chapter 4 under "Tariff Preference Levels," certain textile and apparel goods receive preferential NAFTA and CCFTA tariff treatment even though they are non-originating. See the *North American Free Trade Agreement*, 17 December 1992, Can. T.S. 1994 No. 2 [NAFTA] and CCFTA, above note 3.
6   Subject to the differing staging of tariff elimination referred to above.

produce the good.[7] One producer's good can be another producer's material. Steel is a steel producer's good but is a material to the brake shoe manufacturer who purchases it. The brake shoe is the brake shoe manufacturer's good but is a material to the brake assembly producer who purchases it. The brake assembly is the brake assembler's good but is a material to the vehicle assembler who incorporates it into a finished vehicle.

An originating good is one that satisfies the rules of origin and a non-originating good is one that does not. A material that qualifies as an originating good under the rules of origin that apply to it is an originating material and a material that does not so qualify is a non-originating material. Any material imported from outside the preferential trading area is a non-originating material. A material produced within the preferential trading area is non-originating if it contains imported materials that have not been sufficiently processed to satisfy the rules of origin that apply to the material.

There are two ways of establishing that a good containing non-originating materials is originating. One way requires that the non-originating materials be "substantially transformed" into something that is a new and different good, while the other way requires that a prescribed amount of domestic value be added to the non-originating materials. The NAFTA and CCFTA rules of origin rely on both the substantial transformation and value-added methods of establishing originating status, while the CIFTA rules of origin rely solely on substantial transformation.

d) Establishing that Goods Are Originating Under NAFTA, CIFTA, and CCFTA

There are three basic ways under the NAFTA, CIFTA, and CCFTA rules of origin of establishing that a good is originating.

- A good is originating if it wholly originates within the territories of the NAFTA countries.
- A good is originating if it is produced entirely from originating materials.
- A good containing non-originating materials is originating if it satisfies the specific rule of origin that applies to the good.

The specific rules of origin are largely based on the terminology of the Harmonized System, which was never designed for rules of origin purposes. Therefore, NAFTA, CIFTA, and CCFTA contain special rules to cover certain situations where rules cannot be expressed in HS termi-

---

7   NAFTA, above note 5, art. 415 and UR, above note 3, s. 2(1). Note that in the NAFTA text the expression "material" has a narrower and more technical meaning respecting tracing for heavy duty vehicles referred to below.

nology. There is also a special NAFTA rule that applies to certain automatic data processing equipment and their parts. Once MFN rates on these goods are harmonized among the NAFTA countries (which will occur by 1 January 2004), any of these goods crossing a border between NAFTA countries will be considered as originating. The effect will be to create a sort of mini customs union for these goods.[8]

e) **Wholly Originating Goods**
Wholly originating goods are goods such as trees cut, crops harvested, fish caught, minerals mined, and animals raised and slaughtered within a member country of the free trade area. Generally speaking, none of the materials used in a wholly originating good can be imported. There are, however, a few exceptions. For example, steel made from scrap obtained from used cars will be wholly originating even though the cars were imported. Wholly originating goods are covered by Criterion A in the NAFTA form of Certificate of Origin.

f) **Specific Rules of Origin**
If a good is not a wholly originating good or made entirely of originating materials, the good must satisfy the specific rule of origin that applies to it in order to be originating. The NAFTA specific rules of origin are set out in NAFTA Annex 401 and carried forward in the *Uniform Regulations* as Schedule I. The CIFTA specific rules of origin are set out in CIFTA Annex 3.1, and the CCFTA specific rules of origin are set out in CCFTA Annex D-01. The specific rules of origin in the three agreements are the same or similar for many goods but there are substantial differences in the rules for some goods. The rules are arranged in the order of the Harmonized System, and each rule or set of alternative rules applies to goods of a specified chapter, heading, subheading, or tariff item. The starting point in finding the applicable specific rule of origin is the correct tariff classification of the good being produced.

Most rules in NAFTA Annex 401 and CCFTA Annex D-01 and all the rules in CIFTA Annex 3.1 are based on substantial transformation. The required transformation is almost invariably expressed as a change in tariff classification (see below) that each non-originating material must undergo as it is transformed by processing within the free trade

---

8   See NAFTA, *ibid.*, art. 308 & Annex 308.1, and s. 4(7) of the *UR*, above note 2. See also preference Criterion E on the form of Certificate of Origin. CCFTA, above note 3, art. C-07 & Annex C-07 require the elimination of the MFN tariff on automatic data processing machines and other items, but CCFTA Annex C-07 does not contain an origin rule comparable to that in NAFTA Annex 308.1.

area into the finished good. Some rules also contain process or other requirements. For example, many of the NAFTA rules applicable to apparel goods require that the good be "both cut and sewn or otherwise assembled" in a NAFTA country.

Some NAFTA and CCFTA rules are based on a value-content requirement. A few NAFTA and CCFTA rules combine a change in tariff classification with a mandatory value content requirement.[9] However, in most cases where there is a rule imposing a content requirement, there is an alternative rule based solely on satisfying a change in tariff classification. The producer may choose between the rule with the change in tariff classification alone, or the rule with the value content requirement, which will usually prescribe a less exacting change in tariff classification (such as one that permits processing non-originating parts rather than upstream materials into the finished good).

The CIFTA rules do not contain value content requirements. However, alternative rules are provided for many goods. For example, consider the CIFTA rule for goods under HS subheading 8704.94 (steering wheels, steering columns, and steering boxes). The first rule permits originating status so long as none of the parts are non-originating. The alternative rule permits the use of non-originating parts provided that at least one category of identical or similar parts used is originating.[10]

g) Change in Tariff Classification or Tariff Shift
A change in tariff classification rule is expressed as follows:

> A change to [tariff classification of the good being produced] from [tariff classifications of non-originating materials from which a change confers "originating" status] except [tariff classifications from which a change does not confer originating status].

The rule is applied to each non-originating material used to produce the good. The "change" is the change that occurs through processing each non-originating material into the finished good. The rule operates by comparing the tariff classification of each non-originating material with the tariff classification of the good. The tariff classifications are expressed in terms of the chapters, headings, and subheadings of the Harmonized

---

9 In the case of NAFTA, *ibid.*, pesticides, plastics, spark-ignition and diesel engines, certain colour television sets, motor vehicles, McPherson struts, and certain other automotive parts, yachts and pleasure boats, and parts for watches and clocks.

10 See the rules for subheadings 8708.40-8708.94 in *Canada–Israel Free Trade Agreement*, in force 1 January 1997, see http://www.dfait-maeci.ca/english/trade/agrement.htm [CIFTA], Annex 3.1. These subheadings cover various automotive parts.

System and in some instances may be expressed as individual tariff items. A change in tariff classification is frequently referred to as a tariff shift.

Consider the rule in NAFTA Annex 401 for rear view mirrors falling under HS subheading 7009.10. The rule is:

> A change to heading 70.03 through 70.09 from any heading outside that group.

The "change" is the change in tariff classification of each non-originating material that results from processing it into a rear view mirror. Suppose that the producer uses a non-originating mirror frame classified under HS heading 83.06. Heading 83.06 is outside the group 70.03 through 70.09 so processing the frame into the mirror satisfies the rule. Suppose, however that the producer uses non-originating glass classified under heading HS 70.05. Heading 70.05 is within the group 70.03 through 70.09. Processing glass under heading 70.05 into a mirror under subheading 7009.10 does not satisfy the rule. In effect, the rule says that transforming non-originating glass into a rear view mirror is not a substantial enough transformation to confer originating status on the mirror.

The change does not have to be satisfied by materials that are originating or by packaging materials, packing materials, accessories, or indirect materials (such as fuel, lubricants, catalysts, production machinery and equipment, and the like). The change also does not have to be satisfied if the *de minimis* rule (described below) applies.

h) When a Change in Tariff Classification Cannot Occur

There are some circumstances in which processing or assembling a good will not result in a change in tariff classification because of the manner in which the Harmonized System is structured. HS General Rule of Interpretation 2(a) provides that unassembled or disassembled goods have the same tariff classification as the finished goods.[11] A tariff classification cannot take place through assembling the unassembled good. Also, parts for some goods such as barber chairs are classified under the same HS heading or subheading as the goods themselves.[12] NAFTA and CCFTA rules permit originating status to be established in these cases solely through application of the regional value content requirement. CIFTA rules do not cover the unassembled/disassembled good situation

---

11 See s. 4(4)(a) of the *UR*, above note 2.
12 See s. 4(4)(b) of the *UR*, *ibid.*, which must be read together with s. 4(5) of the *UR*. As to whether a heading or subheading includes the parts is based on its wording or that of the relevant HS Section or Chapter notes. Parts of parts are not covered by the rule.

but address the parts situation by providing that originating status is established so long as at least one category of identical or similar parts in the heading or subheading used to produce the good is originating.[13]

i) The *De Minimis* Rule

One difficulty with tariff shift requirements is that they are rigid. A small quantity of non-originating material that does not meet the required change in tariff classification can result in a good with very high domestic content being non-originating. To solve this problem, the NAFTA, CIFTA, and CCFTA rules of origin contain *de minimis* provisions.

The NAFTA *de minimis* rule[14] provides that if the value of non-originating materials that do not undergo a required change in tariff classification is less than 7 percent of the transaction value or total cost of the good,[15] the good will nonetheless originate as long as other requirements in the rules are satisfied. These rules also relieve a producer from having to satisfy the content requirement if the value of all non-originating materials is less than 7 percent of the transaction value or total cost of the good. Yarns, textile, and apparel goods are not covered by the foregoing but by a special *de minimis* rule for non-originating fibres and yarns, based on weight. There are a number of exceptions that include various agricultural products, dairy products, juices, certain sugar and cocoa products, lard, printed circuit assemblies, and various appliances such as stoves and trash compactors.[16]

CIFTA Articles 3.2 and 3.12 and CCFTA Article D-05 set out *de minimis* provisions that are similar to those in NAFTA, with a threshold of 10 percent in the case of CIFTA and 9 percent in the case of CCFTA rather than 7 percent.[17] The exceptions in the CIFTA and CCFTA *de minimis* provisions are similar to those in NAFTA but there are some differences.

---

13 These rules of NAFTA, above note 5, CCFTA, above note 3, and CIFTA, above note 10, cannot be applied to goods classified under HS chapters 61–63 (apparel goods and textile made-up articles).
14 NAFTA, *ibid.*, art. 405. See also *UR*, above note 2, s. 5. The NAFTA *de minimis* provisions can also be applied to avoid having to satisfy a value-content requirement.
15 The transaction value is, essentially, the selling price, adjusted in accordance with the principles set out in the *Agreement on Implementation of Article VII of the General Agreement on Tariffs and Trade 1994*, set out in Annex 1A of the *Agreement Creating the World Trade Organization*, 15 April 1994 (Dobbs Ferry, N.Y.: Oceana Publications, 1997) (*Valuation Agreement*) [*VA*]. If that price would be "unacceptable" as the basis for value for duty under the *VA*, "total cost" is used.
16 NAFTA, above note 5, art. 405(3). See also *UR*, above note 2, s. 5(4).
17 There are some technical differences in the calculations between the *de minimis* rules of NAFTA, *ibid.*, and CIFTA, above note 10.

j) The NAFTA and CCFTA Value-Content Requirement

The NAFTA and CCFTA value-content requirements are complex and highly technical. The following description is intended to convey a general idea of how these requirements are applied.

i) Transaction Value Method and Net Cost Method

Generally speaking, a producer may choose between the transaction value method and the net cost method. These are as follows:

Transaction Value Method:

$$\frac{TV \text{ minus } VNM}{TV}$$ must be at least 60 percent (NAFTA) or 35 percent (CCFTA).[18]

Net Cost Method:

$$\frac{NC \text{ minus } VNM}{NC}$$ must be at least 50 percent (NAFTA) and 25 percent (CCFTA).[19]

Where:
TV = transaction value
NC = the net cost of the good
VNM = value of non-originating materials used by the producer in the production of the good.

The transaction value method cannot be used for footwear, word processing machines (NAFTA only), motor vehicles, and certain auto-

---

18   These are the most usual percentages. In some instances under NAFTA, *ibid.*, the applicable percentage is 65 percent. See, for example, goods described in HS chapters 34 (soaps, washing preparations, waxes, dental preparations), 35 (albuminoidal substances, modified starches, glues, enzymes), and 36 (explosives, pyrotechnic products, matches, pyrophoric alloys, certain combustible preparations). For pesticides under HS heading 3808, the NAFTA percentage can be 80 percent in the particular circumstances described in the rule. The rules of CCFTA, above note 3, also contain a number of exceptions to the 35 percent rule.
19   These are the most usual percentages. The NAFTA, *ibid.*, percentages for automotive goods will be increased over a phase-in period to 62.5 percent for light duty vehicles and 60 percent for heavy duty vehicles and most parts. The phase-in will be complete by 2002. The NAFTA percentage applicable to pesticides under HS heading 3808 can be 70 percent in some instances. The CCFTA rules also contain a number of exceptions to the 25 percent rule. CCFTA, *ibid.*, arts. D-02(13) & (14) provide for a sliding scale of percentages for various types of footwear. The applicable percentage for automotive goods identified in CCFTA Annex D-03.1 is 30 percent.

motive parts.[20] The transaction value method also cannot be used in certain circumstances in which the producer is selling the goods to related parties or in circumstances described in the Valuation Agreement.

ii) Use of the Valuation Agreement
Application of the NAFTA and CCFTA value content requirements utilize the principles of the *Valuation Agreement* to resolve transfer pricing issues and to adjust both the selling prices of goods and the purchase price of materials. Acceptability of a selling price of a good as the basis for the transaction value method or the purchase price of a material in applying either method is determined in accordance with the principles in the *Valuation Agreement* for determining whether a price paid or payable is acceptable as the basis for value for duty. For example, if a producer purchases a material from a related supplier and the relationship has affected the price, the value of the material will be determined using one of the alternative methods set out in the *Valuation Agreement* (see chapter 3 under "Valuation").[21] If the material is purchased from an unrelated supplier, the purchase price of the material will be subject to the same adjustments as are applied to the price paid or payable under the *Valuation Agreement*.

iii) Transaction Value
The transaction value upon which the transaction value method is based is, essentially, the selling price of the good. This price is "adjusted to an F.O.B. basis," which means that transportation and associated costs to the point of direct shipment to the buyer are added and costs beyond this point are excluded. There are some other adjustments which are required by *Valuation Agreement* principles.[22]

iv) Net Cost
The net cost upon which the net cost method is based is the producer's total cost minus excluded costs, which are sales promotion, marketing and after-service costs, royalties,[23] shipping and packing costs, and non-

---

20 In the case of NAFTA, *ibid.*, the parts are those listed on the tracing lists described below. In the case of CCFTA, *ibid.*, the parts are those listed in CCFTA Annex D-03.1.
21 The principles of the *VA*, above note 15, have been rewritten for rules of origin purposes. In the case of NAFTA, *ibid.*, see Schedules III and VIII of the *UR*, above note 2.
22 See Schedule II of the *UR, ibid.* For example, buying commissions, royalties, and assists are all added to the selling price.
23 Not including royalty costs included in the value of materials. See s. 6(13)(b) of the *UR, ibid.*

allowable interest costs.²⁴ In calculating total cost, the value of all materials, whether originating or not, is the price paid by the producer for the materials, subject to the adjustments required under the principles of the *Valuation Agreement*.²⁵ If the price paid is unacceptable under the principles of the *Valuation Agreement*, the value is determined using one of the other valuation methods in the *Valuation Agreement*.²⁶ The value of indirect materials, packing materials, and containers and all other costs are as recorded in the producer's books, which must be maintained in accordance with the generally accepted accounting principles of the Party in which it is situated.

v) Value of Non-Originating Materials (VNM)
Except in the case of automotive goods under NAFTA, in applying the transaction value method or the net cost method, VNM is determined just as described for the value of all materials in calculating net cost. The only values that are included in VNM are those for materials for which the producer does not have a certificate of origin or other evidence of originating status from the supplier. The value of any non-originating material that is contained in an originating material that is used by the purchaser is *not* included in VNM. For example, suppose that a sailboat manufacturer purchases an originating engine that contains parts that are imported from a non-Party.²⁷ The value of the imported parts is not included in VNM because their value has been "rolled up" into the originating engine. There is a procedure in both NAFTA and CCFTA under which the same result will follow even if the producer produced the engine itself. The producer can designate the originating self-produced engine as an "intermediate material" and the value of the imported parts will not be included in VNM. If a purchased engine is non-originating, its entire value must be included in VNM, despite the fact that it may contain domestic value-added.²⁸

---

24 These expressions are defined in s. 2(1) of the *UR*, *ibid*. Non-allowable interest costs are interest costs that exceed federal government rates defined in the *UR* by 700 basis points. Normal interest charges should not be captured by this definition.
25 See para. 5 of Schedule VIII of the *UR*, *ibid*. For example, buying commissions, royalties, and assists are all added to the price paid or payable.
26 As rewritten in paras. 6 through 11 of Schedule VIII to the *UR*, *ibid*.
27 Pleasure boats under HS heading 89.03 are subject to a mandatory value content requirement under both NAFTA, above note 5, and CCFTA, above note 3.
28 While CIFTA, above note 10, does not make provision for a regional value content requirement, CIFTA art. 3.8 permits a producer to designate a self-produced material used in the production of a good as an originating or non-originating material in determining whether a good satisfies relevant origin requirements.

vi) Value of Non-Originating Materials (VNM): Automotive Goods under NAFTA
The determination under NAFTA of VNM for trucks,[29] buses,[30] passenger vehicles[31] (light duty vehicles), and their parts is based on different principles. NAFTA Annex 403.1[32] sets out a tracing list of HS headings, subheadings, and tariff items. These tariff provisions cover many parts of a motor vehicle, such as engines and their parts, rubber tubes and belts, tires, rear view mirrors, locks, bearings, bearing housings, transmission shafts, transmissions, flywheels, and so on. However, tariff provisions in the light vehicle tracing list do not cover all parts. For example, the tariff provisions for spark plugs, batteries (other than for electric cars), brake linings, and plastic tubes are not on the tracing list.

In applying the net cost method to light duty vehicles or to parts for light duty vehicles included on the tracing list, VNM is equal to the value of all parts incorporated into that vehicle or part that were imported from a non-NAFTA country under tariff provisions on the tracing list. The fact that the imported tracing list part may be incorporated into a material that is originating is irrelevant. For example, unlike the sailboat manufacturer who can disregard the value of the imported parts incorporated into the originating engine, the vehicle manufacturer must (because engine parts are listed) include the value of the parts in VNM, regardless of whether the engine is originating or non-originating.

However, the light duty vehicle manufacturer may disregard the value of any part imported from a non-NAFTA country under a tariff provision that is not on the tracing list. If a sailboat manufacturer imports batteries from a non-NAFTA country, the value of the batteries must be included in VNM. However, a vehicle manufacturer does not have to include the value of imported batteries in VNM because the tariff provision for batteries (except for electric cars) is not on the tracing list.

The rule for tractors,[33] larger trucks,[34] buses,[35] and specialty vehicles[36]

---

29 HS tariff subheadings 8704.21 or 8704.31 (motor vehicles for the transport of goods with g.v.w. not exceeding 5 tonnes).
30 Public-transport type passenger motor vehicles under HS heading 8702 for the transport of fifteen or fewer persons.
31 HS tariff subheadings 8703.21 to 8703.90.
32 Above note 5. See Schedule IV of the *UR*, above note 2.
33 Vehicles under HS heading 8701.
34 Vehicles under HS subheading 8704.10 (dumpers), 8704.22, 8704.23, and 8704.32 (motor vehicles for the transport of goods exceeding 5 tonnes g.v.w.), 8704.90 (other trucks).
35 Public-transport type passenger motor vehicles under HS heading 8702 for transporting sixteen or more persons.
36 Special purpose motor vehicles under HS heading 8705, and chassis fitted with engines under HS heading 8706.

(heavy duty vehicles) is a hybrid. Except for engines and transmissions, VNM for heavy duty vehicles is calculated in the same manner as for non-automotive goods. However, a form of tracing applies for specified engine and transmission parts that are set out in NAFTA Annex 403.2.[37]

vii) *Averaging*
Calculations under NAFTA using the net cost method can be averaged over various accounting periods. Averaging rules for automotive goods are set out in Sections 11 and 12 of the *Uniform Regulations* and averaging options for non-automotive goods are set out in Section 6(15) of the *Uniform Regulations*. CCFTA Article D-03(2) and (3) set out averaging options for vehicles and the parts listed in Annex D-03.1 that are similar to those in NAFTA.

k) **Fungible Goods and Materials**
Fungible goods and fungible materials are goods or materials that are interchangeable for commercial purposes. The NAFTA rules of origin set out rules that permit a producer to use accounting rules to distinguish originating from non-originating fungible goods that it is selling, and originating from non-originating fungible materials that it purchases. Without these rules, the purchaser would have to physically segregate these items. CIFTA Article 3.7 and CCFTA Article D-06 contain similar rules.

l) **Accumulation**
The NAFTA rules permit a producer to "accumulate" its production with that of another producer regardless of whether the other producer is in another NAFTA country.[38] Accumulation applies both to meeting a required change in tariff classification and a value content requirement. CCFTA Article D-04 contains virtually the same provisions. CIFTA does not provide for accumulation.

m) **CIFTA Rules and Free Trade Arrangements with the United States**
Several CIFTA provisions take into account the fact that Israel and Canada both have entered into free trade arrangements with the United States.

i) *Certain Originating Goods*
The effect of CIFTA Article 3.6 is that a good, which if imported into Canada from the United States would be originating under NAFTA rules of ori-

---

37 Carried forward as Schedule V to the *UR*, above note 2.
38 NAFTA, above note 5, art. 404. See also *UR*, above note 2, s. 14.

gin, will be treated as originating when imported into Israel and used as a material in the production of a good in Israel. Under this rule, an Israeli producer who imports NAFTA originating goods from the United States for use as materials in producing a good in Israel may treat the materials as originating when determining whether the good is originating under CIFTA rules of origin and eligible for CIFTA tariff treatment when entering Canada. The same would apply to a Canadian producer who imported goods that are originating under the *Israel–United States Free Trade Agreement* and used those goods as materials in a good to be exported to Israel.

ii) Special Transshipment Rule
The usual transshipment rule in rules of origin is that any further processing in the territory of a non-Party will cause a good to lose its originating character. The transshipment rule in CIFTA Article 3.5(1)(c) permits goods transshipped through the United States to undergo minor processing there without losing their originating character. CIFTA Article 3.5(2) contemplates that certain specifically identified goods may undergo more than minor processing while being transshipped through the United States and not lose their originating character.

n) CCFTA Rules and Chilean Accession to NAFTA
CCFTA Article D-15 provides that upon the accession of Chile to NAFTA, the CCFTA rules of origin will be replaced by the rules negotiated as part of the terms of accession.

2) Rules of Origin for Canada's Autonomous Trade Regimes

Canadian regulations establish rules of origin for Canada's various autonomous trade regimes (the General Preferential Tariff, the Least Developed Developing Country Tariff, the British Preferential Tariff, the New Zealand and Australia Tariff, and the Commonwealth Caribbean Countries Tariff). The rules of origin differ slightly from program to program but are generally based on a concept of wholly originating goods, coupled with simple value content requirements applied to goods that are not wholly originating.

3) *Rules of Origin Agreement*

Annex II of the *Rules of Origin Agreement* contains a common declaration respecting preferential rules of origin that sets out general criteria that must be satisfied by WTO member countries that apply preferential rules of origin. The criteria are generally directed at ensuring that preferential rules be clear and that basic principles of procedural fairness be applied in their application.

4) Establishing Originating Status

a) NAFTA, CIFTA, and CCFTA
Originating status of goods is established under each of NAFTA, CIFTA, and CCFTA by means of a certificate of origin being issued by the exporter or the producer of the good. A commonly agreed form of certificate of origin is used under each agreement. The importer of the goods must have the certificate of origin in its possession at the time that the goods are imported and the claim for preferential NAFTA, CIFTA, or CCFTA tariff treatment is made.

NAFTA, CIFTA, and CCFTA establish requirements respecting customs procedures that must be incorporated into the laws of each member country. A prime objective of these provisions is to ensure procedural fairness in the application of rules of origin and the granting of tariff preferences. Obligations of importers claiming preferential tariff treatment and exporters or producers issuing certificates of origin are specified. Exporters or producers must maintain records for prescribed periods of time. Rules are established for conducting origin verifications. Provision is made for advance rulings, and criteria are established for review and appeal. Each agreement establishes a working group to address rules of origin issues and to attempt to resolve disputes.[39]

b) General Preferential Tariff and Least Developed Developing Country Tariff
In the case of goods for which the benefit of the General Preferential Tariff or the Least Developed Developing Country Tariff is claimed, the importer must present a certificate of origin signed by the exporter and certified by a government body of the beneficiary developing country.

5) Observations

Preferential rules of origin are essential to the administration of any trade arrangement that provides for preferential tariff treatment. However, rules of origin impede trade in that they create an additional administrative hurdle that exporters must surmount if their goods are

---

39   See generally NAFTA, *ibid.*, Chapter Five; CIFTA, above note 10, Chapter Five; and CCFTA, above note 3, Chapter E.

to receive preferential tariff treatment and the proliferation of bilateral preferential trading arrangements (as with Israel and Chile) compound the problem. Rules of origin must be kept reasonably simple and administratively workable in order not to defeat the purpose of preferential trading arrangements.

B. NON-PREFERENTIAL RULES OF ORIGIN

As mentioned above, non-preferential rules of origin are rules for determining the country of origin of goods for purposes other than the granting of preferences. The effect of the application or misapplication of non-preferential rules of origin can range from the irritating to the devastating. Unfairly drafted country of origin marking rules can result in a good having to be marked as a good of a country where one of its inputs was manufactured. Manipulative country of origin rules applied in the administration of quantitative restrictions can result in a denial of market access.

The application of non-preferential rules of origin was not covered under GATT 1947 but has been addressed in the *Rules of Origin Agreement*. The NAFTA negotiators attempted to deal with the problem but failed to establish commonly agreed rules. This failure has created a number of problems that will likely only be resolved through the processes being undertaken under the *Rules of Origin Agreement*. The CIFTA and CCFTA negotiators did not address the question of non-preferential rules of origin because the *Rules of Origin Agreement* was already in effect by the time that CIFTA and CCFTA negotiations commenced, and issues respecting non-preferential rules of origin are being addressed at the WTO level.

Unlike preferential rules of origin, which permit a negative answer (i.e., a good is non-originating), the application of country of origin rules must result in a positive answer (i.e., the identification of a country). Country of origin can be determined by a rule that provides that the country of origin is the country of "last substantial manufacture" or "last substantial transformation." More complex rules establish rule hierarchies through which one progresses until a country of origin is determined.

1) GATT 1994 and *Rules of Origin Agreement*

a) GATT 1994 and Country-of-Origin Marking

Article IX of GATT 1994 sets out rules respecting country-of-origin marking. GATT Article IX:1 establishes an MFN requirement that products of other member countries be no less favourably treated respecting marks of origin than goods from third countries. Inconvenience is to be kept to a minimum. Marking should be permitted at the time of importation and not seriously damage products or reduce their value. No special penalties should be imposed except in the case of unreasonable delay or deception.

b) The *Rules of Origin Agreement*

The objective of the *Rules of Origin Agreement* is to harmonize the non-preferential rules of origin applied by all WTO countries for the purposes listed in Article 1, which include rules for applying MFN requirements under GATT 1994, antidumping and countervailing duty measures, safeguard measures, marking requirements, quantitative restrictions, tariff rate quotas and government procurement requirements.[40] Part IV of the agreement establishes a work program for the harmonization of rules of origin for the purposes mentioned in Article 1 and sets out basic principles to be followed in the development of the harmonized rules. The Committee on Rules of Origin established by the agreement is directed to develop certain key definitions[41] and to consider the use of change in tariff classification and supplemental requirements (such as value and process requirements) for applying the criterion of substantial transformation.

The agreement sets out disciplines that are to be applied during the transition period to harmonization and following harmonization. For example, non-preferential rules of origin shall not, during the transition period, be used as instruments to pursue trade objectives and shall not create restrictive, distorting or disruptive effects on international trade.[42] The disciplines that apply both during and after the transition period contain procedural requirements to ensure that rules of origin are applied fairly.

---

40 *Rules of Origin Agreement*, above note 1, art. 1:2. Trade statistics are also mentioned.
41 Definitions of goods that are wholly obtained in one country and of minimal operations and processes that do not confer origin to a good. See *ibid.*, art. 9:2(c)(i).
42 The changes to the U.S. country-of-origin rules for textile and apparel goods referred to below, which became effective on 1 July 1996, violate both these provisions.

2) Non-Preferential Rules of Origin under NAFTA

a) The Marking Rules

The NAFTA text that was signed by the prime minister of Canada and the presidents of the United States and Mexico on 17 December 1992 incorporated the concept of "Marking Rules." NAFTA Annex 311 required that the NAFTA countries establish Marking Rules for the country-of-origin marking purposes and for several other purposes identified in the NAFTA text (including determining whether a good is Canadian, U.S., or Mexican for the purposes of ascertaining which tariff elimination schedule to apply).[43] The Marking Rules did not exist at this time, and the NAFTA text did not (and still does not) contain any norms to which the Marking Rules must conform.

i) Negotiation of the Marking Rules

Between 17 December 1992 and 1 January 1994 (the date NAFTA became effective), the NAFTA countries negotiated Marking Rules. However, the versions of the Marking Rules adopted by each country, although similar in structure, were not the same. The NAFTA text does not squarely address the question of amendments to the Marking Rules by each NAFTA country. On 1 July 1996, the United States unilaterally substituted entirely new country-of-origin rules for textile and apparel goods that operate on different principles from the Marking Rules that were originally negotiated and have the effect of denying market access to certain products produced in Canada that were formerly admitted.[44] While there is a good argument to the effect that material changes to a NAFTA country's Marking Rules must be trilaterally agreed, the United States has adopted the position (which has yet to be challenged) that each NAFTA country is free to change its Marking Rules in whatever manner it chooses.

ii) Hierarchy of Rules and NAFTA Override

The Marking Rules that came into effect in each NAFTA country at the time that NAFTA became effective establish a hierarchy of rules such that if a country of origin is not determined under the first tier of rules, one applies successive tiers until a country of origin is identified.

The first tier of rules provides that the country of origin is the country from which the good was wholly obtained or produced, or the country

---

43 As discussed below, Canada applies the Marking Rules for these purposes only for textile and apparel goods and agricultural goods.
44 60 Fed. Reg. 46, 188 (1996).

in which the good was produced from domestic materials, or the country in which all foreign materials satisfy the requirements set out in the tariff shift rules annexed to the regulations. The tariff shift rules contain prescribed changes in tariff classification and, in some instances, process requirements. If a country of origin is not found under the first tier of rules, one moves to the next tier of rules, which establishes the country of origin by identifying the country of origin of the single material that imparts the "essential character" to the good.[45] Essential character is not defined, but each country's regulations set out factors to be taken into consideration in making this determination. If a country of origin cannot be established under any of these rules, the final tier of rules provides that the country of origin of the good is the last country in which the goods underwent production, other than by "simple assembling" or "minor processing."

The substituted U.S. rules respecting textile and apparel goods which became effective on 1 July 1996 are also based on a hierarchy of rules, but the hierarchy is differently structured.

Each country's regulations set out an override provision that applies to any good that is originating under the NAFTA rules of origin. If a single NAFTA country is not established as the originating good's country of origin, the country of origin will be the last NAFTA country in which the good underwent production that was more than minor processing. The purpose of this rule is to avoid having the country of origin of an originating good being a non-NAFTA country.

b) Country-of-Origin Marking

i) NAFTA Rules

NAFTA Annex 311 sets out rules respecting the application by the NAFTA countries of requirements that goods be marked with their country of origin. Each NAFTA country may require that goods of another NAFTA country, determined in accordance with the Marking Rules, be marked with the name of the country of origin. Country-of-origin marking in English, French, or Spanish must be permitted, but a NAFTA country may require that a good be marked with its country of origin for general consumer information purposes in the same manner as its domestic goods. As under the GATT, difficulties, costs, and inconveniences are to be minimized.

---

45 There are separate rules that apply if the good is classified as a set or a composite good.

NAFTA countries are to exempt certain goods from the marking requirement.[46] Except for repeat violators, importers are to be permitted to mark goods subsequent to their being imported. No special duty or penalty is to be applied for failure to comply with marking requirements except in the case of importers who have been notified that goods must be marked prior to importation, or where goods are removed from customs custody and control without being marked, or where there has been deceptive marking.

ii) Canadian Marking Requirements

There are two separate sets of regulations under Canadian law respecting the marking of goods with their country of origin. One set of regulations applies to goods imported from NAFTA countries.[47] These regulations set out the Canadian version of the Marking Rules and carry forward a number of the requirements of NAFTA Annex 311. The other set of regulations applies to goods imported from non-NAFTA countries.[48] The country of origin under these rules is the country of "substantial manufacture." Schedule I in each set of rules lists the goods that must be marked.[49]

c) Country of Origin for NAFTA Tariff Preference Purposes

As discussed above, the NAFTA rules of origin determine whether a good is originating but do not identify the NAFTA country of the good's origin. As tariff elimination progresses at different rates among the NAFTA countries, the NAFTA country of origin must be determined in order to apply the correct tariff schedule. The United States and Mexico apply their respective versions of the Marking Rules to determine the NAFTA country of origin of originating goods, as does Canada with respect to originating agricultural goods and textile and apparel goods. However, Canada follows a different approach with respect to other goods. To be a "U.S." good (and eligible for the United States Tariff), an originating good must be originating under the NAFTA rules of origin

---

46 Building bricks, semiconductors, and electronic integrated circuits, microassemblies, goods incapable of being marked, and goods that cannot be marked without causing injury.
47 *Determination of Country of Origin for the Purposes of Marking Goods (NAFTA Countries) Regulations*, SOR/94-23.
48 *Determination of Country of Origin for the Purposes of Marking Goods (Non-NAFTA Countries) Regulations*, SOR/94-16.
49 These two sets of regulations must be read together with the *Marking of Imported Goods Regulations*, SOR/94-10, which sets out a number of general requirements respecting the marking of goods.

applied as if Mexico were not a NAFTA country, with permissible Mexican value-added not exceeding 7 percent. To be a "Mexican" good, and eligible for the Mexico Tariff, an originating good must be originating under the NAFTA rules of origin applied as if the United States were not a NAFTA Country, with permissible U.S. value-added not exceeding 7 percent. An originating good that is neither a U.S. good nor a Mexican good will be eligible for the Mexico–United States Tariff.

d) **Qualifying Goods**
Certain provisions of the bilateral arrangement respecting agricultural goods between Canada and Mexico in Section B of NAFTA Annex 703.2 apply to "qualifying goods." For example, the disciplines respecting import and export restrictions under NAFTA Articles 309(1) and 309(2) apply only to qualifying goods. A qualifying good is a good that is determined to be originating by applying the NAFTA preferential rules of origin as if the United States were not a NAFTA country.[50]

e) **Other Country-of-Origin Issues under NAFTA**
The NAFTA Marking Rules are used only for the purposes discussed above and for the application of certain provisions of NAFTA Annex 300-B (Textile and Apparel Goods). They are not used for the administration of national treatment obligations (see chapter 2), obligations respecting import and export restrictions (see chapter 4), safeguard actions or antidumping or countervailing duties (see chapter 6), or government procurement (see chapter 7). Once the harmonization process under the *Rules of Origin Agreement* is complete, rules for determining the country of origin for all these purposes will be in accordance with the harmonized rules that emerge from that process.

---

50   Paragraph 14 of Section B of NAFTA, above note 5, Annex 703.2.

CHAPTER 6

ANTIDUMPING AND COUNTERVAILING DUTIES, SUBSIDIES, AND SAFEGUARDS

The international trade agreements to which Canada is a party permit member countries to levy special duties to offset the effect of dumping or subsidizing goods. The concept in international trade law of what constitutes dumping has always been fairly clear. Goods are "dumped" when they are sold at a price in the importing country that is lower than the price at which they are sold in the country in which they are produced, or at a price that is insufficient to recover costs. Dumping that causes material injury to domestic producers of like goods can be offset with an antidumping duty.

Until the *Subsidies Agreement* became effective, there was little consensus as to what subsidies were unfair trade practices and, as such, actionable. The *Subsidies Agreement* establishes guidelines for ascertaining which subsidies are actionable and which are not. If a subsidy is actionable and if imports of the subsidized goods cause material injury to domestic producers of like goods, the subsidization can be offset by a countervailing duty.

Dumping actions are governed by the *Antidumping Agreement* and subsidy actions by the *Subsidies Agreement*. NAFTA does not alter the substantive antidumping or countervailing duty laws of the NAFTA countries or their respective obligations under these WTO agreements. However, NAFTA provides for binational review of certain important determinations made in the course of antidumping and countervailing duty cases. CCFTA provides for the elimination of antidumping investigations once certain events occur, but otherwise does not alter the rules established by the *Antidumping Agreement* and the *Subsidies Agreement*.

Subsidies create a variety of problems under international trade law. Massive domestic and export subsidies of agricultural goods of the European Union, the United States, and Canada have resulted in oversupply and depressed prices. The Uruguay Round of negotiations came close to failure over the question of agricultural subsidies. GATT 1994 prohibits export subsidies other than for primary products and the *Subsidies Agreement* elaborates upon the theme of prohibited subsidies. The *Agriculture Agreement* establishes commitments from member countries respecting both domestic and export subsidies of agricultural goods. NAFTA and CCFTA also contain disciplines respecting agricultural subsidies.

Safeguard or emergency actions differ from antidumping and countervailing duty actions in that they are not based on the existence of an unfair practice of another member country but, rather, the existence of volumes of imports from another member country in such increased quantities that serious injury to domestic producers is caused or threatened. The importing country may impose duties or quantitative restrictions but the action must be preceded by consultations, and the country against which the action is taken must receive compensation in the form of substantially equivalent concessions. Several of the trade agreements to which Canada is a party contain special safeguard provisions that apply to agricultural goods and to textile and apparel goods.

A. ANTIDUMPING AND COUNTERVAILING DUTIES, SUBSIDIES DISCIPLINES

Antidumping or countervailing duty actions begin with an investigation that is initiated upon the filing of a complaint or petition or application by a person or persons representing the domestic industry. Occasionally, investigations are self-initiated. The investigation results in a determination of whether or not imports have been dumped or subsidized and, if a dumping or subsidization determination is made, administrative authorities initiate a second investigation to determine whether the domestic industry has suffered material injury as a result of the dumping or subsidization. If the investigation determines that material injury has occurred, antidumping or countervailing duties are levied.

Article VI of GATT 1994 sets out general requirements that apply to both antidumping and countervailing duty actions. The *Antidumping Agreement* establishes procedural requirements for antidumping actions. The *Subsidies Agreement* sets out procedural requirements respecting countervailing duty actions, as well as disciplines that apply to the granting of subsidies.

1) Article VI of GATT 1994

a) Antidumping Duties
Article VI:1 of GATT 1994 describes dumping as introducing a product into the commerce of a country at less than its "normal value." The normal value is the domestic price of a like product in the exporting country. If there is no domestic price, the normal value is the highest comparable price for a like product for export to a third country or the cost of production in the exporting country, plus an allowance for selling costs and profit. The excess of the normal value over the price at which the product is introduced into the commerce of the importing country is the "margin of dumping." Article VI:2 of GATT 1994 permits member countries to offset dumping by an antidumping duty no greater than the margin of dumping.

b) Countervailing Duties
Article VI:3 of GATT 1994 requires that no countervailing duty levied against an imported product shall be greater than the estimated subsidy granted on the manufacture, production, or export of the product in the country of origin or exportation. Article VI does not define the types of subsidies against which countervailing duties may be levied.

c) Material Injury Requirement
An antidumping or countervailing duty may be imposed only if the dumping or subsidy causes or threatens to cause material injury to an established domestic industry or materially retards the establishment of a domestic industry.

2) Antidumping Duties and the *Antidumping Agreement*

The *Antidumping Agreement* establishes rules that elaborate the general provisions in Article VI:1 of GATT 1994. Article 2 sets out detailed rules for the determination of "normal value" and "export price" (the price at which the product is introduced into the commerce of the importing country). Article 3 sets out rules for the determination of injury to a domestic industry, and Article 4 defines "domestic industry" for this purpose. Articles 5, 6, and 12 set out procedural requirements to be followed in dumping investigations. Article 7 establishes the rules for the application of provisional measures, such as provisional duties. An investigation must have been initiated, a public notice must have been published, and a preliminary affirmative determination must have been made.

Article 8 sets out rules permitting the resolution of dumping proceedings through the acceptance of price undertakings under which exporters voluntarily agree to revise prices or cease exporting at dumped prices so as to eliminate the injurious effects of dumping. Articles 9, 10 and 11 cover the imposition and collection of antidumping duties, their application, and their duration. Article 13 requires that member countries provide for judicial review of administrative actions leading to final determinations in antidumping investigations. The balance of the agreement establishes a committee on antidumping practices and provides that the *Dispute Settlement Understanding* applies to disputes arising under the *Antidumping Agreement*.

3) The *Subsidies Agreement*

Article XVI of GAAT 1994 prohibits export subsidies other than those on primary products[1] and provides for consultations if subsidization practices of a member country seriously prejudiced the interests of another member country. As discussed above, Article VI of GATT 1994 provides for a remedy in the form of a countervailing duty to offset the effects of subsidization. However, Articles VI and XVI of GATT 1994 are not connected. A subsidy against which a countervailing duty action was taken does not have to be a subsidy prohibited in Article XVI. The Tokyo Round code on subsidies established procedural requirements to be followed in the imposition of countervailing duties and elaborated upon the disciplines imposed by Article XVI but did not establish a link between GATT subsidy disciplines and the countervailing duty remedy.

The *Subsidies Agreement* sets out much more explicit rules respecting subsidies than its Tokyo Round predecessor and establishes a link between subsidies disciplines and the countervailing duty remedy. Parts I to IV of the *Subsidies Agreement* establish disciplines respecting subsidies. Part V of the agreement sets out the substantive rules respecting countervailing measures. The balance of the agreement establishes a Committee on Subsidies and Countervailing Measures, sets out rules respecting developing countries and certain transitional provisions, and provides that the *Dispute Settlement Agreement* applies to disputes arising under the agreement.

---

1 *General Agreement on Tariffs and Trade 1994*, set out in Annex 1A of the *Agreement Creating the World Trade Organization*, 15 April 1994 (Dobbs Ferry, N.Y.: Oceana Publications, 1997) [*WTO Agreement*] [GATT 1994], art. XVI:4. Article XVI:3 sets out very loose rules respecting export subsidies on primary products.

a) Subsidies Disciplines

i) Definition of Subsidy and "Specific" Subsidies

Article 1 of the *Subsidies Agreement* defines a subsidy as a financial contribution by government or a public body where there is a direct transfer of funds, government revenue is forgone, goods or services other than general infrastructure is provided, or goods are purchased by government. In any of these instances, a benefit must be conferred for there to be a subsidy.

The status of a subsidy under the *Subsidies Agreement* depends largely on whether it is specific. Article 2 sets out rules for determining whether a subsidy is "specific to an enterprise or group of enterprises or industries." A subsidy is specific if access to it is limited to certain enterprises[2] or to certain enterprises within a designated geographical region.[3] However, specificity will not be created where the granting authority or enabling legislation establishes objective criteria or conditions governing eligibility, as long as eligibility is automatic and the criteria and conditions are strictly adhered to.[4] Article 2 sets out other factors that may be taken into account in determining whether a subsidy is specific.

ii) Prohibited Subsidies

Part II of the *Subsidies Agreement* sets out rules respecting prohibited subsidies. Except as provided in the *Agriculture Agreement*, subsidies that are contingent on export performance or the use of domestic over imported goods are prohibited.[5] An illustrative list of prohibited subsidies is set out in Annex I of the *Subsidies Agreement*.[6] Article 4 sets out procedures that may be invoked by a member country if another member country is maintaining prohibited subsidies. A subsidy must be specific to be prohibited.[7]

---

2   *Agreement on Subsidies and Countervailing Measures*, set out in Annex 1A of the *WTO Agreement*, ibid. [*Subsidies Agreement*], art. 2.1(a).
3   Ibid., art. 2.2.
4   Ibid., art. 2.1(b).
5   Ibid., art. 3. As discussed below, the *Agreement on Agriculture*, set out in Annex 1A of the *WTO Agreement*, ibid. [*Agriculture Agreement*] requires that export subsidies of agricultural goods be reduced in accordance with commitments but does not require that they be eliminated.
6   Note that duty drawback and duty deferral programs described in chapter 3 are contingent upon export performance. However, it is clear from paragraph (h) of the *Subsidies Agreement*, above note 2, Annex I, that these programs are not prohibited subsidies.
7   *Subsidies Agreement*, above note 2, art. 1.2.

iii) Actionable and Non-Actionable Subsidies

Part III of the *Subsidies Agreement* sets out rules respecting actionable subsidies. An actionable subsidy is a subsidy that causes injury to the domestic industry of another member country, or nullifies and impairs benefits under GATT 1994, or causes serious prejudice to the interests of another member country. A member country can nullify and impair the benefit of a tariff concession under GATT 1994 by granting a subsidy to domestic producers to offset the concession.[8] Article 6 defines rules for determining whether "serious prejudice" has occurred. For example, an indication of serious prejudice is if the subsidy has the effect of displacing or impeding the imports of another member country. Article 7 sets out procedures that may be invoked by a member country if another member country is maintaining actionable subsidies. A subsidy must be specific to be actionable.[9]

Part IV of the *Subsidies Agreement* establishes rules respecting non-actionable subsidies. A subsidy that is not specific is non-actionable.[10] Provided that certain conditions are satisfied, subsidies for research activities, for disadvantaged regions, and for adaptation of existing facilities to new environmental requirements are non-actionable even if they are specific.[11]

b) Countervailing Duty Actions

Part V of the *Subsidies Agreement* sets out rules respecting the application of countervailing measures.

i) Subsidies to Which Part V Applies

Countervailing duties that are sanctioned by Article VI of GATT 1994 and Part V of the *Subsidies Agreement* may only be applied to subsidies that are specific[12] and may not be applied to non-actionable subsidies.[13]

---

8   As occurred in *EEC — Payments and Subsidies Paid to Processors and Producers of Oilseeds and Related Animal-Feed Proteins (U.S. v. EEC)* (1989), GATT Doc. L/6627, 37th supp. B.I.S.D. (1989–1990) 86 [*EEC — Oilseeds*].
9   *Subsidies Agreement*, above note 2, art. 1.2.
10 *Ibid.*, art. 8.1.
11 *Ibid.*, art. 8.2. If a subsidy program covered by art. 8.2 results in a serious adverse effect to another member, that member can request consultations and ultimately refer the matter to the Committee on Subsidies and Countervailing Measures. The committee can recommend that the program be modified, and if the modifications are not effected within six months, the committee may authorize the requesting member to take countermeasures.
12 *Ibid.*, art. 1.2.
13 *Ibid.*, art. 8.2.

Subsidies that fully satisfy the criteria of Annex 2 of the *Agriculture Agreement* (described below) are non-actionable subsidies for these purposes.[14]

ii) Procedural Requirements
Articles 11 through 23 of the *Subsidies Agreement* set out the procedural requirements that must be observed in countervailing duty actions. Article 11 defines rules respecting the conduct of investigations. For example, Article 11.4 provides that an investigation shall not be initiated unless the application requesting the investigation is supported by a prescribed proportion of the domestic industry, and Article 11.6 permits self-initiation of an investigation "in special circumstances." Article 16 establishes rules for determining what constitutes the domestic industry. Article 12 sets out rules respecting the presentation of evidence. Article 13 requires that consultations with affected member countries take place before the initiation of any investigation. In this regard, it should be kept in mind that, unlike a dumping case, which involves pricing decisions made by individual exporters, a subsidy case amounts to a challenge of policies maintained by the government of another member country.

Article 14 establishes rules for calculating the amount of a subsidy in terms of benefit to recipients, and Article 15 sets out the rules for determining whether injury has occurred. Article 17 sets out rules for the application of provisional measures. Article 18 provides for undertakings, either by the government of the exporting member country to eliminate or reduce the subsidy or by the exporter to revise its prices to eliminate the injurious effect of the subsidy. Articles 19 to 21 cover the imposition and collection of countervailing duties, limit their retroactive application, and set out rules for the duration and review of both countervailing duties and undertakings. Article 22 sets out notice requirements, and Article 23 requires that provision be made for judicial review of final determination.

4) Subsidies Disciplines and Agricultural Goods

a) GATT Article XVI and Primary Products
As mentioned above, the prohibition of export subsidies in Article XVI of GATT 1994 does not apply to primary products. The only restriction imposed on export subsidies of primary products is that the subsidy not result in the subsidizing member country having "more than an

---

14   Article 13(a)(i) of the *Agriculture Agreement*, above note 5.

equitable share of the world export trade" in the subsidized product, having regard to the shares of other member countries over "a previous representative period." This weak provision had no effect in disciplining export subsidies of agricultural products by developed countries, particularly those of the European Union as well as the United States.

GATT 1947 did not contain any meaningful disciplines of domestic support programs. Exported goods that were subsidized could be subjected to countervailing duties, and domestic programs specifically aimed at negating GATT tariff concessions could be challenged as nullifying and impairing GATT benefits.[15] However, these factors did nothing to prevent the developed countries from maintaining massive domestic support programs for their agricultural sectors.

b) The *Agriculture Agreement*
The *Agriculture Agreement* addresses both export subsidies and domestic support programs.

i) *Export Subsidies*
Part V of the *Agriculture Agreement* lists the types of export subsidies subject to reduction commitments,[16] and the reduction commitments are set out in a schedule for each member country. Reductions are to be implemented over a six-year period that commenced in 1995 and will be complete by 2001.[17] An export subsidy that falls within a member country's commitments is not a prohibited subsidy under the *Subsidies Agreement*.

ii) *Domestic Support Programs*
Part IV of the *Agriculture Agreement* provides that member countries are required to reduce domestic support to agricultural producers in accordance with commitments set out in a schedule.[18] The reduction commitments do not apply to domestic measures that satisfy the criteria set out in Annex 2 of the *Agriculture Agreement*. The list of programs in Annex 2 includes various general services (such as research, pests, and disease control, etc.), public stockholding for food security purposes, domestic food aid, certain direct payments to producers and income support programs, payments for relief from natural disasters and certain structural adjustment, environmental, and regional assistance

---

15 See *EEC — Oilseeds*, above note 8.
16 See *Agriculture Agreement*, above note 5, art. 9:1.
17 *Ibid.*, art. 9:2(a). Some relaxation is permitted in art. 0:2(b).
18 *Ibid.*, art. 6:1.

programs. Each category of program is subject to criteria that must be satisfied for the program to fall within Annex 2.

c) NAFTA: Subsidy Disciplines on Agricultural Goods

i) General NAFTA Obligations
NAFTA Article 704 makes reference to domestic support measures but contains no substantive obligations. NAFTA Article 705 sets out minimal obligations respecting export subsidies. An exporting NAFTA country must notify an importing NAFTA country prior to adopting export subsidy measures and enter into consultations with a view to eliminating the subsidy or minimizing its adverse impact. The NAFTA countries recognize that export subsidies are inappropriate when there are no other subsidized imports of the subsidized good into the importing NAFTA country. The NAFTA countries agree to take each other's interests into account when using export subsidies.

ii) Canada and the United States
The NAFTA subsidy disciplines between the United States and Canada are those set out in CUFTA Article 701, which is incorporated by reference into NAFTA by NAFTA Annex 702.1. CUFTA Article 701(2) prohibits export subsidies on trade in agricultural goods between Canada and the United States. This obligation is more onerous than that imposed by the *Agriculture Agreement*. CUFTA Article 701(3) requires that the governments of Canada and the United States not sell agricultural goods for export to the other country at prices below the cost of acquisition plus storage, handling or other costs.[19] CUFTA Article 701(4) requires each of Canada and the United States to take into account the export interests of the other in applying subsidies to exports to third countries. CUFTA Article 701(5) requires that Canada exclude from the transport rates under the *Western Grain Transportation Act* agricultural goods originating in Canada and shipped via west coast ports for consumption in the United States.[20]

---

19 This provision was considered by a *Canada–United States Free Trade Agreement*, 22 December 1987, Can. T.S. 1989 No. 3, 27 I.L.M. 281 [CUFTA] Chapter Eighteen panel in *Interpretation of and Canada's Compliance with Article 701.3 with Respect to Durum Wheat Sales*, [1993] F.T.A.D. No. 2, para 47 (Ch. 18 Panel) (QL).
20 R.S.C. 1985, c. W-8. This legislation was repealed by the *Budget Implementation Act, 1995*, S.C. 1995, c. 17, s. 26, which was deemed in force 31 July 1995.

Antidumping and Countervailing Duties, Subsidies, and Safeguards 155

d) CCFTA: Export Subsidies on Agricultural Goods

CCFTA Article C-14 requires that, effective 1 January 2003, neither Party introduce or maintain any export subsidy on agricultural goods originating in its territory and exported to the other Party. Until 1 January 2003, if a Party introduces an export subsidy of an agricultural product, the other Party may raise its duty on the exports to the MFN tariff. This article also provides for consultation between Canada and Chile respecting export subsidies maintained by non-Parties.

5) Provisions of NAFTA Respecting Antidumping and Countervailing Duty Matters

a) Antidumping and Countervailing Duty Procedures in NAFTA Countries

i) Canada and the United States

The legislation governing antidumping and countervailing duty cases in Canada and the United States follows the procedures outlined in the *Antidumping Agreement* and the *Subsidies Agreement*. The relevant Canadian legislation is the *Special Import Measures Act*[21] (*SIMA*), and the corresponding U.S. legislation is Title VII of the *Tariff Act of 1930*.[22] In Canada, functions respecting the determination of dumping or subsidization are performed by the deputy minister of National Revenue for Customs and Excise (deputy minister). The corresponding administrative functions in the United States are performed by the International Trade Administration of the United States Department of Commerce (Commerce). In Canada, functions respecting the determination of material injury are performed by the Canadian International Trade Tribunal (CITT). The corresponding functions in the United States are performed by the United States International Trade Commission (ITC).

The deputy minister in Canada or Commerce in the United States may on his/her or its own initiative or in response to a complaint (Canada)[23] or petition (United States)[24] initiate an investigation if there is evidence that dumping or subsidizing of goods is causing or likely to cause material injury to an established domestic industry or is retarding the establishment of a domestic industry.

---

21 R.S.C. 1985, c. S-15 [*SIMA*].
22 19 U.S.C. §§1671–1677g (West 1982 and West Supp. III 1985).
23 See *SIMA*, above note 21, ss. 31–34 for the rules governing complaints.
24 *Tariff Act of 1930*, 19 U.S.C. (1988). See §1671a (countervailing duties) & §1673a (antidumping duties).

The deputy minister makes a preliminary determination of whether there has been dumping or subsidization within ninety days of the initiation of the investigation. Commerce in the United States makes the corresponding determination within eighty-five days in countervailing duty actions or 160 days in the case of antidumping actions of the filing of the petition or the initiation of the investigation, provided that the ITC has made a preliminary determination of injury. The *SIMA* does not provide for preliminary determinations of injury. In each country, once preliminary determinations of dumping or subsidization are made, antidumping or countervailing duties can be levied.

Once a preliminary determination of dumping or subsidization is made, the deputy minister has ninety days to make a final determination. The CITT commences its injury investigation and must make a final determination of whether or not the dumping or subsidization has caused injury within 120 days of the date that the CITT was notified of the preliminary determination of dumping. Unlike the procedures followed by the deputy minister, which are purely administrative, the CITT is a quasi-judicial body that conducts a formal hearing. In the United States, the ITC proceeds to make a final determination of injury once Commerce makes an affirmative final determination of dumping.

The law of each country sets out procedures for assessing and collecting antidumping or countervailing duties once final determinations of injury are made, as well as procedures for periodic review. The law of each country also makes provision for the resolution of antidumping or countervailing duty actions through the acceptance of undertakings.

ii) Mexico

Mexican antidumping and countervailing duty procedures correspond roughly to those described above for Canada and the United States. Antidumping and countervailing duty matters are administered by the *Secretaria de Comercio y Fomento Industrial* (SECOFI) and dumping, subsidy, and injury investigations are undertaken by SECOFI officials.[25] NAFTA Annex 1904.15 required that extensive amendments be made to Mexican antidumping and countervailing duty laws and procedures.

b) Retention of Laws

Each NAFTA country reserves the right to apply its antidumping and countervailing duty law to goods imported from other NAFTA coun-

---

25 Secretariat of Commerce and Industrial Development.

tries.²⁶ NAFTA countries also reserve the right to change or modify antidumping or countervailing laws.²⁷ However, amendments apply to goods from other NAFTA countries only if the amending statute expressly so provides and the NAFTA country enacting the amendment must notify the other NAFTA countries affected by the amendment in advance and must consult on request.

i) Minimal Norms

NAFTA Article 1902(2)(d) sets out minimal norms to which amendments of antidumping and countervailing duty statutes must conform. Amendments cannot be inconsistent with GATT 1994 or the *Antidumping Agreement* or the *Subsidies Agreement*.²⁸ The NAFTA countries are bound to observe the requirements of these agreements in any event. Amendments also cannot be inconsistent with the "object and purpose" of NAFTA, which NAFTA Article 1902(2)(d)(ii) describes as being "to establish fair and predictable conditions for the progressive liberalization of trade between the Parties to this Agreement while maintaining effective and fair disciplines on unfair trade practices." This seems a nebulous basis for challenging an amendment to a NAFTA country's antidumping or countervailing duty laws, particularly if the amendment is consistent with relevant WTO requirements.²⁹

ii) Panel Review

NAFTA Article 1903 makes provision for review by a binational panel of amendments to antidumping or countervailing duty laws to determine whether they conform to the requirements of NAFTA Article 1902(2)(d) or whether they have the effect of overturning a decision of a NAFTA binational panel convened under NAFTA Article 1904 respecting a final determination in an antidumping or countervailing duty case (see below). The review results in a declaratory opinion. CUFTA Article 1903 set out similar procedures that were never invoked. In the case of an amendment to a NAFTA country's anti-

---

26 *North American Free Trade Agreement*, 17 December 1992, Can. T.S. 1994 No. 2 [NAFTA], art. 1902(1).
27 *Ibid.*, art. 1902(2).
28 *Ibid.*, art. 1902(2)(d) actually refers to the predecessor agreements but provides that the successor agreements apply.
29 Article VI of GATT 1994, above note 1, and whichever agreement is applicable: the *Subsidies Agreement*, above note 2, or the *Agreement on Implementation of Article VI of the General Agreement on Tariffs and Trade 1994*, set out in Annex 1A of the *WTO Agreement*, above note 1 [*Antidumping Agreement*].

dumping or countervailing duty laws that contravened WTO requirements, other NAFTA countries would likely achieve better results through pursuing WTO remedies rather than proceeding under NAFTA Article 1903.

c) Panel Review of Final Determinations

NAFTA Article 1904(1) requires that NAFTA countries replace judicial review of certain final antidumping and countervailing duty determinations with panel review. A NAFTA country may initiate a request for panel review on its own initiative and must initiate a request on the request of any person who would be entitled to initiate domestic judicial review proceedings under the law of the importing country. In the absence of a request, the normal procedures of judicial review under the laws of the importing country apply.

The objective of the panel review is to determine whether the determination was made in accordance with the antidumping or countervailing duty laws of the importing NAFTA country.[30] The expression "final determination," as defined in NAFTA Article 1911 by reference to NAFTA Annex 1911, is a list of specific orders and determinations under the antidumping and countervailing duty law of each NAFTA country.

The provisions of NAFTA Article 1904 apply only to goods that the competent investigating authority of an importing NAFTA country, in applying that country's antidumping or countervailing duty laws to a particular case, determines are goods of another NAFTA country. These are defined as domestic products as understood in the GATT, which need not be "originating goods" under the NAFTA Rules of Origin.[31]

i) Final Determinations Subject to Panel Review

Canadian final determinations: The Canadian final determinations subject to panel review are as follows:

- an order or finding of material injury by the CITT under *SIMA* section 43(1);

---

30 The antidumping and countervailing duty law of an importing NAFTA country consists of the relevant statutes, legislative history, regulations, administrative practice, and judicial precedents to the extent that a court of the importing NAFTA country would have relied on them. See NAFTA, above note 26, art. 1904(2).
31 See definition in NAFTA, *ibid.*, art. 1911. See discussion in chapter 2 of the definition of "goods of a Party" in NAFTA art. 201. The definition of "goods of a Party" in NAFTA art. 1911 is the same except that it does not refer to originating goods or contemplate other agreements of NAFTA countries as to what constitutes a "good of a Party."

- an order by the CITT under *SIMA* section 76(4) arising from a review of its own prior order or finding of material injury;
- a final determination of the deputy minister under *SIMA* section 41 as to whether there has been dumping or subsidization;
- a decision of the deputy minister under *SIMA* section 59 arising from his or her redetermination of the determination or redetermination of a customs appraiser of normal value and export price (for assessing antidumping duties) or the amount of subsidy (for assessing countervailing duties);
- a decision by the CITT under *SIMA* section 76(3) not to review an order or finding of material injury;
- a reconsideration by the CITT under *SIMA* section 91(3) of a decision as to which of two or more persons is an importer;
- a decision of the deputy minister under *SIMA* section 53(1) arising from the periodic review of undertakings.

These determinations are all subject to judicial review by the Federal Court of Appeal.[32]

U.S. final determinations: The U.S. final determinations subject to panel review are as follows:

- final determinations made by Commerce as to the occurrence of subsidization or dumping, and the ITC as to material injury under Sections 705 and 735 of the *Tariff Act of 1930*;
- a determination arising from the annual review by Commerce of antidumping and countervailing duty orders under Section 751 of the *Tariff Act of 1930*;
- a determination of the ITC under Section 751(b) of the *Tariff Act of 1930* not to review a determination based on changed circumstances;
- a determination by Commerce as to whether a particular type of merchandise is within a class or kind subject to an existing finding of dumping or antidumping or countervailing duty order.

Each of these determinations is subject to judicial review by the United States Court of International Trade.

---

32 Note that a decision of the deputy minister under *SIMA*, above note 21, s. 59, is subject to review by the CITT. An appeal from the CITT to the Federal Court of Appeal may be made only on a question of law. See *SIMA*, s. 62.

Mexican final determinations: The Mexican final determinations subject to panel review are as follows:

- a final resolution (i.e., determination) by SECOFI respecting dumping, subsidization, or injury;
- a final resolution in an annual application for review of antidumping or countervailing duty rates;
- a final resolution by SECOFI as to whether a particular type of merchandise is within the class or kind of merchandise described in an existing antidumping or countervailing duty resolution.

Panel review is available only for the final determinations referred to above. Other determinations made in the course of an antidumping or countervailing duty matter (such as preliminary findings of dumping, subsidization, material injury, or the imposition of provisional duties) are not subject to panel review.

ii) Formation of Panels

Chapter Nineteen panels are always binational, with five members chosen from the rosters of candidates maintained by the importing NAFTA country and the NAFTA country making the request.[33] Each NAFTA country chooses two members from its own roster and a fifth member is chosen by agreement of the two NAFTA countries.[34] A majority of the panelists must be lawyers in good standing and the chairman must be a lawyer. NAFTA Annex 1901.2 details the procedures for panel selection and establishes time limits for each step of the process.[35]

iii) Panel Review

The review is to be based on the administrative record which, unless otherwise agreed by the NAFTA countries and other persons appearing before the panel, consists of all documentary or other information presented to or obtained by the investigating authority including governmental memoranda and records of *ex parte* proceedings, the final determination including reasons, transcripts, and records of conferences and hearings, and all published notices in the official journal of the importing NAFTA country.

---

33 As discussed below in chapter 10, Chapter Twenty panels can consist of members of all three NAFTA countries.
34 Each NAFTA country is allowed four pre-emptory challenges to members proposed by the other NAFTA country. See para. 2 of NAFTA, above note 26, Annex 1901.2.
35 The panel selection procedures set out in NAFTA, *ibid.*, Annex 1901.2, apply to binational panels convened under NAFTA, art. 1903, as well as to panels convened under NAFTA, art. 1904.

The standard of review applied by the panel is defined in NAFTA Annex 911 by reference to the laws of each NAFTA country. For example, a binational panel reviewing a Canadian final determination applies the standard of review set out in subsection 18.1(4) of the *Federal Court Act*, which sets out the grounds for review by the Federal Court of Appeal of CITT decisions.[36] A binational panel reviewing a U.S. final determination applies the applicable U.S. standard of review and a binational panel reviewing a Mexican final determination would apply the applicable Mexican standard of review.[37]

The NAFTA text sets out tight time frames for the various stages of a proceeding, and the panel review process is intended to be completed within 315 days.[38]

The panel may uphold a final determination or remand[39] it back to the competent investigating authority for action consistent with its decision. An investigating authority shall give notice of the action that it has taken by filing a Determination on Remand with the responsible Secretariat. A participant in the proceedings may challenge the action taken by filing a written submission within a prescribed time period.[40] If the action taken by the investigating authority in response to the remand must be reviewed, the same panel shall do so and issue its "final decision" within ninety days.[41] Actions taken by investigating authorities in response to remands were challenged on several occasions under CUFTA, most notably in *In the Matter of Fresh, Chilled and Frozen Pork from Canada (Pork Case)*.[42]

---

36 Acting without jurisdiction, acting beyond its jurisdiction, or refusing to exercise jurisdiction; failing to observe a principle of natural justice; erring in law in making a decision or order; or basing a decision on an erroneous finding of fact made in a perverse or capricious manner or without regard for the evidence presented; acting or failing to act by reason of fraud or perjured evidence; and acting in any other way contrary to law.
37 As set out in NAFTA, above note 26, Annex 911, by reference to specific statutory provisions of each country.
38 NAFTA, *ibid.*, art. 1904(14).
39 NAFTA, *ibid.*, art. 911 defines "remand" as "a referral back for a determination not inconsistent with the panel or committee decision."
40 See *Article 1904 Panel Rules*, C. Gaz. 1994.I.1012 at 1012. Rule 75 sets out the procedures for panel review of actions taken by investigating authorities on remand.
41 NAFTA, above note 26, art. 1904(8).
42 See (1990), 3 T.C.T. 8308 (Art. 1904 Panel) and the second decision is reported at (1991), 4 T.C.T. 7026 (Art. 1904 Panel).

iv) Extraordinary Challenge

NAFTA binational panel decisions are binding on the NAFTA countries involved and may not be appealed in the ordinary course. However, the NAFTA text makes provision for challenging a binational panel decision if certain actions "materially affect" the panel's decision and "threaten" the integrity of the panel process.[43] The actions listed are: a member of the panel was guilty of gross misconduct, bias, a serious conflict of interest, or otherwise materially violated the rules of conduct; the panel seriously departed from a fundamental rule of procedure; or the panel manifestly exceeded its powers, authority or jurisdiction set out in NAFTA 1904.[44] Extraordinary challenges may only be initiated by the government of a NAFTA country and not by a party to an action. The challenge is heard by an Extraordinary Challenge Committee of three judges or former judges. The NAFTA text sets out tight time frames for the various stages of the proceeding. If grounds for challenge exist, the panel decision will be vacated or remanded back to the panel for action not inconsistent with the committee's decision.

The extraordinary challenge procedure is clearly intended to cover aberrant circumstances and is not a routine appeal procedure. Under CUFTA, the extraordinary challenge procedure was invoked by the United States in the *Pork Case* referred to above,[45] and also in *In the Matter of Live Swine from Canada*,[46] and *In the Matter of Certain Softwood Products from Canada* (*Softwood Case*).[47] None of the challenges was successful, although the sole U.S. committee member in the *Softwood Case* issued a dissenting opinion that was scathingly critical of the entire Chapter Nineteen process.

d) Safeguarding the Panel Process

NAFTA Article 1905 sets out procedures by a NAFTA country that may be invoked if the domestic law of another NAFTA country frustrates the panel process. The complaint is heard by a panel and if the panel makes an affirmative finding and the problem is not rectified within a certain time frame, the complaining NAFTA country may suspend the operation of NAFTA Article 1904 with respect to the non-complying NAFTA country and may suspend other NAFTA benefits.

---

43 NAFTA, above note 26, art. 1904(13)(b). Both these circumstances must exist for a challenge to be successful.
44 NAFTA, *ibid.*, art. 1904(13)(a).
45 See *In the Matter of Fresh, Chilled and Frozen Pork from Canada* (1991), 4 T.C.T. 7037 (Ex. Chall. Ctee.).
46 [1993] F.T.A.D. No. 4 (Ex. Chall. Ctee.) (QL).
47 [1994] F.T.A.D. No. 8 (Ex. Chall. Ctee.) (QL).

e) Concluding Remarks

The binational panel process has been extensively used and has worked very well from a Canadian perspective. Binational panels have remanded a number of determinations made by U.S. investigating authorities that were viewed as inappropriate. U.S. views on Chapter Nineteen are mixed. The U.S. trade bar has generally been very supportive of the binational panel process. However, certain U.S. industries, most notably the softwood lumber industry, are highly critical of the process and would like to see it done away with.[48] These special interests will certainly oppose its extension to other countries in any NAFTA accession negotiations.

6) Provisions of CIFTA Respecting Antidumping and Countervailing Duty Matters

Each of Canada and Israel reserves the right to apply its antidumping and countervailing duty laws against goods of the other.[49] Canada and Israel have also agreed that their rights and obligations respecting subsidies and countervailing measures and antidumping measures shall be governed, respectively, by the *Subsidies Agreement* and the *Antidumping Agreement*.[50] CIFTA does not make any provision for binational panel review of determinations in antidumping or countervailing duty actions.

7) Provisions of CCFTA Respecting Antidumping and Countervailing Duty Matters

CCFTA Article M-01 provides for the reciprocal exemption by each of Canada and Chile of goods of the other Party[51] from the application of its antidumping laws. The provisions of Article M-03 will apply to all goods of the other Party either on the date upon which the tariff of both Parties is eliminated at the subheading level or on 1 January 2003, whichever comes first. CCFTA Article M-04 provides for consultations in exceptional cases.

---

48 At the time of writing, a court challenge to the NAFTA, above note 26, Chapter Nineteen binational panel process was working its way through the U.S. courts. The challenge alleged that the substitution of binational panel review for judicial review by a U.S. court amounted to a denial of due process under the U.S. constitution. This challenge was dismissed on procedural grounds, without a decision on the merits.
49 *Canada–Israel Free Trade Agreement*, in force 1 January 1997, see http://www.dfait-maeci.gc.ca/english/trade/agreement.htm [CIFTA] art. 9.2(3).
50 *Ibid.*, arts. 9.2(1) & 9.2(2).
51 As defined in the *Canada–Chile Free Trade Agreement*, in force 5 July 1997, see http://www.dfait-maeci.gc.ca/english/trade/agrement.htm [CCFTA], art. B-01.

Aside from the exemption set out in CCFTA Article M-01, antidumping and countervailing duty matters as between Canada and Chile are to be governed by applicable WTO agreements.[52] CCFTA Articles M-07(4) to (9) set out dispute resolution rules that apply to procedures between the two countries conducted pursuant to the *Dispute Settlement Understanding* involving antidumping or countervailing duty matters. However, CCFTA does not replicate for Chile and Canada the binational panel process provided for in NAFTA Chapter Nineteen.

B. SAFEGUARD (EMERGENCY) ACTIONS

Article XIX of GATT 1994 permits member countries to take emergency action if imports of a product from another member country increase to an extent that causes or threatens serious injury to domestic producers of like or directly competitive products. Unlike antidumping and countervailing duties, which are to counteract wrongful trade practices (dumping or subsidization), "emergency" or "safeguard" actions are not based on wrongdoing. Member countries are permitted to take emergency action because GATT/WTO concessions (such as tariff reductions) may, in some cases, result in significant increases in imports. Rules governing emergency action procedures require that the action be offset by concessions in other areas.

The obligations of WTO member countries are amplified by the *Safeguards Agreement*. As discussed in chapter 4, the *Agriculture Agreement* contains safeguards respecting agricultural products respecting which member countries have made concessions, and the *Textile Agreement* contains transitional safeguard provisions.

NAFTA and CCFTA set out obligations that apply when Parties invoke WTO safeguard procedures involving goods of other Parties or the other Party. NAFTA and CCFTA also define two sets of bilateral procedures that apply as between the Parties, one of which applies specifically to textile and apparel goods and the other to other goods.

1) Article XIX of GATT 1994

Article XIX of GATT 1994 requires as a condition for emergency action that there be increased imports that are the result of "unforeseen . . . circumstances" and the obligations under GATT 1994 (including tariff

---

52 *Ibid.*, art. M-07(3).

concessions) into the member country taking the action. The increased imports must cause or threaten serious injury to domestic producers. The importing country may withdraw or modify GATT concessions respecting the product being imported to the extent and for the time necessary to remedy the injury. The importing country must first consult with other member countries with a substantial interest as exporters. If the consultations do not result in an agreement, the importing country may nonetheless proceed with its emergency action. As the emergency action remedy is not based on wrongdoing, Article XIX of GATT 1994 permits the exporting country to retaliate by suspending substantially equivalent concessions.

2) The *Safeguards Agreement*

The *Safeguards Agreement* defines "serious injury" and "threat of serious injury" and sets out procedural requirements to be observed by a member country before applying safeguard measures.[53] The *Safeguards Agreement* sets time limits on the duration of safeguard measures. A member country may apply safeguard measures only so long as is necessary to prevent or remedy the injury, with a maximum period of eight years,[54] or ten years for developing countries.[55] Provisional measures may be applied where delay would cause damage that would be difficult to repair, provided that the duration of the measure not exceed 200 days.[56] The agreement establishes respecting the suspension of concessions or obligations by countries whose goods are affected by safeguard actions.[57] The *Safeguards Agreement* prohibits member countries from seeking, taking, or maintaining "voluntary export restraints," "orderly marketing arrangements," or similar measures and requires that such existing arrangements be phased out.[58]

---

53 See *Agreement on Safeguards*, set out in the *WTO Agreement*, above note 1, arts. 3 & 4. The definitions are set out in arts. 4:1(a) & (b). Article 1 defines "safeguard measures" as "those measures provided for in Article XIX of GATT 1994."
54 *Ibid.*, arts. 7:1 & 7:3.
55 *Ibid.*, art. 9:2.
56 *Ibid.*, art. 6.
57 *Ibid.*, art. 8.
58 *Ibid.*, art. 11:1(b).

3) NAFTA and CCFTA Safeguard Provisions

a) Global Actions

NAFTA Article 802 and CCFTA Article F-02 set out rules that apply when a Party applies a safeguard measure in circumstances that goods of another Party are affected. A Party taking emergency action under Article XIX of GATT 1994 or the *Safeguards Agreement*[59] must exclude imports from the other Party or Parties unless the imports from a Party account for a "substantial share" of total imports and "contribute importantly" to the serious injury or threat of serious injury. Imports from a Party will not normally constitute a "substantial share" if the Party has not been among the top five suppliers of the good. NAFTA Article 805 and CCFTA Article F-05 define "contribute importantly" as being an important cause but not necessarily being the most important cause of the injury.[60] Imports from a Party initially excluded from an action may, following notice and consultations, be subsequently included if a surge of imports from that Party undermines the effectiveness of the action.[61] NAFTA Article 802(6) and CCFTA Article F-02(6) require that the Party initiating the action provide "mutually agreed trade liberalizing compensation" and if agreement is not reached the Party against which the action is taken may take action having substantially equivalent effect to the action taken against its goods.[62]

b) Bilateral Actions: Goods Other Than Textile and Apparel Goods

NAFTA Chapter Eight sets out two separate procedures that permit a NAFTA country to suspend further tariff reduction in respect of a good of another NAFTA country and to increase tariffs to MFN levels. One set of procedures, which applies only between Canada and the United States, is set out in CUFTA Article 1101, which is incorporated by reference into NAFTA by NAFTA Annex 801.1. The other set of procedures, which applies between Mexico and each of Canada and the United States, is set out in NAFTA Article 801. CCFTA Article F-01 sets out

---

59 NAFTA, above note 26, art. 802(1) refers to "Article XIX of the GATT or any safeguard agreement pursuant thereto."
60 NAFTA, *ibid.*, art. 802(2)(b), and CCFTA, above note 51, art. F-02(2)(b) elaborate upon the concept of "contribute importantly."
61 NAFTA, *ibid.*, art. 802(3), and CCFTA, *ibid.*, art. F-02(3).
62 Assuming that the changes to the *Customs Tariff* set out in the Ways and Means Motion become effective on 1 January 1998, following that date the Canadian statutory authority for global emergency measures will be set out in Sections 54 to 67 of the *Customs Tariff*. The requirements described above are reflected in these sections in relation to "free trade partners."

procedures that are modelled on those set out in NAFTA Article 801. None of these procedures applies to textile and apparel goods to which NAFTA Annex 300-B or CCFTA Annex C-00-B apply. These goods are subject to special emergency procedures described below.[63]

Each set of procedures permits action to be taken if increases in imports from another Party "alone constitute a substantial cause of serious injury, or threat thereof" to a domestic industry producing a like or directly competitive good.[64] There must be a causal link between the increase in imports and the reduction or elimination of tariffs and, accordingly, the goods against which the action is taken must be originating goods. Action may be taken only during a transition period which, between Canada and the United States expires on 31 December 1998, and between Mexico and the other two NAFTA countries expires on 31 December 2003.[65] The CCFTA transition period expires on 31 December 2002.[66] Action may only be taken once against a particular good.[67] Notification and consultation must precede the action and no action can last for more than three years.[68] Once the action is over, the rate reverts to what it would have been had tariff elimination proceeded in the ordinary course.[69]

The Party taking the action must provide "mutually agreed trade liberalizing compensation" in the form of concessions that have "substantially equivalent trade effects" or that are "equivalent to the value of the additional duties expected to result from the action."[70] If agreement

---

63 Assuming that the changes to the *Customs Tariff* set out in the Ways and Means Motion become effective on 1 January 1998, following that date provisions for bilateral emergency measures for U.S. goods will be set out in Section 69 of the *Customs Tariff*, for Mexican and MUST goods in Section 70 of the *Customs Tariff*, and for goods of Chile in Section 71 of the *Customs Tariff*.

64 CUFTA, above note 19, art. 1101(1), and NAFTA, *ibid.*, art. 801(1). "Serious injury" is not defined in CUFTA but is defined in NAFTA art. 805 as "a significant overall impairment of a domestic industry." See also CCFTA, above note 51, art. F-01(1).

65 Except for goods in Staging Category C+ in the schedules of the United States and Mexico, for which the transition period expires on 31 December 2008 (NAFTA, *ibid.*).

66 Except for goods for which the staging for tariff elimination extends beyond this date.

67 NAFTA, above note 26, art. 801(2)(d), and CCFTA, above note 51, art. F-01(2)(d).

68 Under NAFTA, above note 26, art. 801, four years in the case of goods in Staging Category C+, which applies only between the United States and Mexico.

69 There are some elaborations of this in NAFTA, *ibid.*, art. 801.

70 CUFTA, above note 19, art. 1101(4); NAFTA, *ibid.*, art. 801(4); and CCFTA, above note 51, art. F-01(4).

is not reached, the country against which the action is taken may take tariff action having substantially equivalent effect to the action taken against its goods.

c) Bilateral Actions: Textile and Apparel Goods

NAFTA Annex 300-B and CCFTA Annex C-00-B set out two special bilateral emergency action procedures for textile and apparel goods that can be invoked up until 1 January 2004 under NAFTA and 1 July 2003 under CCFTA. One procedure permits action to be taken in respect of tariffs and the other permits the imposition of quantitative restrictions. The condition for invoking either procedure is that goods must be imported from another Party in such increased quantities as to cause or threaten serious damage to a domestic industry producing like or directly competitive goods.

i) Tariff Actions

The tariff action procedures, which are set out in Section 4 of NAFTA Annex 300-B and Section 3 of CCFTA Annex C-00-B, permit suspension of tariff reduction and increases in tariffs to MFN levels in a manner similar to that in NAFTA Article 801 and CCFTA Article F-01.[71] The procedures apply only to goods that are eligible for tariff elimination (i.e., originating goods and goods eligible for entry under tariff preference levels). The increase in imports causing or threatening the injury must result from the reduction or elimination of tariffs. Actions may be maintained for no more than three years and, when the action expires, tariffs revert in a manner similar to that provided in NAFTA Article 801[72] and CCFTA Article F-01.[73] The trade liberalizing compensation requirements are the same as set out in NAFTA Article 801 and CCFTA Article F-01 except that the concessions must be restricted to textile and apparel goods.[74]

---

71 Assuming that the changes to the *Customs Tariff* set out in the Ways and Means Motion become effective on 1 January 1998, following that date provisions for bilateral emergency measures for textile and apparel goods imported from a NAFTA country will be set out in Section 75 of the *Customs Tariff* and for textile and apparel goods imported from Chile will be set out in Section 76 of the *Customs Tariff*.
72 NAFTA, above note 26, Annex 300-B, s. 4, para. 4(c).
73 CCFTA, above note 51, Annex C-00-B, s. 3, para. 4(c).
74 NAFTA, above note 26, Annex 300-B, s. 4, para. 5. CCFTA, *ibid.*, Annex C-00-B, s. 3, para. 5.

ii) *Quantitative Restrictions*
The procedures permitting the imposition of quantitative restrictions are set out in Section 5 of NAFTA Annex 300-B and Section 4 of CCFTA Annex C-00-B. The NAFTA procedures do not apply between Canada and the United States. The quantitative action procedure may be invoked only against non-originating goods that have not been integrated into GATT 1994 under the *Textile Agreement* (see chapter 4). The goods covered by these procedures can include goods eligible for entry under tariff preference levels. The procedures require that consultations take place and establish time frames. The quantitative restrictions that are imposed must comply with the requirements set out in Section 5 (NAFTA) or Section 4 (CCFTA) and cannot extend beyond the end of the applicable transition period. There is no provision for trade liberalizing compensation.[75]

d) Procedural Requirements
NAFTA Annex 803.3 and CCFTA Annex F-03.3 set out extensive procedural requirements respecting the administration of emergency action proceedings, whether invoked under Article XIX of GATT 1994 or NAFTA Chapter Eight or CCFTA Chapter F. However, these procedural requirements do not apply to the bilateral procedures provided for in Annex 300-B in respect of textile and apparel goods.

4) Provisions of CIFTA

CIFTA Article 4.6 sets out provisions respecting global actions that are similar to those provided for in NAFTA Article 802. CIFTA Article 4.5 provides for bilateral emergency actions in a manner that closely follows that in NAFTA Article 801.[76] As under NAFTA Article 801, the maximum period that an action can be maintained is three years, and no action can be taken after 1 July 1999. Unlike NAFTA and CCFTA, CIFTA does not contain special emergency action procedures respecting textile and apparel goods.

---

75 Canadian statutory authority for these procedures is set out in Section 6.1 of the *Export and Import Permits Act*, R.S.C. 1985, c. E-19.
76 Assuming that the changes to the *Customs Tariff* set out in the Ways and Means Motion become effective on 1 January 1998, following that date provisions for bilateral emergency measures for goods of Israel or any other CIFTA beneficiary will be set out in Section 72 of the *Customs Tariff*.

CHAPTER 7

UNDESIGNED PARALLELISM

As discussed in chapter 1, Canada is bound under the WTO agreements and NAFTA by parallel sets of somewhat different obligations in respect of sanitary and phytosanitary measures, technical barriers to trade, intellectual property, and government procurement. The NAFTA trade-in-goods provisions also have counterparts in GATT 1994 with the result that parallel obligations exist with trade in goods. However, with these provisions there was a conscious effort by the drafters of NAFTA and its predecessor, CUFTA, to incorporate certain GATT obligations as a starting point and to improve upon them. With sanitary and phytosanitary measures, technical barriers, government procurement, and intellectual property, parallel obligations evolved not through a conscious effort to improve upon a pre-existing set of obligations but, rather, as the result of obligations in each of these areas being negotiated contemporaneously in separate negotiations. The Uruguay Round negotiations clearly influenced the outcome of the NAFTA negotiations, but the NAFTA outcome cannot be seen as an improvement upon the corresponding WTO agreements. In some instances the NAFTA regime is more rigorous but in some other instances, the WTO regime is clearly more stringent.

The *SPS Agreement* and the *TBT Agreement*, both multilateral agreements by which all NAFTA countries are bound, have their parallels in Section B of NAFTA Chapter Seven (Sanitary and Phytosanitary Measures) and in NAFTA Chapter Nine (Standards-Related Measures) respectively. The *TRIPS Agreement*, also a multilateral agreement, is paralleled by NAFTA Chapter Seventeen (Intellectual Property) and the plurilateral *Government Procurement Agreement* (by which Canada and the United States but not Mexico are bound) is matched by NAFTA Chapter Ten (Government Procurement).

As to which agreement applies in any given instance is governed by the considerations discussed in chapter 1 under "Inconsistencies between Agreements: Which Agreement Prevails?" The practical result for lawmakers is that laws must conform to the more stringent of the two sets of parallel but somewhat differing norms.

CIFTA does not create parallel obligations but, rather, provides that the rights and obligations of Canada and Israel are to be governed in each of these areas by the relevant WTO agreement.[1] CCFTA does not provide for rights and obligations in any of these areas. The rights and obligations of Canada and Chile in respect of sanitary and phytosanitary measures, technical barriers to trade, and intellectual property are governed by the relevant WTO agreements. As Chile is not a signatory to the *Government Procurement Agreement*, there is no agreement respecting government procurement between Canada and Chile.

A. SANITARY AND PHYTOSANITARY MEASURES AND TECHNICAL BARRIERS TO TRADE

While clearly necessary, standards[2] can be turned into effective trade barriers, particularly if they are applied in a discriminatory manner or if they are not transparent. The Tokyo Round of GATT negotiations produced a single code that applied to "technical barriers to trade." The Uruguay Round negotiators carried forward and elaborated upon the Tokyo Round code in the *TBT Agreement* and created an entirely new

---

1   Article 4.2, referring to the *Agreement on Technical Barriers to Trade*, set out in Annex 1A of the *Agreement Creating the World Trade Organization*, 15 April 1994 (Dobbs Ferry, N.Y.: Oceana Publications, 1997) [*WTO Agreement*] [*TBT Agreement*]; art. 4.3, referring to the *Agreement on the Application of Sanitary and Phytosanitary Measures*, set out in Annex 1A of the *WTO Agreement, ibid.,* [*SPS Agreement*]; art. 6.1, referring to the *Agreement on Government Procurement*, set out in Annex 4 of the *WTO Agreement, ibid., [Government Procurement Agreement]*; and art. 9.1, referring to the *Agreement on Trade-Related Aspects of Intellectual Property Rights*, set out in Annex 1C of the *WTO Agreement, ibid., [TRIPS Agreement]*.
2   This expression is used here in a generic sense. As discussed below, the expression "standards" has a defined and narrower meaning in the *TBT Agreement, ibid.,* and in Chapter Nine of the *North American Free Trade Agreement*, 17 December 1992, Can. T.S. 1994 No. 2 [NAFTA].

set of rules for sanitary and phytosanitary measures in the *SPS Agreement*. NAFTA also contains two separate sets of rules, with Section B of Chapter Seven applying to sanitary and phytosanitary measures and Chapter Nine (Technical Barriers to Trade) applying to "standards-related measures."

The correct categorization of a measure is critical to applying these WTO and NAFTA provisions. The first question to ask in applying these provisions is whether the measure is a "sanitary or phytosanitary measure" as defined in the SPS Agreement and NAFTA. If it is, the *SPS Agreement* and Section B of NAFTA Chapter Seven apply to the exclusion of the *TBT Agreement* and NAFTA Chapter Nine.[3] If the measure is not a sanitary or phytosanitary measure, the next question to ask is whether the measure is a "technical regulation," a "standard," or a "conformity assessment procedure" as defined in the *TBT Agreement* and NAFTA Chapter Nine. If it is, the *TBT Agreement* and NAFTA Chapter Nine apply. If the measure does not fall within any of these definitions, neither of these WTO agreements nor these NAFTA provisions apply.

1) Definition of a Sanitary and Phytosanitary Measure

Annex A of the *SPS Agreement* defines a "sanitary and phytosanitary measure" as any measure applied:

(a) to protect animal or plant life or health within the territory of the member from risks arising from the entry, establishment or spread of pests, diseases, disease-carrying organisms, or disease-causing organisms;

(b) to protect human or animal life or health within the territory of the member from risks arising from additives, contaminants, toxins, or disease-causing organisms in foods, beverages or feedstuffs;

(c) to protect human life or health within the territory of the member from risks arising from diseases carried by animals, plants or products thereof, or from the entry, establishment, or spread of pests; or

(d) to prevent or limit other damage in the territory of the member from the entry, establishment, or spread of pests.

The definition of "sanitary or phytosanitary measure" in NAFTA Article 724 is based on the *SPS Agreement* definition, with similar branches (a), (b), (c), and (d), but there are wording differences. For example, branch (c) of the NAFTA definition reads:

---

3   See art. 10, para. 1.5 of the *TBT Agreement*, *ibid.*, and NAFTA, *ibid.*, art. 901.

(c) protect human life or health in its territory from risks arising from a disease-causing organism or pest carried by an animal or plant, or a product thereof.

The correct categorization of a measure as a sanitary or phytosanitary measure requires a careful reading of all four branches of each of the *SPS Agreement* and NAFTA definitions. Consider, for example, a compulsory requirement respecting health warnings on cigarette packages. Branch (a) of the *SPS Agreement* (and its NAFTA counterpart) do not apply because this branch concerns only animal and plant health. Branch (b) of the *SPS Agreement* definition (and its NAFTA counterpart) do not apply because the additive, contaminant, toxin, or disease-causing organism must be contained in a food, beverage, or feedstuff, and cigarettes are none of these. Branch (c) of the *SPS Agreement* definition does not apply because tobacco-related diseases are not "carried" by animals or plants or their products. However, branch (c) of the NAFTA definition arguably does apply because a tobacco leaf could be considered to be a "disease-causing organism" and risks do arise from its use. The contrary argument is that it is the smoke from burning the tobacco leaf that causes tobacco-related diseases and not the tobacco leaf itself. Branch (d) of the *SPS Agreement* definition (and its NAFTA counterpart) do not apply because no pests are involved. As a result of this analysis, the *SPS Agreement* clearly does not apply to the measure but, on a somewhat tortured reading of branch (c) of the NAFTA definition, Section B of NAFTA Chapter Seven might apply.

2) Definitions of Technical Regulation, Standard, and Conformity Assessment Procedure

The expressions "technical regulation," "standard," and "conformity assessment procedure" are defined in Annex 1 of the *TBT Agreement* and in NAFTA Article 915. NAFTA Article 915 also defines a "standards-related measure" as being any one of a technical regulation, standard, and conformity assessment procedure. The following descriptions of the definitions are based on the *TBT Agreement* but the NAFTA definitions are virtually the same.[4]

---

[4] The NAFTA definitions of "technical regulation" and "standard" refer to services as well as to goods. However, as discussed below, NAFTA Chapter Nine applies only to land transportation and telecommunication services and not to other services.

a) Technical Regulation

A technical regulation is a document that lays down product "characteristics or their related processes and production methods, with which compliance is mandatory."[5] A technical regulation may also include or deal exclusively with terminology, symbols, packaging, marking, or labelling requirements as they apply to a product, process, or production method. The health warning requirement on cigarette packages referred to above, non-compliance with which results in a penalty, is clearly a technical regulation.

b) Standard

A standard is a document "approved by a recognized body, that provides, for common and repeated use, rules, guidelines or characteristics for goods or related processes and production methods, . . . with which compliance is not mandatory." As with technical regulations, a standard may also include or deal exclusively with terminology, symbols, packaging, marking, or labelling requirements as they apply to a product, process, or production method. Standards established by standards associations fall within this definition.

c) Conformity Assessment Procedure

A conformity assessment procedure is any procedure used, directly or indirectly, to determine that relevant requirements in technical regulations or standards are fulfilled.[6]

3) Common Themes

The WTO and NAFTA provisions covering sanitary and phytosanitary measures and technical barriers to trade (i.e., technical regulations, standards, and conformity assessment procedures or, to use the collective NAFTA expression, standards-related measures) create norms that follow common themes. However, the WTO and NAFTA provisions respecting sanitary and phytosanitary (SPS) measures differ markedly from those respecting technical barriers to trade (TBT), and each cate-

---

5   The NAFTA definition also includes the words "or services' characteristics or their related operating methods" (*ibid.*).

6   A "conformity assessment procedure," as defined in NAFTA, *ibid.*, art. 915, does not include an "approval procedure," which is separately defined as "registration, notification or other mandatory administrative procedure for granting permission for a good or service to be produced, marketed or used for a stated purpose or under stated conditions." The effect is that NAFTA requirements respecting conformity assessment procedures do not apply to approval procedures. The *TBT Agreement*, above note 1, does not make this distinction.

gory of provisions within the WTO differs in a number of significant respects from its NAFTA counterpart.

- *Right to adopt*: The SPS provisions contain a positive affirmation of the right of member countries to adopt SPS measures while the TBT provisions are less clear on this issue.
- *Risk assessment*: Governments adopt sanitary and phytosanitary measures, technical regulations, and similar measures to protect the public against risks. The assessment of risk may be a rigorous scientific process or may be based on anecdotal evidence or belief. The concern from a trade perspective is that the measure be adopted in response to a real risk and not as a means for favouring local goods over imports.
- *Level of protection and use of international standards*: Upon the determination, by whatever means, that there is a risk, the responsible body must decide upon the level of protection it wishes to establish against the risk materializing. The level of protection may range from zero tolerance (under which a risky product may be banned) to lesser levels of protection (such as labelling requirements warning of the risk). International standards exist for many products and processes. The TBT provisions encourage and the SPS provisions require the use of recognized international standards. However, each set of provisions contains the concept that member countries may choose their own level of protection.
- *Non-discrimination*: The SPS and TBT provisions both establish non-discrimination requirements, although the approach to discrimination taken in respect of sanitary and phytosanitary measures differs significantly from that taken in respect of technical barriers to trade.
- *No unnecessary obstacles*: The SPS and TBT provisions express in some manner the concept that the measures covered not create unnecessary obstacles to trade.
- *Procedural fairness — conformity assessment*: The SPS and TBT provisions set out rules governing procedures for determining that the requirements imposed by measures have been fulfilled.
- *Transparency*: The SPS and TBT provisions require that measures covered be published before implementation (with exceptions being made for emergency situations) and that member countries establish inquiry points so interested parties can receive information about the measures.

4) Scope and Coverage

a) Sanitary and Phytosanitary Measures

The *SPS Agreement* and Section B of NAFTA Chapter Seven apply to any sanitary or phytosanitary measure that directly or indirectly affects international trade or, in the case of NAFTA, trade between the NAFTA countries.[7] These provisions apply only to trade in goods and not to trade in services.

b) Technical Barriers to Trade

The *TBT Agreement* and NAFTA Chapter Nine apply to measures that are technical regulations, standards, or conformity assessment procedures that are not sanitary or phytosanitary measures.[8] The *TBT Agreement* and NAFTA Chapter Nine do not apply to specifications prepared by government bodies for government procurement purposes that are covered by the *Government Procurement Agreement* and NAFTA Chapter Ten.[9] The *TBT Agreement* applies to goods but not to services, while NAFTA Chapter Nine applies to land transportation and telecommunication services as well as to goods.[10]

5) Application to Provincial and State Laws and to Non-Governmental Organizations

a) Sanitary and Phytosanitary Measures

Article 13 of the *SPS Agreement* states that member countries are "fully responsible" for the observance of all obligations under the *SPS Agreement*. This could be construed as a requirement to ensure compliance by local governments, although no mention is made of local governments other than a requirement that member countries not take measures that require or encourage non-compliance by local governments. Member countries are obliged to take "such reasonable measures as may be available to them" to ensure compliance by non-governmental organizations.

Except for notification requirements, the NAFTA provisions respecting sanitary and phytosanitary measures are subject to NAFTA Article 105 that obliges NAFTA countries to take all necessary measures to ensure compliance by state and provincial governments. Federal governments of NAFTA countries must "seek, through appropriate measures," to ensure provincial and state compliance with notification requirements.[11]

---

7   Article 1:1 of the *SPS Agreement*, above note 1, and NAFTA, *ibid.*, art. 709.
8   The carve-out of sanitary and phytosanitary measures is in para. 1.5 of the *TBT Agreement*, above note 1, and NAFTA, *ibid.*, art. 901(1).
9   Paragraph 1.4 of art. 1 of the *TBT Agreement*, *ibid.*, and NAFTA, *ibid.*, art. 901(2).
10 See the definition of "services" in NAFTA, *ibid.*, art. 915.
11 NAFTA, *ibid.*, art. 718(2).

b) Technical Barriers to Trade

With the exception of some notification requirements, the *TBT Agreement* requires member countries to take such reasonable measures as may be available to them to ensure compliance by local governments and by non-governmental bodies.[12]

NAFTA Article 105 does not apply to the substantive provisions of NAFTA Chapter Nine. The federal government of each NAFTA country must "seek, through appropriate measures, to ensure observance" by states and provinces and by non-governmental standardizing bodies. The dictionary definition of "seek" is "to try to bring about or effect."[13] The obligation imposed is one of "best efforts" which, while not without meaning, is clearly weaker than the strong positive obligation imposed by NAFTA Article 105.

6) Right to Adopt

a) Sanitary and Phytosanitary Measures

Both the *SPS Agreement* and Section B of NAFTA Chapter Seven positively affirm the right of member countries to adopt sanitary or phytosanitary measures, so long as the requirements of the *SPS Agreement* or, in the case of NAFTA, Section B are complied with.[14] These provisions suggest that the *SPS Agreement* and Section B of NAFTA Chapter Seven are self-contained codes and that if a sanitary or phytosanitary measure satisfies their respective requirements, other WTO or NAFTA provisions may be disregarded.

b) Technical Barriers to Trade

The preamble of the *TBT Agreement* recognizes that countries should not be prevented from taking measures to ensure the quality of exports or to protect human, animal, or plant life or health or the environment or to prevent deceptive practices. However, the body of the *TBT Agreement* does not contain a positive affirmation of the right of a member country to adopt such measures.

---

12 See *TBT Agreement*, above note 1, para. 3.1 of art. 3 for Technical Regulations; para. 4.1 of art. 4 for Standards; para. 7.1 of art. 7 (Local Government Bodies); and para. 8.1 of art. 8 (Non-Governmental Bodies) for Assessment of Conformity.
13 See *The Shorter Oxford English Dictionary on Historical Principles*, vol. 2, 3d ed. (Oxford: Clarendon Press, 1973) at 1830, which contains a number of definitions of "seek," the most likely of which is intended to apply in NAFTA, above note 2, is "to try to bring about or effect."
14 Article 2:1 of the *SPS Agreement*, above note 1, and NAFTA, *ibid.*, art. 712(1).

NAFTA Article 904(1) provides that a NAFTA country "may, in accordance with this Agreement, adopt, maintain or apply any standards-related measure, including any such measure relating to safety, the protection of human, animal or plant life or health, the environment or consumers, and any measure to ensure its enforcement or implementation." As the "Agreement" is NAFTA, this provision is tautological because a NAFTA country may adopt, maintain, or apply any measure that is in accordance with NAFTA. The tautological aspect of Article 904(1) may give rise to interpretative difficulties because although its drafters may have intended it as a meaningless provision to give comfort to environmentalists, a NAFTA panel could be persuaded to give meaning to the provision on the basis of the principle of effectiveness enunciated by the Appellate Body in *Japan — Taxes on Alcoholic Beverages* discussed in chapter 1 under "Tautological Provisions and the Principle of Effectiveness."

7) Risk Assessment

a) Sanitary and Phytosanitary Measures
Both the *SPS Agreement* and Section B of NAFTA Chapter Seven require that sanitary and phytosanitary measures be based on an assessment of risk and on scientific evidence or scientific principles.[15] Each agreement lists the factors that are to be taken into account in assessment of risk.[16]

b) Technical Barriers to Trade
Neither the *TBT Agreement* nor NAFTA Chapter Nine requires that technical regulations or standards be based upon an assessment of risk. The *TBT Agreement* is silent on the subject of risk assessment. NAFTA Article 907(1) provides that a NAFTA country may conduct a risk assessment and lists the factors that may be taken into account.

8) Level of Protection and Use of International Standards

a) Sanitary and Phytosanitary Measures
Both the *SPS Agreement* and Section B of NAFTA Chapter Seven require that member countries base their sanitary or phytosanitary measures on

---

15 See *SPS Agreement*, ibid., art. 5:1 (assessment of risk) & art. 2:2 (scientific evidence). The corresponding (but differently worded) NAFTA, ibid., provisions are arts. 712(3)(c) & (a). The *SPS Agreement* art. 5:7 and NAFTA art. 715(4) each permits provisional measures when relevant scientific information is not available.
16 See *SPS Agreement*, ibid., art. 5, para. 2 & 3. See NAFTA, ibid., art. 715.

international standards, guidelines, or recommendations where they exist,[17] and each agreement creates a presumption that sanitary or phytosanitary measures that conform to international standards, guidelines, or recommendations are consistent with the requirements of the *SPS Agreement* or, in the case of NAFTA, NAFTA requirements.[18] However, Article 5:3 of the *SPS Agreement* permits member countries to introduce or maintain sanitary or phytosanitary measures that provide for a higher level of protection than would be achieved through international standards, provided that there is scientific justification for the higher level of protection.[19] NAFTA contains a stronger affirmation of the right of NAFTA countries to choose the appropriate level of protection. NAFTA Article 712(2) states that, notwithstanding any other provision in Section B of NAFTA Chapter Seven, NAFTA countries may establish appropriate levels of protection in accordance with Article 715. Article 715(2) lists factors that must be considered in establishing an appropriate level of protection respecting the introduction, establishment, or spread of an animal or plant pest or disease.

b) Technical Barriers to Trade

The *TBT Agreement* and NAFTA Chapter Nine both require that member countries use relevant international standards[20] as the basis for technical regulations and standards unless their use would be ineffective or inappropriate.[21] The *TBT Agreement* also provides that, where appropriate, technical regulations and standards be based on product requirements in terms of performance rather than design or descriptive characteristics.[22] NAFTA Chapter Nine does not contain a comparable provision.

The *TBT Agreement* does not contain a positive affirmation to the effect that a member country may establish the level of protection that it considers appropriate. However, NAFTA Article 904(2) provides that a NAFTA country may, in pursuing its legitimate objectives of "safety or the protection of human, animal or plant life or health, the environ-

---

17 *SPS Agreement*, ibid., art. 3:1. NAFTA, *ibid.*, art. 713(1). The expression "international standard, guideline or recommendation" is defined in the *SPS Agreement*, Annex A, para. 3 and in NAFTA, art. 724.
18 *SPS Agreement*, ibid., art. 3:2. NAFTA, *ibid.*, art. 713(2).
19 *SPS Agreement*, ibid., art. 5:3.
20 See definitions of "international standard" and "international standardizing body" in NAFTA, above note 2, art. 915.
21 *TBT Agreement*, above note 1, art. 2, para. 2.4 (technical regulations) and Annex 3, para. F (standards). NAFTA, *ibid.*, art. 905(1).
22 *TBT Agreement, ibid.*, art. 2, para. 2.8 (technical regulations) and Annex 3, para. I (standards).

ment or consumers," establish the level of protection that it considers appropriate.[23] The level of protection chosen may be higher than that afforded by a relevant international standard.

9) Non-Discrimination

a) Sanitary and Phytosanitary Measures

The *SPS Agreement* and NAFTA both require that member countries ensure that sanitary and phytosanitary measures do not arbitrarily or unjustifiably discriminate between members where identical or similar conditions prevail.[24] The *SPS Agreement* provides that sanitary or phytosanitary measures not be applied in a manner that would constitute a disguised restriction on international trade.[25] The *SPS Agreement* and Section B of NAFTA Chapter Seven also require that member countries avoid arbitrary or unjustifiable discrimination when applying or establishing the appropriate level of protection.[26]

These provisions impose a lower standard than national treatment because the prohibited discrimination must be arbitrary and unjustifiable, suggesting that discrimination that is non-arbitrary or justifiable is permitted.[27] NAFTA Article 710 specifically excludes sanitary and phytosanitary measures from the application of the national treatment requirements of NAFTA Article 301. The *SPS Agreement* does not specifically exclude the application of the national treatment requirements of Article III of GATT 1994, but the general interpretative note to Annex 1A of the *WTO Agreement*[28] coupled with the affirmation of the right of member countries to take sanitary and phytosanitary measures consistent with the *SPS Agreement*[29] have the same effect.

---

23 Subject to certain principles of non-discrimination in NAFTA, above note 2, art. 907(2), discussed below.
24 *SPS Agreement*, above note 1, art. 2:3. NAFTA, *ibid.*, art. 712(4).
25 *SPS Agreement*, *ibid.*, art. 2:3.
26 *SPS Agreement*, *ibid.*, art. 5:5. NAFTA, above note 2, art. 715(3)(b).
27 The considerations raised by the Appellate Body in its decision in *U.S. — Standards for Reformulated and Conventional Gasoline*, WT/DS2/AB/R, Appellate Body Report (AB-1996-1), are relevant to interpreting this language. See discussion in chapter 2 under "Third Element: Inconsistent Measure Satisfies Introductory Clause of Article XX."
28 Which provides that the other agreements listed in Annex 1A of the *WTO Agreement*, above note 1, prevail over the *General Agreement on Tariffs and Trade 1994* [GATT 1994] set out in Annex 1A to the *WTO Agreement* to the extent of any inconsistency.
29 *SPS Agreement*, above note 1, art. 2:1, discussed above.

b) Technical Barriers to Trade

The non-discrimination provisions of the *TBT Agreement* and NAFTA Chapter Nine are based on national treatment. The provisions of the *TBT Agreement* respecting technical regulations and standards both require that products of other member countries be accorded no less favourable treatment than like products of national origin.[30] Unlike the NAFTA sanitary and phytosanitary provisions, which provide that Article 301 does not apply, NAFTA Article 904(3) expressly requires that NAFTA countries accord national treatment in accordance with NAFTA Article 301 and its services counterpart, NAFTA Article 1202 in respect of its standards-related measures.

10) No Obstacles to Trade

a) Sanitary and Phytosanitary Measures

Both the *SPS Agreement* and Section B of NAFTA Chapter Seven require that in determining the appropriate level of protection, a member country should take into account the objective of minimizing negative trade effects.[31] Article 5:6 of the *SPS Agreement* requires that a measure not be more trade restrictive than necessary to achieve the appropriate level of protection determined by the member country. NAFTA Article 712(5) adopts a slightly different approach by requiring that a sanitary or phytosanitary measure be applied only to the extent necessary to achieve the level of protection that the NAFTA country has determined to be appropriate.

b) Technical Barriers to Trade

Both the *TBT Agreement* and NAFTA Chapter Nine require that technical regulations and standards not create unnecessary obstacles to international trade or, in the case of NAFTA, trade between the Parties (i.e., the NAFTA countries).[32] To be inconsistent with this provision, a measure must create an obstacle to the trade between countries and not just to trade within a single country. The *TBT Agreement* also requires that technical regulations be no more trade-restrictive than necessary to achieve a legitimate objective.[33] NAFTA Chapter Nine does not contain a counterpart to this provision.

---

30 *TBT Agreement*, above note 1, art. 2, para. 2.1 (technical regulations) and Annex 3, para. D (standards).
31 *SPS Agreement*, above note 1, art 5:4. NAFTA, above note 2, art. 715(3)(a).
32 *TBT Agreement*, above note 1, art. 2, para. 2.1 (technical regulations) and Annex 3, para. E (standards). NAFTA, *ibid.*, art. 904(4) (all standards-related measures).
33 *TBT Agreement, ibid.*, art. 2, para. 2.2. The concept of "legitimate objective" is discussed below.

The *TBT Agreement* and NAFTA Chapter Nine deem certain provisions that achieve "legitimate objectives" not to be obstacles to trade. Both agreements include safety and the protection of human, animal, or plant life or health and the environment as "legitimate objectives."[34] The *TBT Agreement* also includes national security requirements and the prevention of deceptive practices, while the NAFTA definition includes protection of consumers and sustainable development. The deeming provision in the *TBT Agreement* covers only technical regulations that are in accordance with relevant international standards. Such technical regulations are rebuttably presumed not to create obstacles to international trade.[35] The deeming provision in NAFTA Chapter Nine is much broader. NAFTA Article 904(4) provides that an unnecessary obstacle to trade "shall not be deemed to be created" where the demonstrable purpose of the measure is to achieve a legitimate objective and the measure does not exclude goods of other NAFTA countries that meet that objective. NAFTA Article 905(2) also provides that standards-related measures that are in accordance with international standards shall be presumed to be consistent with NAFTA requirements respecting non-discrimination and not creating unnecessary obstacles to trade.

11) Procedural Fairness: Conformity Assessment

a) Sanitary and Phytosanitary Measures
Annex C of the *SPS Agreement* and NAFTA Article 717 set out provisions respecting control, inspection, and approval procedures which require that these procedures be applied expeditiously and in a manner consistent with both national treatment and MFN treatment. The provisions also establish norms respecting processing periods, fees, confidential and proprietary information, siting of facilities, and minimization of inconvenience.

b) Technical Barriers to Trade
Article 5 of the *TBT Agreement*[36] and NAFTA Article 908 set out requirements respecting conformity assessment. Procedures must be expeditious and the processing of applications must be undertaken in a non-discriminatory order. These requirements also establish norms respecting

---

34 *TBT Agreement*, ibid., art. 2, para. 2.1. NAFTA, above note 2, art. 915, under the definition of "legitimate objective."
35 *TBT Agreement*, ibid., art. 2, para. 2.5.
36 *Ibid.*, art. 5 applies to central government bodies. Article 7 sets out procedures for assessment of conformity by local bodies.

publishing or communicating processing periods, processing applications, information that may be requested, treatment of confidential and proprietary information, imposition of fees, location of facilities, requiring samples, and dealing with modifications subsequent to approval. Article 6 of the *TBT Agreement* and NAFTA Article 907(6) require that member countries accept the results of the conformity assessment procedures conducted in other member countries where they are satisfied that the procedure offers an assurance of compliance with its own technical regulations or standards.

12) Transparency

a) Sanitary and Phytosanitary Measures
Both the *SPS Agreement* and Section B of NAFTA Chapter Seven set out requirements respecting notification, publication, and provision of information respecting the adoption and modification of sanitary and phytosanitary measures, and the establishment of inquiry points to answer reasonable inquiries from affected persons.[37]

b) Technical Barriers to Trade
NAFTA Articles 909 and 910 set out provisions respecting notification, publication, provision of information, and establishment of inquiry points that closely resemble those in Section B of NAFTA Chapter Seven. The requirements of the *TBT Agreement* are less stringent. Proposed technical regulations and conformity assessment procedures need be published only when there is no international standard or guide or recommendation or the regulation or procedure is not in accordance with a relevant international standard or guide or recommendation.[38] Once adopted, all technical regulations and conformity assessment procedures must be published.[39] Standards must be published before adoption, with opportunity for comment, and once adopted standards must be published.[40]

---

37 *SPS Agreement*, above note 1, Annex B. NAFTA, above note 2, arts. 718 & 719.
38 *TBT Agreement*, above note 1, art. 2, paras. 2.9 & 2.10 for technical regulations; art. 5, paras. 5.6 & 5.7 for conformity assessment procedures.
39 *Ibid.*, art. 2, para. 2.11 for technical regulations and art. 5, para. 5.8.
40 *Ibid.*, Annex 3, paras. L & O.

13) Application of Exceptions in Article XX of GATT 1994

The exceptions in Article XX of GATT 1994 apply only to the provisions of GATT 1994 and not to the other multilateral agreements, including the *SPS Agreement* and the *TBT Agreement*. A measure that does not comply with the provisions of the *SPS Agreement* or the *TBT Agreement* cannot be justified under either agreement on the basis of an exception in Article XX of GATT 1994.

Section B of NAFTA Chapter Seven is included in Part Two of NAFTA (Trade in Goods) and, as such, is subject to the exceptions in Article XX that are incorporated by NAFTA Article 2101 (see chapter 2). However, NAFTA Article 710 expressly provides that the human, animal, and plant life or health exception in Article XX(b) does not apply to sanitary or phytosanitary measures. It is unlikely that any of the other exceptions in Article XX would be relevant to a sanitary or phytosanitary measure.

The Article XX exceptions incorporated by NAFTA Article 2101 apply to Part III of NAFTA (Technical Barriers to Trade), except to the extent that Part III applies to services. Therefore, a measure that did not meet the requirements of NAFTA Chapter Nine could nonetheless be justified under Article XX, provided that the requirements of that Article were satisfied.

14) Environmental Issues

Despite the obvious linkages between trade matters and measures taken to protect the environment (such as restrictions of imports of hazardous products, technical regulations imposing product and process standards, etc.), neither the WTO agreements nor the NAFTA text deal with environmental issues in any sort of comprehensive way.[41] GATT 1947, which was drafted at a time when environmental issues were not regarded as significant, does not mention the environment. The drafters of the WTO agreements were more sensitive about environmental issues. Environmental protection is included as a "legitimate objective" in the *TBT Agreement* and, provided that certain conditions are satisfied, subsidies for the adaptation of existing facilities to new environmental requirements are not actionable under the *Subsidies Agreement*. The *Decision on Trade and the Environment* made at Marrakesh established a Committee on Trade and

---

41 The same observation applies to the *Canada–Israel Free Trade Agreement*, in force 1 January 1997, see http://www.dfait-maeci.gc.ca/english/trade/agrement.htm and the *Canada–Chile Free Trade Agreement*, in force 5 July 1997, see http://www.dfait-maeci.gc.ca/english/trade/agrement.htm.

the Environment to address trade and environmental issues. The drafters of the NAFTA text went a little further. In addition to expressly clarifying that measures necessary to protect the environment are included in the exception in GATT Article XX(b), NAFTA Article 104 provides that the provisions of a number of major environmental and conservation agreements prevail over NAFTA to the extent of inconsistencies.[42]

As mentioned in the "Overview," the *Environmental Cooperation Agreement* was negotiated and entered into by the three NAFTA countries as a result of pressure exerted by U.S. environmental groups during the NAFTA approval process. The *Environmental Cooperation Agreement* (sometimes referred to as the NAAEC) is a comprehensive arrangement among the three NAFTA countries that establishes the North American Commission for Environmental Cooperation (CEC) composed of a council (consisting of the cabinet level or equivalent representatives of the NAFTA countries), a secretariat, and a Joint Public Advisory Committee. The CEC is responsible for promoting environmental enforcement as well as providing a forum for dispute resolution. Disputes are settled through an arbitral process under which the government of a NAFTA country can complain that another NAFTA country is engaging in a "persistent pattern" of not enforcing its environmental laws. The process begins with consultations and, failing resolution, proceeds to an arbitral panel. Failure to implement recommendations of a panel can result in a monetary assessment and suspension of benefits or failure to pay same.[43]

15) Labour Issues

Neither the WTO agreements nor NAFTA deal specifically with labour issues.[44] However, the *Labour Cooperation Agreement* came into being as a direct result of pressure from labour groups in the United States and their political supporters during the U.S. NAFTA approval process.

---

42 *Convention on International Trade in Endangered Species of Wild Fauna and Flora*, 3 March 1973, U.K.T.S. 1976 101, 12 I.L.M. 1085, am. 22 June 1979, U.K.T.S. 1980 33; *Montreal Protocol on Substances that Deplete the Ozone Layer*, 16 September 1987, U.K.T.S. 1990 19, 26 I.L.M. 1550, am. 29 June 1990; *Basel Convention on the Control of Transboundary Movements of Hazardous Wastes and Their Disposal*, 22 March 1989, 28 I.L.M. 657; as well as several bilateral agreements described in Annex 104.1. CCFTA, *ibid.*, art. A-04 contains a similar provision respecting these international conventions. There are no comparable provisions in CIFTA, *ibid.*

43 There is a special procedure that applies to Canada set out in Annex 36A of the *North American Agreement on Environment Cooperation*, 14 September 1993, Can. T.S. 1994 No. 3.

44 The same observation applies to CIFTA, above note 41, and CCFTA, above note 41.

Their concerns were expressly directed at potential competitive disadvantages to U.S. workers resulting from substandard Mexican labour standards and their lax enforcement. Like its environmental counterpart, this agreement does not contain any substantive requirements in respect of the laws and regulations that it covers (other than the somewhat vague requirement that the standards provided be "high") but is concerned with their enforcement. As under the *Environmental Cooperation Agreement*, a complaint by a NAFTA country commences with consultations and, provided that the matter is "trade-related," proceeds to evaluation by an Evaluation Committee of Experts. If the report of the committee discloses a persistent pattern of failure to enforce laws or regulations respecting occupational safety and health, child labour or minimum wages, further consultations take place and ultimately the matter proceeds to an arbitral panel. A NAFTA country against which a finding is made that does not implement the recommendations of a panel may have to pay an enforcement assessment.

B. INTELLECTUAL PROPERTY

The *TRIPS Agreement* and NAFTA Chapter Seventeen create parallel obligations respecting intellectual property rights. NAFTA Chapter Seventeen is based on the draft version of the TRIPS Agreement that existed at the time that NAFTA was being negotiated. The *TRIPS Agreement* and NAFTA Chapter Seventeen are structured in a similar manner, cover more or less the same intellectual property rights and contain roughly similar provisions. However, there are significant differences between the two agreements.

International recognition of intellectual property rights is not new. International conventions covering patents, trademarks, and trade names, industrial designs, and copyright have existed in one form or another for more than a century. More recent conventions cover such subject matter as phonograms (sound recordings), integrated circuits, and new plant varieties. The problem perceived by the Uruguay Round negotiators (at least those representing developed countries) and their NAFTA counterparts was that the means for enforcing internationally recognized intellectual property rights, both at the international level and through the legal systems within many countries, were woefully inadequate.

The *TRIPS Agreement* and NAFTA Chapter Seventeen each contains the following basic provisions:

- *International conventions*: Each agreement requires that member countries comply with or give effect to the substantive provisions of major international intellectual property conventions.

- *Creation of norms*: Each agreement establishes norms for various categories of intellectual property that expand upon the norms set out in the conventions.
- *Procedural fairness*: Each agreement sets out requirements that must be incorporated into the domestic law of each member country respecting civil and administrative procedures for enforcement of intellectual property rights, provision of interim relief in infringement cases, criminal procedures, and penalties for trademark counterfeiting and copyright piracy, and enforcement of intellectual property rights at the border.
- *Dispute resolution*: Each agreement provides for full access to dispute settlement procedures for claims arising both from breaches of the *TRIPS Agreement* provisions or those of NAFTA Chapter Seventeen *and* from breaches of the international intellectual property conventions to which effect must be given.

1) Scope and Coverage

The *TRIPS Agreement* and NAFTA Chapter Seventeen provide for the protection of "intellectual property rights" which, in both agreements, include copyright and related rights, trademark rights, patent rights, rights in layout designs of semiconductor integrated circuits, trade secret rights, rights in geographic indications, and industrial design rights.[45] The NAFTA definition of intellectual property rights also includes plant breeder rights.

2) Use of International Conventions

The *TRIPS Agreement* requires that member countries comply with specified provisions of the *Paris Convention for the Protection of Industrial Property*, 1967 (*Paris Convention*),[46] the *Berne Convention for the Protection of Literary and Artistic Works*, 1971 (*Berne Convention*),[47] and the *Treaty on Intellectual Property in Respect of Integrated Circuits*, opened

---

45 For the definitions, see *TRIPS Agreement*, above note 1, art. 1:2, and NAFTA, above note 2, art. 1721.
46 *TRIPS Agreement*, ibid., art. 2:1. The provisions of the *Paris Convention for the Protection of Industrial Property*, 20 March 1883, 828 U.N.T.S. 305 [*Paris Convention*] referred to are arts. 1 through 12 and art. 19.
47 *TRIPS Agreement*, ibid., art. 9:1. The provisions of the *Berne Convention for the Protection of Literary and Artistic Works*, September 1886, Can. T.S. 1948 No. 2 [*Berne Convention*] referred to are art. 1 through 21.

for signature on 26 May 1989 (*Integrated Circuits Treaty*).[48] NAFTA Article 1701(2) requires that NAFTA countries give effect to the substantive provisions of the *Paris Convention* and the *Berne Convention*, as well as to the *Geneva Convention for the Protection of Producers of Phonograms Against Unauthorized Duplication of their Phonograms*, 1971 (*Geneva Convention*), the *International Convention for the Protection of New Varieties of Plants*, 1978 (*UPOV Convention 1978*), and the *International Convention for the Protection of New Varieties of Plants*, 1991 (*UPOV Convention 1991*). NAFTA Article 1710(1) also requires that NAFTA countries protect layout designs in accordance with specified provisions of the *Integrated Circuits Treaty*.

The *TRIPS Agreement* and NAFTA also make reference to the *International Convention for the Protection of Performers, Producers of Phonograms and Broadcasting Organizations*, adopted at Rome on 26 October 1961 (*Rome Convention*), although neither agreement requires that member countries give effect to its provisions.

a) **Paris Convention**
The original version of the *Paris Convention* entered into force in 1884 and the *Paris Convention* was revised in 1900, 1911, 1925, 1934, 1958, and 1967. The *Paris Convention* provides for the protection by member countries of patents, utility models, industrial designs, trademarks, service marks, trade names, and indications of source or appellations of origin. Article 4 provides that a person who files an application for a patent, utility model, industrial design, or trademark in one Union country will have a right or priority for twelve months for patents and utility models and six months for industrial designs and trademarks for filing in other Union countries. Article 6*quinquies* provides that, with certain exceptions,[49] a trademark registered in its country of origin shall be accepted for filing and protected *as is* in other member countries. Article 6*bis* requires countries of the Union, where confusion is likely, to refuse or to cancel the registration and prohibit the use of a trademark which is a reproduction, imitation, or translation of a trademark that is already the trademark of a person entitled to the benefits of the convention and that is well known. The *Paris Convention* also sets out general

---

48 *TRIPS Agreement*, ibid., art. 35. The provisions of the *Treaty on Intellectual Property in Respect of Integrated Circuits*, 26 May 1989, 28 I.L.M. 1484 [*Integrated Circuits Treaty*] referred to are arts. 2 through 7 (other than para. 3 of art. 6), art. 12, & para. 3 of art. 16.

49 For example, if the mark infringes rights acquired by third parties, or if it is devoid of distinctive character, or if it is contrary to morality or public order.

requirements respecting the repression of unfair competition. Article 10*bis* requires that member countries assure nationals of other member countries effective protection against unfair competition, which is broadly defined as "[e]very act of competition contrary to honest practices in industrial or commercial matters."[50]

b) *Berne Convention*

The *Berne Convention* was originally signed in 1886 and was revised in 1908, 1928, 1948, 1967, and 1971. The *Berne Convention* covers "literary and artistic works," which are broadly defined to include books and various other written works; musical composition; cinematographic works; works of drawing, painting, architecture, sculpture, engraving, and lithography; photographic works; works of applied art; and illustrations, maps, plans, sketches, and three-dimensional works relative to geography, topography, architecture, and science. These works are to be protected in all member countries and the protection operates to the benefit of the "author" of the work and his or her successors. The basic protection required by the *Berne Convention* lasts for the life of the author and fifty years after the author's death.

c) *Geneva Convention* and the *Rome Convention*

The *Geneva Convention* was done at Geneva on 29 October 1971 and applies to producers of phonograms. A phonogram is an "exclusively aural fixation of sounds of a performance or of other sounds" such as a record, a cassette tape, or a CD disc, and the producer is the person or legal entity who first fixes the sounds.[51] Copyright in phonograms or sound recordings exists independently from the copyright in the work that is recorded. While the producer of a sound recording needs the authorization of the holder of the copyright in the work being recorded, the producer will hold an independent copyright in the resulting sound recording. The *Geneva Convention* obliges member countries to protect producers of phonograms who are nationals of other member countries against making duplicates of phonograms without consent for distribution to the public or importing duplicates for such distribution.

The *Rome Convention* provides protection to performers and broadcasting organizations as well as to producers of phonograms.

---

50 *Paris Convention*, above note 46, art. 10*bis*, para. 2.
51 *Geneva Convention for the Protection of Producers of Phonograms Against Unauthorized Duplication of their Phonograms*, 29 October 1971, 866 U.N.T.S. 67, T.I.A.S. 7808 [*Geneva Convention*], art. 1(a).

d) UPOV Convention 1978 and UPOV Convention 1991

The original *UPOV Convention* was done in 1961 and was revised in 1972, 1978, and 1991. The NAFTA text makes reference to both the *UPOV Convention 1978* and the *UPOV Convention 1991*. The purpose of both conventions is to protect the rights of breeders in new varieties of plants. To be entitled to protection, the variety must be new, distinguishable (1978) or distinct (1991), homogeneous (1978) or uniform (1991), and stable. The minimum period of protection under the *UPOV Convention 1978* is fifteen years and under the *UPOV Convention 1991* is twenty-five years for trees and vines and twenty years for other plants.

e) Integrated Circuits Treaty

The *Integrated Circuits Treaty* was adopted in Washington on 26 May 1989 and obliges each member country to provide intellectual property protection to layout designs of integrated circuits within its territory.[52] The layout design must be original (i.e., the work of the creator's own intellectual effort) and not commonplace.

3) Extension of Protection to "Nationals"

The protection of intellectual property rights afforded by the *TRIPS Agreement* and NAFTA Chapter Seventeen extends to "nationals of other Members" in the case of the *TRIPS Agreement* and "nationals of another Party" in the case of NAFTA. These expressions are defined in each agreement as persons who would be eligible for protection under the international convention that applies to the category of intellectual property under consideration.[53]

If the intellectual property right is a patent, utility model, industrial design, trademark, service mark, trade name, or an indication of source or appellation of origin (i.e., geographic indication), a national of another member or Party is a person who would be eligible for protection under the *Paris Convention*. The protection afforded by the *Paris Convention* applies to nationals of a member country and to nationals of other countries who are domiciled in a member country or have "real and effective commercial establishments" in a member country. A national of another member or Party for copyright purposes is a person eligible for protection under the *Berne Convention*. A national of another member or Party for purposes of layout designs is a person eligible for

---

52 Above note 48. See F.M. Abbott, "Introductory Note" (1989) 28 I.L.M. 1477.
53 See *TRIPS Agreement*, above note 1, art. 1, para. 3, and the definition of "nationals of another Party" in NAFTA, above note 2, art. 1721.

protection under the *Integrated Circuits Treaty*. A national of another Party for right to protection of a phonogram under NAFTA is a person eligible for protection under the *Geneva Convention*,[54] whereas a national of a member for protection of phonograms and broadcasts under the *TRIPS Agreement* is a person eligible for protection under the *Rome Convention*.[55] Under NAFTA, a national of another Party for breeders' rights purposes is a person who would be eligible for protection under the *UPOV Convention 1978* or the *UPOV Convention 1991*.

If the intellectual property right in question is not covered by one of the conventions, as is the case with trade secret rights, a national under the *TRIPS Agreement* is a person, legal or natural, who is domiciled or who has a real and effective industrial or commercial establishment in a member country,[56] while under NAFTA a national is an individual who is a citizen or permanent resident of a NAFTA country.[57]

4) Establishment of Norms: General Provisions

a) Principles of Non-Discrimination

i) National Treatment
The *TRIPS Agreement* and NAFTA Chapter Seventeen each set out national treatment obligations requiring that member countries accord to nationals of other member countries treatment no less favourable than they accord to their own nationals.[58] The *TRIPS Agreement* obligation is subject to the exceptions in the *Paris Convention*, the *Berne Convention*, the *Rome Convention*, and the *Integrated Circuits Treaty*, whereas the NAFTA obligation is not so qualified.

---

54 The definition of "nationals of another Party" in NAFTA, *ibid.*, art. 1721, refers to both the *Geneva Convention*, above note 51, and the *International Convention for the Protection of Peformers, Producers of Phonograms and Broadcasting Organizations*, 26 October 1961, 496 U.N.T.S. 43, U.K.T.S. 1964 38 [*Rome Convention*], both of which cover phonograms. Presumably the *Geneva Convention* determined the definition of "national" in respect of phonograms because NAFTA requires that effect be given to the *Geneva Convention* but not to the *Rome Convention*.
55 The *Geneva Convention*, *ibid.*, and the Rome Convention, *ibid.*, both cover phonograms. However, unlike NAFTA, *ibid.*, the *TRIPS Agreement*, above note 1, does not refer to the *Geneva Convention* but does refer to the *Rome Convention* in art. 1, para. 3.
56 See footnote 1 in *TRIPS Agreement*, *ibid.*, art. 1, para. 3.
57 NAFTA, above note 2, art. 1721.
58 *TRIPS Agreement*, above note 1, art. 3. NAFTA, *ibid.*, art. 1703. Each agreement permits limited derogations from the national treatment obligation in respect of its judicial or administrative procedures to the extent permitted by the relevant convention. See *TRIPS Agreement*, art. 3, para. 2, and NAFTA, art. 1703(3).

ii) Most-Favoured-Nation Treatment

Article 4 of the *TRIPS Agreement* sets out a most-favoured-nation obligation that requires that advantages, favours, privileges, and immunities granted to one member country be extended to all member countries. NAFTA does not contain a comparable provision.

b) Control of Abusive or Anticompetitive Practices

Both the *TRIPS Agreement* and NAFTA recognize the potential conflict between protection of intellectual property rights and the objective of competition policy of restricting anticompetitive conduct. Each agreement permits member countries to specify licensing practices or conditions that constitute an abuse of intellectual property rights because they have an adverse effect on competition and to take appropriate measures consistent with the *TRIPS Agreement* or NAFTA, as the case may be, to prevent or control such practices or conditions.[59]

5) Establishment of Norms: Requirements Respecting Specific Categories of Intellectual Property

The *TRIPS Agreement* and NAFTA set out specific requirements respecting copyright, sound recordings, trademarks, geographical indications, industrial designs, patents, layout designs of integrated circuits, and protection of undisclosed information (trade secrets). NAFTA also sets out provisions respecting encrypted program-carrying satellite signals. The requirements of each agreement supplement and, to some extent modify, the obligations set out in the relevant conventions. The requirements of each agreement respecting each category of intellectual property are briefly summarized below.

a) Copyright

The *TRIPS Agreement* and NAFTA both provide that computer programs and compilations of data are literary works within the meaning of the *Berne Convention* and shall be protected as such.[60] The *Berne Convention* does not specifically mention computer programs or compilations of data. Article 11 of the *TRIPS Agreement* requires that member countries provide authors with the right to authorize or prohibit the rental of computer programs and cinematographic works. NAFTA

---

59 *TRIPS Agreement*, ibid., art. 40. NAFTA, ibid., art. 1704.
60 *TRIPS Agreement*, ibid., art. 10. NAFTA, ibid., art. 1705(2). In the case of compilations of data, the protection does not extend to the data itself.

Article 1705(2) sets out a similar right respecting computer programs, as well as other actions in respect to copyright that authors can authorize or prohibit, such as importation. Article 13 of the *TRIPS Agreement* and NAFTA Article 1705(4) provide that (except for photographic works and works of applied art) where the duration of protection is based other than on the life of a natural person, the term of protection must be at least fifty years from the end of the calendar year in which the first authorized publication occurred or, failing that, the end of the calendar year of making.

b) Sound Recordings

Article 14 of the *TRIPS Agreement* provides that performers, producers of phonograms (sound recordings), and broadcast organizations shall have the right to prohibit certain acts undertaken without their authorization. For example, a performer shall have the right to prohibit the fixation on a phonogram of an unfixed performance and the reproduction of such a fixation.[61] A broadcasting organization can also prohibit the fixation of broadcasts and the reproduction of fixations, as well as the rebroadcasting of broadcasts.[62] The protection accorded to performers and producers of phonograms is to last fifty years from the end of the year in which the performance took place or the fixation was made. The duration of the protection for broadcast organizations is twenty years.[63]

NAFTA Article 1706 sets out requirements respecting sound recordings but, unlike the *TRIPS Agreement*, does not cover performers or broadcast organizations.[64] NAFTA Article 1706(1) requires each NAFTA country to provide the producer of a sound recording with the right to authorize or prohibit acts such as the direct or indirect reproduction of the sound recording, importation of copies of the sound recording, and the first public distribution (by sale, rental or otherwise). Like the *TRIPS Agreement*, NAFTA Article 1706(2) requires a term of protection for sound recordings of fifty years from the calendar year of fixation, which is a significantly more stringent standard than the twenty-year term provided for in the *Geneva Convention*.

---

61 *TRIPS Agreement*, ibid., art. 14:1.
62 *TRIPS Agreement*, ibid., art. 14:3.
63 *TRIPS Agreement*, ibid., art. 14:5.
64 Note, however, that art. 2006 of the *Canada–United States Free Trade Agreement*, 22 December 1987, Can. T.S. 1989 No. 3, 27 I.L.M. 281 [CUFTA], sets out rules respecting cable retransmission of transmissions carried on distant signals intended for free television. The effect of NAFTA, above note 2, Annex 2106, is to incorporate this provision into NAFTA.

c) Trademarks

Article 15:1 of the *TRIPS Agreement* defines a trademark as being any "sign or any combination of signs, capable of distinguishing the goods and services of one undertaking from those of other undertakings" and NAFTA Article 1708(1) defines a trademark in virtually the same terms. The *TRIPS Agreement* and NAFTA establish the basic right of a trademark holder to prevent persons, without consent, from using identical or similar signs in connection with goods or services for which the trademark is registered where such use would cause confusion.[65] The *TRIPS Agreement* and NAFTA permit member countries to make registrability depend on use but prevent a member country from refusing registration solely because intended use has not occurred within three years of the application date.[66]

The *TRIPS Agreement* and NAFTA both provide that the nature of goods or services to which a trademark is to be applied will not form an obstacle to registration.[67] The *TRIPS Agreement* and NAFTA both extend application of the *Paris Convention* provision in Article 6bis respecting well-known marks to services.[68] NAFTA Article 1708(7) provides for a minimum initial registration term of ten years and that registrations be renewable indefinitely for successive ten-year terms, while Article 18 of the *TRIPS Agreement* provides for an initial seven-year term and that registrations be renewable indefinitely. NAFTA Article 1708(8) requires that a trademark must be used for registration to be maintained and that registration may, subject to some extenuating circumstances, be cancelled after two uninterrupted years of non-use. Article 19:1 of the *TRIPS Agreement* is permissive as to requiring use, and the period of non-use is three years.

Article 20 of the *TRIPS Agreement* and NAFTA Article 1708(10) both provide that the use of a trademark may not be encumbered with special requirements, such as a use that reduces the trademark's function as an indication of source or a use with another trademark. The *TRIPS Agreement* provision uses the expression "unjustifiably encumber," suggesting that some encumbrances may be justified. The NAFTA text does not contain a similar qualifier.

Article 21 of the *TRIPS Agreement* and NAFTA Article 1708(11) permit member countries to determine the conditions of licensing and

---

65 *TRIPS Agreement*, above note 1, art. 16:1. NAFTA, *ibid.*, art. 1708(2).
66 *TRIPS Agreement*, *ibid.*, art. 15:3. NAFTA, *ibid.*, art. 1708(3).
67 *TRIPS Agreement*, *ibid.*, art. 15:4. NAFTA, *ibid.*, art. 1708(5). There is a similar provision in art. 7 of the *Paris Convention*, above note 46, that refers only to goods.
68 *TRIPS Agreement*, *ibid.*, art. 16:2. NAFTA, *ibid.*, art. 1708(6).

assignment of trademarks, but prohibit compulsory licensing. These provisions also affirm the right of a trademark owner to assign its trademark.

NAFTA Article 1708(13) requires NAFTA countries to prohibit the registration of words that generically describe goods or services in English, French, or Spanish and to refuse to register trademarks that consist of immoral, deceptive, or scandalous matter. These provisions do not have counterparts in the *TRIPS Agreement*.

d) Geographical Indications

A geographic indication is an indication identifying a good as originating in a particular country or a region or locality of a country where particular quality, reputation, or other characteristic of the good is essentially attributable to its geographical origin.[69] Article 22 of the *TRIPS Agreement* and NAFTA Article 1712 contain various provisions that give the legal means to interested persons of preventing the use of various methods of misrepresenting the true origin of goods so as to mislead the public as to their geographical origin. Article 23 of the *TRIPS Agreement* also sets out specific provisions for additional protection for geographical indications respecting wine and distilled spirits.

e) Industrial Designs

The requirements respecting industrial designs are set out in Articles 25 and 26 of the *TRIPS Agreement* and NAFTA Article 1713. Member countries must provide for the protection of independently created industrial designs that are new and original. An owner of a protected design will have the right to prevent other persons from making or selling articles for commercial purposes bearing or embodying a design that is a copy or substantially a copy of the protected design. The term of protection in both the *TRIPS Agreement* and NAFTA is ten years.

f) Patents

The requirements respecting patents are set out in Articles 27 to 34 of the *TRIPS Agreement* and NAFTA Article 1709. Member countries must make patents available for any invention, whether products or processes, in all fields of technology provided that the inventions are new, result from an inventive step, and are capable of industrial application.[70] Patents must be available and patent rights enjoyable without discrimination as to the field of technology, the place where the invention was

---

69 *TRIPS Agreement*, ibid., art. 22:1. NAFTA, ibid., art. 1721.
70 *TRIPS Agreement*, ibid., art. 27. NAFTA, ibid., art. 1709(1).

made and whether products are imported or locally produced.[71] However, patentability of an invention may be excluded if preventing the commercial exploitation of the invention is necessary to protect *ordre public* or morality, or human, animal or plant life or health, or the environment[72] and certain other exclusions are permitted, such as diagnostic, therapeutic, and surgical methods for the treatment of humans and animals.[73]

The *TRIPS Agreement* and NAFTA provide that if the subject matter of a patent is a product, the patent holder may prevent other persons from making, using, or selling the product without the holder's consent and if the subject matter is a process, the holder can prevent other persons from using the process or using, selling, or importing products directly obtained from the process without the holder's consent.[74] Patent holders must be permitted to assign patents or transfer patents by succession and to conclude licensing contracts.[75]

Article 33 of the *TRIPS Agreement* provides for a term of protection of twenty years from the date of filing the application for the patent, whereas NAFTA Article 1709(12) requires a term of protection of twenty years from the date of filing or seventeen years from the date of the grant of the patent. The *TRIPS Agreement* requires that a process of judicial review be available if a patent is revoked or forfeited, whereas NAFTA prescribes the circumstances under which a patent may be revoked.[76] Both agreements set out rules respecting the burden of proof in infringement actions involving process patents.[77]

Article 31 of the *TRIPS Agreement* and NAFTA Article 1709(10) set out provisions respecting compulsory licensing (i.e., the permitted use of the patent without the consent of the owner). Both agreements provide much stronger disciplines than Article 5 of the *Paris Convention*. Both agreements permit compulsory licensing but a proposed user must have made efforts to obtain authorization from the owner on reasonable commercial terms and conditions and such efforts must have failed to be successful within a reasonable period of time. There are exceptions to this requirement for national emergencies and also to remedy practices judicially determined to be anticompetitive. The scope and duration of the use must be limited to the purpose for which it was autho-

---

71 *TRIPS Agreement, ibid.,* art. 27:1. NAFTA, *ibid.,* art. 1709(7).
72 *TRIPS Agreement, ibid.,* art. 27:2. NAFTA, *ibid.,* art. 1709(2).
73 *TRIPS Agreement, ibid.,* art. 27:3. NAFTA, *ibid.,* art. 1709(3).
74 *TRIPS Agreement, ibid.,* art. 28. NAFTA, *ibid.,* art. 1709(5).
75 *TRIPS Agreement, ibid.,* art. 28:2. NAFTA, *ibid.,* art. 1709(9).
76 *TRIPS Agreement, ibid.,* art. 32. NAFTA, *ibid.,* art. 1709(8).
77 *TRIPS Agreement, ibid.,* art. 34. NAFTA, *ibid.,* art. 1708(11).

rized. The use shall be non-exclusive and non-assignable except as part of the enterprise or goodwill enjoying the use. The use must be primarily for the domestic market of the member country imposing the compulsory licensing. Subject to some protections, the authorized use may be terminated if the circumstances that gave rise to it have ceased to exist. The patent holder must be paid adequate remuneration, taking into account the economic value of the authorization. The legal validity of decisions relating to authorizations and remuneration must be subject to judicial or other independent review.

g) Layout Designs of Integrated Circuits

As mentioned above, the *TRIPS Agreement* and NAFTA both require that effect be given to specified provisions of the *Integrated Circuits Treaty*. Each agreement excludes the application of Article 6(3) of the treaty, which permits compulsory licensing, and NAFTA Article 1705(5) expressly prohibits NAFTA countries from permitting compulsory licensing. Both agreements set out provisions respecting unauthorized importing, selling, and distributing similar to those in Article 6(1) of the treaty.[78] Both agreements prohibit member countries from considering as unlawful an act respecting an integrated circuit incorporating an unlawfully reproduced layout design when the person involved did not know or had no reasonable grounds for believing that the layout design was unlawfully produced, and set out requirements that apply after such person receives notice that the reproduction was unlawful.[79] Each agreement provides for protection of ten years from the date of filing an application for registration or first commercial exploitation anywhere in the world.[80]

h) Protection of Undisclosed Information (*TRIPS Agreement*) or Trade Secrets (NAFTA)

Both the *TRIPS Agreement* and NAFTA expand upon the obligation to provide effective protection against unfair competition required under Article 10*bis* of the *Paris Convention* by requiring that undisclosed information (*TRIPS Agreement*) or trade secrets (NAFTA) be

---

78 *TRIPS Agreement, ibid.*, art. 36. NAFTA, *ibid.*, art. 1710(2).
79 *TRIPS Agreement, ibid.*, art. 37. NAFTA, *ibid.*, arts. 1710(3) & 1710(4). Article 6(4) of the *Integrated Circuits Treaty*, above note 48, addresses the same problem but is permissive as to whether the member country treats the act as lawful or unlawful.
80 *TRIPS Agreement, ibid.*, art. 38. NAFTA, *ibid.*, art. 1710(6). Unlike NAFTA, art. 38 of the *TRIPS Agreement* takes into account that some members may not provide for registration and permits members to provide for protection to lapse after fifteen years.

protected.[81] Each agreement obliges member countries to provide the possibility (*TRIPS Agreement*) or legal means (NAFTA) for persons to prevent undisclosed information (*TRIPS Agreement*) or trade secrets (NAFTA) from being disclosed to, acquired by, or used by others without consent of the person lawfully in control of the information in a manner "contrary to honest commercial practice."[82] The information must be secret and have actual or potential commercial value and the person in control must have taken reasonable steps to keep it secret. Duration of the protection cannot be limited so long as these conditions exist.

i) Encrypted Program-Carrying Satellite Signals
NAFTA Article 1707 obliges each NAFTA country to make it a criminal offence to make available devices for decoding an encrypted program-carrying satellite signal without authorization from the lawful distributor and a civil offence to receive such a signal without authorization in connection with commercial activities or further distribution. There is no counterpart to this provision in the *TRIPS Agreement*.

6) Exceptions to the Norms

a) General Exceptions

i) TRIPS Agreement
Article 8:1 of the *TRIPS Agreement* permits measures consistent with the *TRIPS Agreement* necessary to "protect public health and nutrition" and to promote the public interest in sectors of vital importance to "socio-economic and technological development." Article 8:2 permits measures consistent with the *TRIPS Agreement* to prevent practices that "unreasonably restrain trade or adversely affect the international transfer of technology." The requirement in each of these provisions that the measures be consistent with the *TRIPS Agreement* is tautological and raises the same interpretative problems as NAFTA Article 904(1) because a member

---

81 *TRIPS Agreement, ibid.,* art. 39. NAFTA, *ibid.,* art. 1711.
82 Defined in footnote 10 to the *TRIPS Agreement, ibid.,* art. 39, and NAFTA, *ibid.,* art. 1721, as practices such as a breach of contract, breach of confidence, and inducement to breach, and includes the acquisition of information by third parties who knew or were grossly negligent in failing to know that such practices were involved in acquiring the information. The expression "contrary to honest practices" appears, without definition, in para. 2 of art. 10*bis* of the *Paris Convention,* above note 46.

country can adopt *any* measure that is consistent with the *TRIPS Agreement*. The scope of these provisions is unclear but they are not true "exceptions" such as those in Article XX of GATT 1994. However, based on the principle of effectiveness enunciated by the Appellate Body in *Japan — Taxes on Alcoholic Beverages* discussed in chapter 1, it is likely that a WTO panel or the Appellate Body would attribute some meaning to them. For example, they could be applied to broaden or narrow the scope of provisions of the *TRIPS Agreement* that leave latitude for interpretation.

ii) NAFTA

NAFTA Chapter Seventeen does not contain any general exceptions, and the exceptions of Article XX of GATT 1994 that are incorporated into NAFTA by NAFTA Article 2101 do not apply to any of the obligations set out in NAFTA Chapter Seventeen.

b) **Limited Exceptions in the *TRIPS Agreement* and NAFTA for Trademarks, Patents, and Industrial Designs**

The *TRIPS Agreement* and NAFTA provisions respecting trademarks, patents, and industrial designs permit "limited exceptions" to the rights conferred or protection accorded by the intellectual property right in question.[83] Although the wording varies from provision to provision, each provision requires (in general terms) that in making a limited exception a member country take into account or not prejudice the legitimate interests of the owner of the intellectual property right while taking into account legitimate interests of other persons. The wording of the NAFTA provisions closely follow those of the *TRIPS Agreement*.

Article 8 of the *TRIPS Agreement* may affect the interpretation of these limited exception provisions. In order to give some meaning to Article 8, a panel construing the *TRIPS Agreement* might, on the basis of the principle of effectiveness, apply a more generous interpretation of the concept of limited exception when applied to a measure covered by Article 8, such as one concerned with "public health," than to a measure that is not. As indicated above, NAFTA has no counterpart to Article 8 of the *TRIPS Agreement*.

It has been suggested to the author that the positioning of the limited exception provision in the text may affect its scope. For example, in the *TRIPS Agreement* requirements respecting trademarks, the limited

---

83   For trademarks, see *TRIPS Agreement*, *ibid.*, art. 17, and NAFTA, *ibid.*, art. 1708(12). For industrial designs, see *TRIPS Agreement* art. 26:2, and NAFTA art. 1713(4). For patents, see *TRIPS Agreement* art. 30, and NAFTA art. 1709(6). See also the provisions respecting copyright limitations or exceptions in *TRIPS Agreement* art. 13 and NAFTA art. 1705(5).

exception provision is placed before the provision prohibiting encumbering while in the corresponding NAFTA provisions the limited exception provision appears after the provision prohibiting encumbering. One might argue that the positioning indicates an intent in the *TRIPS Agreement* that the limited exception provision not modify the provision prohibiting encumbering and an opposite intent in the NAFTA text. As to whether this argument would succeed is, at this point, pure speculation.

7) Procedural Fairness: Enforcement of Intellectual Property Rights

Articles 42 through 60 of the *TRIPS Agreement* and NAFTA Articles 1714 to 1718 provide for the enforcement of intellectual property rights within and at the borders of member countries. Each agreement prescribes the civil and administrative procedures, interim relief provisions, criminal sanctions and enforcement rights at the border that must be available in each member country's domestic legal system. The following briefly describes the highlights of these provisions.

- *Civil and administrative procedures*: Articles 42 to 48 of the *TRIPS Agreement* and NAFTA Article 1715 establish basic codes of civil procedure which require that judicial authorities be empowered to grant relief by way of injunction or damages and prescribe the circumstances under which such relief may be granted. These provisions cover such matters as the giving of notice, the right to counsel, the identification and protection of confidential information, and the production of evidence. Member countries are required to ensure that judicial authorities be empowered to dispose of infringing goods.
- *Interim relief*: Article 50 of the *TRIPS Agreement* and NAFTA Article 1716 require that member countries make provision for interim relief (referred to in the *TRIPS Agreement* and NAFTA texts as "provisional measures") pending judicial determination of the merits of a case. Judicial authorities must be able to take action to prevent infringing goods from entering commerce. Applicants for interim relief must produce evidence that their goods are being infringed and that delay will result in irreparable harm or the destruction of evidence. Defendants must be entitled to compensation if it is subsequently found that there has been no infringement.
- *Criminal procedures*: Article 61 of the *TRIPS Agreement* and NAFTA Article 1717 require that each member country provide for criminal procedures and penalties in the case of wilful trademark counterfeiting and copyright piracy on a commercial scale.

- *Enforcing rights at the border*: Articles 51 of the *TRIPS Agreement* and NAFTA Article 1718 require that member countries provide the means for the holders of intellectual property rights to enforce their rights at the border so as to prevent the importation of infringing goods. Applicants must establish that there is a *prima facie* infringement under the laws of the importing country and describe the goods sufficiently for Customs to identify them. Competent authorities may require that security be posted. These provisions also provide for protection of importers whose goods are affected and require that competent authorities be empowered to order damages against applicants if goods are wrongfully detained. Competent authorities must have the right to destroy or dispose of infringing goods.

8) Dispute Resolution

Article 64 of the *TRIPS Agreement* provides that the dispute settlement procedures of Articles XXII and XXIII of GATT 1994, as modified by the *Dispute Settlement Understanding* apply to disputes arising under the *TRIPS Agreement*.[84] The dispute resolution provisions of NAFTA Chapter Twenty apply with full effect to disputes arising under NAFTA Chapter Seventeen.[85] WTO or NAFTA dispute settlement procedures may be invoked not only for disputes arising from the provisions of the TRIPS Agreement or NAFTA but also in respect of the provisions of the intellectual property conventions that must be complied with (*TRIPS Agreement*) or to which effect must be given (NAFTA).

9) Transitional Provisions

Article 70 of the *TRIPS Agreement* and NAFTA Article 1720 contain certain transitional provisions. For example, Article 70:1 of the *TRIPS Agreement* and NAFTA Article 1720(1) have the effect of providing that neither agreement gives rise to obligations in respect of acts that

---

84 Paragraph 2 of art. 64 of the *TRIPS Agreement, ibid.*, provides that subparas. 1(b) & 1(c) of art. XXIII of GATT 1994, above note 28 (the non-violation nullification and impairment provisions) do not apply to the *TRIPS Agreement* until the *TRIPS Agreement* has been in effect for five years.

85 In contrast to para. 2 of art. 64 of the *TRIPS Agreement, ibid.*, para. 1 of NAFTA, above note 2, Annex 2004 permits NAFTA dispute settlement procedures to be invoked in respect of disputes arising under NAFTA Part Six based on non-violation nullification and impairment.

occurred before the date of application of the relevant provisions of the agreement.[86]

The *TRIPS Agreement* provides for delay in the application of certain provisions. For example, developing country members can delay application of all provisions of the *TRIPS Agreement*, other than Articles 3 (national treatment), 4 (MFN treatment) and 5 (exception to Articles 3 and 4 for multilateral agreements concluded under auspices of WIPO) for a period of five years from the time that the *WTO Agreement* became effective.[87] For least developed developing countries, the period of delay is ten years.[88] No delays are allowed under NAFTA.

C. GOVERNMENT PROCUREMENT

Governments have a significant effect on the trade in goods and services through their own procurement practices because governments are significant consumers of goods and services.[89] Government procurement decisions are driven not only by cost factors but also by policy objectives such as creating employment, as well as by purely political considerations. Governments are frequently willing to pay more for goods if using local as opposed to foreign suppliers will stimulate job creation or buy political goodwill.

Other than Article XVII (State Trading Enterprises), GATT 1994 does not address the question of discrimination in government procurement practices. In fact, Article III:8 expressly excludes government procurement from the GATT national treatment requirements. However, the question of the trade distorting effects of government procurement practices was addressed in the Tokyo Round and the result was the *Agreement on Government Procurement* which came into effect on 1 January 1981.[90]

The *Government Procurement Agreement* that emerged from the Uruguay Round is based on the Tokyo Round code but expands the scope of coverage to include not only goods but also services and construction

---

86 There is one exception to this in NAFTA, *ibid.*, art. 1720(1), which relates to certain U.S. obligations respecting motion pictures described in NAFTA Annex 1705.7.
87 *TRIPS Agreement*, above note 1, art. 65, para. 2.
88 *TRIPS Agreement*, *ibid.*, art. 66, para. 1.
89 In its *North American Free Trade Agreement Canadian Statement on Implementation*, the Canadian government has estimated that the government procurement markets of the three NAFTA countries have a combined value of about US$1 trillion. See C. Gaz. 1994.I.68 at 140.
90 Above note 1. This code was amended on 20 November 1986.

services. As mentioned above, the *Government Procurement Agreement*, which became effective on 1 January 1996, is a plurilateral agreement that binds only those WTO member countries that are signatories. Canada, the United States, and Israel are signatories to the *Government Procurement Agreement*, together with the fifteen countries of the European Union, Hong Kong, Korea, Norway and Switzerland.[91] Mexico and Chile are not signatories to the *Government Procurement Agreement*. NAFTA Chapter Ten (which is based on the 1991 draft text of the *Government Procurement Agreement*) became effective on 1 January 1994 and applies among Canada, the United States, and Mexico.

As discussed in chapter 8, government procurement is expressly excluded from the NAFTA and CCFTA services chapters and the non-discrimination requirements of the NAFTA and CCFTA investment chapters.

To summarize:

- Government procurement between Canada and the United States is governed by the parallel obligations under both the *Government Procurement Agreement* and NAFTA Chapter Ten.
- Government procurement between Canada and Israel, the countries of the European Union, Hong Kong, Korea, Norway, and Switzerland is governed by the *Government Procurement Agreement*.
- Government procurement between Canada and Mexico is governed solely by NAFTA Chapter Ten.
- Government procurement between Canada and Chile, as well as all other countries not mentioned above, is not governed by any agreement.

1) Common Themes

The *Government Procurement Agreement* and NAFTA Chapter Ten are based on common themes:

- *Limited scope and coverage*: The *Government Procurement Agreement* and NAFTA Chapter Ten apply only to procurements:[92]
  – *by* specified government departments and enterprises;

---

91 These countries were the signatories to the *Government Procurement Agreement*, *ibid.*, at Marrakesh. The European Union (referred to as the European Communities in the document) is also a signatory.
92 Procurement under each agreement includes procurement by way of purchase, lease, or rental, with or without an option to buy. See *Government Procurement Agreement*, *ibid.*, art. I, para. 3, and NAFTA, above note 2, art. 1001(5). NAFTA 1001(5) lists certain activities that are not covered, such as non-contractual government assistance.

- *of* specified goods, services, and construction services; and
- *above* specified monetary thresholds.
- *Non-discrimination*: The *Government Procurement Agreement* and NAFTA Chapter Ten set out principles of non-discrimination respecting goods and suppliers (of both goods and services) of other member countries and locally based suppliers on the basis of foreign affiliation.
- *Creation of norms*: The *Government Procurement Agreement* and NAFTA Chapter Ten create norms respecting a number of aspects of the government procurement process.
- *Transparency and procedural fairness*: The *Government Procurement Agreement* and NAFTA Chapter Ten contain transparency requirements and require member countries to establish bid challenge procedures.

2) Scope and Coverage

The scope and coverage of the *Government Procurement Agreement* and NAFTA Chapter Ten is determined by reference to the annexes to each agreement. The *Government Procurement Agreement* contains an appendix for each signatory member country and each appendix is divided into five annexes. NAFTA Chapter Ten also sets out annexes that largely correspond to those set out in the *Government Procurement Agreement*.

a) Specified Government Departments and Enterprises

i) Central (Federal) Government Entities

- *Government Procurement Agreement*: Annex 1 of each member country's appendix to the *Government Procurement Agreement* lists the central government entities whose procurements are subject to the agreement. Annex 1 for Canada lists 100 departments and other entities of the Canadian federal government. Annex 1 for the United States lists 87 departments and other entities of the U.S. federal government. Annex 1 for Israel lists various ministries and other entities (such as the Knesset and the Prime Minister's Office) of the Israeli government.
- *NAFTA*: The corresponding NAFTA annex is Annex 1001.1a-1, which sets out schedules of federal government entities for the three NAFTA countries. The schedule of Canada lists the same entities as are listed in Canada's Annex I to the *Government Procurement Agreement*. The schedule of the United States includes the first fifty-six entities listed in the U.S. Annex I to the *Government Procurement Agreement* but not the remaining entities. NAFTA Annex 1001.1a-1 also sets out a schedule of Mexico that lists various ministries and other entities of the Mexican federal government.

ii) Subcentral (Provincial and State) Government Entities

- *Government Procurement Agreement*: Annex 2 of each member country's appendix to the *Government Procurement Agreement* lists subcentral government entities whose procurements are subject to the agreement. Annex 2 for Canada does not list any entities. However, Annex 2 of the United States lists various entities for the states of California, Colorado, Connecticut, Delaware, Florida, Hawaii, Idaho, Illinois, Louisiana, Maine, Maryland, Michigan, Mississippi, Missouri, New York, Oregon, Pennsylvania, South Dakota, Tennessee, Texas, Washington, Wisconsin and Wyoming. Annex 2 for Israel lists the municipalities of Jerusalem, Tel-Aviv, and Haifa and the company for economy and management of the Center of Local Government.
- *NAFTA*: Provision is made in NAFTA for an Annex 1001.1a-3 to include provincial and state entities and enterprises negotiated pursuant to Article 1024. At the time of writing, no entities or enterprises of any Canadian province or U.S. or Mexican state have been added to this annex, and the scope and coverage of NAFTA Chapter Ten remains confined to the federal level of government of each NAFTA country.

iii) Other Enterprises

- *Government Procurement Agreement*: Annex 3 of each member country's appendix to the *Government Procurement Agreement* lists all other entities that procure in accordance with the agreement. Annex 3 for Canada lists nine entities, all of which are emanations of the federal government, such as Canada Post. Annex 3 for the United States lists the Tennessee Valley Authority, various power marketing administrations, and the St. Lawrence Seaway Development Corporation.[93] Annex 3 for Israel lists eleven entities (e.g., Israel Airports Authority).
- *NAFTA*: The corresponding NAFTA annex is Annex 1001.1a-2, which sets out schedules of government enterprises whose procurements are subject to NAFTA Chapter Ten. The schedules for Canada and the United States each list the same entities as Annex 3 for each country to the *Government Procurement Agreement*.[94] The schedule of Mexico lists thirty-six enterprises.

---

93 *Government Procurement Agreement, ibid.*, Annex 3 also waives Buy American restrictions on Rural Electrification Administration financing to rural cooperatives.

94 *Ibid.* The schedule of Canada also includes Canadian National Railway Company, which is not listed in Annex 3 of the *Government Procurement Agreement*. However, Canadian National Railway Company is no longer included because it has been privatized. See NAFTA, above note 2, art. 1023. The schedule of the United States does not mention waiving Buy American restrictions on Rural Electrification Administration financing to rural cooperatives.

b) Specified Goods

i) Government Procurement Agreement

The *Government Procurement Agreement* applies to all goods subject to restrictions in the case of Canada in respect of purchases by the Department of National Defence, the Coast Guard, and the Royal Canadian Mounted Police,[95] and in the case of the United States of purchases by the Department of Defense.[96] In the case of the United States, procurements by the entities of certain states of construction grade steel, motor vehicles, and coal are also excluded.[97] In the case of Israel, the procurement of certain goods by the Ministry of Health are excluded,[98] as are the procurements of certain goods by certain enterprises.[99]

ii) NAFTA

NAFTA Chapter Ten applies to all goods subject to a number of restrictions set out in Annex 1001.1b-1. Procurements by the Canadian Department of National Defence and the Royal Canadian Mounted Police[100] and by the U.S. Department of Defense are subject to virtually the same restrictions as under the *Government Procurement Agreement*. There are similar restrictions in the case of Mexico respecting purchases by the *Secretaria de la Defensa Nacional* and the *Secretaria de Marina*.

c) Specified Services

i) Government Procurement Agreement

Annex 4 of each signatory country's appendix specifies services, whether positively or negatively, that are covered by the agreement. Annex 4 for Canada sets out a positive list of services identified by the United Nations Central Product Classification (CPC) services classification system. If a service is not on the list, it is not covered.[101] Annex 4 for Israel also sets out a positive list of services covered by the agree-

---

95 See the *Government Procurement Agreement, ibid.*, Annex 1. Note that goods are identified by Federal Supply Classification (FSC) numbers in the *Government Procurement Agreement* and NAFTA, *ibid.*, annexes. The FSC is a U.S. system of classifying goods.
96 See *Government Procurement Agreement, ibid.*, Annex 1.
97 See *ibid.*, Annex 2.
98 See *ibid.*, Note to Annex 1.
99 See *ibid.*, Notes to Annex 3. For example, procurement of cables by the Israel Ports and Railways Authority is excluded.
100 Reference is not made to the Coast Guard.
101 See also *Government Procurement Agreement*, above note 1, Notes to Annex 4, which set out some qualifications and exclusions.

ment. Annex 4 for the United States sets out a negative list of services, meaning that if a service is not on the list, it is covered by the agreement.

ii) NAFTA
The services covered by NAFTA Chapter Ten are set out in Annex 1001.1b-2. The general rule in NAFTA is that all services are covered unless they are excluded which, in the case of Canada, is the opposite from the approach under the *Government Procurement Agreement*. The schedules of Canada and the United States each list services that are excluded. If a service is not included on these lists, its procurement by the specified Canadian and U.S. entities and enterprises is covered. Appendix 1001.1b-2-A sets out a temporary positive list of services for Mexico. The procurement by a specified Mexican entity or enterprise of a service not on the list is not covered by NAFTA Chapter Ten. Once Mexico completes its negative list of services (i.e., a list of services that are not covered), the positive list in Appendix 1001.1b-2-A will cease to be operative.

d) Specified Construction Services

i) Government Procurement Agreement
Annex 5 of each signatory country's appendix specifies construction services covered by the agreement. Annex 5 for Canada and Annex 5 for the United States each include all services in Division 51 of the CPC system. Annex 5 for Canada specifically excludes dredging services and construction services tendered on behalf of the Department of Transport (DOT). Annex 5 for Israel sets out a positive list of construction services in Division 51 of the CPC system identified by CPC code numbers.

ii) NAFTA
The construction services covered by NAFTA Chapter Ten are set out in Annex 1001.1b-3. Appendix 1001.1b-3-A sets out a list of construction services that applies to all three NAFTA countries and is based on CPC Division 51.[102] Schedule B of Annex 1001.1b-3 sets out the same exclusions for Canada as in Annex 5 for Canada of the *Government Procurement Agreement* and in the case of the United States excludes Mexico.

---

102 The practical result is substantially the same as with Annex 5 for each of Canada and the United States in the *Government Procurement Agreement*, ibid. However, setting out a list rather than simply referencing Division 51 means that the approach is static rather than dynamic.

e) General Notes (Exclusions)

i) Government Procurement Agreement

The appendix of each signatory to the *Government Procurement Agreement* sets out (after the five annexes) general notes that contain exclusions. For example, the general notes for both the Canadian and U.S. appendices exclude set-asides for small and minority businesses. The general notes in the appendix for each signatory country must be reviewed before concluding that a procurement is covered.

ii) NAFTA

Annex 1001.2b is entitled "General Notes" and sets out schedules for the three NAFTA countries. The schedules for Canada and the United States are similar to their respective general notes set out in their appendices to the *Government Procurement Agreement*. The schedule for Mexico sets out exclusions and also permits set-asides in respect of *Petroleos Mexicanos* (Pemex) and the *Comisión Federal de Electricidad* (CFE) and permits local content requirements in respect of certain contracts. Annex 1001.2a sets out transitional provisions that apply to Mexico.

f) Above Specified Monetary Thresholds

The requirements of the *Government Procurement Agreement* and NAFTA apply only to procurements with a value that exceeds specified thresholds. Procurements below the thresholds are not covered.

i) Government Procurement Agreement

The monetary thresholds in the *Government Procurement Agreement* are expressed in terms of Special Drawing Rights (SDRs), an international unit created by the International Monetary Fund.[103] The thresholds for goods, services, and construction services are set out in Annex 1 for each signatory country. The thresholds for goods and services is 130,000 SDRs for each of Canada, the United States, and Israel.[104] The threshold for construction services is 5,000,000 SDRs for each of Canada and the United States and 8,500,000 SDRs for Israel.

---

103 See the *Bretton Woods and Related Agreements Act*, R.S.C., c. B-7, Schedule 1, for the text of this agreement.
104 On 9 May 1997, the *Financial Post* reported (at 38) that the Canadian dollar equivalent of one SDR was $1.8994.

ii) NAFTA
For NAFTA Chapter Ten to apply, the estimated value of the contract to be awarded must be equal to or exceed the thresholds set out in NAFTA Article 101(1)(c). The thresholds for procurements of goods or services or a combination of them by federal government entities is US$50,000 and by government enterprises is US$250,000. The thresholds for procurements of construction services by federal government entities is US$6,500,000 and by government enterprises is US$8,000,000. Annex 1001.1c sets out currency conversion formulae to convert U.S. dollars into Canadian dollars and pesos and provides for indexation of the thresholds with an indexation formula based on the U.S. Producer Price Index, with adjustments taking place every two years.

Annex 1001.2c provides that between Canada and the United States, the threshold in CUFTA Chapter Thirteen of US$25,000 applies to contracts for goods (with incidental services) entered into by the government entities listed in Annex 1001.1a-1. The currency conversion provisions of Annex 1001.1c apply but the indexation provisions do not. This lower threshold does not apply to procurements by the government enterprises listed in Annex 1001.1a-2.

iii) Valuation of Contracts
Article II of the *Government Procurement Agreement* and NAFTA Article 1002 set out rules respecting the valuation of contracts. The objective of these provisions is to maintain the integrity of the monetary thresholds that determine whether or not a procurement contract is covered.

g) Denial of Benefits under NAFTA

A supplier of a NAFTA country is a national of that country or an enterprise constituted or organized under its laws that has provided or could provide goods or services in response to a call for tender.[105] A supplier that is an enterprise does not have to be controlled by nationals of a NAFTA country to be entitled to the benefits of NAFTA Chapter Ten. However, NAFTA Article 1005 permits a NAFTA country to deny the benefits of NAFTA Chapter Ten to a supplier owned or controlled by persons of a non-NAFTA country that has no substantial business activities in any NAFTA country. A NAFTA country may also deny NAFTA Chapter Ten benefits to suppliers controlled by nationals of a non-NAFTA country if the NAFTA country does not maintain diplomatic

---

105 See the definition of "supplier" in NAFTA, above note 2, art. 1025, and the definitions of "person," "enterprise," and "person of a Party" in NAFTA art. 201.

relations with the non-NAFTA country or if measures adopted by that NAFTA country respecting the non-NAFTA country would be violated if the benefits were accorded to the supplier.

3) Non-Discrimination

a) Non-Discrimination Obligations

Article III of the *Government Procurement Agreement* and NAFTA Article 1003 set out non-discrimination obligations. The *Government Procurement Agreement* requires in respect of measures covered by the agreement that products, services, and suppliers of other Parties[106] be accorded treatment no less favourable than the treatment accorded to domestic products, services and suppliers or to those of another Party. The NAFTA provision is worded slightly differently but has similar effect. Both agreements prohibit discrimination against locally established suppliers on the basis of foreign affiliation or because the goods or services being supplied are those of another member country.

b) Rules of Origin

Article IV of the *Government Procurement Agreement* and NAFTA Article 1004 provide that member countries not apply rules of origin to products and services (*Government Procurement Agreement*) or goods (NAFTA) different or inconsistent with the rules of origin applied in the "normal course of trade." Under NAFTA, these rules of origin are not the preferential rules of origin in NAFTA Chapter Four but, rather, those used to determine whether a good is eligible for MFN tariff treatment.

NAFTA Article 1004 states that the rules used in the ordinary course of trade may be the Marking Rules. Given the confused state of the Marking Rules under NAFTA, this reference is probably meaningless. Paragraph 2 of Article III of the *Government Procurement Agreement* requires the Parties to take into account the results of the work program undertaken under the *Rules of Origin Agreement*. Article 1:2 of the *Rules of Origin Agreement* includes rules of origin used for government procurement purposes as among the non-preferential rules of origin to which the provisions of the Rules of Origin Agreement apply. As discussed in chapter 5, these provisions include the work program for

---

106 Unlike the other WTO agreements, the *Government Procurement Agreement*, above note 1, uses the expression "Party" to refer to a government that is a signatory, and in the context of the *Government Procurement Agreement*, a "Party" is the government of a signatory country.

harmonization (Article 9) and the disciplines during the transition period (Article 2).

4) Creation of Norms

Both the *Government Procurement Agreement* and NAFTA Chapter Ten establish norms in respect of technical specifications and tendering procedures, and each agreement prohibits offsets.

a) Technical Specifications

Article VI of the *Government Procurement Agreement* and NAFTA Article 1007 set out requirements respecting the technical specifications prepared or adopted by government entities. Technical specifications must not create unnecessary obstacles to trade and must, where appropriate, be specified in terms of performance criteria rather than design or descriptive characteristics and be based on international standards.[107]

b) Tendering Procedures

Articles VI through to XV of the *Government Procurement Agreement* and NAFTA Articles 1008 through to 1016 set out a complete code of requirements respecting the tendering process. Tendering procedures must be applied in a non-discriminatory manner and be consistent with the respective sets of requirements. The requirements of each agreement are similar but there are some differences in wording. Each agreement defines open tendering procedures as those under which all interested suppliers may submit tenders, selective tendering procedures as those under which suppliers invited to do so may submit tenders, and limited tendering procedures as those under which the procuring government entity contacts suppliers.[108] Articles X and XV of the *Government Procurement Agreement* and their counterparts in NAFTA Articles 1011 and 1016 set out requirements covering selective and limited tendering procedures respectively.

Article VIII of the Government Procurement Agreement and NAFTA Article 1009 set out requirements respecting the qualification of suppliers. Article IX of the *Government Procurement Agreement* and NAFTA Article 1010 establish rules respecting the invitation to participate,

---

[107] There are several other requirements respecting technical specifications in both art. VI of the *Government Procurement Agreement*, above note 1, and in NAFTA, *ibid.*, art. 1007.

[108] Article VII of the *Government Procurement Agreement*, *ibid.*, and NAFTA, *ibid.*, art. 1025.

made by procuring entities to suppliers. Each agreement requires that an invitation to participate be published. NAFTA Article 1010 requires that the notice contain certain information, although the corresponding provision of the *Government Procurement Agreement* is permissive.[109] Article XI of the *Government Procurement Agreement* and NAFTA Article 1012 contain requirements respecting prescribing time limits for tendering and delivery. Article XII of the *Government Procurement Agreement* and NAFTA Article 1013 establish requirements respecting the content of tendering documentation and its forwarding to suppliers. Article XIV of the *Government Procurement Agreement* and NAFTA Article 1014 establish disciplines that must be observed by procuring entities in conducting negotiations with suppliers. Article XIII of the *Government Procurement Agreement* and NAFTA Article 1015 contain requirements respecting the submission, receipt, and opening of tenders and the awarding of contracts.

c) Prohibition of Offsets

The *Government Procurement Agreement* defines offsets as "measures used to encourage local development or improve balance of payments accounts by means of domestic content, licensing of technology, investment requirement, counter-trade or similar requirements."[110] The NAFTA concept of offset is similar. Article XVI of the *Government Procurement Agreement* and NAFTA Article 1006 both prohibit offsets.

5) Transparency and Procedural Fairness

a) Transparency

Article XIX of the *Government Procurement Agreement* and NAFTA Article 1019 each set out publication obligations which require that member countries publish laws, regulations, judicial decisions, administrative rulings and the like regarding procurements covered by the relevant agreement. Member countries must also make available information respecting the characteristics and relative advantages of winning tenders. These obligations are subject to the qualification that member countries are not required to disclose confidential information and must not disclose confidential information that would prejudice the legitimate interests of a particular person without that person's consent.

---

109 *Government Procurement Agreement, ibid.,* art. IX, paras. 2 & 6.
110 See *ibid.,* Note 1 to para. 1 of art. XVI.

b) Procedural Fairness: Bid Challenge Procedures

Article XX of the *Government Procurement Agreement* and NAFTA Article 1017 require that member countries establish procedures under which suppliers may challenge the procurement process. The grounds for a challenge under Article XX of the *Government Procurement Agreement* is that the agreement has been breached.[111] NAFTA Article 1017(1)(a) is more general in that it requires that suppliers be allowed to submit bid challenges concerning "any aspect of the procurement process." Article XX of the *Government Procurement Agreement* and NAFTA Article 1017 set out procedural requirements that must be available to suppliers wishing to initiate a challenge. The requirements of Article XX of the *Government Procurement Agreement* are more extensive in that they prescribe requirements respecting the composition of the review body and the procedures that it must follow in its deliberations. For example, the procedures must enable participants to be heard before an opinion is given or a decision reached.[112] There is no NAFTA counterpart to this provision.

The Canadian authority for bid challenges is the Canadian International Trade Tribunal and the procedures are set out in the *Canadian International Trade Tribunal Act*[113] and the *North American Free Trade Agreement Procurement Inquiry Regulations*.[114]

6) Other Provisions

a) Exceptions

Article XXIII of the *Government Procurement Agreement* and NAFTA Article 1018 each contain an unqualified exception in respect of essential security interests. These articles also provide that, subject to "arbitrary or unjustifiable discrimination" and "disguised restriction on international trade" qualifiers, the respective agreements will not be construed to prevent member countries from imposing measures necessary to protect public morals, order or safety or human, animal or plant life, or health, or relating to goods or services of handicapped persons or philanthropic institutions or prison labour.[115]

---

111 See *ibid.*, para. 2 of art. XX.
112 See *ibid.*, para. 6(a) of art. XX.
113 S.C. 1988, c. C-56.
114 SOR/93-602.
115 The Appellate Body jurisprudence discussed in chapter 2 under "General Exceptions" and, in particular, the *Gasoline Case* discussed under "Third Element: Inconsistent Measure Satisfies Introductory Clause of Article XX" is relevant in interpreting this exception.

b) NAFTA and Privatization

NAFTA Article 1023 provides that nothing in NAFTA Chapter Ten shall be construed to prevent a NAFTA country from divesting an entity covered by the chapter. Enterprises listed in a NAFTA country's schedule to Annex 1001.1a-2 may be removed from the schedule once the entity ceases to be controlled by the federal government. The schedule to Annex 1001.1a-2 for Canada includes the Canadian National Railway Company, which has since been privatized. By the operation of NAFTA Article 1023, this enterprise has been removed from the schedule and its procurements are no longer subject to NAFTA Chapter Ten.

CHAPTER 8

INVESTMENT, SERVICES, AND OTHER MATTERS

NAFTA and CCFTA set out provisions respecting investment, services, telecommunications and temporary entry, and NAFTA (but not CCFTA) covers financial services. There is no counterpart to the NAFTA investment chapter among the WTO agreements but the GATS and its annexes set out provisions affecting services, telecommunications, financial services, and temporary entry. CIFTA does not cover any of these areas.

GATT 1994, the GATS, NAFTA, CIFTA, and CCFTA all contain provisions affecting monopolies and state enterprises, and the GATS, NAFTA, CIFTA, and CCFTA set out tentative provisions respecting competition law.

A. COMMON THEMES

The obligations created by the trade agreements to which Canada is a party affecting investment, services, telecommunications, financial services, and temporary entry are based on common themes.

1) Non-Discrimination

The investment and services chapters of both NAFTA and CCFTA impose national treatment and MFN treatment obligations. The NAFTA financial services chapter also incorporates modified national treatment and MFN treatment obligations. The GATS sets out a general MFN treatment obligation. The NAFTA, CCFTA, and GATS provisions respecting telecommunications and monopolies and state enterprises all contain non-discrimination requirements.

2) Creation of Norms

The NAFTA and CCFTA investment, services, and telecommunications chapters and the NAFTA financial services chapter all establish norms that go beyond non-discrimination. The NAFTA and CCFTA temporary entry provisions are based on norms which require that certain otherwise applicable entry requirements not be applied to citizens of other member countries.

3) Transparency

The NAFTA and CCFTA telecommunications chapters, the GATS Annex on Telecommunications, and the NAFTA financial services chapter each set out transparency requirements.

4) Limitation of Scope through Exceptions and Reservations

The scope of the NAFTA and CCFTA investment and services provisions, the NAFTA financial services provisions, and the GATS services provisions are all subject to exceptions and reservations.

B. INVESTMENT

NAFTA Chapter Eleven, which is a comprehensive investment treaty among the three NAFTA countries, is based on CUFTA Chapter Sixteen and on the *Model Bilateral Investment Treaty* developed by the U.S. government in the early 1980s for use in its bilateral investment treaty program. CCFTA Chapter G (Investment) is based on and closely follows the provisions of NAFTA Chapter Eleven. The provisions of the *TRIMs Agreement* are limited to requiring the elimination of certain "trade-related investment measures" and will be discussed below under "Performance Requirements." Canada is currently negotiating a *Multilateral Agreement on Investment* (MAI) with other OECD countries. If and when the MAI becomes effective, its provisions will resemble those of NAFTA and CCFTA.

1) Scope and Coverage: NAFTA and CCFTA

The requirements of NAFTA Chapter Eleven and CCFTA Chapter G apply to "investors of another Party" (NAFTA) or "investors of the other

Party" (CCFTA) and to their "investments" in the territory of a Party. The expression "Party" under NAFTA means any of Canada, the United States, or Mexico, and under CCFTA means either Canada or Chile. A "non-Party" under NAFTA is any country other than Canada, the United States, and Mexico, and a "non-Party" under CCFTA is any country other than Canada or Chile.

Between the United States and Canada under NAFTA, the provisions of Chapter Eleven apply to "investors of the United States" and their "investments" in Canada and to "investors of Canada" and their "investments" in the United States.[1] Between Canada and Chile under CCFTA, the provisions of Chapter G apply to "investors of Canada" and their "investments" in Chile and to "investors of Chile" and their "investments" in Canada. The scope and coverage of the investment provisions in each of NAFTA and CCFTA depend upon the definitions of investor of a Party and investment.

a) Investor of a Party

An investor of a Party under both NAFTA and CCFTA is:[2]

- the government or a state enterprise of a Party; or
- a natural person who is a citizen or resident of a Party; or
- an "enterprise of a Party" (i.e., a corporation, trust, partnership, sole proprietorship, joint venture or other association organized under the laws of a Party)

that seeks to make or is making or has made an investment.[3]

An enterprise of a Party need not be owned or controlled by citizens or residents of a member country to fall within the definition of investor of a Party. Thus a corporation constituted under New York state law but owned by citizens of Japan is an "investor of the United States" for NAFTA purposes. Similarly, a corporation constituted under the laws of Canada and owned by citizens of France is an "investor of Canada" for both NAFTA and for CCFTA purposes. However, each of NAFTA and CCFTA permit a Party to deny benefits to an "enterprise of a Party" that does not have substantial business activities in the Party under whose

---

1   The same applies between Canada and Mexico, substituting "Mexico" for the "United States."
2   See the *North American Free Trade Agreement*, 17 December 1992, Can. T.S. 1994 No. 2 [NAFTA], art. 1139, and the *Canada–Chile Free Trade Agreement*, in force 5 July 1997, see http://www.dfait-maeci.gc.ca/english/trade/agrement.htm [CCFTA], art. G-40.
3   See NAFTA, *ibid.*, art. 201, and CCFTA, *ibid.*, art. B-01.

laws it is organized.[4] Accordingly, Canada could deny benefits to the New York state corporation owned by Japanese if the corporation did not have substantial business activities in the United States. Similarly, the United States could deny NAFTA benefits and Chile could deny CCFTA benefits to the Canadian corporation owned by French citizens if that corporation did not have substantial business activities in Canada.

b) Investment

The NAFTA and CCFTA definitions of "investment" are broad and include not only controlling interests in business enterprises but also passive investments such as debt securities of and loans to affiliated enterprises or with terms exceeding three years, interests in income or profits of enterprises, tangible or intangible property acquired for economic benefit, and certain contractual interests.[5] A Canadian measure affecting a passive real estate investment owned by an investor of the United States would be covered by NAFTA Chapter Eleven. A Chilean measure affecting a mining concession in Chile owned by an investor of Canada would be covered by CCFTA Chapter G.

Some interests are not included in the definition of investment. For example, an account receivable arising from the sale of goods or services by an enterprise in one member country to an enterprise in another is not an "investment" for the purposes of either NAFTA Chapter Eleven or CCFTA Chapter G.[6]

If the New York state corporation referred to above owned all the shares of an Ontario corporation, the shares in the Ontario corporation would be the "investment" of the New York state corporation, which would be the "investor." If the Ontario corporation owned a parcel of real estate in Ontario, the real estate would also be an "investment" of that investor because the definition of "investment of an investor of a Party" includes investments that are held indirectly.

c) Exclusion of Financial Institutions

NAFTA Chapter Eleven does not apply to measures covered by NAFTA Chapter Fourteen (Financial Services). However, as discussed below, certain provisions of Chapter Eleven are incorporated by reference into NAFTA Chapter Fourteen. CCFTA Chapter G, other than Article G-09

---

4   See NAFTA, *ibid.*, art. 1113, and CCFTA, *ibid.*, art. G-13. There are several other grounds for denying benefits set out in these articles.
5   See NAFTA, *ibid.*, art. 1139, and CCFTA, *ibid.*, art. G-40.
6   See branch (i) of each definition, *ibid.*

(transfers) and Article G-10 (expropriation and compensation) does not apply to investors or investments in financial institutions.[7]

d) Application to Provinces and States
The obligations of NAFTA Chapter Eleven apply to measures adopted by the Canadian provinces and the U.S. and Mexican states, and the obligations of CCFTA Chapter G apply to the Canadian provinces.

2) Non-Discrimination: NAFTA and CCFTA

NAFTA and CCFTA both require that Parties accord to investors of other Parties, and to their investments, the better of national treatment and MFN treatment.[8]

a) National Treatment
NAFTA Article 1102 and CCFTA Article G-02 require that each Party accord to investors of other Parties and their investments treatment no less favourable than that accorded in like circumstances to its own investors and their investments. The treatment relates to the establishment, acquisition, expansion, management, conduct, operation, and sale or other disposition of investments. When applied to provinces and states, the treatment accorded must be the most favourable accorded by the province or state to the investors (and their investments) of the Party of which it forms a part. Thus the province of Quebec must treat investors of the United States, Mexico, and Chile (and their investments) no less favourably than it treats Quebec investors and investments, even though it may treat Newfoundland investors and their investments less favourably.

The national treatment provisions in NAFTA and CCFTA prohibit minimum equity requirements and forced dispositions on the basis of nationality.

b) MFN Treatment
NAFTA Article 1103 and CCFTA Article G-03 require that Parties accord to investors of other Parties and their investments treatment no less favourable than the treatment accorded in like circumstances to investors of other Parties and of non-Parties, and their investments. As with

---

7   A "financial institution" is defined in art. G-40 as a financial intermediary or other enterprise authorized to do business or regulated or supervised as a financial institution under the law of the Party in whose territory it is organized. As discussed below, the NAFTA, *ibid.*, definition of financial institution is similar.
8   NAFTA, *ibid.*, art. 1104, and CCFTA, above note 2, art. G-04.

national treatment, the treatment relates to the establishment, acquisition, expansion, management, conduct, operation, and sale or other disposition of investments.

3) Creation of Norms: NAFTA, CCFTA, and TRIMs

NAFTA and CCFTA create norms respecting minimum standard of treatment, performance requirements, senior management and boards of directors, transfers, and expropriation and compensation. The *TRIMs Agreement* creates norms respecting performance requirements only.

a) Minimum Standard of Treatment

NAFTA Article 1105 and CCFTA Article G-05 require each Party to accord to investments of another Party and to their investments "treatment in accordance with international law, including fair and equitable treatment and full protection and security."

The significance of this provision is that it incorporates standards of public international law into each of NAFTA and CCFTA. Opponents of the U.S. *Cuban Solidarity (LIBERTAD) Act of 1996*[9] (the *LIBERTAD Act* or *Helms-Burton*) take the position that it violates international law because of its extraterritorial application.[10] If this is correct, the application of the *LIBERTAD Act* against investors of Canada or Mexico or their investments would be contrary to NAFTA. Although principles of public international law apply among countries regardless of NAFTA, the effect of NAFTA Article 1105 is that a breach of principles of public international law adversely affecting investments of other Parties (as may be the case with the *LIBERTAD Act*) can be pursued through the NAFTA dispute settlement procedures, including the investor/state dispute settlement procedures described in chapter 10. The same observations apply with respect to CCFTA.

b) Performance Requirements

i) *NAFTA and CCFTA*

NAFTA Article 1106(1) and CCFTA Article G-06(1) prohibit Parties from imposing certain requirements in connection with the establishment, acquisition, expansion, management, conduct or operation of an

---

9 Pub.L. No. 104-114, 110 Stat. 785.
10 For a discussion of this, see P. Lichtenbaum & W. Kunze, "The Cuba 'LIBERTAD' Act and Its Implications for Canadian Companies," (1996) 28 The Canadian Law Newsletter 5 at 11 (published by the Committee on Canadian Law Section of International Law and Practice, American Bar Association).

investment by an investor of a Party or a non-Party. The prohibited requirements are:

- exporting given levels or percentages of goods and services;
- achieving given levels of domestic content;
- purchasing or preferring local goods or services;
- trade or foreign exchange balancing requirements;
- restrictions on domestic sales or relating such sales to exports; technology transfer requirements; and
- exclusive supplier (world product mandate) requirements.

NAFTA Article 1106(3) and CCFTA Article G-06(3) prohibit certain of these requirements as conditions for investments of investors of a Party or non-Party receiving advantages such as subsidies or tax advantages. The prohibited requirements are:

- achieving given levels of domestic content;
- purchasing or preferring local goods or services;
- trade or foreign exchange balancing requirements;
- restrictions on domestic sales or relating such sales to exports.

Subsidies subject to conditions other than these are not prohibited[11] and some requirements (such as locating production, providing a service, training or employing workers, constructing or expanding particular facilities, carrying out research and development) are expressly permitted.[12]

The inclusion of investors of non-Parties in these prohibitions is consistent with the MFN principle. If an investment of an investor of a Party cannot receive a subsidy that is conditional on one of the prohibited requirements, investors of non-Parties should not be more favourably treated by being permitted to receive the subsidy.

NAFTA Articles 1106(6) and CCFTA Article G-06 contain certain exceptions to these provisions that include measures necessary to protect human, animal, or plant life or health and for the conservation of living or non-living exhaustible natural resources. NAFTA Article 1108(8) and CCFTA Article G-08(8) provide further that certain of the prohibited performance requirements described above do not apply to export promotion and foreign aid programs, government procurement, or content requirements necessary for preferential tariff or quotas.

---

11 NAFTA, above note 2, art. 1106(5). CCFTA, above note 2, art. G-6(5).
12 NAFTA, *ibid.*, art. 1106(4). CCFTA, *ibid.*, art. G-04.

ii) TRIMs Agreement

The *TRIMs Agreement* is the only WTO agreement that addresses any of the matters covered by NAFTA Chapter Eleven and CCFTA Chapter G.

The *TRIMs Agreement* declares that certain performance requirements (which are referred to as trade-related investment measures or TRIMs) that are mandatory or enforceable under domestic law or administrative rulings or that must be complied with to obtain an advantage, are inconsistent with Article III (national treatment) and Article XI (import and export restrictions) of GATT 1994. TRIMs that are inconsistent with GATT Article III[13] are:

- the purchase or use by an enterprise of products of domestic origin or any from domestic source . . . ;
- . . . an enterprise's purchases or use of imported products be limited to an amount related to the volume or value of local products that it exports.

TRIMs that are inconsistent with Article XI of GATT 1994 are measures that restrict an enterprise from:

- [importing products] . . . used in or related to its local production, [either] generally or to an amount related to . . . [its] exports;
- [importing products] . . . used in or related to its local production by restricting its access to foreign exchange to an amount related to . . . [its] foreign exchange inflows . . . ;
- [exporting or selling products for export].

The effect of the *TRIMs Agreement* is that programs based on any of these requirements will be found to be inconsistent with Article III or Article XI of GATT 1994. The TRIMs listed above are similar to some of the prohibited performance requirements in NAFTA except that TRIMs, in being tied to GATT 1994, do not include services. Member countries were required to give notice of their TRIMs within ninety days of the *WTO Agreement* entering into force and, in the case of developed countries such as Canada, to eliminate notified TRIMs within two years of such date (i.e., by 1 January 1997).[14]

---

13 Items 1 and 2 in the Illustrative List in the Annex to the *Agreement Respecting Trade-Related Investment Measures*, set out in Annex 1A of the *Agreement Creating the World Trade Organization*, 15 April 1994 (Dobbs Ferry, N.Y.: Oceana Publications, 1997) [*WTO Agreement*] [*TRIMs Agreement*].

14 *Ibid.*, art. 5, paras. 1 & 2. The time period for elimination for developing countries is five years and for least-developed developing countries is seven years.

c) Senior Management and Boards of Directors

NAFTA Article 1107 and CCFTA G-07 prohibit requirements that the senior management of businesses owned by investors of other Parties be of any particular nationality. Resident or nationality requirements are permitted for the majority of boards of directors or committees of boards so long as the ability of the investor to control the investment is not impaired.

d) Transfers

NAFTA Article 1109 and CCFTA G-09 require Parties to permit the free transfer of profits, dividends, interest, royalties, management and other fees, proceeds from sale and various other payments relating to investments of investors of other Parties. Also, no Party may require its own investors to transfer earnings, profits and other amounts derived from their investments in other Parties. These requirements are subject to the right of Parties to prevent transfers through the "non-discriminatory and good faith" application of laws respecting such matters as bankruptcy and insolvency, securities trading and dealing, criminal offences, the reporting of currency transfers and ensuring the satisfaction of judgments.

e) Expropriation and Compensation

NAFTA Article 1110 and CCFTA Article G-10 provide that no Party may directly or indirectly nationalize or expropriate an investment of an investor of another Party or take a measure tantamount to nationalization or expropriation of such investment except:

- for a public purpose;
- on a non-discriminatory basis;
- in accordance with due process;[15] and
- on payment of full compensation.

Neither NAFTA nor CCFTA define "nationalization" or "expropriation"; whether a measure is a nationalization or expropriation or a measure tantamount to a nationalization or expropriation must be determined in any given situation under principles of public or customary international law.[16] Public international law distinguishes between state action

---

15 As well as the obligation to accord treatment in accordance with international law in NAFTA, above note 2, art. 1105, and CCFTA, above note 2, art. G-05.
16 There is extensive jurisprudence in both Canada and the United States on the compensable taking versus non-compensable regulation issue. However, the relevant body of law is international law and not the domestic law of any Party. See NAFTA, *ibid.*, art. 1131, and CCFTA, *ibid.*, art. G-32. International jurisprudence on the subject of taking versus regulation is not nearly as well developed as Canadian or U.S. jurisprudence.

that amounts to an "expropriation" or "taking" that requires that compensation be paid, and state action that amounts to "regulation" that does not require compensation. Public international law clearly recognizes that states have the right to take property for public purposes provided that certain requirements are satisfied. For example, governments frequently take land for road building or road widening purposes. In so doing, governments are fulfilling legitimate public functions and the actions are consistent with international law requirements as long as compensation is paid to the landowners.

However, many actions taken by the state which adversely affect the value of property would nonetheless be considered as non-compensable regulation because to hold otherwise would make it impossible for governments to carry out their legitimate functions. For example, land use bylaws, taxation measures, rent or price control regimes, and environmental laws can impair the value of property but are usually regarded as non-compensable regulation. Some laws that result in people being deprived of wealth do not amount to compensable taking. For example, laws that impose fines for committing crimes or provide civil remedies for breach of contract or injury resulting from tortious conduct clearly fall within the power of the state to regulate.

The requirements of NAFTA Article 1110 and CCFTA Article G-10 that must be observed if an expropriation takes place reflect the requirements of international law.[17] The "public purpose" requirement is obvious. The "non-discrimination" requirement is quite broad and precludes any sort of non-discriminatory application of the expropriating measure. The "due process" requirement extends beyond following domestic legal requirements. For example, an expropriating law duly passed by a legislature and proclaimed into force that expressly precluded access to the courts to review compensation awards could be found to be inconsistent with this requirement.

The standard of compensation required under international law is prompt, adequate, and effective compensation at fair market value. NAFTA Articles 1110(2) through (6) and CCFTA Articles G-10(2)

---

17   This is as perceived by the United States and Canada. Latin American countries have, historically at least, adopted a different view. The "Calvo" doctrine, which has been applied by Mexico and other Latin American countries, requires that foreigners waive diplomatic protection which means, in a situation involving nationalization or expropriation, that foreigners receive no better treatment than nationals and that if nationals receive less than full compensation, so do foreigners. The fact that Mexico is a Party to NAFTA, *ibid.*, and Chile a Party to CCFTA, *ibid.*, reflects a significant departure from this position.

through G-10(6) set out specific rules respecting compensation that carry forward and make this standard more explicit.

The provisions do not apply to compulsory licensing or revocation or limitation of intellectual property rights consistent with, in the case of NAFTA, NAFTA Chapter Seventeen, and in the case of CCFTA, the *TRIPS Agreement*,[18] nor to certain actions taken in respect of debt securities.[19]

f) Environmental Matters

NAFTA Article 1114 and its counterpart, CCFTA Article G-14, are entitled "Environmental Matters" but neither provision contains any obligations in respect of the environment that could be described as substantive. NAFTA Article 1114(1) and CCFTA Article G-14(1), in providing that nothing in the chapter in question prevents a Party from adopting or maintaining measures to protect the environment "otherwise consistent with this Chapter," are tautologous.[20] NAFTA Article 1114(2) provides that Parties *should* not waive or derogate from environmental measures to attract investment. The use of the word "should" rather than "shall" may cast doubt on the utility of these provisions. However, as discussed in chapter 2 under "Article III:1: No Protection to Domestic Production," the Appellate Body in *Japan — Taxes on Alcoholic Beverages* attributed meaning to Article III:1 of GATT 1994 notwithstanding the use in that provision of the word "should."

4) Exceptions: NAFTA and CCFTA

NAFTA Article 1108(7) and CCFTA Article G-08(6) provide that the following provisions do not apply to procurement by a Party or a state enterprise or to subsidies provided by a Party or a state enterprise:

- national treatment (NAFTA Article 1102 and CCFTA Article G-02);
- MFN treatment (NAFTA Article 1103 and CCFTA Article G-03);
- senior management and boards of directors (NAFTA Article 1106 and CCFTA Article G-06).

Procurement under NAFTA is subject to the disciplines of NAFTA Chapter Ten. Subsidies under both agreements are subject to the restrictions on performance requirements set out in NAFTA Article 1106 and CCFTA Article G-6.

---

18 NAFTA, *ibid.*, art. 1110(7). CCFTA, *ibid.*, art. G-10(7).
19 NAFTA, *ibid.*, art. 1110(8). CCFTA, *ibid.*, art. G-10(8).
20 See the discussion in chapter 1 under "Tautological Provisions and the Principle of Effectiveness."

C. SERVICES PROVISIONS: NAFTA AND CCFTA

NAFTA Chapter Twelve and CCFTA Chapter H (which is based on NAFTA Chapter Twelve) set out general principles of non-discrimination (national treatment and MFN treatment) that apply to the cross-border provision of services as well as certain other requirements.

1) Scope and Coverage

NAFTA Chapter Twelve and CCFTA Chapter H apply to measures that affect the cross-border provision of services by service providers of another or the other Party.

a) Services Covered

Unlike CUFTA Chapter Fourteen, which covered only those services (covered services) that were specifically identified in a list, NAFTA Chapter Eleven and CCFTA Chapter H cover all services other than financial services and air services (except for aircraft repair and maintenance when an aircraft is withdrawn from service and specialty air services, which are covered). Financial services are covered by NAFTA Chapter Fourteen, which has no CCFTA counterpart.

b) Cross-Border Provision of a Service

Cross-border provision of a service means providing a service:

- from the territory of one Party into the territory of another Party;
- in the territory of a Party by a person of that Party to a person of another Party;
- by a national of a Party in the territory of another Party.[21]

Cross-border provision of a service includes:

- a service provider providing a service from Canada into the United States;
- a service provider in Canada providing a service to a U.S. company;
- a Canadian citizen providing a service in the United States.

Provision of services by a U.S. subsidiary of a Canadian company within the United States is not included in the cross-border provision of a service. A U.S. measure affecting this service provider would be covered by NAFTA Chapter Eleven (Investment) and not by Chapter Twelve.

21　See definition of "cross-border provision of a service" in NAFTA, *ibid.*, art. 1213, and CCFTA, *ibid.*, art. H-12.

c) Service Provider of a Party

A service provider of a Party can be a national or an enterprise of a Party. An "enterprise of a Party" means an enterprise organized under the laws of a Party and can include a branch. The equity interests in the enterprise need not be owned by nationals of a Party. A company organized under Canadian law, whose shares are owned by Europeans, that is providing services into the United States or Chile is a "service provider of a Party" for the purposes of NAFTA Chapter Twelve or CCFTA Chapter H. However, as under the NAFTA and CCFTA investment chapters, each of NAFTA and CCFTA permit a Party to deny benefits to an enterprise of a Party that does not have substantial business activities in the Party under whose laws it is organized.[22] Thus the United States or Chile could deny benefits if the Canadian company owned by the Europeans did not have substantial business activities in Canada.

d) Application to Provinces and States

The obligations of NAFTA Chapter Twelve apply to measures adopted by the Canadian provinces and the U.S. and Mexican states, and the obligations of CCFTA Chapter H apply to the Canadian provinces.

2) Non-Discrimination

NAFTA and CCFTA both require that Parties accord to service providers of other Parties the better of national treatment and MFN treatment.[23]

a) National Treatment

NAFTA Article 1202 and CCFTA Article H-02 require that each Party accord to service providers of other Parties treatment no less favourable than that accorded in like circumstances to its own service providers and their investments. As under the investment chapter, when applied to provinces and states, the treatment accorded must be the most favourable accorded by the province or state to the service providers of the Party of which it forms a part.

b) MFN Treatment

NAFTA Article 1203 and CCFTA Article H-03 require that Parties accord to investors of other Parties and their investments treatment no less favourable than the treatment accorded in like circumstances to investors of other Parties and of non-Parties, and their investments.

---

22   NAFTA, *ibid.*, art. 1211, and CCFTA, *ibid.*, art. H-11. There are several other grounds for denying benefits set out in these articles.
23   NAFTA, *ibid.*, art. 1204, and CCFTA, *ibid.*, art. H-04.

3) Local Presence

NAFTA Article 1205 and CCFTA Article H-05 prohibit residency requirements or requirements that service providers establish or maintain representative offices or any form of enterprise (such as a subsidiary corporation or a branch).

4) Licensing and Certification Procedures

NAFTA Article 1210 and CCFTA Article H-10 set out general requirements regarding measures respecting the licensing or certification of nationals of other NAFTA countries in regard to the provision of services. The measures are to be based on objective and transparent criteria, are not to be more burdensome than necessary to ensure the quality of a service, and are not to constitute a disguised restriction on the cross-border provision of a service.

Notwithstanding the MFN requirements described above, NAFTA Article 1210(2) and CCFTA Article H-10(2) permit a Party to unilaterally recognize various qualifications from other countries without having to accord the same recognition to such qualifications obtained in the territory of another Party. However, the other Party must be given the opportunity to demonstrate that the qualifications obtained in its territory should be recognized.

Annex 1210.5 and CCFTA Annex H-10.5 set out more extensive requirements respecting the licensing and certification of professional services, foreign legal consultants, and temporary licensing of engineers.

5) Quantitative Restrictions and Liberalization Commitments

NAFTA Article 1207 and CCFTA Article H-07 require the Parties to list non-discriminatory quantitative restrictions and to meet periodically to negotiate their liberalization or removal. The lists are set out in NAFTA Annex V and CCFTA Annex IV. NAFTA Annex VI and CCFTA Annex V set out specific liberalization commitments.

6) Exceptions

NAFTA Chapter Twelve and CCFTA Chapter H do not apply to government procurement and subsidies. Under NAFTA, government procurement is covered by Chapter Ten, which has no counterpart in CCFTA.

D. RESERVATIONS RESPECTING NAFTA AND CCFTA INVESTMENT AND SERVICES OBLIGATIONS

NAFTA Article 1108 and CCFTA Article G-08 make provision, respectively, for reservations to certain provisions of NAFTA Chapter Eleven and CCFTA Chapter G. Similarly, NAFTA Article 1206 and CCFTA Article H-06 make provision, respectively, for reservations to certain provisions of NAFTA Chapter Twelve and CCFTA Chapter H.

1) Reservations Respecting Existing Non-Conforming Measures at the Federal (National) Level

An "existing non-conforming" measure is one that existed at the time that the relevant agreement became effective (1 January 1994 in the case of NAFTA and 5 July 1997 in the case of CCFTA) and that does not conform to NAFTA or CCFTA requirements. Both NAFTA and CCFTA adopt a "list it or lose it" approach to such measures maintained at the federal (in the case of Chile, national) level. Unless the non-conforming measure is identified in a NAFTA or CCFTA annex, the government maintaining it must bring the measure into conformity with NAFTA or CCFTA obligations.

NAFTA Articles 1108(1) and 1206(1) and CCFTA Articles G-08(1) and H-06(1) provide that the following articles do not apply to existing non-conforming measures at the federal (in the case of Chile, national) level listed in Annex I of each agreement and, in the case of NAFTA Chapter Eleven, Annex III:

- national treatment (NAFTA Articles 1102 and 1202 and CCFTA Articles G-02 and H-02);
- MFN treatment (NAFTA Articles 1103 and 1203 and CCFTA Articles G-03 and H-03);
- performance requirements (NAFTA Article 1106 and CCFTA Article G-06);
- senior management and boards of directors (NAFTA Article 1106 and CCFTA Article G-06);
- local presence requirements (NAFTA Article 1205 and CCFTA Article H-05).

Non-conforming measures may not be made more non-conforming and if a measure is made less non-conforming, it cannot subsequently be amended to be made more non-conforming.

a) Annex I Reservations: NAFTA and CCFTA

The schedules to Annex I of each of NAFTA and CCFTA identify specific measures at the federal (in the case of Chile, national) level. Some reservations contain liberalization commitments, which may modify the measure or phase it out over time. Each reservation identifies the measure in the "Measures" element, as well as the relevant industry classification by sector or subsector, and the NAFTA or CCFTA articles to which the reservation applies. Liberalization commitments are identified under the "Phase-out" element and may also appear in the "Description" of the measure. The preamble to Annex I of each agreement sets out rules for interpreting each reservation. For example, phase-out prevails over all other elements of the reservation, and a liberalization commitment contained in the description of the measure prevails over the measures element.

The following briefly describes the reservations of each country set out in their respective schedules.

i) Schedule of Canada (NAFTA and CCFTA)

The schedules of Canada in NAFTA Annex I and CCFTA Annex I are virtually the same, with only a few minor differences.[24]

- *Investment Canada*: The reservation respecting the *Investment Canada Act* and the *Investment Canada Regulations* in NAFTA Annex I carries forward on a trilateral basis the commitments that were made by Canada under CUFTA and the counterpart in CCFTA Annex I extends the same benefits to investors of Chile. These Canadian measures provide for review by Investment Canada of both direct and indirect investments by non-Canadian investors. NAFTA and CCFTA eliminate review of indirect investment and set the threshold for review of direct investments at a level for 1996 of Cdn$168,000,000, subject to annual adjustment to account for inflation.[25] Each reservation retains the *Investment Canada Act* concept that an investor of a Party must be a national or an entity controlled by nationals of a

---

24 The CCFTA, *ibid.*, Annex I schedule of Canada contains a reservation from CCFTA arts. H-02 (national treatment — services) and H-03 (local presence) for auditing services in respect of financial institutions that does not have a NAFTA counterpart. There are slight differences in some of the "Measures" elements and a few "Phase-out" elements differ.

25 By way of example, an indirect investment occurs when the shares of a U.S. company with a Canadian subsidiary are acquired by another U.S. company. Ownership of the shares of the Canadian subsidiary has not changed but ownership of the U.S. holding company has changed.

Party to be eligible for benefits. The higher thresholds do not apply to uranium production and ownership of uranium-producing properties, oil and gas, financial services, transportation services, and cultural businesses.

- *Other reservations*: The schedules of Canada in NAFTA and CCFTA Annex I also set out reservations respecting a number of federal measures, the more significant of which are:
  - the *Farm Credit Act* and regulations;
  - foreign ownership restrictions respecting shares of privatized Crown corporations (such as Air Canada) and reservation of the right to limit foreign ownership of federal or provincial Crown corporations that may be privatized;
  - constrained share provisions and majority resident-Canadian requirements in federal corporate statutes such as the *Canada Business Corporations Act* and the *Canada Corporations Act*;
  - the performance-based duty remission programs discussed in chapter 3 under "Automotive Duty Remission";
  - citizenship, permanent residency, and other requirements respecting customs brokers, operators of duty-free shop, and patent and trademark agents;[26]
  - foreign ownership and other restrictions respecting the oil and gas sector, uranium mines, fisheries, air transportation,[27] land transportation, and water transportation.

ii) Schedule of Mexico (NAFTA)

The schedule of Mexico in NAFTA Annex I includes the following reservations:

- Mexican laws and regulations respecting investment; these measures prescribe foreign ownership limits in a number of sectors and provide for investment screening; the reservations include significant liberalization commitments;
- the maquiladora program and the ALTEX and PITEX programs (duty deferral programs based on export requirements); these programs will be phased out by 2001;

---

26 Citizenship and permanent residency requirements respecting patent and trademark agents have been phased out pursuant to a liberalization commitment in these reservations and pursuant to NAFTA, above note 2, art. 1210(3).
27 Subject to liberalization commitments respecting certain specialized air transport services such as heli-logging.

- foreign ownership restrictions in various mining activities, activities respecting agriculture, livestock, forestry and lumber, construction activities, entertainment and media, explosives, commercial air services (subject to liberalization commitments respecting certain specialty services), fisheries, and other maritime activities;
- foreign ownership restrictions respecting the auto parts industry (to be phased out by 1999) and the Mexican Automotive Decree (to be phased out by 2004 as provided in NAFTA Annex 300-A);
- restrictions respecting land transportation services subject to some liberalization commitments;
- restrictions respecting provision of educational services, customs brokers, law firms, and various other professional activities subject to some liberalization commitments;
- foreign ownership restrictions on border and coastal lands;
- activities relating to the distribution and sale of various petroleum products and to exploration for petroleum and gas.

iii) Schedule of the United States (NAFTA)
The schedule of the United States in NAFTA Annex I includes the following reservations:

- licensing requirements respecting nuclear materials;
- restrictions respecting insecticides, fungicides, and rodenticides;
- restrictions respecting rights-of-way for oil and gas pipelines;
- restrictions on availability of Overseas Private Investment Corporation insurance and loan guarantees;
- restrictions respecting air transportation services (subject to liberalization commitments respecting some specialty services) and land transportation services (subject to liberalization commitments respecting Mexico);
- citizenship requirements respecting customs brokers;
- performance requirements respecting materials used in waste treatment plants.

iv) Schedule of Chile (CCFTA)
The schedule of Chile in CCFTA Annex I includes the following reservations:

- foreign ownership restrictions respecting certain lands disposed of by the state;
- reservation of the right to limit foreign ownership of equity interests in state enterprises that may be disposed of by the state;
- requirements that a minimum of 85 percent of employees of employers employing more than twenty-five persons be Chilean natural persons;
- certain performance requirements respecting the automotive industry;

- restrictions on foreigners performing certain services related to fisheries, exploration, and archaeology;
- restrictions respecting oil and gas exploration, nuclear energy, aquaculture and fisheries, and mining;
- restrictions respecting the provision of various professional services (including auditing, engineering, legal, customs brokers);
- restrictions respecting air transportation, land transportation, and water transportation.

b) Annex III Reservations: NAFTA

NAFTA Annex III applies only to Mexico and sets out certain activities that are reserved to the state, including petroleum, other hydrocarbons and basic petrochemicals, electricity, nuclear power and treatment of radioactive minerals, satellite communications, telegraph services, radiotelegraph services, postal services, railroads, issuance of currency and minting, and activities related to maritime and inland ports, airports, and heliports. This annex sets out rules that apply if an activity is deregulated, including a right to limit foreign ownership in the initial sale of state-owned assets or ownership interests in state enterprises.

2) Reservations Respecting Existing Non-Conforming Measures at the Provincial, State, and Local Level

NAFTA Articles 1108(1)(a)(ii) and 1206(1)(a)(ii) originally contemplated that non-conforming provincial and state measures that existed on 1 January 1994 would be specifically listed in each Party's schedule to NAFTA Annex I by 1 January 1996. The time limit for listing was extended to 31 March 1996 and extensive lists of non-conforming provincial and state measures were exchanged. However, the federal governments of the three NAFTA countries agreed that the required listing of non-conforming provincial and state measures would consist of a simple reference to all existing non-conforming measures of provinces and territories (in the case of Canada) and states (in the case of Mexico and the United States).[28] The lengthy lists of specific measures that had been prepared were exchanged for "transparency" purposes. The effect of the foregoing is that all non-conforming provincial and state measures that existed on 1 January 1994

---

28 NAFTA, above note 2, art. 1108(1)(a)(ii) and art. 1206(1)(a)(ii) refer to states and provinces but not to territories. Presumably territorial governments were considered as local govern-ments and there never was any need under NAFTA to list their measures. Obviously the inclusion of a reference to territories in the listing suggests some unease with this interpretation.

have been grandfathered. NAFTA Article 1108(1)(a)(iii) grandfathers non-conforming measures of local governments that existed on 1 January 1994. The articles affected by the grandfathering are those to which the reservations respecting existing non-conforming federal measures apply.

The approach under CCFTA is the same as that under NAFTA, as modified by the subsequent events just described. CCFTA Article G-08(1)(a)(i) requires that non-conforming provincial measures existing on 5 July 1997 be listed in Annex I, but the reference in the schedule of Canada to Annex I is simply to "all existing non-conforming measures of all provinces and territories," the effect of which is to grandfather all such measures. CCFTA Article G-08(1)(a)(ii) grandfathers non-conforming measures of local governments that existed on 5 July 1997. The articles affected by the grandfathering are those to which the reservations respecting existing federal or national measures apply.

Under each agreement, the non-conforming provincial, state (NAFTA only) and local government measures cannot be made more non-conforming and if a measure is made less non-conforming, it cannot subsequently be made more non-conforming.

3) Sectoral Reservations under NAFTA and CCFTA Annex II

NAFTA Articles 1108(3) and 1206(3) and CCFTA Articles G-08(3) and H-06(3) provide that the NAFTA and CCFTA articles listed above respecting national treatment, MFN treatment, performance requirements, senior management and boards of directors, and local presence do not apply to sectors, subsectors, and activities listed in the schedule of each Party in NAFTA or CCFTA Annex II. This reservation is much more extensive than that provided in NAFTA Articles 1108(1) and 1206(1) and CCFTA Articles G-08(1) and H-06(1). New non-conforming measures may be introduced and existing non-conforming measures may be made more non-conforming. The only constraint is imposed by NAFTA Article 1108(4) and CCFTA Article G-08(4), which prevent a Party introducing a measure covered by Annex II that requires an investor of another Party to dispose of an investment by reason of the investor's nationality.

The rules for interpreting Annex II reservations are set out in the preamble to NAFTA and CCFTA Annex II and they differ from those respecting Annex I. The schedules of Canada in NAFTA Annex II and CCFTA Annex II are virtually identical.

a) Social Services
The schedules of Canada (NAFTA and CCFTA), Mexico (NAFTA), the United States (NAFTA), and Chile (CCFTA) each contain a reservation

respecting public law enforcement and correctional services and "the following services to the extent that they are social services established or maintained for a public purpose: income security or insurance, social security or insurance, social welfare, public education, public training, health, and child care." Concern has been expressed in Canada respecting the extent to which this reservation insulates Canada's publicly funded health care system from NAFTA disciplines. The reservation certainly provides some protection but, given the wording, it is difficult to ascertain its extent.

b) Other Annex II Reservations
Annex II reservations also cover matters that include:

- rights and privileges of socially or economically disadvantaged minorities and (in the case of Canada and Chile) rights and privileges provided to aboriginal peoples;
- ownership of oceanfront land (Canada, the United States) and control of use of beaches and other such properties for the issuance of maritime concessions (Chile);
- acquisition, sale, or other distribution of government debt instruments (Canada, Mexico, Chile);
- various aspects of the telecommunications and radiocommunications industries;
- various aspects of air transportation (Canada, Mexico), water transportation (Canada, Mexico, the United States), and control of certain aspects of commercial fishing (United States, Chile);
- legal services (Mexico, United States), newspaper publishing (the United States);
- postal services and railways, certain entertainment services and services related to energy and basic petrochemical goods (all Mexico);
- construction services, educational services, environmental services relating to water such as the distribution of potable water and the collection and disposal of waste (all Chile).

4) Reservations Respecting MFN Treatment: NAFTA Annex IV and CCFTA Annex III

NAFTA Annex IV sets out exceptions for each Party to NAFTA Article 1103 for all international agreements in force or signed prior to NAFTA becoming effective and for international agreements entering into force or signed after NAFTA became effective respecting aviation, fisheries, maritime matters, and telecommunications. The reason for these exceptions is that international agreements affecting areas such as aviation set out reciprocal commitments that may grant privileges to the country or countries signing the agreement that are not granted to NAFTA countries. CCFTA Annex III sets out similar exceptions between Canada and Chile.

E. SERVICES: *GENERAL AGREEMENT ON TRADE IN SERVICES*

The structure of the GATS follows that of GATT 1994 but its provisions are not as comprehensive in respect of services as are those of GATT 1994 in respect of goods.

1) Scope and Coverage

The scope and coverage of the GATS depends upon the definition "service supplier" and related definitions[29] and the GATS concept of "trade in services."

a) Service Supplier and Related Definitions

A service supplier is a person that provides a service. A "person" is a natural person or a juridical person. A "natural person of another member" is a natural person who resides in the territory of a member who is a national of that member or, subject to some qualifications, a person who has right of permanent residence. A "juridical person of another member" is a legal entity[30] constituted under the laws of a member with substantive business operations in the territory of that member or any other member.[31] The effect of these definitions is that a "service supplier of a member" includes a company organized under the laws of a member but not owned by nationals of that member, as long as it has substantive business operations in the territory of that member or another member.

b) Trade in Services

The GATS concept of trade in services[32] is similar to the concept of "cross-border provision of a service" in NAFTA Chapter Twelve and CCFTA Chapter H, but there are some differences. Trade in services includes supply of a service:

---

29 The relevant definitions are set out in the *General Agreement on Trade in Services*, set out in Annex 1B of the *WTO Agreement*, above note 13, [GATS], art. XXVIII.
30 See definition of "juridical person," *ibid.*
31 There is a second branch of this definition covering supply of a service through a commercial presence (*ibid.*).
32 *Ibid.*, art. 1, para. 1.

- from the territory of one member into the territory of another member; and
- in the territory of a member to the service customer of another member.

These two branches are similar to the first two branches of the NAFTA and CCFTA definitions described above. However, the third branch of the GATS definition is the supply of a service:

- by a service supplier of one member, through commercial presence in the territory of any other member.[33]

Measures affecting the supply of services under this branch would be covered by the NAFTA and CCFTA investment provisions rather than the services provisions.

The fourth branch of the GATS definition is the supply of a service:

- by a service supplier of one member, through the presence of natural persons of a member in the territory of any other member.

This branch is slightly different from the third branch of the NAFTA and CCFTA definition, which covers nationals of one Party providing services in the territory of another Party.

c) Application to Regional and Local Governments
Member countries must take such reasonable measures as are available to them to ensure observance by regional (i.e., provincial and state) and local governments.[34]

2) General Obligations

The GATS sets out a number of obligations that apply generally to measures affecting trade in services.

a) Non-Discrimination: MFN Obligation
GATS Article II requires that each member accord to services and service suppliers of other members treatment no less favourable than that accorded to services and service suppliers of any other country. Members may maintain inconsistent measures listed in GATS Annex II.

b) Transparency and Procedural Fairness
GATS Article III requires that members (other than in emergency situations) publish all measures that relate to the operation of the GATS.

---

33 See definition in *ibid.*, art. XXVIII, para. (d).
34 *Ibid.*, art. 1, para. 3.

Members must also respond promptly for requests for information and establish enquiry points for this purpose.

GATS Article VI requires that all measures of general application affecting trade in services be administered in a reasonable, objective, and impartial manner. Members must establish procedures for the review of administrative decisions affecting the trade in services. Applications for authorization to supply a service must be dealt with within a reasonable period of time.

c) Recognition of Education, Experience

GATS Article VII permits a member to recognize the education, experience obtained, requirements met, or licences or certifications granted in a particular country. However, the member must grant another interested member the opportunity to negotiate accession to such arrangements or comparable arrangements and to demonstrate that education, experience, licences or certifications obtained there should be recognized.[35]

d) Subsidies

GATS Article XV provides for the WTO member countries to enter into negotiations to develop multilateral disciplines to avoid the trade-distorting effects of subsidies on the trade in services. The negotiations are also to address the appropriateness of countervailing procedures. GATS Article XV does not contain any firm obligations.

3) Reduction of Barriers: Specific Commitments

Rather than addressing the issue of market access through a general national treatment obligation, the GATS requires that each member country set out its specific market access commitments in a schedule. Paragraph 1 of Article XVI requires that each member country accord to services and services suppliers of other members treatment no less favourable than set out in its schedule. Article XVII sets out a national treatment obligation in respect of the sectors set out in its schedule. Article XIX contemplates future rounds of negotiations to progressively liberalize the trade in services. Just as successive rounds of GATT negotiations have improved market access for goods by lowering tariffs, successive rounds of GATS negotiations should improve market access for

---

35 This provision is analogous to the provision in NAFTA, above note 2, art. 1210(2), and CCFTA, above note 2, H-10(2) described above.

services by improving access in sectors listed on members' schedules and adding commitments for new service sectors.

GATS Article XI requires that, subject only to the balance of payments exception in Article XII, members not apply restrictions on international transfers and payments for current transactions relating to its specific commitments.

GATS Article XXI makes provision for the modification of schedules. A member may modify or withdraw a commitment after three years from the time that the commitment entered into effect. Notice must be given and provision is made for compensatory adjustments.

4) Exceptions and Qualifications

The obligations set out in the GATS are subject to a number of exceptions.

a) General Exceptions

GATS Article XIV is based on its counterpart in Article XX of GATS 1994 and sets out exceptions covering measures:

- necessary to protect public morals or to maintain public order;
- necessary to protect human, animal, or plant life or health;
- necessary to ensure compliance with laws not inconsistent with the GATS;
- inconsistent with GATS Article XVII (members' national treatment commitments) where the different treatment is aimed at ensuring the equitable or effective imposition or collection of direct taxes;
- inconsistent with the MFN obligation in GATS Article II provided that the difference is the result of an agreement to avoid double taxation.

The wording of the chapeau of GATS Article XIV contains the same "arbitrary or unjustifiable discrimination" and "disguised restriction" language as Article XX of GATT 1994. The approach to the application of the exceptions in Article XX of GATT 1994 described in chapter 2 under "Approach to Interpretation of Article XX Exceptions" will doubtless be followed by WTO panels and the Appellate Body when WTO member countries invoke the exceptions in GATS Article XIV.

b) National Security and Balance of Payments

Article XIV*bis* sets out a national security exception that closely follows the wording of its counterpart in Article XXI of GATT 1994. Article XII sets out a balance of payments exception that is similar to its GATT 1994 counterpart. These exceptions are discussed in chapter 9.

c) Government Procurement

Article XIII excludes government procurement from GATS obligations. As discussed in chapter 7, the plurilateral *Government Procurement Agreement* covers services and construction services.[36]

d) Economic Integration

Article V provides that the GATS will not prevent members from entering into agreements liberalizing trade in services provided that the agreements have substantial sectoral coverage and provide for the elimination of substantially all discriminatory measures in the sectors covered. This article is analogous to Article XXIV of GATT 1994, which permits member countries to enter into agreements creating customs unions or free trade areas. But for GATS Article V, the fulfilment by Canada, the United States, and Mexico of their obligations under NAFTA Chapters Twelve and Fourteen and by Canada and Chile of their obligations under CCFTA Chapter H would be inconsistent with the MFN obligation set out in GATS Article II unless the benefit of these provisions were extended to all WTO members.

5) Sectoral Annexes

The GATS sets out sectoral annexes on telecommunications, financial services, and movement of natural persons that are discussed below. The GATS also sets out sectoral annexes respecting air transport services and maritime transport services.

a) Annex on Air Transport Services

The effect of this annex is to exclude traffic rights and services directly related to the exercise of traffic rights from the GATS. Traffic rights are defined as the right for scheduled and unscheduled services to operate and/or carry passengers, cargo, and mail for remuneration or hire from, to, within, or over the territory of a member.[37] The annex provides that

---

36 *Agreement on Government Procurement*, set out in Annex 4 of the *WTO Agreement*, above note 13, [*Government Procurement Agreement*], para. 2, art. XIII, provides that there will be multilateral negotiations under the GATS, above note 29, within two years of the entry into force of the *WTO Agreement*. This suggests that it is contemplated that there will be government procurement obligations under the multilateral GATS. If so, there is a question how these will interrelate with the existing obligations under the plurilateral *Government Procurement Agreement*.

37 See para. 6(d) of the Annex on Air Transport Services, GATS, above note 29.

aircraft repair and maintenance services, the selling and marketing of air transport services, and computer reservation services are covered by the GATS.[38]

b) Annex on Negotiations on Maritime Transport Services

The effect of this annex is to postpone the application of Article II (most-favoured-nation obligations) and the requirement to list non-conforming measures respecting international shipping, auxiliary services, and access to and use of port facilities pending the outcome of negotiations being conducted pursuant to the *Ministerial Decision on Negotiations on Maritime Transport Services*. The annex also permits members to modify specific commitments in this sector without compensation, provided that the modification is made between the time that the negotiations are concluded and the time that they are implemented.[39]

F. TELECOMMUNICATIONS

NAFTA Chapter Thirteen and CCFTA Chapter I (which is based on NAFTA Chapter Thirteen) set out requirements respecting telecommunications, as does the GATS Annex on Telecommunications.

1) NAFTA and CCFTA

NAFTA Chapter Thirteen and CCFTA Chapter I set out provisions that address some unique aspects of the telecommunications sector. This sector is otherwise subject to NAFTA Chapters Eleven and Twelve and to CCFTA Chapters G and H. NAFTA Chapter Thirteen prevails over other NAFTA chapters and CCFTA Chapter I prevails over other CCFTA chapters.

a) NAFTA Chapter Thirteen and CCFTA Chapter I

NAFTA Chapter Thirteen and CCFTA Chapter I are largely concerned with access to public telecommunications networks and basic services provided over those networks.[40] Basic services include communication

---

38   These three expressions are defined in *ibid.*, paras. 6(a), 6(b), & 6(c).
39   See para. 3 of the Annex on Negotiations on Maritime Transport Services, GATS, *ibid.*, and para. 5 of *Ministerial Decision on Negotiations on Maritime Transport Services* (GATS Decision).
40   See the definitions of "public telecommunication transport network," "network termination point," and "public telecommunications transport service" in NAFTA, above note 2, art. 1310, and CCFTA, above note 2, art. I-10.

by telephone, telegraph or telegram, telex and facsimile. The essence of a basic service is that the information is carried through the telecommunications network without being changed. More sophisticated telecommunications services involve customer interaction and are referred to as "enhanced or value-added."[41] Examples include voicemail, e-mail, and electronic data interchange. The distinction between basic services on the one hand and enhanced or value-added services on the other is critical because NAFTA and CCFTA requirements respecting enhanced or value-added services are more rigorous than with basic services.

NAFTA Article 1302 and CCFTA I-02 require each Party to ensure that persons of other Parties have access to the public network and the basic services offered within its territory and across its borders on reasonable and non-discriminatory terms and set out rules respecting various aspects of accessing public networks and basic services. However, Parties are not obliged to permit persons of other Parties to establish or acquire public networks.

NAFTA Article 1303 and CCFTA Article I-03 establish principles of non-discrimination and transparency respecting licensing, permits, registration, and other procedures regarding the provision of enhanced or value-added services. NAFTA Article 1304 and CCFTA Article I-04 set out requirements regarding standards-related measures respecting attaching terminal or other equipment to public telecommunications networks. NAFTA Article 1305 and CCFTA Article I-05 require that a monopoly designated or maintained for the purpose of providing basic services and that also competes in providing enhanced or value-added services or other telecommunications-related services or goods does not use its monopoly position to engage in anticompetitive conduct in these areas in which it is competing.

b) NAFTA Chapters Eleven and Twelve and CCFTA Chapters G and H
Canada, the United States, and Mexico have taken Annex II reservations respecting telecommunications networks and basic services from various obligations under NAFTA Chapters Eleven and Twelve, and Mexico has taken an Annex III reservation that reserves the provision of telegraph services and radio telegraph services to the state. Canada and Chile have each taken similar corresponding reservations respecting various obligations under CCFTA Chapters G and H. The effect is largely to exclude telecommunications networks and the provision of basic services from the NAFTA and CCFTA investment and services

---

41   This expression is defined in NAFTA, *ibid.*, art. 1310, and CCFTA, *ibid.*, art. I-10.

obligations. Enhanced and value-added services are expressly excluded from these reservations.[42] These reservations do not affect the obligations imposed by NAFTA Article Thirteen or by CCFTA Article I.

2) GATS Annex on Telecommunications

The GATS Annex on Telecommunications addresses matters of access, non-discrimination, and transparency similar to those described above in respect of NAFTA Chapter Thirteen and CCFTA Chapter I. Paragraph 2 of the annex provides that its scope extends to public telecommunications transport networks and services[43] but not to cable or broadcast distribution of radio or television programming. Paragraph 4 of the annex requires that member countries ensure that relevant information on conditions affecting access to and use of public telecommunications transport networks and services is publicly available. Paragraph 5 of the annex requires that service suppliers of other member countries be accorded access to and use of public telecommunications transport networks and services on reasonable and non-discriminatory terms.[44]

On 15 February 1997 the WTO members concluded three years of negotiations on improving market access in the basic telecommunications services sector. The negotiations produced fifty-five offers by sixty-nine governments (the European Union having made a single offer) of market access improvements. The resulting commitments will be annexed to a protocol to the GATS and added to the schedules of specific commitments of the member countries that made them. The GATS Annex on Negotiations on Basic Telecommunications deferred the entry into force of GATS Article II (MFN treatment) pending the outcome of these negotiations. Upon the protocol becoming effective on 1 January 1998, basic telecommunications services will be covered by this GATS provision.[45]

---

42 *Ibid*. The United States and Mexico have taken certain Annex I reservations affecting the provision of enhanced services.
43 These are defined expressions. See subparas. 3(c) & 3(b) of the Annex on Negotiations on Basic Telecommunicating, GATS, *ibid*.
44 The details of the application of this obligation are set out in subparas. 5(b) through (g), *ibid*.
45 For a summary of the results of these negotiations and the commitments made by each member, see the *World Trade Organization Negotiations on Basic Telecommunications: Informal Summary of Commitments and M.f.n. Exemptions*, 6 March 1997, http://www.wto.org/press/bt-summ3.htm. Canadian improvements include the elimination of Teleglobe's monopoly on overseas facilities-based service in October 1998 and of Telesat's exclusive rights on satellite facilities and earth stations serving the U.S./Canada market as of March 2000. Certain foreign equity limitations will also be relaxed.

G. FINANCIAL SERVICES

NAFTA Chapter Fourteen sets out comprehensive provisions based on principles of non-discrimination covering financial institutions and the cross-border provision of financial services. There is no counterpart to NAFTA Chapter Fourteen in any of the other trade agreements to which Canada is a party. The GATS contains two annexes respecting financial services, but neither is comparable to NAFTA Chapter Fourteen.

1) NAFTA Chapter Fourteen

a) Scope and Coverage

NAFTA Chapter Fourteen is a free-standing code covering financial institutions and the provision of financial services. Chapter Eleven (Investment) does not apply to measures adopted or maintained by Parties to the extent that they are covered by Chapter Fourteen.[46] Chapter Twelve (Services) does not apply to financial services as defined in Chapter Fourteen.[47]

i) Financial Institutions

Chapter Fourteen covers measures of Parties that affect financial institutions of other Parties. Chapter Fourteen also covers measures affecting the ability of investors of Parties to invest in financial institutions of other Parties. The scope of Chapter Fourteen as it relates to financial institutions is governed by the definitions of "financial institution" and "financial institution of a Party."

A financial institution is any financial intermediary or other enterprise authorized to do business and regulated or supervised as a financial institution under the laws of the Party in which it is located.[48] It is significant that a financial institution is not defined in terms of its activities but, rather, in terms of how it is regulated in the country where it is located. A financial institution of another Party is a financial institution, including a branch, located in one Party that is controlled by persons of another Party. Persons are natural persons who are citizens or permanent residents of a Party or enterprises of a Party but do not include branches of enterprises of non-NAFTA countries. A financial institution in Canada controlled by a U.S. subsidiary of a Japanese

---

46 NAFTA, above note 2, 1101(3).
47 NAFTA, *ibid.*, art. 1201(2).
48 NAFTA, *ibid.*, art. 1416.

bank would be included in the definition, but a financial institution controlled by a U.S. branch of a Japanese bank would not be included in the definition.

Chapter Fourteen covers measures taken by a Party:

- affecting the operation within its territory of financial institutions of other Parties;
- affecting the ability of investors of other Parties (as defined in Chapter Eleven) to invest in financial institutions within its territory;
- specifically directed at financial institutions of other Parties affecting their ability to make investments[49] in its territory.

However, a measure of general application taken by a Party affecting the ability of investors of other Parties to make investments within its territory would be covered by Chapter Eleven, even though the investor of the other Party is a financial institution.

ii) Financial Services

Chapter Fourteen also covers measures affecting the cross-border provision of financial services.

"Financial services" are defined in NAFTA Article 1416 as services of a financial nature or services ancillary to such services. The definition includes insurance but does not mention any other activity, and "financial nature" is not defined. Besides insurance, such services include lending, various other banking services, services relating to the securities industry such as brokerage and underwriting, financial advisory services, financial leasing, factoring, providing bonding services and dealing in foreign exchange. Financial services need not be provided by a financial institution and a service provided by a "financial institution" has to be "of a financial nature" in order to be a "financial service."

A "financial service provider of a Party" is a national or an enterprise of a Party that provides financial services within that Party. A financial service provider may be but does not have to be a financial institution.

The concept of cross-border is identical to that in Chapter Twelve. Cross-border provision of trade in financial services means providing financial services:

- from one Party into another (such as from Canada into the United States);
- within a Party by one of its nationals or enterprises to a national or enterprise of another Party (such as within Canada by Canadians or Canadian enterprises to U.S. nationals or U.S. enterprises); or

---

49   As defined in NAFTA, *ibid.*, art. 1139, with some modifications.

- by a national (i.e., individual) of a Party within another Party (such as a Canadian providing financial advisory services in the United States).

iii) Denial of Benefits
NAFTA Article 1401(2) incorporates NAFTA Articles 1113 (denial of benefits — investment) and 1211 (denial of benefits — services) into Chapter Fourteen. The denial of benefits provisions in NAFTA Articles 1113 and 1211 set out the "substantial business activities" test and the other circumstances in which benefits can be denied when an "enterprise of a Party" is controlled by investors of non-Parties. The incorporation of NAFTA Article 1113 into Chapter Fourteen would permit Canada to deny benefits in respect of a financial institution in Canada controlled by a U.S. corporate entity owned by Japanese investors if the corporate entity did not have substantial business activities in the United States. Similarly, the incorporation of NAFTA Article 1211 would permit the United States to deny benefits to a cross-border financial services provider of Canada if the financial services provider was a Canadian corporate shell owned by European investors and without substantial business activities in Canada.

iv) Provinces and States
The obligations of NAFTA Chapter Fourteen apply to measures adopted by the Canadian provinces and the U.S. and Mexican states.

b) Non-Discrimination

i) National Treatment: Financial Institutions
NAFTA Articles 1405(1) and (2) set out obligations to provide no less favourable treatment that closely follow those set out in NAFTA Article 1102 described above. These obligations cover measures affecting the establishment, acquisition, expansion, management, conduct, operation, and sale or other disposition of financial institutions and investments in financial institutions within a party. These obligations benefit investors of other Parties, investments of those investors in financial institutions within a Party and financial institutions of other Parties.

ii) Prospective Rules Respecting Establishment of Financial Institutions
NAFTA Article 1403 provides for the recognition of certain principles respecting the establishment of financial institutions that are not consistent with practices followed at the time that NAFTA became effective.

Under NAFTA Article 1403(1), the Parties recognize that an investor of another Party should be able to establish a financial institution in the territory of a Party in a juridical form of its choosing. Canadian law required, and at the time of writing continues to require, that foreign banks operate through subsidiaries incorporated under Schedule II of the *Bank Act*. Mexican banking law contains a similar requirement.

Under NAFTA Article 1403(2), the Parties recognize that investors of other Parties should be able to participate widely in a Party's market through providing a range of financial services through separate financial institutions as a Party may require; geographic expansion; and ownership of financial institutions without being subject to ownership requirements. The separation of functions under the U.S. *Glass-Steagall Act* restrict the provision by commonly owned financial institutions providing diverse financial services such as banking and securities underwriting. At the time that NAFTA became effective, U.S. rules restricted interstate branching by banks. Canadian and Mexican laws respecting financial institutions contain foreign ownership restrictions.[50]

NAFTA Article 1403(4) allows a Party to require that an investor of another Party that does not own a financial institution in that Party's territory incorporate under that Party's laws. However, NAFTA Article 1403 provides that once the United States permits commercial banks to expand substantially throughout its territory, the Parties shall review their market access requirements with a view to permitting investors to choose their own juridical form (such as a branch). At the time of writing, the U.S. government had largely dismantled its restrictions on interstate branching and, as discussed below, Canada has agreed in GATS negotiations to allow foreign banks to establish branches in Canada.

iii) National Treatment: Cross-Border Trade in Financial Services
NAFTA Article 1405(3) requires each NAFTA country to accord no less favourable treatment to cross-border service providers than it accords to its own service providers. However, this obligation applies only when a NAFTA country permits the cross-border provision of a financial service and is subject to NAFTA Article 1404. NAFTA Article 1404(1) is, in effect, a standstill provision that prohibits future restrictions on cross-border trade that a Party permitted when NAFTA became effective (except to the extent set out in Section B of Annex VII). NAFTA Article 1404(2) requires that Parties permit persons within their territory to purchase financial service from cross-border financial service providers, but states that this obligation does not require that a Party permit such

---

50 U.S. investors were exempted from Canadian federal ownership restrictions respecting banks, insurance companies, investment companies, and loan and trust companies. See *Canada–United States Free Trade Agreement*, 22 December 1987, Can. T.S. 1989 No. 3, 27 I.L.M. 281, art. 1703(1).

financial service providers to do business or solicit within its territory. Subject to the standstill provision in Article 1404(1), each Party may define "doing business" and "solicitation."

iv) Application to Provinces and States
Much financial regulation in Canada and the United States is at the provincial or state level. Whereas bank regulation in Canada is an exclusive preserve of the federal government, jurisdiction respecting insurance companies and loan and trust companies exists at both levels of government, and provinces have exclusive responsibility for regulating the securities industry. While U.S. regulation in the securities industry is primarily federal, jurisdiction respecting banks is divided between the federal government and the states, and regulation of insurance companies occurs wholly at the state level.

NAFTA Article 1405(4) sets out rules that describe how the principles of national treatment described above are to be applied by provinces and states that are based on and elaborate upon the most-favourable-treatment approach that appears elsewhere in the NAFTA text in relation to provinces and states.

v) Equal Competitive Opportunities
NAFTA Article 1405(5) provides that the obligation to accord national treatment described above has been fulfilled if the treatment affords "equal competitive opportunities" and NAFTA Articles 1405(6) and (7) describe the application of this principle. The "equal competitive opportunities" test is consistent with the GATT jurisprudence respecting Article III:4 of GATT 1994 described in chapter 2 under "Article III:4: No Less Favourable Treatment."

vi) Most-Favoured-Nation Treatment
NAFTA Article 1406(1) sets out a most-favoured-nation obligation analogous to that set out in the investment and financial services chapters. However, NAFTA Article 1406(2) sets out an important qualification by providing that a Party may recognize prudential measures of another Party or a non-Party, either unilaterally, through harmonization or other means or by agreement or other arrangement. If this occurs, the Party according the recognition must give a Party to which recognition has not been accorded the opportunity to demonstrate that its prudential measures are comparable and should also be recognized and provide the other Party with an opportunity to negotiate accession to the agreement or arrangement or negotiate something comparable. However, the obligations of a Party in these circumstances to other Parties do not extend beyond this.

c) Creation of Norms

i) Provisions Incorporated from Other NAFTA Chapters

NAFTA Article 1401(2) incorporates NAFTA Articles 1109 (transfers),[51] 1110 (expropriation and compensation), 1111 (special formalities), and 1114 (environmental measures) into Chapter Fourteen. All these provisions have been discussed above. The investor-state dispute settlement procedures described in chapter 10 are also incorporated into NAFTA Chapter Fourteen solely for breaches of the incorporated provisions of Chapter Eleven. Therefore, if a Party expropriates a bank owned by investors of another Party, NAFTA Article 1110 applies and those investors can invoke these procedures to secure a remedy. However, the investor-state dispute settlement procedures do not apply to other provisions of NAFTA Article Fourteen.

ii) Preservation of Concessions under CUFTA

Under CUFTA Chapter Seventeen, Canada exempted U.S. residents and companies controlled by U.S. residents from the ownership restrictions that applied and continue to apply to banks and federally chartered insurance companies, loan companies, trust companies, and investment companies. Canada also exempted U.S.–controlled Schedule II banks from limitations on total domestic assets that applied and continues to apply to foreign bank subsidiaries and from having to obtain the approval of the minister of finance to open branches in Canada. These concessions were extended to Mexico in Canada's Schedule C to Annex VII.

NAFTA Annex 1401.4 preserves the U.S. concessions in CUFTA 1702(1) and CUFTA 1702(2) by incorporating them into NAFTA. CUFTA Article 1702(1) required that domestic and foreign banks and bank holding companies in the United States be permitted to deal in, underwrite, and purchase debt instruments backed by the government of Canada and Canadian provincial governments. Under CUFTA Article 1702(2), the United States agreed not to adopt any federal measure that would accord to Canadian-controlled banks treatment less favourable than that existing on 4 October 1987 respecting their ability to establish and operate any state branch, state agency, or bank, or lending company subsidiary outside their home states.

---

51 NAFTA, above note 2, art. 1410(4), elaborates on NAFTA art. 1109(4) by permitting a NAFTA country to prevent or limit transfers by financial institutions and financial service providers to affiliates in the application of measures relating to the maintenance of the "safety, soundness, integrity or financial responsibility of financial institutions or cross-border financial service providers."

iii) New Financial Services and Data Processing

Subject to some requirements, NAFTA Article 1407(1) requires each Party to permit financial institutions of other NAFTA countries to provide any new financial services[52] that it permits its own financial institutions to provide. NAFTA Article 1407(2) requires each Party to permit financial institutions of other NAFTA countries to transfer information out of its territory for data processing required in the ordinary course of business.

iv) Senior Management and Boards of Directors

NAFTA Article 1408 sets out a provision similar to that in NAFTA Article 1107 above respecting senior management and boards of directors that applies to financial institutions of other Parties. Like NAFTA Article 1107, NAFTA Article 1407 permits nationality or residency requirements respecting boards of directors but without the qualification that the requirement does not impair the ability to exert control.

d) Transparency

NAFTA Article 1411 sets out transparency requirements respecting publication of measures and applications to provide financial services.

e) Exceptions

NAFTA Article 1401(3) provides that Chapter Fourteen shall not prevent a NAFTA country or its public entities from exclusively conducting or providing activities or services forming part of a public retirement plan or statutory system of social security.

NAFTA Article 1410(1) provides that nothing in Part Five of NAFTA (which includes not only Chapter Fourteen but also Chapters Eleven, Twelve, Thirteen, Fifteen, and Sixteen) prevents a NAFTA country from adopting and maintaining reasonable measures for prudential reasons (such as measures to protect investors, depositors, financial market participants, policy holders, policy claimants, and persons to whom fiduciary duties are owed). NAFTA Article 1410(2) provides that Part Five does not apply to non-discriminatory measures of general application taken by public entities in pursuit of monetary and related credit policies or exchange rate policies.

f) Reservations and Specific Commitments

NAFTA Chapter Fourteen addresses the question of non-conforming measures existing at the time NAFTA became effective in much the

---

52   See definition in NAFTA, *ibid.*, art. 1416.

same manner as described above in respect of investment and services. The reservations of each Party are set out in its schedule to Annex VII, and each Party's schedule is divided into Sections A, B, and C. Reservations set out in Annexes I through IV in respect of the national treatment and MFN treatment requirements of NAFTA Articles 1102, 1103, 1202, and 1203 also constitute reservations respecting Articles 1405 (national treatment) and 1406 (MFN treatment).[53]

i) Section A Reservations
NAFTA Article 1409(1) provides that NAFTA Articles 1403 (establishment of financial institutions), 1404 (cross-border trade), 1405 (national treatment), 1406 (MFN treatment), 1407 (new financial services and data processing), and 1408 (senior management and boards of directors) do not apply to federal non-conforming measures or those of provinces or states set out in Section A of each Party's schedule to Annex VII. Reservations at the federal level were set out in the original NAFTA text signed on 17 December 1992. Provinces and states had until 1 January 1994 or, in the case of some U.S. states, until 1 January 1995 to list their non-conforming measures. Unlike with NAFTA Chapters Eleven and Twelve where the grandfathering approach described above was ultimately adopted, provincial and state non-conforming measures were actually listed. NAFTA Article 1409(1) grandfathers non-conforming measures of local governments.

As under NAFTA Articles 1108 and 1206, these provisions apply only to measures that existed on 1 January 1994. Non-conforming measures made less non-conforming or eliminated cannot subsequently be amended or replaced with a new measure that is more non-conforming.

Canada and the United States have each taken limited reservations under Section A of Annex VII. Section A for Canada includes reservations for certain provincial laws affecting loan and trust corporations, credit unions and caisse populaires, mortgage brokers, and the insurance and securities industries. The Mexican reservations under Section A of Annex VII are extensive and carry forward Mexican laws and regulations that limit foreign investment in a wide range of financial institutions.

ii) Section B Reservations and Section C Commitments
NAFTA Article 1409(2) provides that NAFTA Articles 1403 to 1408 do not apply to non-conforming measures adopted and maintained by a Party in accordance with Section B of its schedule. Section C of each Party's schedule sets out specific commitments.

---

53   NAFTA, *ibid.*, art. 1409(4).

Section B of the Annex VII schedules of each of Canada and the United States sets out reservations respecting the cross-border trade in securities services. Section B of the Canadian schedule to Annex VII also reserves the right to adopt or maintain measures requiring enterprises of other Parties to be controlled by residents of those Parties in order to be entitled to the benefits of Chapter Fourteen. Section C of the Canadian schedule extends CUFTA benefits to Mexico as described above and Section B of the U.S. schedule sets out a very limited exception to certain provisions of the *Glass-Steagall Act*.

Sections B and C of the Mexican schedule to Annex VII are extensive and complex. Essentially, these sections establish a process of liberalization that will be phased in over a transition period ending on 1 January 2000. Once the transition period is complete, Mexico will have partially liberalized its financial services sector for investors of other Parties.[54]

2) GATS Annexes on Financial Services

The GATS sets out an Annex on Financial Services (First Annex) and a Second Annex on Financial Services (Second Annex). Paragraph 2 of the First Annex affirms the right of member countries to adopt prudential measures and that the GATS does not require the disclosure of confidential information. GATS Article 3 is similar to NAFTA 1406(2) described above in that it permits member countries to enter into arrangements that recognize the prudential measures of other member countries. However, these arrangements must give to other interested member countries the opportunity to negotiate accession to such arrangements or to negotiate comparable ones. The Second Annex extended the time for the listing of measures inconsistent with the MFN obligation in GATS Article II and provided a further opportunity for member countries to improve, modify, or withdraw their specific commitments.

In December 1997 negotiators of seventy WTO member countries, including Canada, reached agreement on specific commitments that will significantly liberalize financial services markets. For example, Canada has agreed to allow foreign banks to open branches in Canada but will not permit loans by foreign bank branches of less than $150,000. The agreement is scheduled to take effect in March 1999.

---

54 The details of this liberalization process are described at 368 to 372 of J.R. Johnson, *The North American Free Trade Agreement: A Comprehensive Guide* (Aurora: Canada Law Book, 1994).

H. TEMPORARY ENTRY

NAFTA Chapter Sixteen and CCFTA Chapter K set out requirements respecting the temporary entry of business persons. The GATS also sets out an Annex on Movement of Natural Persons Supplying Services under the Agreement (Natural Persons Annex).

The NAFTA and CCFTA temporary entry provisions are ancillary to services and investment provisions of each of those agreements and the Natural Persons Annex complements the GATS. The provisions exist to prevent a member country from subverting its market access commitments under the services and investment chapters by refusing entry to service providers or investors or their employees. These provisions apply only to measures respecting non-immigrants and do not affect laws respecting persons seeking permanent residence. None of NAFTA or CCFTA or the GATS purports to incorporate a principle of free movement of people like the European Union. Canada and the United States may have the longest undefended border in the world but that applies only in the military sense. Each country's border is well-defended by immigration officials who screen those who enter from the other.

Policy respecting temporary entry is driven by a number of factors. Persons seeking entry from other countries may be security risks or carriers of disease, so screening is necessary for national security and public health purposes. Temporary entry rules are usually designed to restrict access by temporary entrants to job markets through employment authorization/validation or labour certification requirements; it must be established that there is no one available locally to do the work proposed to be performed by a temporary entrant. Persons entering a country for reasons other than pleasure or short business visits usually must obtain entry documentation, which may include a visa.

1) NAFTA Chapter Sixteen and CCFTA Chapter K: Creation of Norms

NAFTA and CCFTA each simplify procedures for temporary entry by prohibiting employment validation or labour certification requirements for various categories of business persons.

NAFTA Article 1603(1) and CCFTA Article K-03(1) require each Party to grant temporary entry to business persons who otherwise qualify for entry under the immigration regulations respecting public health, safety, and national security standards in accordance with the provisions of NAFTA Chapter Sixteen. A "business person" is defined in each agreement as a citizen of a Party engaged in trade in goods, provision of services, or in the conduct of investment activities.[55]

The categories of business person and the basis upon which temporary entry will be granted to each category are set out in NAFTA Annex 1603 and in CCFTA Annex K-03(1). The four categories of business persons covered by these annexes are business visitors, traders and investors, intracompany transferees, and professionals. The annexes set out the specific requirements and commitments that apply to each category.

2) GATS Natural Persons Annex

The Natural Persons Annex applies to measures affecting natural persons who are service suppliers of a member country and natural persons of a member employed by a service supplier of a member. The annex does not apply to natural persons seeking access to the employment market of a member or to measures respecting permanent residence. The annex makes provision for the negotiation of specific commitments respecting the movement of natural persons covered by the agreement.

I. MONOPOLIES AND STATE ENTERPRISES

Government-created monopolies exist to varying degrees in almost all countries. While fewer monopolies exist in the United States than in most countries, postal services are still delivered by the U.S. Postal Service, a monopoly created and owned by the U.S. federal government. In many countries activities such as the provision of basic telecommunication services are conducted through monopolies. The Canadian Wheat Board maintains a monopoly over a significant portion of Canada's interprovincial and international trade in grain and grain products. Provincial hydro-electric utilities have a monopoly over most power generation, and provincial governments require that at least some alcoholic beverages be bought and sold within the province by provincial liquor monopolies.

Most governments have at least some state enterprises. Both the federal and the provincial governments in Canada conduct certain activities through state enterprises generally referred to as Crown corporations. Some of these, like Canada Post and the provincial liquor boards and hydroelectric power commissions, function as monopolies in at least some of their activities. Others are businesses owned by the government that compete in the private sector. Some state enterprises have

---

55 NAFTA, above note 2, art. 1608. CCFTA, above note 2, art. K-08.

delegated authority to exercise government functions. For example, licences to import and export grain products are issued by the Canadian Wheat Board.

Monopolies and state enterprises can discriminate and pursue other activities that distort the trade in goods or services or that adversely affect goods and service providers of other countries. For example, a monopoly can engage in anticompetitive practices by using profits from the monopolized sector to give it an unfair advantage when trading in non-monopolized sectors. An effective trade agreement must discipline the activities of monopolies and state enterprises but cannot prohibit them because of their widespread use and the legitimate social needs that some fulfil.

1) Common Themes

The obligations imposed by the WTO agreements and by NAFTA, CIFTA, and CCFTA respecting monopolies and state enterprises revolve about common themes.

a) Right to Designate
NAFTA, CIFTA, and CCFTA affirm the right to designate monopolies and state enterprises.

b) Non-Discrimination
All the trade agreements set out some form of non-discrimination requirement that must be observed by monopolies and state enterprises in the conduct of their activities.

c) Commercial Considerations
All the trade agreements require at least to some degree that monopolies and state enterprises base their purchases and sales on commercial considerations.

d) Anticompetitive Practices
All the trade agreements address to some extent the use by monopolies of profits derived from the monopolized sector to create unfair competitive advantages in non-monopolized sectors.

e) Regulatory Authority
NAFTA, CIFTA, and CCFTA require that monopolies and state enterprises exercise regulatory authority in a manner consistent with the NAFTA, CIFTA, or CCFTA obligations.

2) WTO Agreements

a) Provisions of GATT 1994

The principal GATT provisions respecting state trading enterprises and monopolies are set out in Article XVII of GATT 1994. Article II:4 of GATT 1994 applies to import monopolies, and an Interpretative Note to Articles XI, XII, XII, XIV, and XVIII of GATT 1994 provides that "import restrictions" and "export restrictions" used in these articles include those made effective through state trading enterprises.

Article XVII:1 of GATT 1994 applies to state enterprises or enterprises to which exclusive or special privileges (which need not amount to a monopoly) have been granted. The requirements of Article XVII:1 are as follows:

- *Non-discrimination*: Such enterprises must act, in their purchases or sales involving imports or exports, in a manner consistent with the general principles of non-discriminatory treatment prescribed by the GATT for measures affecting imports and exports by private traders.
- *Commercial considerations*: Such enterprises must make such purchases or sales solely in accordance with commercial considerations.

Article XVII:2 of GATT 1994 provides that the obligations imposed by GATT Article XVII do not apply to purchases by government for its own use.

Article II:4 of GATT 1994 addresses the question of mark-ups that can be charged by import monopolies on products listed on a contracting party's Schedule of Concessions and covered by bound tariffs. The effect of this provision is that an import monopoly cannot apply mark-ups to imported products that protect the domestic industry more than would be the case if the products were imported by private traders subject to the bound tariff.[56]

b) GATS Article VIII

GATS Article VIII sets out requirements respecting monopolies and exclusive service suppliers.

- *Non-discrimination*: Member countries must ensure that monopoly suppliers of services act consistently with the MFN requirements of Article II and the members' specific commitments.

---

56 If the product is not covered by a concession, art. XVII(4)(b) of the *General Agreement on Tariffs and Trade 1994*, set out in Annex 1A of the *Agreement Creating the World Trade Organization*, 15 April 1994 (Dobbs Ferry, N.Y.: Oceana Publications, 1997) [GATT 1994], obliges a contracting party to provide mark-up information upon the request of another contracting party with a substantial trade in the product concerned.

- *Anticompetitive practices*: Member countries must ensure that monopoly suppliers that supply services outside of the scope of the monopoly that are subject to that member's specific commitments do not abuse their monopoly position.

3) NAFTA, CIFTA, and CCFTA

a) Monopolies

i) Right to Designate

NAFTA Article 1502(1), CIFTA Article 7.2(1), and CCFTA Article J-02(1) each provide that nothing in the agreement shall be construed to prevent a Party from designating a monopoly. In the case of NAFTA and CCFTA, this provision must be considered together with NAFTA Article 1110 and CCFTA Article G-10, which require the payment of full compensation in the event of a nationalization or expropriation. One could argue that the requirement to pay compensation would, for all practical purposes, prevent the designation of a monopoly where the designation put investments of other investors of other Parties out of business and therefore that the compensation provision should not apply in such instances. It is unlikely that a panel or tribunal would accept this argument because NAFTA Article 1502(1) and CCFTA Article J-02(1) are, in effect, exceptions to the obligations under the investment and services chapters of each of these agreements and will be narrowly construed, and because the result would be egregiously unfair. However, the requirement to pay full compensation would defeat the entire purpose of a monopoly established for the purpose of supplying an essential service at a lower cost to the public.

A Party designating a monopoly must "wherever possible" provide prior written notification to the other Party or other Parties whose persons' interests will be affected and "endeavour" to introduce conditions on the operation of the monopoly that will minimize or eliminate nullification or impairment.[57]

ii) Requirements

NAFTA Article 1502(3), CIFTA Article 7.3, and CCFTA Article J-02(3) set out requirements that must be fulfilled by "government" monopolies and "privately owned" monopolies. The NAFTA and CCFTA provisions

---

57 NAFTA, above note 2, art. 1502(2); *Canada–Israel Free Trade Agreement*, in force 1 January 1997, see http://www.dfait-maeci.gc.ca/english/trade/agrement.htm [CIFTA], art. 7.2(2); and CCFTA, above note 2, art. J-02(2).

are virtually identical, while the CIFTA provisions differ in a number of respects, mainly because CIFTA does not contain an investment or services chapter. While privately owned monopolies include those designated by both federal and provincial (or, in the case of NAFTA, state) governments, under NAFTA and CCFTA a government monopoly is defined as one owned or controlled by the federal government.[58] Monopolies owned by provincial governments, such as the provincial liquor boards and hydroelectric utilities, are not covered by these NAFTA and CCFTA provisions. The CIFTA provisions use the expression "government monopoly" in the same context as their NAFTA and CCFTA counterparts but, as the expression is undefined in CIFTA, the expression could be read to include Canadian provincial government monopolies.

Monopolies covered by these provisions are subject to the following requirements:

- *Regulatory authority*: These monopolies must act in a manner not inconsistent with the Party's obligations under the agreement in exercising any regulatory or administrative authority delegated to them in connection with the monopoly good or service.[59]
- *Non-discrimination*: Under NAFTA and CCFTA, these monopolies must provide non-discriminatory treatment (the better of national treatment and MFN treatment) to investments of investors of other Parties and to goods and service providers of other Parties in its purchases and sales of the monopoly good or service.[60]
- *Anticompetitive practices*: These monopolies must not engage in anticompetitive practices in non-monopolized markets that adversely affect investments of the other Party (NAFTA) or other Parties (CIFTA and CCFTA).
- *Commercial considerations*: These monopolies must act solely in accordance with commercial considerations in their purchases and sales of the monopoly good or service in the relevant market (subject to a right to deviate from this requirement to the extent necessary to comply with the terms of its designation, as long as the terms of the

---

58 NAFTA, *ibid.*, art. 1505, and CCFTA, above note 2, art. J-05.
59 NAFTA, *ibid.*, art. 1502(3)(a); CIFTA, above note 57, art. 7.2(3)(a); and CCFTA, *ibid.*, art. J-02(3)(a). Examples given include the power to grant import and export licences, approve commercial transactions, or impose quotas, fees, or charges.
60 NAFTA, *ibid.*, art. 1502(3)(c), and CCFTA, *ibid.*, art. J-02(3)(c). See the definition of "non-discriminatory treatment" in NAFTA art. 1505 and CCFTA art. J-05. CIFTA, *ibid.*, art. 7.3(2) does not contain a corresponding provision because CIFTA does not include an investment or a services chapter.

designation are not inconsistent with the obligations respecting non-discrimination and anticompetitive practices described above).[61]

b) State Enterprises

i) Right to Designate

NAFTA Article 1503(1), CIFTA Article 7.3, and CCFTA Article J-03 provide that nothing in these agreements prevents a Party from designating a state enterprise.[62]

ii) Requirements

The requirements of NAFTA Article 1503, CIFTA Article 7.3, and CCFTA Article J-03 apply to state enterprises of both the federal and provincial (and, in the case of NAFTA, state) governments.

- *Regulatory authority:* Under NAFTA Article 1503(2) and CCFTA Article J-03(2), state enterprises must exercise regulatory, administrative or other authority delegated to them in a manner not inconsistent with the Party's obligations in the investment chapter and, in the case of NAFTA, the financial services chapter. CIFTA Article 7.3(2) sets out a comparable provision but the reference to the "Party's obligations" is general and not restricted to any particular CIFTA chapter.
- *Non-discrimination*: State enterprises under NAFTA Article 1503(3) and CCFTA Article J-03(3) must accord non-discriminatory treatment in the sale of goods and services to investments of investors of other Parties. This obligation is narrower than the non-discrimination requirement that applies to monopolies that includes purchases as well as sales and goods and service providers as well as investments of investors of other Parties. This obligation is meaningful in the case of a provincial hydroelectric utility that sells power to investments of investors of other Parties (such as U.S.–owned businesses in Canada) but does not affect provincial liquor boards whose sales for the most part are to individuals rather than to investments and whose purchasing practices are not covered. The corresponding provision in CIFTA Article 7.3(3) requires that state enterprises accord non-discriminatory treatment in the sale of its goods. The obligation does not extend to purchases.

---

61 NAFTA, *ibid.*, art. 1502(3)(b); CIFTA, *ibid.*, art. 7.2(3)(b); and CCFTA, *ibid.*, art. J-02(3)(b). Note by way of contrast that the "commercial considerations" requirement in art. XVII(1)(b) of GATT 1994, above note 56, is not subject to qualification.
62 Note the country specific definitions of "state enterprise" in NAFTA, *ibid.*, Annex 1505, and CCFTA, *ibid.*, Annex J-04.

J. COMPETITION LAW

The objective of both international trade policy (as implemented through international trade agreements) and competition policy is to make markets work more effectively. International trade agreements limit the extent to which governments can distort the operation of markets through discriminatory measures applied to foreign goods, service providers, and investors, whereas competition policy is directed at regulating and in some instances prohibiting conduct that is or can be anticompetitive. Despite some obvious linkages, however, between trade policy and competition policy, the trade agreements to which Canada is a party deal minimally with competition law issues.

1) WTO Agreements

In GATS Article IX, member countries recognize that certain practices may restrain competition and restrict trade in services. Article IX:2 requires each member to enter into consultations at the request of any other member with a view to eliminating such practices. The WTO agreements do not otherwise address competition law issues.

2) NAFTA, CIFTA, and CCFTA

NAFTA Article 1501(1), CIFTA Article 7.1(1), and CCFTA Article J-01 require that each Party adopt or maintain measures to proscribe anticompetitive conduct and to appropriate measures respecting such conduct. None of these agreements defines "anticompetitive conduct" or establishes standards that must be incorporated into each Party's domestic laws. Under NAFTA Article 1501(2), CIFTA Article 7.1(2), and CCFTA Article J-01(2), the Parties recognize the importance of cooperation and coordination among their authorities in competition law enforcement and agree to cooperate on issues of competition law enforcement policy. The cooperation includes mutual legal assistance, notification, consultation, and exchange of information relating to enforcement of competition laws and policies. NAFTA Article 1501(3), CIFTA Article 7.1(3), and CCFTA Article J-01(3) limit the utility of these provisions by providing that a Party may not have recourse to dispute resolution procedures for any matter arising under them.

CHAPTER 9

FURTHER EXCEPTIONS

The obligations set out in several WTO agreements, as well as NAFTA, CIFTA, and CCFTA are subject to general exceptions. The exceptions in Article XX of GATT 1994, which have been incorporated by reference into each of NAFTA, CIFTA, and CCFTA, are discussed in chapter 2. GATT 1994, the GATS, NAFTA, CIFTA, and CCFTA also contain further exceptions respecting national security and balance of payments. NAFTA, CIFTA, and CCFTA contain exceptions respecting cultural industries. The GATS, NAFTA, CIFTA, and CCFTA contain exceptions respecting taxation measures, and the GATS, NAFTA, and CCFTA contain exceptions respecting the disclosure of information.

A. NATIONAL SECURITY

Article XXI of GATT 1994 provides that nothing in GATT 1994 will require a contracting party to disclose information that it considers necessary to its essential security interests or prevents a contracting party from "taking any action which it considers necessary for the protection of its essential security interests" relating to such matters as arms traffic, supplying military and security establishments and the non-proliferation of nuclear weapons, or "taken in time of war or other emergency in international relations." GATS Article XIV*bis*, Article 73 of the *TRIPS*

Agreement, NAFTA Article 2102, CIFTA Article 10.2, and CCFTA Article O-02 all contain similarly worded exceptions.[1]

The difficulty with assessing the scope of these exceptions lies in their self-judging nature. Other than CIFTA Article 10.2, the exceptions are worded in such a manner that it is up to the government that takes the action to judge whether the action is necessary for the protection of its essential security interests. The U.S. government has consistently taken the position that it is in the exclusive judgment of the government taking the action to determine what actions are necessary for the protection of its essential security interests. In *U.S. — Trade Measures Affecting Nicaragua*,[2] which involved a U.S. embargo on trade with Nicaragua, the U.S. government insisted that the panel's terms of reference be so narrowly defined that the panel was precluded from examining or judging the validity of or the motivation for the invocation by the United States of Article XXI of GATT 1947, the identically worded predecessor of Article XXI of GATT 1994.

It is certainly arguable that these exceptions are not open-ended and that there are limits on the ability of governments to take actions under their cover. As discussed in chapter 2, exceptions in international agreements are construed narrowly and GATT jurisprudence on the meaning of "necessary" has concluded that a member cannot rely on an exception to justify a measure as necessary if less inconsistent measures can be employed to address the problem. Also, while the provisions may be self-judging insofar as the "actions taken" in response to, say, an "emergency in international relations," the self-judging language does not apply to the question as to whether there is in fact an emergency, and it is clearly arguable that this question should be assessed by objective standards and not be left to be judged by the government taking the

---

1 There are slight differences in wording in all these provisions. However, all the provisions except for the *Canada–Israel Free Trade Agreement*, in force 1 January 1997, see http://www.dfait-maeci.gc.ca/english/trade/agrement.htm [CIFTA], art. 10.2(1)(b), are self-judging in that they provide that nothing in the relevant agreement will prevent the Party from taking actions that it *considers* necessary for the protection of its essential security interests taken in time of war or other emergency in international relations. The CIFTA version of this provision in art. 10.2(b) is similar but without the self-judging words "it considers." There are also national security exceptions in the *North America Free Trade Agreement*, 17 December 1992, Can. T.S. 1994 No. 2 [NAFTA], arts. 607 (relating to energy goods) & 1018 (government procurement), and in NAFTA art. 1603(1) and *Canada–Chile Free Trade Agreement*, 5 July 1997, see http://www.dfait-maeci.gc.ca/english/trade/agrement.htm [CCFTA], art. K-03(1), respecting temporary entry.

2 [1986] GATTPD LEXIS 1. The report of the panel is dated 13 October 1986.

action. For example, the U.S. government has treated the presence of a Communist government in Cuba as a continuing emergency in international relations, justifying actions against that country, such as trade embargoes, that are clearly inconsistent with U.S. WTO obligations. The fact that most countries have normal relations with Cuba suggests that applying an objective standard could result in a finding that the presence of a Communist government in Cuba does not constitute an emergency in international relations.

The scope of these national security exceptions has yet to be determined by a panel.

B. BALANCE OF PAYMENTS

Article XII of GATT 1994, GATS Article XII, NAFTA Article 2104, and CCFTA Article O-04 all contain exceptions for measures taken by member countries experiencing balance-of-payments difficulties. CIFTA Article 10:4 provides that balance-of-payments matters will be governed by the relevant provisions of GATT 1994.

1) Common Themes

Restrictions imposed under the balance-of-payments exceptions described above must all adhere to the following principles:

- restrictions must be applied on a non-discriminatory basis;[3]
- restrictions must not be more burdensome than is necessary to resolve the problem and must be progressively phased out as the situation improves and eliminated when no longer needed;[4]

---

3 See art. XII of the *General Agreement on Tariffs and Trade 1994*, set out in Annex 1A of the *Agreement Creating the World Trade Organization*, 15 April 1994 (Dobbs Ferry, N.Y.: Oceana Publications, 1997) [*WTO Agreement*] [GATT 1994] (subject to exceptions in art. XIV); para. 2(a) of the *General Agreement on Trade in Services*, set out in Annex 1B of the *WTO Agreement* [GATS], art. XII; NAFTA, above note 1, art. 2104(3)(e); and CCFTA, above note 1, art. O-04(3)(e).

4 Paragraphs 2(a) & (b) of art. XII of GATT 1994, *ibid.*; paragraphs 2(d) & (e) of GATS, *ibid.*, art. XII; NAFTA, *ibid.*, arts. 2104(3)(b) & (c); and CCFTA, *ibid.*, art. O-04(3)(b) & (c).

- restrictions must avoid unnecessary damage to the commercial or economic interests of other member countries.[5]

2) IMF Agreement

The *Articles of Agreement of the International Monetary Fund* (*IMF Agreement*) set out a number of requirements that must be satisfied by countries seeking to impose restrictions on international payments and transfers.[6] For example, Article VIII(2)(a) of the *IMF Agreement* provides that no member of the International Monetary Fund (IMF) shall impose restrictions on the making of payments and transfers for current international transactions without IMF approval. Article XII of GATT 1994 does not refer to the *IMF Agreement*,[7] but GATS Article XII requires that balance-of-payments restrictions be consistent with the *IMF Agreement* and NAFTA Article 2104 and CCFTA Article O-4 are closely tied to the requirements of the *IMF Agreement*.

3) Article XII of GATT 1994

Article XII of GATT 1994 permits a contracting party to limit imports in order to safeguard its external financial position. Import restrictions must not exceed those necessary to forestall an imminent drop in monetary reserves or, in the case of a party with low monetary reserves, achieve a reasonable rate of increase in its reserves. Besides incorporating the principles described above, Article XII prohibits restrictions on the importation of commercial samples or that would prevent compliance with patent, trademark, copyright, or similar procedures. Quantitative restrictions are subject to the requirements of Article XIII.[8] Article XII also sets out guidelines to be followed by countries in dealing with balance of payments matters[9] and provides for consultations under certain circumstances.

---

5   Paragraph 3(c)(i) of art. XII of GATT 1994, *ibid.*; para. 2(c) of GATS, *ibid.*, art. XII; NAFTA, *ibid.*, art. 3(a); and CCFTA, *ibid.*, art. O-04(3)(a).
6   See Schedule I to the *Bretton Woods Agreements Act*, R.S.C. 1985, c. B-7.
7   Article XV of GATT 1994, above note 3, entitled "Exchange Arrangements," deals with the IMF in a somewhat different context.
8   Note the exceptions to *ibid.*, art. XIII in art. XIV.
9   See, for example, para. 3(a) of art. XII, *ibid.*, which requires contracting parties to pay due regard for the need to maintain balance-of-payments equilibrium on a sound and lasting basis, and para. 3(d), which provides that a contracting party need not sacrifice full employment policies in order to avoid the need to impose restrictions under art. XII.

4) GATS

Subject to the principles described above, GATS Article XII permits member countries to adopt or maintain restrictions on trade in services in the event or threat of serious balance-of-payments and external financial difficulties. Restrictions must be notified to the Committee on Balance-of-Payments Restrictions and provision is made for consultations.

5) NAFTA and CCFTA

NAFTA Article 2104(1) and CCFTA Article O-04(1) provide that nothing in NAFTA or CCFTA will be construed to prevent a Party from restricting transfers when it is experiencing or threatened with serious balance-of-payments difficulties. NAFTA Article 2104 and CCFTA Article O-04 incorporate the principles described above, with non-discrimination being specifically described as being the better of national treatment or MFN treatment.

As mentioned above, the exceptions in NAFTA Article 2104 and CCFTA Article O-04 are closely tied to obligations imposed upon the Parties by the *IMF Agreement*.[10] If a Party imposes a measure under these provisions, it must submit any current exchange restrictions to the IMF for review, enter into consultations with the IMF on economic adjustment measures to address the economic problems causing the difficulties, and adopt or maintain policies consistent with such consultations. Measures protecting specific industries are permitted only if consistent with the provisions of Article VIII(3) of the *IMF Agreement*, which requires IMF approval of a restriction, and with the policies required as a result of the consultations with the IMF referred to above.

Restrictions on transfers are subject to further requirements set out in NAFTA 2104(5)[11] and CCFTA Article O-04(5). Restrictions on payments for current international transactions must be consistent with Article VIII(3) of the *IMF Agreement*. Restrictions on international capital transactions may only be imposed in conjunction with measures imposed on current international transactions and must be consistent with Article VI of the *IMF Agreement*. Article VI permits members to exercise controls necessary to regulate international capital movements but provides that, subject to limited exceptions, no member may exercise these controls so as to restrict payments for current transactions or

---

10 Canada, the United States, Mexico, and Chile are all IMF members.
11 NAFTA, above note 1, art. 2104(5) does not apply to the cross-border trade in financial services.

unduly delay transfer of funds in settlement of commitments. Restrictions on transfers covered by NAFTA Article 1109 and CCFTA Article G-09 and on transfers related to trade in goods may not "substantially" impede such transfers from being made in a freely convertible currency at a market rate of exchange. Restrictions on transfers may not take the form of trade restrictions such as tariff surcharges, quotas, licences, or similar measures.[12]

NAFTA Articles 2104(6) and 2104(7) set out rules respecting the cross-border trade in financial services that has no counterpart in CCFTA Article O-04. A Party may not impose more than one measure on any transfer unless it is consistent with the Article VIII(3) of *IMF Agreement* and the outcome of the consultations with the IMF referred to above. Once a restriction is imposed, the Party imposing the restriction must notify and consult with the other Parties to assess its balance of payments situation and the measures adopted.

C. CULTURAL INDUSTRIES

Cultural industries include such activities as film and video and music production and distribution, publication and distribution of books, newspapers, magazines and periodicals, and radio and television broadcasting. Cultural industries are sensitive sectors for many countries, Canada being among them. The Canadian government has gone to considerable lengths in its trade negotiations to preserve the ability of Canadian governments to protect cultural industries. Canadian policies to protect cultural industries have been and continue to be a trade irritant between Canada and the United States. The U.S. government and U.S. business view activities such as film and video production and distribution, radio and television broadcasting, and publishing books and magazines as commercial activities that are no more deserving of protection than other commercial activities.

1) Canadian Cultural Policies

Canadian policy respecting cultural industries has been directed not at excluding U.S. cultural products or those of other countries but, rather, at ensuring that cultural products of Canadian origin based on Canadian themes are available to the Canadian consumer. U.S. penetration of the Canadian market is considerable in all cultural industries and Canadian

---

12 Note that such measures are not prohibited by art. XII of GATT 1994, above note 3.

cultural policies do not inhibit in any significant way the ability of U.S. producers of cultural products (such as films or magazines) and providers of cultural services (such as cable television programming) to access the Canadian consumer. However, Canadian cultural policies are rooted in discrimination in one form or another and thus have the potential to be inconsistent with obligations under international trade agreements that are largely based on principles of non-discrimination.

Canadian cultural policies are based on the following themes:

- *Content requirements*: Television programming by Canadian stations must contain prescribed levels of Canadian content. Films must contain prescribed levels of Canadian content to be eligible for subsidies or tax benefits. Content is measured in terms of nationality of writer, director, lead actor or actress. In trade terms, these are "performance requirements" that are subject to disciplines under several trade agreements to which Canada is a party.
- *Trade restrictions*: Tariff Code item 9958 in Schedule VII of the *Customs Tariff*[13] (which is the only Canadian trade restriction specifically directed at a cultural product) prohibits the importation of split-run editions of periodicals. Split-runs are issues of a periodical using substantially the same editorial content but differing in some local content and advertising.[14] The objective of the restriction is to prevent Canadian advertising revenues from being siphoned into U.S. periodicals that are directed at the Canadian market but have little Canadian content. Without the cover of an exception, import restrictions are inconsistent with Canada's obligations under a number of trade agreements. As discussed below, Tariff Code item 9958 has been successfully challenged by the United States in *Canada — Certain Measures Concerning Periodicals*.
- *Foreign ownership restrictions*: Television stations and cable companies must be effectively owned and controlled by Canadians. Absent an exception, foreign ownership requirements are inconsistent with the national treatment and right of establishment requirements of investment obligations.
- *Other discriminatory practices*: Under the Investment Canada film distribution policy, foreign film distribution businesses establishing new

---

13 Following 1 January 1998, this prohibition is set out in tariff item 9897.00.00 in the schedule to the *Customs Tariff*.

14 This tariff code item also prohibits the importation of issues of periodicals, more than 5 percent of the advertising space in which indicate sources of availability or terms or conditions for the sale of goods in Canada. This tariff code item is directed only at split-runs and not at foreign periodicals generally.

businesses in Canada may only distribute film product in Canada in which they have proprietorial rights.[15] Split-run periodicals printed in Canada are subject to a special 80 percent excise tax on advertising revenue while Canadian periodicals benefit from preferential postal rates.[16] Expenses for advertising in newspapers or periodicals are not deductible unless the newspaper or periodical is Canadian-owned. Canadian cable companies may not carry programming of foreign (i.e., U.S.) cable service providers if there is a competing Canadian cable service.[17] All these policies are subject to attack under the trade agreements to which Canada is a party unless an exception applies. As discussed below, the 80 percent excise tax and the preferential postal rates have both been successfully challenged by the United States in *Canada — Certain Measures Concerning Periodicals*.

2) WTO Agreements

None of the WTO agreements single out cultural industries for special treatment and there are no exceptions for the products produced or the services provided by any of these industries. Like GATT 1994, the GATS does not contain any exception that is directed at cultural industries. However, unlike GATT 1994, the national treatment and market access provisions of the GATS apply only to those sectors identified by member countries in their schedules of specific commitments. Canada has created exceptions for most cultural services by not including them on its schedule.[18]

---

15   This policy became effective in 1987. At that time, U.S. majors such as Twentieth Century Fox, Tristar, Columbia, and Warner had long established film distribution activities in Canada and they were unaffected by the policy.
16   This provision was enacted in response to the circumvention by *Sports Illustrated* of Tariff Code item 9958 by transmitting its Canadian split-run edition electronically to Canada and having it printed in Canada, thereby bypassing the border. The effect of the 80 percent excise tax was to make the Canadian split-run edition uneconomic.
17   For example, Canadian cable companies do not carry ESPN because it competes directly with TSN. The application of this policy led to a major trade dispute when the CRTC required that a U.S. country music cable service cease being provided by Canadian cable companies because a competing Canadian cable service had been established. The dispute was ultimately settled through negotiation outside the formal dispute settlement process.
18   The Film Distribution Policy described above may be inconsistent with Canada's GATS MFN obligation under GATS, above note 3, art. II, in that it does not apply to the U.S. majors that were distributing film in Canada before the policy came into effect. The Film Distribution Policy is not included in Canada's Schedule of Exemptions and the GATS does not grandfather existing non-conforming measures.

Canadian policies respecting periodicals had been a long-standing irritant between Canada and the United States. The United States initiated proceedings under the WTO (in *Canada — Certain Measures Concerning Periodicals*[19]) forthwith upon the imposition by Canada of the 80 percent excise tax on the advertising revenue of split-run periodicals in December, 1995. In addition to challenging the 80 percent excise tax, the United States also challenged Tariff Code Item 9958 and the preferential postal rates for Canadian periodicals. The WTO panel and the Appellate Body both held that the 80 percent excise tax was inconsistent with Article III:2 of GATT 1994.[20] The panel held that Tariff Code Item 9958 was inconsistent with Article XI:1 of GATT 1994 and rejected Canada's argument that the measure was justified under the exception in Article XX(d).[21] Canada did not appeal this finding to the Appellate Body. As discussed in chapter 2 under "Article III:8: Exceptions," the Appellate Body held that the preferential postal rates were inconsistent with GATT Article III. As a result of these panel and Appellate Body decisions, the deduction in Section 19 of the *Income Tax Act* for expenses for advertising in periodicals and newspapers that are Canadian-owned is the only Canadian policy respecting periodicals that remains intact.[22]

3) NAFTA, CIFTA, and CCFTA

a) Cultural Industries Defined

The NAFTA, CIFTA, and CCFTA definitions of "cultural industries" all read as follows:

> Cultural industries means persons engaged in any of the following activities:
>
> (a) the publication, distribution, or sale of books, magazines, periodicals, or newspapers in print or machine readable form but not including the sole activity of printing or typesetting any of the foregoing;

---

19 WT/DS31/R, Panel Report; WT/DS31/AB/R, Appellate Body Report (AB-1997-2).
20 As discussed in note 21 of chapter 2, the reasoning of the panel and the Appellate Body were different (*ibid.*).
21 Discussed in chapter 2 under "First Element: Policy Objective Falls within the Exception."
22 At the time of writing, the Canadian government had agreed to abide by the WTO panel and Appellate Body decisions, above note 19, but the offending provisions had not been repealed.

(b) the production, distribution, sale or exhibition of film or video recordings;

(c) the production, distribution, sale or exhibition of audio or video music recordings;

(d) the publication, distribution, or sale of music in print or machine readable form; or

(e) radio communications in which the transmissions are intended for direct reception by the general public, and all radio, television, and cable broadcasting undertakings and all satellite programming and broadcast network services.[23]

b) CIFTA and CCFTA

Cultural industries are exempted from the provisions of both CIFTA and CCFTA except for those respecting tariff elimination.[24]

c) NAFTA

NAFTA Annex 2106 reads as follows:

> Notwithstanding any other provision of this Agreement, as between Canada and the United States, any measure adopted or maintained with respect to cultural industries, except as specifically provided in Article 302 (Market Access-Tariff Elimination), and any measure of equivalent commercial effect taken in response, shall be governed under this Agreement exclusively in accordance with the provisions of the *Canada–United States Free Trade Agreement*. The rights and obligations between Canada and any other party with respect to such measures shall be identical to those applying between Canada and the United States.

NAFTA Annex 2106 has the effect, between Canada and the United States, of incorporating into NAFTA the entirety of the CUFTA provisions as they affect cultural industries. While CUFTA does not apply between Canada and Mexico, the effect of the last sentence of NAFTA Annex 2106 is to apply the CUFTA provisions as they affect cultural industries between Canada and Mexico. Thus the provisions of the CUFTA govern measures affecting cultural industries between Canada and each of the United States and Mexico, and not those of NAFTA (other than tariff elimination under NAFTA Article 302). Between the United States and Mexico, measures affecting cultural industries are governed by NAFTA.

---

23 NAFTA, above note 1, art. 2107; CIFTA, above note 1, art. 10.6; and CCFTA, above note 1, art. O-07.

24 CIFTA, *ibid.*, art. 10.6, and CCFTA, *ibid.*, art. O-06 & Annex O-06.

i) CUFTA Article 2005

CUFTA Article 2005(1) provides that, subject to certain exceptions described below, cultural industries are exempt from the CUFTA requirements. However, CUFTA Article 2005(2) permits a Party to take "measures of equivalent commercial effect" in response to actions of the other in respect of a cultural industry that are inconsistent with CUFTA but for CUFTA Article 2005(1). Exemption of cultural industries from CUFTA comes at the price of exposure to possible retaliation in the form of measures of equivalent commercial effect. However, the right to retaliate does not apply if the action is consistent with the CUFTA without having to rely upon the CUFTA 2005(1) exemption.

Many Canadian measures relating to cultural industries are "not inconsistent" with CUFTA requirements for reasons other than the application of CUFTA Article 2005(1). As a result of the blanket grandfathering in the CUFTA investment and service chapters, ownership restrictions and performance requirements that came into effect prior to CUFTA are unaffected by CUFTA requirements and thus "not inconsistent" with CUFTA.[25] The CUFTA services chapter and the provisions of the CUFTA investment chapter respecting the conduct and operation of businesses apply only to "covered services," which exclude virtually all services provided by cultural industries.[26] As under the GATS, Canada created an exception for cultural industries by keeping them off the list. Canadian measures affecting the conduct and operation of cultural industries that do not provide covered services are not covered by CUFTA requirements and therefore are not inconsistent with CUFTA. None of the measures just described depends on Article 2005(1) for its consistency with CUFTA requirements and, therefore, none of these measures is open to retaliation under CUFTA Article 2005(2). By way of example, the decision of the Canadian Radio-television and Telecommunications Commission (CRTC) to require Canadian cable companies to substitute the U.S. Country Music Television with a competing Canadian cable service affected the cross-border provision of a service that is not a covered service. The national treatment requirements of CUFTA Chapter Fourteen do not apply and, for this reason, the decision was not inconsistent with CUFTA requirements.

---

25 For example, Canadian ownership requirements under the *Broadcasting Act*, S.C. 1991, c. 11, and quota requirements for Canadian content predated *Canada–United States Free Trade Agreement*, 22 December 1987, Can. T.S. 1989 No. 3, 27 I.L.M. 281 [CUFTA].

26 Covered services do include one cultural industry, namely "establishments primarily engaged in the wholesale dealing in books, periodicals and newspapers." See Canadian SIC No. 5991, which is listed in CUFTA Annex 1408.

The Canadian measures respecting periodicals that were successfully challenged in *Canada — Certain Measures Concerning Periodicals* are all inconsistent with CUFTA requirements but for the application of CUFTA Article 2005(1). The 80 percent excise tax, which was found to be inconsistent with Article III:2 of GATT 1994, is inconsistent with CUFTA 501, which incorporates GATT Article III by reference.[27] Tariff Code 9958, which was found to be inconsistent with Article XI of GATT 1994, is also inconsistent with CUFTA Article 407(1) under which Canada and the United States affirm their GATT rights and obligations with respect to prohibitions or restrictions on bilateral trade in goods. CUFTA Article 1201 incorporates the GATT Article XX exceptions, which are unchanged in Article XX of GATT 1994. The reasoning applied by the WTO panel and the Appellate Body respecting the inapplicability of Article XX of GATT 1994 would apply equally to CUFTA Article 1201. CUFTA does not make provision for further exceptions other than the qualified exemption in CUFTA Article 2005(1). Respecting the postal rate subsidy, Canada would have had to rely on the same exception (namely that in GATT Article III:8 as incorporated by CUFTA Article 501) as it attempted to do in the periodicals case, and would face the same logic for denying the applicability of the exemption that was applied by the Appellate Body.

The only difference between the application of the exemption in CUFTA Article 2005 to these CUFTA-inconsistent measures and the exercise of WTO rights is one of process. However, the difference is significant. Under CUFTA Article 2005, the United States could have applied measures of "equivalent commercial effect" without resort to any proceedings but instead of doing this, the U.S. government elected to invoke the WTO dispute settlement procedures. By so doing, the U.S. government obtained a ruling from a respected international body that the Canadian measures were inconsistent with Canada's international obligations. As the Canadian government clearly cannot ignore the ruling, the U.S. Government will have achieved its objective of having the offending measures repealed. This is clearly a more satisfactory result from a U.S. perspective than applying measures of "equivalent commercial effect" that would not have been found to be justified in any proceeding and that may never have achieved the desired U.S. objective of the repeal by the Canadian government of the inconsistent measures.

---

27 CUFTA, *ibid.*, art. 501, refers to the "existing" provisions of GATT, art. III, which means those that were in effect as at 1 January 1989, the date that CUFTA became effective. However, the text of art. III of GATT 1994, above note 3, is the same as that of GATT III that was incorporated by CUFTA, art. 501.

ii) Exceptions to CUFTA Article 2005
There are four exceptions to the exemption provided in CUFTA Article 2005.

- *Tariff elimination*: The exemption does not apply to tariff elimination.
- *Forced divestiture*: The exemption does not apply to CUFTA Article 1607(4), which requires Canada to purchase a business from an investor of the United States at fair open market value in circumstances in which Canada requires the divestiture of a business enterprise in a cultural industry pursuant to its review of a direct acquisition.
- *Retransmission rights*: The exemption does not apply to CUFTA Article 2006 which protects copyright holders of television programming in respect of retransmission rights.
- *Print-in-Canada requirements*: CUFTA Article 2007 required that Section 19 of the *Income Tax Act* (Canada) be amended to eliminate the requirement that a Canadian issue be printed and typeset in Canada in order that an advertising expense placed in such an issue be deductible.

iii) Concluding Remarks
Although Canada has been able to shield a number of its cultural policies under NAFTA and CUFTA exemptions, the status of cultural policies under Canada's international trade agreements is far from satisfactory. The effect of NAFTA is to create a non-regime without disciplines. While Canada may be able to shield some of its policies from NAFTA disciplines, Canadian cultural industries are not protected from U.S. discriminatory measures. The United States has also bypassed NAFTA on at least one occasion, namely the periodicals case referred to above, by utilizing WTO rather than NAFTA dispute settlement procedures. Whether the decision in this case is specific to its fact situation or has broader implications for Canadian cultural policies remains to be seen.

D. TAXATION MEASURES

International trade agreements such as GATT 1994, NAFTA, CIFTA, and CCFTA set out substantive requirements affecting a variety of taxation measures. Article II of GATT 1994 imposes tariff bindings on contracting parties, and NAFTA, CIFTA, and CCFTA provide for the elimination of tariffs on originating goods. All of these agreements establish norms that affect other commodity taxes. For example, paragraph 2 of Article III of GATT 1994, which is incorporated into NAFTA, CIFTA, and CCFTA, requires that imported products of other contracting parties not be subject to internal taxes or charges higher than those imposed on like domestic products. The trade agreements to which Canada is a party serve as international commodity tax conventions.

Taxes on income, capital gains, and inheritances are covered by international bilateral tax conventions designed to avoid the double taxation. Unlike the trade agreements, which are based largely on national treatment, the bilateral tax conventions are generally based on principles of reciprocity. As long as the subject matter of trade agreements was confined to trade in goods, the taxation measures affected were restricted to commodity taxes. However, the national treatment requirements of trade agreements such as NAFTA and CCFTA apply to measures affecting services and investment. Without an exception, these provisions would cover taxes on income and capital gains that are already subject to different requirements under bilateral tax conventions.

1) GATS Exception for Taxation Measures

The general exceptions in Article XIV of the GATS includes an exception for measures that are inconsistent with the MFN requirements of GATS Article II provided that the difference in treatment is the result of an agreement on the avoidance of double taxation.[28]

2) NAFTA, CIFTA, and CCFTA Exceptions for Taxation Measures

NAFTA Article 2103, CIFTA Article 10.3, and CCFTA Article O-03 all contain exceptions for taxation measures. NAFTA Article 2103 and CCFTA Article O-03 are virtually identical in their wording. NAFTA, CIFTA, and CCFTA all provide that:

- Except as provided in NAFTA Article 2103, CIFTA Article 10.3, and CCFTA Article O-03, nothing in the agreement affects taxation measures (which for these purposes exclude customs duties, antidumping, and countervailing duties and importation fees).[29]

---

28 GATS, above note 3, art. XIV, para. (e).
29 See definition of "taxation measure" in NAFTA, above note 1, art. 2107; CIFTA, above note 1, art. 10.6; and CCFTA, above note 1, art. O-07. Also excluded in the case of NAFTA are fees applied pursuant to the U.S. *Agricultural Adjustment Act*, U.S.C. §22 (1998).

- Nothing in the agreement affects the rights of the Parties under a tax convention, and in the event of an inconsistency, the tax convention prevails.[30]
- The national treatment provisions of NAFTA Article 301, CIFTA Article 4.1, and CCFTA Article C-01 apply to taxation measures. Commodity taxes such as GST are covered by these provisions.
- The prohibition of export taxes in NAFTA Article 314 and 604, CIFTA Article 4.7, and CCFTA Article C-12 apply to taxation measures.

In addition, because NAFTA and CCFTA (unlike CIFTA) cover services and investment, NAFTA Article 2103 and CCFTA O-03 also provide that the national treatment and MFN requirements of NAFTA and CCFTA affecting investment, cross-border trade in services, and, in the case of NAFTA, financial services do not apply to:

- taxation measures on income, capital gains, or on the taxable capital of corporations unless they relate to the purchase or consumption of particular services; or
- taxes on estates, inheritances, gifts, and generation-skipping transfers;

but they do apply to other taxes such as Canada's goods and services tax. The application of these NAFTA provisions to the taxation measures that they do cover is subject to general grandfathering of non-conforming taxation measures existing on 1 January 1994 (NAFTA) or 5 July 1997 (CCFTA). These NAFTA and CCFTA provisions also do not apply to MFN obligations in tax conventions, new taxation measures aimed at the equitable and effective imposition of taxes that do not arbitrarily discriminate or nullify and impair NAFTA or CCFTA benefits, or to certain Mexican excise taxes on insurance premiums.[31]

The disciplines in NAFTA Article 1106 and CCFTA Article G-06 prohibiting performance requirements as conditions of receiving advantages apply to all taxation measures. This applies to taxes on income and capital gains as well as to sales, use, and value-added taxes.

NAFTA Article 2103(6) and CCFTA Article O-03(6) provide that the provisions of NAFTA 1110 and CCFTA G-10 respecting expropriation and compensation apply to taxation measures with the significant qualification that the determination of whether a measure is an expropriation must be referred to national taxation authorities. The investor may

---

30 CCFTA, *ibid.*, Annex O-03.1 provides that Canada and Chile will conclude a double taxation agreement within a reasonable period of time after CCFTA enters into force, and will exchange letters setting out the relationship between the agreement and CCFTA, art. O-03.
31 See NAFTA, above note 1, Annex 2103.4.

invoke NAFTA or CCFTA investor-state dispute settlement procedures only if the authorities fail to consider the matter or fail to agree that the measure is not an expropriation. However, NAFTA Article 2103(6) and CCFTA Article O-03(6) do not foreclose the application of the dispute settlement procedures in NAFTA Chapter Twenty or CCFTA Chapter N if the Party of the investor does not agree with the determination.

E. DISCLOSURE OF INFORMATION

GATS Article III*bis* provides that the GATS will not be construed to require any member to provide confidential information, the disclosure of which would impede law enforcement or otherwise be contrary to the public interest or prejudice the commercial interests of particular enterprises. NAFTA Article 2105 and CCFTA Article O-05 provide that NAFTA and CCFTA will not be construed to require a Party to furnish or allow access to information that would impede law enforcement or be contrary to laws protecting personal privacy or the financial affairs and accounts of individual customers of financial institutions. There is no comparable provision in CIFTA.

CHAPTER 10

INSTITUTIONAL STRUCTURE, DISPUTE RESOLUTION, AND CONCLUSION

This chapter will briefly describe the institutional structures of the trade agreements to which Canada is a party and the general dispute settlement procedures available for the resolution of disputes. The chapter will then describe the investor-state dispute settlement procedures provided for in NAFTA and CCFTA that may be invoked by investors who have suffered damage as a result of a breach of the investment provisions of these agreements.

A. INSTITUTIONAL STRUCTURE

Institutional structures under international agreements range from no structure at all to complex and intrusive supranational institutions that have direct authority over the conduct of prescribed matters within member countries. While the *WTO Agreement*, NAFTA, CCFTA, and CIFTA all establish institutional structures, none of these agreements create supranational institutions along the lines of the European Union.

1) WTO Agreement

The *WTO Agreement* established the World Trade Organization (WTO), an international body with a legal personality headquartered in Geneva. Its principal functions are to:

- facilitate the implementation, administration, and operation of the WTO agreements;
- provide the forum for negotiations among members concerning their multilateral trade relations; and
- administer the *Understanding on Rules and Procedures Governing the Settlement of Disputes (Dispute Settlement Understanding* or *DSU).*[1]

a) **Structure**

The WTO consists of a Ministerial Conference composed of representatives of the members who meet every two years. There is also a General Council made up of representatives of the members, as well as:

- a Council for Trade in Goods to oversee the functioning of GATT 1994 and the other Multilateral Trade Agreements in Annex 1A of the *WTO Agreement*;
- a Council for Trade in Services to oversee the functioning of the GATS;
- a Council for Trade-Related Aspects of Intellectual Property to oversee the TRIPS Agreement.[2]

The Ministerial Conference is also directed by the *WTO Agreement* to establish a Committee on Trade and Development, a Committee on Balance of Payments, and a Committee on Budget, Finance, and Administration. These committees are to carry out various functions that are assigned to them.[3] The Multilateral Agreements also establish committees covering the specific subject matter of the agreement. Accordingly, there is a Committee on Agriculture,[4] a Committee on Sanitary and Phytosanitary Measures,[5] a Textile Monitoring Body (TMB),[6] a Committee on Technical Barriers to Trade,[7] a Committee on Trade-Related Invest-

---

1 *Agreement Creating the World Trade Organization*, 15 April 1994 (Dobbs Ferry, N.Y.: Oceana Publications, 1997) [*WTO Agreement*], art. III. The WTO also administers the Trade Policy Review Mechanism discussed in chapter 1.
2 *WTO Agreement*, ibid., art. IV, para. 5.
3 *Ibid.*, art. IV, para. 7.
4 Article 17 of the *Agreement on Agriculture*, set out in Annex 1A of the *WTO Agreement*, above note 1 [*Agriculture Agreement*].
5 Paragraph 1 of art. 12 of the *Agreement on the Application of Sanitary and Phytosanitary Measures*, set out in Annex 1A of the *WTO Agreement*, ibid. [*SPS Agreement*].
6 Article 8 of the *Agreement on Textiles and Clothing*, set out in Annex 1A of the *WTO Agreement*, ibid. [*Textile Agreement*].
7 Article 13 of the *Agreement on Technical Barriers to Trade*, set out in Annex 1A of the *WTO Agreement*, ibid. [*TBT Agreement*].

ment Measures,[8] a Committee on Anti-Dumping Practices,[9] a Committee on Customs Valuation,[10] a Committee on Rules of Origin,[11] a Committee on Subsidies and Countervailing Measures,[12] and a Committee on Safeguards[13].

The WTO has a secretariat and a director-general, whose functions include the presentation of an annual budget to the Committee on Budget, Finance, and Administration. The WTO is funded through contributions from its members.[14]

b) Decisions

Decisions of the WTO are made by consensus or, in the case of a failure to reach a consensus, by voting. Each member has one vote except for the European Union, which has votes equal to the number of its members.[15] The *WTO Agreement* does not contain a general rule stipulating a percentage required to carry a vote but, in the case of granting waivers of obligations of Members, it does provide that the decision must be made by three-fourths of the members.[16]

c) Amendments

Article X of the *WTO Agreement* sets out procedures for making amendments to the *WTO Agreement* or any of the Multilateral Agreements. Generally, amendments to the *WTO Agreement* and the Multilateral Agreements (other than the *Dispute Settlement Understanding* and the

---

8   Article 7 of the *Agreement Respecting Trade-Related Investment Measures*, set out in Annex 1A of the *WTO Agreement*, ibid. [*TRIMs Agreement*]
9   Article 16 of the *Agreement on Implementation of Article VI of the General Agreement on Tariffs and Trade 1994*, set out in Annex 1A of the *WTO Agreement*, ibid.
10 Article 18 of the *Agreement on Implementation of Article VII of the General Agreement on Tariffs and Trade 1994*, set out in Annex 1A of the *WTO Agreement*, ibid. (*Valuation Agreement*), which also establishes a Technical Committee on Customs Valuation.
11 Article 4 of the *Agreement on Rules of Origin*, set out in Annex 1A of the *WTO Agreement*, ibid. [*Rules of Origin Agreement*].
12 Article 24 of the *Agreement on Subsidies and Countervailing Measures*, set out in Annex 1A of the *WTO Agreement*, ibid. [*Subsidies Agreement*].
13 Article 13 of the *Agreement on Safeguards*, set out in Annex 1A of the *WTO Agreement*, ibid. [*Safeguards Agreement*].
14 *WTO Agreement*, ibid., art. VII.
15 *WTO Agreement*, ibid., art. IX, para. 1. See the qualification in note 2 of this provision that states that the number of votes of the European Communities (i.e., European Union) and their member states shall in no case exceed the number of the member states of the European Communities.
16 *Ibid.*, art. IX, para. 3.

Trade Policy Review Mechanism) that alter the rights and obligations of members will take effect for members that have accepted them upon acceptance by two-thirds of the members and will become effective for all members upon acceptance by a three-fourths majority, subject to a right of a non-accepting member to withdraw.[17] Amendments to these agreements that do not alter the rights and obligations of members are binding on all members upon acceptance by two-thirds of the members.[18] A few amendments require unanimity.[19] Amendments to the *Dispute Settlement Understanding* must be made by consensus. These amendments, as well as amendments to the Trade Policy Review Mechanism, become effective upon acceptance by the Ministerial Conference. Amendments to a Plurilateral Agreement are governed by the procedures set out in the agreement.[20]

d) Accession

Like the GATT, the *WTO Agreement* anticipates expansion of its membership and, for this reason, Article XII of the *WTO Agreement* makes provision for accession. Decisions on accession are taken by the Ministerial Conference and must be approved by a two-thirds majority. At the time of writing, accession negotiations were under way with twenty-eight countries, including China, the Russian Federation and other former Soviet republics, Albania, Algeria, Cambodia, Chinese Taipei, Croatia, Macedonia, Nepal, Saudi Arabia, Seychelles, Sudan, Tonga, Vanuatu, and Vietnam.

Accession negotiations are conducted at both a multilateral and a bilateral level. At the multilateral level, the WTO member countries negotiate a protocol with the acceding country that governs the terms

---

17 See *ibid.*, art. X, para. 3, for the general rule and para. 5 for the *General Agreement on Trade in Services*, set out in Annex 1B of the *WTO Agreement, ibid.*, [GATS]. Paragraph 6 also contains a special rule respecting the *Agreement on Trade-Related Aspects of Intellectual Property Rights*, set out in Annex 1C of the *WTO Agreement, ibid.*, [*TRIPS Agreement*].
18 See *WTO Agreement, ibid.*, art. X, para. 4.
19 See *WTO Agreement, ibid.*, art. X, para. 2, which requires unanimity in respect of amendments to art. XI of the *WTO Agreement* (original WTO membership); arts. I & II of the *General Agreement on Tariffs and Trade 1994*, set out in Annex 1A of the *WTO Agreement, ibid.* [GATT 1994] (MFN and Schedules of Concessions); art. II:1 of GATS, above note 17 (MFN); and art. 4 of the *TRIPS Agreement*, above note 17 (MFN).
20 See *WTO Agreement, ibid.*, art. X, para. 10. Paragraph 9 of art. XIV of the *Agreement on Government Procurement*, set out in Annex 4 of the *WTO Agreement, ibid.*, provides that amendments do not enter into force for a Party until that Party accepts them.

of its membership. In the case of China, the draft protocol covers a wide range of matters affecting current Chinese practices, including, for example, a requirement that China progressively liberalize the right to trade so that, within three years of the entry into force of the protocol, all enterprises will have the right to trade in all goods throughout China. The acceding country also negotiates bilateral market access commitments with individual WTO member countries. China is currently negotiating its tariff bindings under GATT 1994 and its specific market access commitments for services under the GATS with Canada, the United States, the European Union, Japan, and other WTO member countries. Once accession occurs, the market access commitments made by China in each bilateral negotiation will be extended to all WTO members under the MFN principle.

2) NAFTA, CIFTA, and CCFTA

The formal institutional structures of NAFTA, CIFTA, and CCFTA are minimal.

a) Commission

Each agreement establishes a commission (in NAFTA and CCFTA, the Free Trade Commission, and in CIFTA the Canada–Israel Trade Commission) consisting of cabinet level officers of the Parties or their designees whose function it is to supervise the implementation of the agreement and to resolve disputes.[21] Under each agreement, decisions of the commission are made by consensus. The commission performs a mediation function in dispute resolution, but disputes are ultimately resolved through a panel process.

b) Secretariat: NAFTA and CCFTA

NAFTA Article 2002 and CCFTA Article N-02 require the commission to establish and oversee a secretariat consisting of national sections. Both agreements require the establishment of a permanent office with a secretary responsible for its administration and management. The secretariat assists the commission generally, and it also provides administrative assistance to panels established under Chapters Nineteen and

---

21 *North American Free Trade Agreement*, 17 December 1992, Can. T.S. 1994 No. 2 [NAFTA], art. 2001; *Canada–Israel Free Trade Agreement*, 1 January 1997, see http://www.dfait-maeci.gc.ca/english/trade/agrement.htm [CIFTA], art. 8.2; and *Canada–Chile Free Trade Agreement*, 5 July 1997, see http://www.dfait-maeci.gc.ca/english/trade/agrement.htm [CCFTA], art. N-01.

Twenty, in the case of NAFTA, and Chapter N, in the case of CCFTA. CIFTA does not require the establishment of a secretariat.

c) Committees and Working Groups
Each agreement establishes various committees and working groups that meet on a periodic basis to consider matters arising under designated provisions of the agreement and, in some cases, to endeavour to resolve disputes.

d) Amendments
NAFTA, CIFTA, and CCFTA all make provision for amendments, which must be agreed to by all Parties.[22]

e) Accession

i) NAFTA

It was originally anticipated that NAFTA membership would expand beyond that of Canada, the United States, and Mexico to include other Latin American countries. Accordingly, NAFTA Article 2204 provides for the accession to NAFTA of any country or group of countries. Accession is subject to such terms and conditions as may be agreed between the acceding country or country and the NAFTA Free Trade commission. As decisions of the commission must be made by consensus, any one NAFTA country can block an accession.

At the time of writing, there have not been any accessions to NAFTA. Chile is the most likely candidate for accession but negotiations in this regard have been delayed by U.S. Congressional politics and growing U.S. scepticism towards the benefit of trade agreements.

The NAFTA accession provision makes reference to "groups of countries" and the drafters may have had in mind customs unions such as MERCOSUR. However, NAFTA is not presently structured to accommodate a customs union with supranational institutions that have substantive jurisdiction over matters such as border measures. NAFTA would have to be modified in a number of significant respects to accommodate a customs union so that supranational institutions and national governments were both bound, regarding measures falling within their respective areas of responsibility.

ii) CIFTA and CCFTA

Neither CIFTA nor CCFTA make provision for accession. CIFTA is intended as a purely bilateral arrangement between Canada and Israel

---

22 NAFTA, *ibid.*, art. 2202; CIFTA, *ibid.*, art. 11.2; and CCFTA, *ibid.*, art. P-02.

and was inspired in part because the United States has a similar arrangement with Israel. CCFTA was negotiated because the U.S. administration was unsuccessful in obtaining the requisite authority from Congress to negotiate Chilean accession to NAFTA, and the Canadian and Chilean governments wanted to establish a free trade arrangement, notwithstanding the U.S. administration's inability to proceed. For the time being, CCFTA is a bilateral interim arrangement between Canada and Chile that will be superseded by NAFTA if and when accession occurs.

B. GENERAL DISPUTE RESOLUTION PROCEDURES

The *Dispute Settlement Understanding*, NAFTA, CIFTA, and CCFTA all contain general procedures for the resolution of disputes.

1) Common Themes

These procedures have the following in common:

- Only federal or national governments of member countries have standing under these procedures. Regional governments (provincial, state, territorial, municipal) have no standing under any of these procedures, even though the consistency of the measures of these governments may be the subject matter of the dispute. Similarly, private individuals and organizations have no standing under these procedures, even though their interests may be directly affected by the resolution of the dispute.
- The procedures are all subject to specific time periods to ensure that resolution is reached within a finite and reasonable period of time.
- The procedures are invoked by a request for consultations made by the government of the complaining party to the government of the other disputing party. The disputing parties must endeavour for a prescribed time period to resolve the dispute through consultations. NAFTA, CIFTA, and CCFTA procedures make provision for mediation by the relevant commission if consultations fail to resolve the dispute. The DSU does not provide for a mediation step.
- If consultations or mediation do not resolve the dispute, the next step is arbitration by a panel, before which the disputing parties may make written and oral representations. Under the DSU and NAFTA, the federal or national governments of other member countries may intervene but other interested parties (such as regional governments or affected private interests) may not intervene.

- Panel proceedings are not public. However, Canada and the United States are now adopting the practice of making their written submissions public.
- The panel must issue its reports (interim and final) within prescribed time frames. The DSU makes provision for one level of appeal, while NAFTA, CIFTA, and CCFTA panel decisions are final.
- Once a final panel report is issued, the parties consult as to how the panel report ought to be implemented. Preference is given to modifying or removing the non-conforming measure over providing compensation.
- If the member or Party against which the report is made fails to implement the recommendations in the report within a prescribed time period, the complaining member or Party may retaliate by withdrawing benefits. There is no other sanction for failure to comply. Panel decisions are not binding on disputing members or Parties in that they are not enforceable under domestic legal systems.
- None of these general procedures confers private legal rights.[23]

2) Dispute Resolution under the WTO Agreements

Disputes under the WTO agreements can arise under:

- the Multilateral Agreements set out in Annex 1A of the *WTO Agreement*, the principal one of which is GATT 1994;
- the GATS;
- the *TRIPS Agreement*;
- the Plurilateral Agreements.

The *Dispute Settlement Understanding* sets out procedures that apply to disputes arising under all of the Multilateral and Plurilateral Agreements.

a) Articles XXII and XXIII of GATT 1994

Articles XXII and XXIII of GATT 1994 apply to disputes arising under GATT 1994 and under most of the Multilateral Agreements. Article XXII of GATT 1994 requires that contracting parties try to resolve disputes through consultation. Article XXIII:1 authorizes a contracting party whose benefits under the GATT are being "nullified or impaired" by the actions of another contracting party to make written representations or proposals to the other contracting party who must give sympa-

---

23 NAFTA, *ibid.*, art. 2021; CIFTA, *ibid.*, art. 8.10; and CCFTA, *ibid.*, art. N-20, expressly prohibit Parties from conferring private rights of action based on a measure being inconsistent with the relevant agreement.

thetic consideration to same. Article XXIII:2 provides that if a resolution does not result from consultations, the matter is referred to the contracting parties for investigation and, if the circumstances are sufficiently serious, the contracting parties may authorize the suspension of benefits. Article XXIII:2 does not set out any procedure to be followed from the point in time that the matter is referred to the contracting parties to the time that the suspension of benefits is authorized. Under GATT 1947, panel procedures evolved over time but were never formally incorporated into the GATT text. The DSU remedied this deficiency by establishing a formal dispute resolution procedure that covers not only the resolution of disputes but also the process of consultations and the suspension of benefits.

i) *Application of Articles XXII and XXIII of GATT 1994 to Other WTO Agreements*

The provisions of Articles XXII and XXIII of GATT 1994, as elaborated and applied by the DSU, apply to disputes arising under the *Agriculture Agreement*,[24] the *SPS Agreement*,[25] the *TBT Agreement*,[26] the *TRIMs Agreement*,[27] the *Preshipment Inspection Agreement*,[28] the *Rules of Origin Agreement*,[29] the *Import Licensing Agreement*,[30] the *Safeguards Agreement*,[31] and the *TRIPS Agreement*.[32]

Under the *Textile Agreement*, dispute resolution commences with consultations and if the dispute remains unresolved, the disputing members refer the matter to the TMB for recommendations.[33] If the matter is still unresolved despite the TMB recommendations, the member may initiate resolution of the dispute by invoking paragraph 2 of Article XXIII of GATT 1994 and the relevant provisions of the DSU.[34]

---

24 Above note 4, art. 19.
25 Above note 5, art. 11, para. 1.
26 Above note 7, art. 14.
27 Above note 8, art. 8.
28 *Agreement on Preshipment Inspection*, set out in Annex 1A of the *WTO Agreement*, above note 1, art. 8.
29 Above note 11, arts. 7 and 8.
30 *Agreement on Import Licensing Procedures*, set out in Annex 1A of the *WTO Agreement*, above note 1, art 6.
31 Above note 13, art. 14.
32 Above note 17, art. 64.
33 *Textile Agreement*, above note 6, arts. 8:4 to 8:9.
34 *Ibid.*, art. 8:10.

Articles XXII and XXIII of GATT 1994, as elaborated and applied by the DSU, apply to disputes arising under the *Subsidies Agreement* except where otherwise provided in that agreement.[35] Articles 4 and 7 of the *Subsidies Agreement* set out remedies that apply in respect of prohibited subsidies and subsidies that result in injury. These articles do not make reference to Articles XXII and XXIII of GATT 1994 but, instead, provide for consultations and, failing resolution through consultations, reference to the Dispute Settlement Body (discussed below) for establishment of a panel.

The *Antidumping Agreement*, the *Valuation Agreement*, and the GATS do not make reference to Articles XXII and XXIII of GATT 1994. Article 17 of the *Antidumping Agreement* and Article 19 of the *Valuation Agreement* permit a member who considers that its benefits under the relevant agreement are being nullified and impaired to request consultations, and provide that the DSU applies to both consultations and dispute resolution. Similarly, GATS Articles XXII and XXIII provide for consultations and recourse to the DSU for dispute resolution.

ii) *Non-Violation Nullification and Impairment under*
    Article XXIII of GATT 1994

Paragraph 1(b) of Article XXIII of GATT 1994 permits the procedures in GATT Article XXIII to be invoked if a measure is nullifying or impairing benefits, even if it does not conflict with a provision of GATT 1994. For example, a contracting party may grant a subsidy to a domestic industry that offsets the benefit of a tariff concession. The subsidy is not contrary to any GATT provision but the competitive advantage which the exporting country anticipated as a result of the tariff concession and for which it paid with its own tariff concessions is nullified by the subsidy. Paragraph 1(c) of GATT Article XXIII permits GATT Article XXIII to be invoked if the nullification or impairment is the result of the "existence of any other situation." Nullification and impairment in respect of measures that do not conflict with a specific provision of a trade agreement is known as "non-violation nullification and impairment."

Non-violation nullification and impairment will apply to the provisions of any of the WTO agreements that refers to Article XXIII of GATT 1994 in its dispute settlement language. In the case of the *TRIPS Agreement*, the application of the nullification and impairment provisions of paragraphs 1(b) and 1(c) of Article XXIII of GATT 1994 are postponed until five years after the *WTO Agreement* became effective.[36]

---

35 *Subsidies Agreement*, above note 12, art. 30.
36 *TRIPS Agreement*, above note 17, art. 64:2.

Conversely, non-violation nullification and impairment will not apply to the provisions of WTO agreements (namely, the *Antidumping Agreement*, the *Valuation Agreement*, and the GATS) that do not make reference to Article XXIII of GATT 1994 in their dispute resolution procedures. In the case of the *Subsidies Agreement*, non-violation nullification and impairment will not apply to provisions covered by the dispute resolution procedures set out in Articles 4 and 7 described above.

Panels convened under GATT 1947 were conservative in their application of the non-violation provisions of Article XXIII. This conservative approach will likely be followed by panels convened under the DSU.

b) The *Dispute Settlement Understanding*

The DSU establishes formal dispute settlement procedures that apply to all Multilateral and Plurilateral Agreements (covered agreements) included in the annexes to the *WTO Agreement*.[37] The DSU also establishes the Dispute Settlement Body (DSB) to administer these procedures and the consultation and dispute settlement procedures set out in the covered agreements. Members seeking redress in respect of any of the covered agreements must use the procedures set out in the DSU.[38] The DSU prohibits members from unilaterally determining that obligations under covered agreements have been violated or that benefits under such agreements have been nullified and impaired. The rules and procedures established by the DSU are subject to special or additional rules and procedures set out in the *SPS Agreement*, the *Textile Agreement*, the *TBT Agreement*, the *Antidumping Agreement*, the *Valuation Agreement*, the *Subsidies Agreement* and the GATS.[39]

i) Consultations

The DSU sets out rules governing requests for consultations under the covered agreements, including time limits following which a complaining party may request a panel. The settlement of a dispute begins with a request for consultations. The usual time period for consultations is

---

37 *Understanding on Rules and Procedures Governing the Settlement of Disputes*, set out in Annex 2 of the *WTO Agreement*, above note 1 [DSU], art. 1:1 & Appendix 1.
38 *Ibid.*, art. 23:1.
39 DSU, *ibid.*, art. 1:2. The special or additional rules and procedures in these Multilateral Agreements are listed in Appendix 2 to the DSU. The list in Appendix 2 also includes the *Ministerial Decision on Certain Dispute Settlement Procedures for the General Agreement on Trade in Services* (GATS Decision), which establishes certain requirements respecting rosters of panelists in disputes involving GATS provisions.

sixty days but this period can be reduced to twenty days in urgent situations, such as those involving perishable goods.

ii) The Panel Process

If a dispute is not resolved through consultations, the complaining party may request a panel. Multiple requests for the establishment of panels can be consolidated and member countries with a substantial interest in the matter in dispute may make submissions to the panel as a "third party." The DSU establishes the terms of reference for panels and sets out rules respecting their composition. Unlike domestic courts, panels must meet in closed session. Normally parties (including third parties) will make written submissions and a first substantive meeting of the panel will take place at which the complaining party will present its case and the party complained against will be invited to express its views. Formal rebuttals will be made at a second substantive meeting of the panel. The panel issues a draft report and the parties may comment in writing. The panel then issues an interim report and, ultimately, a final report that is circulated among the members. The final report will be adopted at a DSB meeting within sixty days of its circulation unless a party appeals or the meeting chooses "by consensus" not to adopt it.[40] Generally, the process from the time the composition and terms of reference of the panel are settled to the issuance of the final report should not take more than six months. In no case can this period be extended to more than nine months.

iii) Appeals

The decision of a panel may be appealed only by parties to a dispute but not by third parties. The appeal is made to the Appellate Body, a permanent institution established by the DSB. The appeal is limited to issues of law in the panel report and legal interpretations developed by the panel.

iv) Implementation of Recommendations, Compensation, and Suspension of Concessions

If a panel or the Appellate Body concludes that a measure is inconsistent with a covered agreement, it shall recommend that the member concerned bring the measure into conformity with the agreement concerned and it may suggest ways for doing so. The DSB must hold a meeting within thirty days of the adoption of the report at which the member concerned will inform the DSB of its intentions respecting the imple-

---

40 The party complained against can no longer block the adoption of a report as was the case under the *General Agreement on Tariffs and Trade*, 30 October 1947, Can. T.S. 1947 No. 27 [GATT 1947].

mentation of the recommendations. Members are granted a reasonable period of time within which to implement recommendations.[41] The DSB keeps the implementation of the recommendations under surveillance and if the recommendations are not implemented within a reasonable time, the DSU permits voluntary compensation and suspension of concessions. Principles and procedures are set out for determining what concessions to suspend. A member will first suspend concessions in the same sector as that in which the violation occurred. If this is impracticable or ineffective, concessions can be suspended in a different sector but under the same covered agreement; and if this is still impracticable or ineffective and the circumstances are sufficiently serious, concessions under another agreement can be suspended.[42]

c) The *Government Procurement Agreement*
As stated above, the *Dispute Settlement Understanding* applies to disputes arising under both the Plurilateral and Multilateral Agreements. Article XXII of the *Government Procurement Agreement* provides that the DSU applies to the *Government Procurement Agreement*, subject to some modifications. For example, paragraph 6 of Article XXII alters some of the DSU time frames, and paragraph 7 provides that disputes arising under other WTO agreements will not result in a suspension of concessions under the *Government Procurement Agreement*. Paragraph 2 of Article XXII incorporates a concept of non-violation nullification and impairment similar to that in Article XXIII of GATT 1994.

3) Dispute Resolution under NAFTA, CIFTA, and CCFTA

The dispute settlement procedures of NAFTA, CIFTA, and CCFTA are set out in Section B of NAFTA Chapter Twenty, CIFTA Articles 8.6 to 8.10, and Section II of CCFTA Chapter N. The provisions of Section B

---

41 A reasonable time is that proposed by the member if approved by the DSB, or that mutually agreed by the parties to the dispute, or that determined through binding arbitration within ninety days of the adoption by the DSB of the recommendations. DSU, above note 37, art. 21:3. An outside period of fifteen months is suggested as a guideline. DSU, art. 21:4.
42 Less stringent results follow from a claim based on claims of non-violation nullification and impairment under arts. XXIII:1(b) & (c) of GATT 1994, above note 19. For example, if a finding of non-violation nullification and impairment is made under GATT, art. XXIII:1(b), the party complained against is under no obligation to withdraw the measure, and compensation may be part of a final settlement of the matter. DSU, *ibid.*, art. 26, paras. 1(b) & (d).

of NAFTA Chapter Twenty and Section II of CCFTA Chapter N are virtually identical. The provisions of CIFTA Articles 8.6 to 8.10 are similar to the corresponding provisions of the other two agreements.

a) Scope of Procedures

Except for matters covered by NAFTA Chapter Nineteen (Antidumping and Countervailing Matters) and except for matters arising under the competition law provisions of NAFTA Article 1501, CIFTA Article 7.1, or CCFTA Article J-01, the dispute resolution procedures in NAFTA Chapter Twenty, CIFTA Chapter Eight, and CCFTA Chapter N apply to all disputes respecting the interpretation or application of the relevant agreement. The investor-state dispute settlement procedures provided for in Section B of NAFTA Chapter Eleven and Section II of CCFTA Chapter G do not preclude the Parties to these respective agreements from using NAFTA Chapter Twenty or CCFTA Chapter N to resolve disputes respecting matters covered by these procedures.[43]

b) Non-Violation Nullification and Impairment

NAFTA Annex 2004 and CCFTA Annex N-04 permit a Party, in prescribed circumstances, to invoke the dispute settlement procedures if a measure adopted by another Party that is not inconsistent with the relevant agreement is nonetheless nullifying or impairing benefits that the Party reasonably expected to receive. These provisions are based on the concept of non-violation nullification and impairment set out in Article XXIII:1(b) of GATT 1994 discussed above. The application of non-violation nullification and impairment is restricted to:

- the trade-in-goods provisions of each agreement (except for the automotive provisions of NAFTA Annex 300-A and CCFTA Annex C-00-A and the provisions of NAFTA Chapter Six on energy insofar as they relate to investment);
- NAFTA Chapter Nine (Standards-Related Measures);
- NAFTA Chapter Twelve and CCFTA Chapter H (Cross-Border Trade in Services);
- NAFTA Chapter Seventeen (Intellectual Property).[44]

---

43 See NAFTA, above note 21, art. 1115, and CCFTA, above note 21, art. G-16.
44 Paragraph 2 of both NAFTA, *ibid.*, Annex 2004, and CCFTA, *ibid.*, Annex N-04 further restricts the application of non-violation and impairment in circumstances involving the exceptions of art. XX of GATT 1994, above note 19 (incorporated into NAFTA by art. 2102 and into CCFTA by art. O-01). However, the drafting is so cryptic that the author has difficulty in deriving clear meaning from these provisions.

Non-violation nullification and impairment does not apply to the excluded provisions mentioned above or to the remaining provisions of these agreements.

CIFTA extends the application of non-violation nullification and impairment to any measure covered by CIFTA except for a measure that falls within the cultural exception in CIFTA Article 10.5. The purpose of this exclusion is to prevent a Party from undermining the cultural exception by claiming that benefits have been nullified and impaired by a measure that falls within the exception and is not inconsistent with CIFTA requirements.

c) Dispute Resolution Process

i) Consultations

NAFTA Article 2003 and CCFTA Article N-03 require Parties to make every attempt to resolve matters through cooperation and consultation. A Party under CCFTA, CIFTA, or NAFTA may request consultations under CCFTA Article N-06, CIFTA Article 8.6(1), or NAFTA Article 2006(1) regarding any actual or proposed measure that it considers will affect the operation of the agreement. The request is delivered to the other Party or Parties and, in the case of NAFTA and CCFTA, to its own section of the secretariat. In the case of NAFTA, a third Party that considers that it has a substantial interest in the matter may participate in the consultations.

ii) Request for Meeting of the Commission

If the dispute is not resolved within thirty days of the request for consultations, any consulting Party may request a meeting of the Free Trade Commission (NAFTA and CCFTA) or the Canada–Israel Trade Commission (CIFTA).[45] A meeting of the commission may be requested under NAFTA and CCFTA if a responding Party in an environmental dispute initiated under the WTO has requested that the matter be considered under NAFTA or CCFTA or if consultations have taken place respecting a matter through certain committees established under the agreement.[46]

---

45 NAFTA, ibid., art. 2007(1); CIFTA, above note 21, art. 8.7(1); and CCFTA, ibid., art. N-07(1). This period is extended in the case of NAFTA to forty-five days if another Party has subsequently requested or participated in consultations respecting the same matter, and in the case of NAFTA and CCFTA is reduced to fifteen days if perishable agricultural goods are involved.

46 See, for example, NAFTA, ibid., art. 513(3)(e), which provides for consultation through a Working Group on Rules of Origin and under CCFTA, ibid., art. C-15(2), which provides for consultations through a Committee on Trade in Goods and Rules of Origin.

Upon a request for a meeting, the commission must convene within ten days in the case of NAFTA and CCFTA and twenty days in the case of CIFTA and try to resolve the dispute promptly. If the matter is not resolved within thirty days after the commission has convened, any consulting Party may request the establishment of an arbitral panel.[47]

iii) Panels

Under each of NAFTA, CIFTA, and CCFTA, the commission is required to establish an arbitral panel upon the delivery of a request. Under NAFTA, a Party not directly involved in the dispute that considers that it has a substantial interest in its outcome may join the proceeding as a complaining Party. Panels are chosen from rosters of individuals maintained by each Party.[48]

NAFTA and CCFTA panels consist of five members. NAFTA 2011 and CCFTA N-11 provide for a reverse selection procedure under which each disputing Party selects panelists from rosters of the other disputing Party or (in the case of NAFTA) Parties and not from its own. The disputing Parties must try to agree on a chair of the panel within fifteen days of the delivery of the request for a panel. If a chair is not agreed upon and there are two disputing NAFTA countries, the disputing Party chosen by lot will choose the chair within five days. Each Party then has fifteen days to select two panelists who are citizens of the other disputing Party and if a selection is not made the panelists shall be selected by lot from the roster of the other disputing Party. NAFTA Article 2011(2) sets out another reverse selection procedure to be applied when there are more than two disputing Parties. Panelists are normally to be chosen from the roster and a disputing Party may exercise a peremptory challenge against any person chosen who is not on the roster within fifteen days of the person being proposed.

CIFTA panels consist of three members. Each Party chooses one member and the commission chooses the third member. If the commission cannot agree on the third member, the member is chosen by lot from the rosters.[49]

NAFTA, CIFTA, and CCFTA each provide for the establishment of a code of conduct for panelists.[50] If a disputing Party under any of these

---

47 NAFTA, *ibid.*, art. 2008(1); CIFTA, above note 21, art. 8.9(2); and CCFTA, *ibid.*, art. N-08(1).
48 NAFTA, *ibid.*, art. 2009; para. 1 of CIFTA, *ibid.*, art. 8.9; and CCFTA, *ibid.*, art. N-09.
49 Paragraph 3 of CCFTA, *ibid.*, Annex 8.9.
50 NAFTA, above note 21, art. 2009(2)(c); CIFTA, above note 21, art. 8.8; and CCFTA, *ibid.*, art. N-09(2)(c).

agreements believes that a panelist has violated the code of conduct, the disputing Parties will consult and if they agree, the panelist shall be removed and a new panelist selected.

iv) Panel Proceedings
Panel proceedings under NAFTA, CIFTA, and CCFTA are conducted in accordance with the Model Rules of Procedure established by the relevant commission,[51] with at least one hearing and an opportunity to provide initial and rebuttal written submissions. Unlike the other two agreements, CIFTA 8.9(5)(b) requires that the CIFTA Model Rules permit counsel chosen by a Party to advise that Party during panel proceedings, including hearings. NAFTA Article 2012(3), CIFTA Article 8.9(4), and CCFTA Article N-12(4) set out terms of reference that will apply unless the disputing Parties agree to other terms. NAFTA and CCFTA make provision for expert evidence and a NAFTA or CCFTA panel may request a written report of a scientific review board on any factual issue concerning environmental, health, safety, or other scientific matters raised by a disputing Party.[52]

A panel must issue its initial report within ninety days of the selection of the last panelist[53] or, in the case of CIFTA, within three months of the selection of the chairperson.[54] Under NAFTA Article 2016(4) and CCFTA Article N-15(4), a disputing Party may submit written comments on the initial report within fourteen days of its presentation. CIFTA Article 8.9(7) allows thirty days for a written statement of objections to the initial report. NAFTA Article 2017(1) and CCFTA Article N-16(1) require that a panel present its final report within thirty days of the initial report. The corresponding time period provided by CIFTA Article 8.9(7) is sixty days.

v) Implementation and Suspension of Benefits
Once the final report of a panel is received, NAFTA Article 2018, CCFTA Article N-17, and CIFTA Article 8.9(9) require the Parties or, in the case of CIFTA, the commission to agree on a resolution of the dispute that shall normally conform with the panel's determinations and recommendations. Wherever possible, the resolution will be by way of non-implementation or removal of non-conforming measures and, failing resolution, there will be compensation. If agreement on resolution

---

51 NAFTA, *ibid.*, art. 2012; CIFTA, *ibid.*, art. 8.9(5); and CCFTA, *ibid.*, art. N-12.
52 NAFTA, *ibid.*, art. 2015, and CCFTA, *ibid.*, art. N-15.
53 NAFTA, *ibid.*, art. 2016(1), and CCFTA, *ibid.*, art. N-15(2).
54 CIFTA, above note 21, art. 8.9(6).

of the dispute is not reached within thirty days of receipt of the final report, the complaining Party may suspend benefits under the agreement. Suspension of benefits should be in the same sector as that affected by the inconsistent measure unless the complaining Party considers this impracticable or ineffective, in which case suspension of benefits may take place in a different sector.

NAFTA Article 1414(5) sets out limitations on the suspension of benefits in respect of matters involving financial services and financial institutions. If a measure found inconsistent with NAFTA obligations affects only the financial services sector, benefits may only be suspended in the financial services sector. If an inconsistent measure affects a sector other than the financial services sector, benefits may not be suspended in the financial services sector. If the inconsistent measure affects the financial services sector and another sector, a NAFTA country may suspend benefits in the financial services sector that have an effect equivalent to the effect of the inconsistent measure in its financial services sector.

vi) Special Situations
NAFTA Article 1606 and CCFTA Article K-06 provide that a Party may not invoke dispute resolution procedures respecting a refusal to grant temporary entry unless the matter involves a pattern of practice and the business person has exhausted available administrative remedies.

NAFTA Article 1414(3) requires each NAFTA country to maintain a separate roster of fifteen individuals with financial services expertise to serve as financial services panelists.

4) Which Procedures Apply?

As noted earlier, there is significant overlap between the provisions of the WTO agreements on the one hand, and the provisions of NAFTA, CIFTA, and CCFTA on the other. The trade-in-goods provisions of NAFTA, CIFTA, and CCFTA incorporate and expand upon the provisions of GATT 1994. As described in chapter 7, the WTO agreements and NAFTA set out parallel obligations covering sanitary and phytosanitary measures, technical barriers to trade, intellectual property and government procurement. Ample potential exists for disputes involving the same subject matter and the same parties to arise under the WTO agreements and NAFTA, CIFTA, or CCFTA.

NAFTA, CIFTA, and CCFTA each set out rules for choice of forum in circumstances in which provisions of both the WTO agreements and NAFTA, CIFTA, or CCFTA can apply. The choice of forum will govern the substantive provisions that govern the matter in dispute.

a) NAFTA and CCFTA

NAFTA Article 2005 and CCFTA Article N-05 set out rules respecting disputes that arise under both NAFTA or CCFTA and the *WTO Agreement*.[55] Dispute settlement proceedings initiated under NAFTA or CCFTA or the *WTO Agreement* precludes the initiation of proceedings under the other forum.

NAFTA Article 2005(1) and CCFTA Article N-05(1) both provide that the choice of forum in these instances is at the discretion of the complaining Party. This rule gives a significant advantage to the complaining Party as it will invariably choose the forum with the provisions most favourable to its case. For example, the United States chose to pursue its complaint against Canada's policies respecting periodicals through the DSU rather than through NAFTA because, unlike NAFTA, the WTO agreements do not contain an exception for cultural matters.[56] However, there are a few constraints on the right of the complaining Party to select the forum. If a responding Party claims that the action that it has taken is subject to NAFTA 104 or CCFTA Article A-04 (which provides that certain environmental agreements prevail over NAFTA or CCFTA) and requests resolution under NAFTA or CCFTA, NAFTA Article 2005(3) and CCFTA Article N-05(2) require that the matter be pursued only through NAFTA or CCFTA dispute resolution procedures. NAFTA Article 2005(4) also provides that complaints respecting measures to protect human, animal, or plant life or health or the environment under Section B of NAFTA Chapter Seven (Sanitary and Phytosanitary Measures) or NAFTA Chapter Nine (Standards-Related Measures) may only be pursued through NAFTA Chapter Twenty if the responding Party so requests.

Under NAFTA, a third Party without direct involvement in the outcome of a matter can affect the choice of forum. NAFTA Article 2005(2) requires a complaining Party to notify a third Party of its intention to initiate a proceeding under the WTO rules. If that Party wants recourse under the NAFTA dispute settlement procedures, it shall inform the complaining NAFTA country, and the NAFTA countries will consult with a view to agreeing to a single forum. In the absence of an agreement, the NAFTA dispute settlement procedures will "normally" be used.

---

55 NAFTA, above note 1, art. 2005(1) refers to the GATT 1947, above note 40, or agreements negotiated thereunder or any successor agreement. The *WTO Agreement*, above note 1, is a successor agreement.
56 See chapter 9 under "WTO Agreements."

b) CIFTA

The CIFTA provisions are set out in CIFTA Article 8.1. If a dispute arises under both the *WTO Agreement* and CIFTA, the choice of forum is at the discretion of the complaining Party and once the choice is made, the procedure chosen shall be used to the exclusion of the other.

5) Concluding Remarks

The dispute settlement procedures set out in the DSU and in each of NAFTA, CIFTA, and CCFTA are comprehensive and, as experience is showing under the DSU, reasonably effective. Disputing parties have an incentive to resolve disputes through consultations because failure of consultations will lead to a panel hearing conducted under tight time frames. The weakness in the process is the complete exclusion of private interests, which are those most directly affected by non-conforming measures adopted by Canada's trading partners. In Canada, at the present at least, the only recourse open to a business that has been adversely affected by a non-conforming measure of a country to which it exports goods or services is to lobby the Department of Foreign Affairs and International Trade to pursue the matter through consultations and dispute resolution. Unfortunately, however, the department may have its own agenda in relation to the importance of matters and it is also possible that its limited resources may not allow it to pursue a perfectly valid complaint.[57] This weakness is remedied only in the area of investment disputes under NAFTA and CCFTA, which are discussed below.

C. INVESTOR-STATE DISPUTE SETTLEMENT PROCEDURES: NAFTA AND CCFTA

Section B of NAFTA Chapter Eleven and Section II of CCFTA Chapter G establish procedures for the settlement of disputes arising between Parties and investors of other Parties respecting the investment obligations

---

57 There are procedures in the United States and the European Union that permit private sector persons, through a formal process, to complain of the practices of U.S. or EU trading partners. For the U.S. procedures, see Sections 301 to 304 of the *Omnibus Trade and Competitiveness Act of 1988*, Pub. L. No. 100–418, 102 Stat. 1186 (1988), and for the EU procedures see Regulation 2641/84 as modified by Regulation 522/94. For a discussion of both the U.S. and the EU procedures, see B.-R. Killmann, "The Access of Individuals to International Trade Dispute Settlement" (1996) 13 J. Int'l Arb. 143.

of the Parties under Section A of NAFTA Chapter Eleven and Section I of CCFTA Chapter G. These procedures also apply to provisions respecting the exercise by state enterprises and monopolies of regulatory, administrative, or other governmental authority set out in NAFTA Articles 1503(2) and 1502(3)(a) and CCFTA Articles J-03(2) and J-02(3)(a). As discussed in chapter 8 under "Financial Services," the NAFTA investor-state dispute settlement procedures established by Section B also apply to NAFTA Articles 1109 through 1111 and Articles 1113 and 1114 as incorporated into NAFTA Chapter Fourteen (Financial Services).

1) Provisions That Could Give Rise to Claims

There are a number of provisions of NAFTA Chapter Eleven and CCFTA Chapter G, the non-compliance with which could result in a claim for damages. These include:

- NAFTA Article 1102 and G-02 respecting national treatment. Damages suffered by an investor of a Party or its investment arising from a discriminatory law enacted by a government of another Party could give rise to a claim.
- NAFTA Article 1105 and CCFTA Article G-05 respecting treatment in accordance with international law. A denial of justice contrary to international law (such as an egregious award of punitive damages in an unfair civil trial coupled with denial of a right to appeal) that results in damage to an investment could give rise to a claim.
- NAFTA Article 1106 and CCFTA Article G-06 respecting performance requirements. An investor of a Party could make a claim on the basis that the government of another or the other Party imposed onerous conditions on its investment with resulting monetary loss.
- NAFTA Article 1109 and CCFTA Article G-09 respecting repatriation. A refusal to permit or an unreasonable delay in permitting repatriation that resulted in damages to an investor of another or the other Party could give rise to a claim.
- NAFTA Article 1110 and CCFTA Article G-10 respecting nationalization or expropriation and compensation. An expropriation or a measure tantamount to an expropriation taken by the government of a Party in respect of an investment of an investor of another or the other Party could give rise to a claim.

Investors and their counsel may attempt to characterize any act of government that adversely affects private interests as a measure tantamount to an expropriation in order to make an investor-state claim. It is submitted that the scope of NAFTA Article 1110 and CCFTA Article

G-10 is not broad enough to allow, in most instances, for such a claim. Many government actions that may be inconsistent with NAFTA or CCFTA obligations and injurious to private interests, would nevertheless amount to non-compensable regulation under international law. An unjustified import restriction may be inconsistent with NAFTA Article 309(1) or CCFTA Article C-08(1) and a matter to which the dispute resolution procedures in NAFTA Chapter Twenty or CCFTA Chapter N properly apply. However, it does not follow that the restriction is a measure tantamount to an expropriation, even if the interests of an investor of another or the other Party may be adversely affected.

Certain matters are expressly excluded from the scope of these NAFTA and CCFTA investor-state dispute settlement procedures. Decisions of Investment Canada or (in the case of NAFTA) the Mexican National Commission on Foreign Investment not to permit an acquisition subject to review are not subject to these procedures or to the procedures in NAFTA Chapter Twenty or CCFTA Chapter N.[58] A decision of a Party to prohibit or restrict the acquisition of an investment pursuant to the national security exceptions in NAFTA Article 2102 or CCFTA Article 0-02 is not subject to these procedures or to NAFTA Chapter Twenty or CCFTA Chapter N.[59]

2) Standing to Submit a Claim

An investor of a Party, on its own behalf or on behalf of an enterprise of another Party that is a juridical person which it owns or controls, may submit a claim that the other or another Party, or the Party of the enterprise, has breached an obligation under the foregoing NAFTA or CCFTA provisions.[60] The investor or the enterprise must have suffered loss or damage as a result of the breach and the claim may not be made if more than three years have elapsed from the time that the investor or the enterprise first acquired or should have first acquired knowledge of the breach and that

---

58 NAFTA, above note 21, Annex 1138.2, and CCFTA, above note 21, Annex G-39.2.
59 NAFTA, *ibid.*, art. 1138(1), and CCFTA, *ibid.*, art. G-39(1).
60 See NAFTA, *ibid.*, art. 1116, and CCFTA, *ibid.*, art. G-17 for claims by investors; NAFTA, art. 1117, and CCFTA, art. G-18, for claims by investors on behalf of enterprises. The provisions of NAFTA art. 1117 and CCFTA art. G-18 to avoid the problem presented by *Barcelona Traction Case (Belgium v. Spain)*, [1970] I.C.J. Rep. 3, in which the International Court of Justice held that Belgium did not have standing to bring a claim on behalf of the Belgium shareholders of a Canadian company, the assets of which had allegedly been expropriated by the government of Spain.

loss or damage has been incurred.⁶¹ Claims arising out of the same facts by investors on behalf of enterprises and by investors on their own behalf or by non-controlling investors in enterprises may be consolidated unless one of the parties making the claim would be prejudiced.⁶²

Suppose that the Canadian federal government arbitrarily expropriated an asset or right belonging to a U.S. company with the result that the U.S. company suffered loss. The U.S. company could bring a claim directly against the Canadian government for loss that it suffered. Suppose that the asset or right was held by a Canadian subsidiary of the U.S. company and the subsidiary and not the U.S. company had suffered the loss. The U.S. company could nevertheless make the claim on behalf of the subsidiary because the subsidiary is an enterprise of a Party (Canada) that is a juridical person (a corporation) that it controls. The subsidiary could not bring the claim on its own behalf.⁶³ Non-controlling U.S. shareholders of the subsidiary could bring a claim if they suffered loss as the result of the value of their shares (investments) in the subsidiary being impaired.

The U.S. company would be an investor of the United States and eligible to make the claim even if it were controlled by Canadians. A question arises as to whether Canadians whose investment in Canada was about to be expropriated could rearrange their affairs prior to the enactment of the expropriating legislation so that at the time that the legislation was passed the investment was held by a U.S. company eligible to make a claim. While such a course of action may seem contrived, the ethical justification is clear enough given the deficiencies in the Canadian constitution respecting the protection of property rights and the fact that expropriation without compensation or with inadequate compensation is contrary to international law.

3) Invoking the Procedures

NAFTA Article 1118 and CCFTA Article G-19 provide that the disputing parties should first attempt to settle the claim through consultation or negotiation.⁶⁴ The investor making the claim (the "disputing investor") must deliver to the Party against which the claim is being made (the "disputing Party") a notice of its intention to submit a claim at least ninety

---

61 NAFTA, above note 21, art. 1116(2), and CCFTA, *ibid.*, art. G-17(2), for claims by investors; NAFTA, art. 1117(2), and CCFTA, art. G-18(2), for claims on behalf of enterprises.
62 NAFTA, *ibid.*, art. 1117(3), and CCFTA, *ibid.*, art. G-18(3).
63 NAFTA, *ibid.*, art. 1117(4), and CCFTA, *ibid.*, art. G-18(4).
64 The use of the word "should" suggests that this step is not mandatory.

days before the claim is submitted to arbitration.[65] The notice must specify the name and the address of the disputing investor and, if applicable, the enterprise, the provisions alleged to be breached, the issues and factual basis, the relief sought, and the approximate amount of damages.

4) Submitting the Claim to Arbitration

a) The Choices
Once six months have elapsed since the events giving rise to the claim, a disputing investor may submit the claim under:

- the *Convention on the Settlement of Investment Disputes between States and Nationals of other States (ICSID Convention)*;[66] or
- the Additional Facility Rules of the International Centre for Settlement of Investment Disputes (ICSID), which is established by the *ICSID Convention*; or
- the arbitration rules of the United Nations Commission on International Trade Law, approved by the United Nations General Assembly on 15 December 1976 (UNCITRAL Arbitration Rules).

b) Constraints on Choice
The *ICSID Convention* can be used only if both the Party of the investor and the disputing Party are parties to the *ICSID Convention*. At the time of writing, Canada was not a party to the *ICSID Convention* but was taking steps to become one. The Additional Facility Rules of ICSID may be used only if the Party of the investor or the disputing Party are parties to the *ICSID Convention*. In a dispute under NAFTA between the United States and an investor of Canada, the investor could choose the Additional Facility Rules even though Canada is not yet a party to the *ICSID Convention*. Subject to these constraints, the choice of the arbitration vehicle is up to the disputing investor. There is no constraint on the use of the UNCITRAL Arbitration Rules.

c) The Arbitration Procedures
The *ICSID Convention*, the Additional Facility Rules, and the UNCITRAL Arbitration Rules each set out a comprehensive body of arbitration procedures that provide for the selection of arbitral tribunals, the

---

65 NAFTA, above note 21, art. 1119, and CCFTA, above note 21, art. G-20.
66 The *ICSID Convention* was done at Washington, 18 March 1965 (4 I.L.M. 532) and entered into force on 14 October 1966. ICSID operates under the aegis of the World Bank.

conduct of proceedings, and the making of awards. Awards are final in each case. The *ICSID Convention* requires that contracting states recognize and enforce awards. The recognition and enforcement of awards is also provided for under the *United Nations Convention on the Recognition and Enforcement of Foreign Arbitral Awards (New York Convention)*[67] and the *Inter-American Convention on International Commercial Arbitration (Inter-American Convention)*.[68]

d) Conditions to Submitting a Claim

A disputing investor may submit a claim to arbitration only if the investor and, if applicable, the enterprise on whose behalf a claim is made, consent in writing to the arbitration and waive the right to commence or continue proceedings respecting the measure before any administrative tribunal or court under the law of any NAFTA country, or other dispute settlement procedures.[69] The waiver does not apply to proceedings for injunctive, declaratory, or other extraordinary relief not involving the payment of damages before an administrative tribunal or court under the law of the disputing NAFTA country. These provisions modify the general rule in international law that a person must exhaust local remedies before resorting to remedies afforded by international law.[70]

NAFTA Article 1122 and CCFTA Article G-23 provide that each Party consents to arbitration and that this consent, together with the written consent of the disputing investor, constitute the written consent required under the *ICSID Convention* and the agreements required for the *New York Convention* and the *Inter-American Convention* to apply.

A disputing Party must deliver notice to the other Parties or Party that a claim has been submitted and, on written notice to the disputing parties, a Party may make submissions to the tribunal on questions of interpretation.[71]

State and provincial governments have no standing in proceedings before tribunals. If the matter in dispute involves a state or provincial

---

67 10 June 1958, Can. T.S. 1986 No. 43. See NAFTA, above note 21, art. 1122(2)(b), and CCFTA, above note 21, art. G-23(2)(b).
68 30 January 1975, 14 I.L.M. 336. See NAFTA, *ibid.*, art. 1122(2)(c), and CCFTA, *ibid.*, art. G-23(2)(c).
69 NAFTA, *ibid.*, arts. 1121(1) & 1121(2); CCFTA, *ibid.*, arts. G-22(1) & G-22(2). The consent and waiver must be included in the submission of the claim to arbitration. For when this occurs, see NAFTA art. 1137(1) and CCFTA art. G-38(1). NAFTA, Annex 1120.1, and CCFTA, Annex G-21.1, place certain constraints on actions against Mexico under NAFTA and Chile under CCFTA.
70 *Restatement (Second) of Foreign Relations Law* §206 (1965).
71 NAFTA, above note 21, arts. 1127 & 1128; CCFTA, above note 21, arts. G-28 & G-29.

measure, the recourse of the disputing investor is against the federal government of the Party of which the state or province forms a part and that federal government will be the party to the proceedings.

e) Arbitral Tribunals and Consolidation

Unless the disputing parties agree otherwise, tribunals are comprised of three arbitrators, with one being appointed by each of the disputing parties and the third and presiding arbitrator being appointed by agreement of the disputing parties.[72] Selection of arbitrators is subject to the requirements of the arbitration procedure chosen by the disputing investor, but NAFTA Article 1124 and CCFTA Article G-25 set out a procedure to be followed if a tribunal is not constituted within ninety days of the date that the claim is submitted to arbitration, or if the disputing parties cannot agree on a presiding arbitrator.

NAFTA Article 1126 and CCFTA Article G-27 set out special rules that apply if more than one investor submits a claim arising from the same event. An arbitration conducted pursuant to this procedure must be established under the UNCITRAL Arbitration Rules, but the panel of three arbitrators is established by the Secretary General of ICSID.

f) Procedure

Procedure under each of NAFTA and CCFTA is governed by the applicable body of arbitration rules except as modified by NAFTA or CCFTA. NAFTA Article 1130 and CCFTA Article G-31 set out rules respecting the place of arbitration.

Issues in dispute are to be decided in accordance with NAFTA and the applicable rules of international law.[73] A matter involving an alleged expropriation by a federal, provincial, or state government in Canada or the United States would be decided not in accordance with the extensive jurisprudence in each of those countries on compensable taking (power of eminent domain) and non-compensable regulation (police power) but, rather, in accordance with international jurisprudence, which is much less comprehensive.

Interpretations of NAFTA or CCFTA provisions by the NAFTA or CCFTA Free Trade Commission are binding on a tribunal. A tribunal must request an interpretation by the commission when a disputing Party raises as a defence that a measure falls under a reservation or exception set out in NAFTA Annexes I through to IV or CCFTA Annexes I to III. If the commission does not issue an interpretation

---

72 NAFTA, *ibid.*, art. 1123, and CCFTA, *ibid.*, art. G-24.
73 NAFTA, *ibid.*, art. 1131(1), and CCFTA, *ibid.*, art. G-32.

within sixty days (which would occur if the Parties could not agree), the tribunal may decide the issue on its own.[74]

A tribunal may appoint experts to report in writing on factual matters concerning environmental, health, safety, or other scientific matters[75] and may order interim measures of protection to preserve the rights of disputing parties.[76]

g) Awards

A tribunal may award monetary damages and applicable interest or restitution of property, but the award in this case must provide that the disputing Party may pay monetary damages and interest in lieu of restitution.[77] Where a claim is made on behalf of an enterprise, the payment must be made to the enterprise. Awards are without prejudice to relief under domestic law.[78] A tribunal may not order punitive damages. NAFTA Article 1136 and CCFTA Article G-37 provide that awards have no binding effect except between the disputing parties in respect of the particular case, and they set out time periods for enforcement.

Parties are obliged to provide for the enforcement of awards and if a disputing Party fails to abide by or comply with a final award after a request to do so from the Party whose investor was a party to the proceedings, the requesting Party may ask for the establishment of a panel under NAFTA Article 2008 or CCFTA Article N-08 without having to first request a meeting of the commission. Disputing investors may seek enforcement of awards under any of the *ICSID Convention*, the *New York Convention*, or the *Inter-American Convention*, regardless of whether a

---

74 NAFTA, *ibid.*, art. 1132, and CCFTA, *ibid.*, art. G-33. NAFTA art. 1415 also requires that the tribunal refer a question of whether NAFTA art. 1410 (which contains certain exceptions to the NAFTA financial services provisions) applies to the Financial Services Committee. The decision of the committee is binding on the tribunal, but if the committee does not decide the matter within sixty days, the disputing Party or the Party of the disputing investor may request the establishment of a panel under NAFTA art. 2008. The decision of the panel is binding on the tribunal. If a panel is not requested within ten days of the expiry of the sixty-day period, the tribunal may decide the matter.
75 NAFTA, *ibid.*, art. 1133, and CCFTA, *ibid.*, art. G-34.
76 NAFTA, *ibid.*, art. 1134, and CCFTA, ibid., art. G-35. This can include an order to preserve evidence. However, a tribunal cannot order attachment or enjoin the application of a measure.
77 The provisions respecting final awards are set out in NAFTA, *ibid.*, 1135, and CCFTA, *ibid.*, art. G-36.
78 Note that the waiver of the right to initiate or continue domestic proceedings does not cover claims for injunctive, declaratory, or other extraordinary relief.

Chapter Twenty panel has been invoked. NAFTA Annex 1137.4 and CCFTA Annex G-38.4 set out rules respecting the publication of awards.

Awards in respect of breaches of NAFTA or CCFTA obligations by state or provincial governments are the responsibility of the federal governments of which they form a part.

5) Concluding Remarks

The NAFTA and CCFTA investor-state dispute settlement procedures are potentially a much more useful vehicle for advancing the commercial interests of private sector parties because they can be initiated directly without the involvement of the complainant's government. As stated above, the fact that the general dispute resolution procedures are the exclusive preserve of government under all the trade agreements to which Canada is a party means that the government sets the agenda in all cases and private interests with legitimate grievances may be left without remedy.

The NAFTA investor-state dispute settlement procedures have been little used under NAFTA despite, at the time of writing, having been in effect for almost four years.[79] Lack of familiarity with the arbitral procedures that must be used may be one reason. The fact that the procedures necessitate suing a host government may be another inhibiting factor. A third factor may be that the applicable body of law is international law, which rarely provides clear answers to hard legal questions. However, at some point in time, a matter will be significant enough and the issues clear enough that an investor will push a claim through to a conclusion and receive an award. Once this happens, the procedures may be more frequently invoked.

These procedures must be viewed with some ambivalence. On the one hand, they do permit aggrieved parties to pursue claims directly and thus afford relief that might not otherwise, for practical purposes, be available. On the other hand, these procedures could result in matters of significant importance to the Canadian public interest being adjudicated before an international tribunal under international law in circumstances in which acceptable Canadian remedies are available and that, as a matter of Canadian public interest, are better dealt with under Canadian law.

---

79 A few cases are pending but none has been decided.

D. CONCLUSION

The trade agreements to which Canada is a party significantly affect Canadian law and Canadian public policy. As a member of the WTO, Canadian lawmakers must ensure that Canadian laws and regulations conform to a comprehensive set of international norms. The WTO is proving to be a dynamic organization with an expanding membership and an evolving jurisprudence. Subsequent rounds of WTO negotiations will likely expand the coverage of certain WTO agreements like the GATS and may extend into new areas, such as investment.

NAFTA will continue for the foreseeable future to be a major factor in relations between Canada, the United States, and Mexico. Its future expansion is, at present, more problematic, mainly because of opposition in the United States. A number of areas in which NAFTA broke ground, such as intellectual property, are now covered by WTO agreements and countries acceding to NAFTA need not be covered by parallel NAFTA provisions. However, the NAFTA investment, services, and financial services provisions set NAFTA apart from the WTO agreements.[80] Regrettably, the opponents to NAFTA expansion in the U.S. Congress are missing an opportunity to extend NAFTA investment norms throughout Latin America and bind Latin American governments to investment rules that protect U.S. direct foreign investment. Most Latin American countries have significantly liberalized their investment laws over the last decade. However, without being bound by an international normative structure, subsequent regimes could revert to previous practices.

CIFTA is likely a one-off arrangement addressing a unique set of circumstances that exist between Canada and Israel. Other than possibly including whatever Palestinian entity emerges from Israeli-Palestinian negotiations, it is improbable that CIFTA will expand to include other countries.

CCFTA may be nothing more than a transition vehicle for Chilean accession to NAFTA. If the U.S. Congress grants fast-track authority to the administration to negotiate Chilean accession, the U.S. negotiators will resist the inclusion into the accession agreement of any CCFTA provisions that are inconsistent with the U.S. negotiating agenda, such

---

80 If the MAI becomes effective, it will establish obligations among OECD countries (which include Canada and the United States) similar to those in the NAFTA and CCFTA investment chapters. Mexico is the only Latin American country that is an OECD country. Neither Chile nor Israel is an OECD country.

as the special provision respecting antidumping matters. However, these provisions could nonetheless continue in effect between Canada and Chile. There may also be considerable resistance to the extension of NAFTA Chapter Nineteen binational panel procedures to Chile. If the U.S. Congress remains intransigent about NAFTA expansion, CCFTA may become a longer-term arrangement and could evolve into a plurilateral arrangement including a number of Latin American countries besides Canada and Chile.

GLOSSARY

AAA *Agricultural Adjustment Act*, 7 U.S.C. (1988), an Act of the U.S. Congress

Agriculture Agreement *Agreement on Agriculture*, a Multilateral Agreement set out in Annex 1A of the *Agreement Creating the World Trade Organization*, 15 April 1994 (Dobbs Ferry, N.Y.: Oceana Publications, 1997)

Antidumping Agreement *Agreement on Implementation of Article VI of the General Agreement on Tariffs and Trade 1994*, a Multilateral Agreement set out in Annex 1A of the *Agreement Creating the World Trade Organization*, 15 April 1994 (Dobbs Ferry, N.Y.: Oceana Publications, 1997)

Appellate Body The Appellate Body established by the Dispute Settlement Body, which in turn has been established pursuant to the *Dispute Settlement Understanding*

Auto Pact *Agreement Concerning Automotive Products between the Government of Canada and the Government of the United States of America*, 16 January 1965, Can. T.S. 1966 No. 14

Beer Agreement *Memorandum of Understanding on Provincial Beer Marketing Practices*, 5 August 1993

Beer Case *Canada — Import, Distribution and Sale of Certain Alcoholic Drinks by Provincial Marketing Authorities (U.S. v. Canada)* (1991), GATT Doc. DS17/R, 39th supp. B.I.S.D. (1991–1992) 27, a GATT panel decision

Berne Convention *Berne Convention for the Protection of Literary and Artistic Works*, 9 September 1886, revised at Berlin, 13 November 1908; Rome, 2 June 1928; Brussels, 26 June 1948, Can. T.S. 1948 No. 22

BPT British Preferential Tariff

CCFTA *Canada–Chile Free Trade Agreement*, in force 5 July 1997, see http://www.dfait-maeci.gc.ca/english/trade/agrement.htm

chapeau The introductory language of a provision in a trade agreement

CIFTA *Canada–Israel Free Trade Agreement*, in force 1 January 1997, see http://www.dfait-maeci.gc.ca/english/trade/agrement/htm

Cigarette Case *Thailand — Restrictions on Importation of and Internal Taxes on Cigarettes (U.S. v. Thailand)* (1990), GATT Doc. DS10/R, 37th supp. B.I.S.D. (1989–1990) 200, a GATT panel decision

CITT Canadian International Trade Tribunal

Commission Under NAFTA, the Free Trade Commission established by NAFTA Article 2001; under CIFTA, the Canada–Israel Trade Commission established by CIFTA Article 8.2; under CCFTA, the Free Trade Commission established by CCFTA Article N-01

contracting party The expression used in GATT 1947 and GATT 1994 to designate a "member" or a "member country"

CRTC Canadian Radio-television and Telecommunications Commission

CUFTA *Canada–United States Free Trade Agreement*, 22 December 1987, Can. T.S. 1989 No. 3, 27 I.L.M. 281

CWB Canada Wheat Board

deputy minister Deputy Minister of National Revenue for Customs and Excise

Dispute Settlement Understanding **or DSU** *Understanding on Rules and Procedures Governing the Settlement of Disputes*, a Multilateral Agreement set out in Annex 2 of the *Agreement Creating the World Trade Organization*, 15 April 1994 (Dobbs Ferry, N.Y.: Oceana Publications, 1997)

DSB The Dispute Settlement Body established by the *Dispute Settlement Understanding*

EC Alcoholic Beverage Agreement *Agreement between Canada and the European Economic Community concerning Trade and Commerce in Alcoholic Beverages*, 28 February 1989, Can. T.S. 1989 No. 4

ECU European Currency Unit

EEC European Economic Community, the former name for the European Union

Environmental Cooperation Agreement North American Agreement on Environmental Cooperation, 14 September 1993, Can. T.S. 1994 No. 3, one of the NAFTA "side agreements"

First Annex GATS Annex on Financial Services

Gasoline Case *U.S. — Standards for Reformulated and Conventional Gasoline*, WT/DS2/R, Panel Report; WT/DS2/AB/R, Appellate Body Report (AB-1996-1), a WTO panel and an Appellate Body decision

GATS *General Agreement on Trade in Services*, a Multilateral Agreement set out in Annex 1B of the *Agreement Creating the World Trade Organization*, 15 April 1994 (Dobbs Ferry, N.Y.: Oceana Publications, 1997)

GATT *General Agreement on Tariffs and Trade*

GATT 1947 The original *General Agreement on Tariffs and Trade* that was negotiated in 1947 and entered into effect in 1948 (30 October 1947, Can. T.S. 1947 No. 27, 55 U.N.T.S. 187, T.I.A.S. No. 1700)

GATT 1994 *General Agreement on Tariffs and Trade 1994*, a Multilateral Agreement set out in Annex 1A of the *Agreement Creating the World Trade Organization*, 15 April 1994 (Dobbs Ferry, N.Y.: Oceana Publications, 1997). GATT 1994 carries forward, with some modifications, the obligations set out in GATT 1947.

Geneva Convention *Geneva Convention for the Protection of Producers of Phonograms Against Unauthorized Duplication of their Phonograms*, 29 October 1971, 866 U.N.T.S. 67, T.I.A.S. 7808

Government Procurement Agreement *Agreement on Government Procurement*, a Plurilateral Agreement set out in Annex 4 of the *Agreement Creating the World Trade Organization*, 15 April 1994 (Dobbs Ferry, N.Y.: Oceana Publications, 1997)

GPT General Preferential Tariff

GST Goods and Services Tax

ICSID International Centre for Settlement of Investment Disputes established by the *ICSID Convention*

ICSID Convention *Convention on the Settlement of Investment Disputes between States and Nationals of other States*, 18 March 1965, 4 I.L.M. 532

IEP Agreement Agreement on an International Energy Program, 18 November 1974, 1040 U.N.T.S. 271, T.I.A.S. 7791

IMF International Monetary Fund

IMF Agreement Articles of Agreement of the International Monetary Fund, 27 December 1945, Can. T.S. 1944 No. 37

Import Licensing Agreement Agreement on Import Licensing Procedures, a Multilateral Agreement set out in Annex 1A of the *Agreement Creating the World Trade Organization*, 15 April 1994 (Dobbs Ferry, N.Y.: Oceana Publications, 1997)

Integrated Circuits Treaty Treaty on Intellectual Property In Respect of Integrated Circuits, 26 May 1989, 28 I.L.M. 1484

Inter-American Convention Inter-American Convention on International Commercial Arbitration, 30 January 1975, 14 I.L.M. 336

ITC United States International Trade Commission

Labour Cooperation Agreement North American Agreement on Labour Co-operation, 13 September 1993, Can. T.S. 1994 No. 4, one of the NAFTA "side agreements"

MAI Multilateral Agreement on Investment

measure A law, regulation, procedure, requirement, or practice

MFN Most-favoured-nation

Modalities Agreement Agreement on Modalities for the Establishment of Specific Binding Commitments under the Reform Programme, The Dunkel Draft (GATT Secretariat) (Buffalo, N.Y.: William S. Hein & Co., 1992) at L.19 to L.28.

Model BIT U.S. Model Bilateral Investment Treaty

Multifibre Arrangement or **MFA** Arrangement Regarding International Trade in Textiles, 20 December 1973, Can. T.S. 1974 No. 26, 930 U.N.T.S. 166

Multilateral Agreement An agreement set out in Annex 1A, 1B, 1C, 2, or 3 of the *Agreement Creating the World Trade Organization*, 15 April 1994 (Dobbs Ferry, N.Y.: Oceana Publications, 1994), which binds all WTO member countries

NAFTA North American Free Trade Agreement, 17 December 1992, Can. T.S. 1994 No. 2

Natural Persons Annex GATS Annex on Movement of Natural Persons Supplying Services under the Agreement

New York Convention *United Nations Convention on the Recognition and Enforcement of Foreign Arbitral Awards*, 10 June 1958, Can. T.S. 1986 No. 43, 330 U.N.T.S. 3

non-Party Under NAFTA, a country that is not Canada, the United States, or Mexico; under CIFTA, a country that is not Canada or Israel; under CCFTA, a country that is not Canada or Chile

OECD Organization for Economic Cooperation and Development

OEM Original equipment manufacturer

Paris Convention *Paris Convention for the Protection of Industrial Property*, 20 March 1883, revised at Brussels, 14 December 1900; Washington, 2 June 1911; The Hague, 6 November 1925; London, 2 June 1934; Lisbon, 31 October 1958; and Stockholm, 14 July 1967, 828 U.N.T.S. 305, T.I.A.S. 6923

Party Canada, Mexico, or the United States under NAFTA; Canada or Israel under CIFTA; Canada or Chile under CCFTA

Periodicals Case *Canada — Certain Measures Concerning Periodicals*, WT/DS31/R, Panel Report; WT/DS31/AB/R, Appellate Body Report (AB-1997-2), a WTO panel and an Appellate Body decision

Plurilateral Agreement An agreement set out in Annex 4 of the *Agreement Creating the World Trade Organization*, 15 April 1994 (Dobbs Ferry, N.Y.: Oceana Publications, 1997), which binds only those WTO member countries that are signatories to the agreement

Pork Case *In the Matter of Fresh, Chilled and Frozen Pork from Canada* (1990), 3 T.C.T. 8308 (Art. 1904 Panel), a U.S. countervailing duty case that was subject to binational panel review under CUFTA Chapter Nineteen

Preshipment Inspection Agreement *Agreement on Preshipment Inspection*, a Multilateral Agreement set out in Annex 1A of the *Agreement Creating the World Trade Organization*, 15 April 1994 (Dobbs Ferry, N.Y.: Oceana Publications, 1997)

PST Provincial Sales Tax

Rome Convention *International Convention for the Protection of Performers, Producers of Phonograms and Broadcasting Organizations*, 26 October 1961, 496 U.N.T.S. 43, U.K.T.S. 1964 38

Rules of Origin Agreement Agreement on Rules of Origin, a Multilateral Agreement set out in Annex 1A of the *Agreement Creating the World Trade Organization*, 15 April 1994 (Dobbs Ferry, N.Y.: Oceana Publications, 1997)

Safeguards Agreement *Agreement on Safeguards*, a Multilateral Agreement set out in Annex 1A of the *Agreement Creating the World Trade Organization*, 15 April 1994 (Dobbs Ferry, N.Y.: Oceana Publications, 1997)

SECOFI *Secretaria de Comercio y Fomento Industrial*, the Mexican Secretariat of Commercial and Industrial Development

Second Annex GATS Second Annex on Financial Services

SIMA *Special Import Measures Act*, R.S.C. 1985, c. S-15

Softwood Case *In the Matter of Certain Softwood Products from Canada*, [1994] F.T.A.D. No. 8 (Ex. Chall. Ctee.) (QL), a U.S. countervailing duty case that was subject to binational panel review under CUFTA Chapter Nineteen

Softwood Lumber Agreement *Softwood Lumber Agreement between the Government of Canada and the Government of the United States of America*, 29 May 1996, Can. T.S. 1996 No. 16

SPS Agreement *Agreement on the Application of Sanitary and Phytosanitary Measures*, a Multilateral Agreement set out in Annex 1A of the *Agreement Creating the World Trade Organization*, 15 April 1994 (Dobbs Ferry, N.Y.: Oceana Publications, 1997)

Subsidies Agreement *Agreement on Subsidies and Countervailing Measures*, a Multilateral Agreement set out in Annex 1A of the *Agreement Creating the World Trade Organization*, 15 April 1994 (Dobbs Ferry, N.Y.: Oceana Publications, 1997)

TBT Agreement *Agreement on Technical Barriers to Trade*, a Multilateral Agreement set out in Annex 1A of the *Agreement Creating the World Trade Organization*, 15 April 1994 (Dobbs Ferry, N.Y.: Oceana Publications, 1997)

Textile Agreement *Agreement on Textiles and Clothing*, a Multilateral Agreement set out in Annex 1A of the *Agreement Creating the World Trade Organization*, 15 April 1994 (Dobbs Ferry, N.Y.: Oceana Publications, 1997)

TMB Textile Monitoring Body established under the *Textile Agreement* (set out in Annex 1A of the *Agreement Creating the World Trade Organization*, 15 April 1994 (Dobbs Ferry, N.Y.: Oceana Publications, 1997)

Tokyo Round codes   The various codes resulting from the Tokyo Round of GATT negotiations

TPLs   Tariff preference levels, pursuant to which annual volumes of certain non-originating textile and apparel goods that satisfy prescribed requirements receive NAFTA or CCFTA preferential duty treatment

transparent   Capable of being readily determined

TRIMs   Trade-related investment measures

TRIMs Agreement   *Agreement Respecting Trade-Related Investment Measures*, a Multilateral Agreement set out in Annex 1A of the *Agreement Creating the World Trade Organization*, 15 April 1994 (Dobbs Ferry, N.Y.: Oceana Publications, 1997)

TRIPS Agreement   *Agreement on Trade-Related Aspects of Intellectual Property Rights*, a Multilateral Agreement set out in Annex 1C of the *Agreement Creating the World Trade Organization*, 15 April 1994 (Dobbs Ferry, N.Y.: Oceana Publications, 1997)

Tuna Case   *U.S. — Restrictions on Imports of Tuna (EEC & Netherlands v. U.S.)* (1994), 33 I.L.M. 839, a GATT panel decision

UPOV Convention 1978   *International Convention for the Protection of New Varieties of Plants*, 2 December 1961, revised at Geneva, 10 November 1972; 23 October 1978, Can. T.S. 1991 No. 5, T.I.A.S. 10199

UPOV Convention 1991   *International Convention for the Protection of New Varieties of Plants*, 1991 (unpublished). A copy can be obtained through the World Intellectual Property Organization in Geneva (tel. 22-730-9111).

UST   United States Tariff

Valuation Agreement   *Agreement on Implementation of Article VII of the General Agreement on Tariffs and Trade 1994*, a Multilateral Agreement set out in Annex 1A of the *Agreement Creating the World Trade Organization*, 15 April 1994 (Dobbs Ferry, N.Y.: Oceana Publications, 1997)

Vienna Convention   *Vienna Convention on the Law of Treaties*, 23 May 1969, 8 I.L.M. 679

Ways and Means Motion   Notice of Ways and Means Motion respecting the imposition of duties of customs and other taxes, to provide relief against the imposition of certain duties and taxes, and to provide for other related matters, introduced by the Canadian minister of finance on 7 October 1997

WIPO World Intellectual Property Organization

WTO World Trade Organization

WTO Agreement Agreement Creating the World Trade Organization, 15 April 1994 (Dobbs Ferry, N.Y.: Oceana Publications, 1997)

WTO agreements The agreements resulting from the Uruguay Round of GATT negotiations, including the *WTO Agreement* and the agreements and understandings set out in the four annexes to the *WTO Agreement*

TABLE OF CASES

Barcelona Traction Case (Belgium v. Spain), [1970] I.C.J. Rep. 3 298

Canada — Certain Measures Concerning Periodicals,
 WT/DS31/AB/R, Appellate Body Report
 (AB-1997-2) 47, 50, 58, 60–61, 69, 267, 268, 269, 272
Canada — Certain Measures Concerning Periodicals,
 WT/DS31/R, Panel Report 47, 50, 58, 61, 68, 69, 267, 268, 269, 272
Canada — Import, Distribution and Sale of Alcoholic Drinks
 by Canadian Provincial Marketing Agencies (EEC v. Canada)
 (1987), GATT Doc. L/6304, 35th supp. B.I.S.D. (1987–1988) 37 63
Canada — Import, Distribution and Sale of Certain Alcoholic
 Drinks by Provincial Marketing Agencies (U.S. v. Canada) (1991),
 GATT Doc. DS17/R, 39th supp. B.I.S.D. (1991–1992) 27 59
Canada — Import Restrictions on Ice Cream and Yoghurt
 (U.S. v. Canada) (1989), GATT Doc. L/6568, 36th supp.
 B.I.S.D. (1988–1989) 68 .... 108, 109
Canada — Measures Affecting Exports of Unprocessed Herring
 and Salmon (U.S. v. Canada) (1987), GATT Doc. L/6368,
 35th supp. (1987–1988) 98 .... 69, 70

Differential and More Favourable Treatment, Reciprocity and
 Fuller Participation of Developing Countries (1979), GATT
 Doc. L/4903, 26th supp. B.I.S.D. (1978–1979) 203 30

EEC — Payments and Subsidies Paid to Processors and Producers
 of Oilseeds and Related Animal-Feed Proteins (U.S. v. EEC) (1989),
 GATT Doc. L/6627, 37th supp. B.I.S.D. (1989–1990) 86 151
EEC — Programme of Minimum Import Prices, Licences and
 Surety Deposits for Certain Processed Fruits and Vegetables
 (U.S. v. EEC) (1978), GATT Doc. L/4687, 25th supp. B.I.S.D.
 (1977–1978) 68 102

EEC — Regime for the Importation, Sale and Distribution
    of Bananas (1994), GATT Doc. DS38/R (unadopted).................................83
EEC — Regime for the Importation, Sale and Distribution of
    Bananas, WT/DS27/AB/R, Appellate Body Report
    (AB-1997-3) 47, 53, 109

Generalized System of Preferences (1971), GATT Doc. L/3545,
    18th supp. B.I.S.D. (1970–1971) 24 30

In the Matter of Article 304 and the Definition of Direct Cost of
    Processing or Direct Cost of Assembling (1992), 5 T.C.T. 8118
    (Ch. 18 Panel) 43
In the Matter of Canada's Landing Requirement for Pacific Coast
    Salmon and Herring (1989), 2 T.C.T. 7162 (Ch. 18 Panel) 43
In the Matter of Certain Softwood Products from Canada, [1994]
    F.T.A.D. No. 8 (Ex. Chall. Ctee.) (QL)..162
In the Matter of Fresh, Chilled and Frozen Pork from Canada
    (1990), 3 T.C.T. 8308 (Art. 1904 Panel) 161
In the Matter of Fresh, Chilled and Frozen Pork from Canada
    (1991), 4 T.C.T. 7026 (Art. 1904 Panel) 161
In the Matter of Fresh, Chilled and Frozen Pork from Canada
    (1991), 4 T.C.T. 7037 (Ex. Chall. Ctee.) 162
In the Matter of Live Swine from Canada, [1993] F.T.A.D. No. 4
    (Ex. Chall. Ctee.) (QL) 162
In the Matter of Lobsters from Canada (1990), 3 T.C.T. 8182
    (Ch. 18 Panel) 43
In the Matter of Puerto Rico Regulations on the Import,
    Distribution and Sale of U.H.T. Milk from Quebec, [1993]
    F.T.A.D. No. 7 (Ch. 18 Panel) (QL) 43
In the Matter of Tariffs Applied by Canada to Certain U.S.-Origin
    Agricultural Products, 2 December 1996, CDA-95-2008-01
    (Ch. 20 Panel) 12, 41, 42, 43, 46, 111
Interpretation of and Canada's Compliance with Article 701.3
    with Respect to Durum Wheat Sales, [1993] F.T.A.D.
    No. 2 (Ch. 18 Panel) (QL) 43, 154

Japan — Taxes on Alcoholic Beverages, WT/DS8/AB/R,
    WT/DS10/AB/R, WT/DS11/AB/R, Appellate Body
    Report (AB-1996-2).......................11, 41, 43, 44, 45, 55, 57, 58, 178, 199, 225
Japan — Taxes on Alcoholic Beverages, WT/DS8/R,
    WT/DS10/R, WT/DS11/R, Panel Report..42, 43, 56, 57

Ministerial Decision on Certain Dispute Settlement Procedures for the
    General Agreement on Trade in Services (GATS Decision).........................287
Ministerial Decision on Negotiations on Basic Telecommunications
    (GATS Decision) 243
Ministerial Decision on Negotiations on Maritime Transport Services
    (GATS Decision) 241

Table of Cases   317

Thailand — Restrictions on Importation of and Internal Taxes on
  Cigarettes (U.S. v. Thailand) (1990), GATT Doc. DS10/R,
  37th supp. B.I.S.D. (1989–1990) 200......................................67, 68, 69, 70, 71
U.S. — Imports of Automotive Products, 20 December 1965,
  14th supp. B.I.S.D. (1966) 37..23
U.S. — Measures Affecting Alcoholic and Malt Beverages
  (Canada v. U.S.) (1992), GATT Doc. DS23/R, 39th supp.
  B.I.S.D. (1991–1992) 206..61
U.S. — Restrictions on Imports of Tuna (EEC & Netherlands
  v. U.S.) (1994), 33 I.L.M. 839 (GATT)..67, 68, 71
U.S. — Restrictions on Imports of Tuna (Mexico v. U.S.) (1991),
  GATT Doc. DS21/R, 39th supp. B.I.S.D. (1991–1992) 155..........................68
U.S. — Section 337 of the Tariff Act of 1930 (EEC v. U.S.) (1988),
  GATT Doc. L/6439, 36th supp. B.I.S.D. (1988–1989) 345................59, 69, 70
U.S. — Standards for Reformulated and Conventional Gasoline,
  WT/DS2/R, Panel Report.......................................41, 55, 59, 60, 67, 69, 70, 74
U.S. — Standards for Reformulated and Conventional
  Gasoline, WT/DS2/AB/R, Appellate Body Report
  (AB-1996-1)..68, 69, 70, 71, 72, 73, 213
U.S. — Trade Measures Affecting Nicaragua, [1986]
  GATTPD LEXIS 1...262

INDEX

AGREEMENT CREATING THE WORLD TRADE ORGANIZATION. *See* WTO AGREEMENT

AGRICULTURAL GOODS
Agriculture Agreement
   domestic support programs, 153
   export subsidies, 153
   generally, 24
   safeguards, 110
   summarized, 24
   tariffication, 108
   tariff rate quotas, 109
Canada–Mexico, 114
Canadian market restrictions
   Canadian Wheat Board control of grains, 108
   supply management for dairy, poultry, eggs
      Canadian programs, 107
      justification under Article XI:2(c), 101
      managed trade, as example of, 24
      upheld by NAFTA panel, 111
CCFTA provisions
   export subsidies, 155
NAFTA provisions
   Canada and Mexico, 114
   Canada and United States
      CUFTA provisions, incorporation of export subsidies, 154
      fresh fruits and vegetables, 110
      generally, 110
      retention of GATT rights, 111
      selling below acquisition cost, 110
      transportation and other domestic subsidies, 154
      wheat, oats, and barley, 110
   country of origin
      NAFTA tariff preference purposes, 144
      qualifying goods, 145
   export subsidies, general provision, 154
   special safeguards, 114
   United States and Mexico, 114
tariff rate quotas
   conversion by Canada, 109
   non-discriminatory application, 109
tariffication, 108
U.S. market restrictions
   Agricultural Adjustment Act, 108
   dairy products, 108
   sugar and sugar-containing products, 108

ALCOHOLIC BEVERAGES
Beer Agreement with United States, 65
CCFTA provisions
   blending, 65
   wine and distilled spirits, 65

CUFTA provisions, wine and distilled
    spirits, 64
discriminatory practices, provincial
    liquor monopolies, 63
EC Alcoholic Beverages Agreement, 64
GATT jurisprudence respecting, 59, 63,
    64
NAFTA provisions
  beer, no special rule, 65
  wine and distilled spirits
    Canada and Mexico, 65
    Canada and United States,
      incorporation of CUFTA
      provisions, 64
WTO jurisprudence respecting, 55, 56, 58

ANTIDUMPING AND
    COUNTERVAILING DUTIES,
    SUBSIDIES
Antidumping Agreement
  export price, 148
  judicial review, requirement for, 149
  normal value, 148
  price undertakings, 149
  summarized, 25
antidumping duties
  margin of dumping, 148
  purpose, 9, 146
antidumping and countervailing duty
    procedures, NAFTA countries
  Canadian and United States, 155
  Mexico, 156
CCFTA provisions
  antidumping laws, reciprocal
      exemption, 163
  dispute settlement rules, 164
  WTO agreements, application of, 164
CIFTA provisions
  no panel review, 163
  reservation of right to apply, 163
  WTO agreements, application of, 163
countervailing duties
  purpose, 10, 146
  Subsidies Agreement, and
    subsidies to which countervailable
      measures apply, 151
    procedural requirements, 152
dumping
  defined, 9, 146
GATT 1994
  antidumping duties, requirements,
      148
  countervailing duties, requirements,
      148

generally, 9, 146
material injury, requirement for, 148
NAFTA provisions
  minimum norms, 157
  panel review of final determinations
    extraordinary challenge
      procedures, 162
    final determinations subject to
        review
      Canadian, 158
      Mexican, 160
      U.S., 159
    formation of panels, 160
    standard of review, 161
    time frames, 161
    safeguarding panel process, 162
    uphold or remand, 161
  retention of existing domestic laws, 156
  statutory amendments, panel review
      of, 157

APPAREL GOODS. See TEXTILE AND
    APPAREL GOODS

AUTOMOTIVE GOODS
CAFE rules and NAFTA, 97
duty remission respecting
  Auto Pact
    background, 94
    CUFTA provisions, 95
    NAFTA, carries CUFTA provisions
        forward, 95
    elimination of parts duty, effect on,
        96
    rule of origin, 96
    export-based duty remission, CUFTA
        and NAFTA, 96
    production-based duty remission,
        CUFTA and NAFTA, 96
Mexican Automotive Decree, dismantled
    under NAFTA, 97
most-favoured-nation, NAFTA, 54 n. 5
rules of origin. See RULES OF ORIGIN
used cars embargo
  CCFTA, continuation of Chilean
      prohibition, 103
  NAFTA, provisions respecting, 97

BALANCE OF PAYMENTS
exceptions respecting
  CCFTA, 265
  NAFTA, 265
  GATS, 265
  GATT 1994, 264

Index   321

restrictions, requirements respecting
  generally, 263
  IMF Agreement, 264

BUSINESS PERSONS. *See* TEMPORARY
  ENTRY

CANADA–CHILE FREE TRADE
  AGREEMENT. *See* CCFTA

CANADA–ISRAEL FREE TRADE
  AGREEMENT. *See* CIFTA

CANADA–UNITED STATES FREE
  TRADE AGREEMENT. *See* CUFTA

CCFTA
  accession, no provision respecting, 282
  agricultural goods. *See* AGRICULTURAL
    GOODS
  alcoholic beverages provisions, 65
  antidumping and countervailing duties.
    See ANTIDUMPING AND
    COUNTERVAILING DUTIES
  balance of payments, exception, 265
  competition law, 260
  copper, exception for, 103
  cultural industries, exemption of, 270
  customs procedures. *See* CUSTOMS
    PROCEDURES
  dispute resolution. *See* DISPUTE
    RESOLUTION
  duties
    repair and alteration, re-entry after, 99
    temporary admission of goods, 99
    waivers under, 99
  effective, 38
  environmental issues. *See*
    ENVIRONMENTAL ISSUES
  export taxes prohibited, 104
  free trade area, creates, 30, 38
  generally, 39
  import and export restrictions. *See*
    TRADE IN GOODS, import and
    export restrictions
  institutional structures. *See*
    INSTITUTIONAL STRUCTURES
  intellectual property, 171
  investment provisions. *See*
    INVESTMENT
  monopolies and state enterprises.
    See MONOPOLIES AND
    STATE ENTERPRISES
  national security, exception for, 262

reservations. *See* RESERVATIONS
rules of origin. *See* RULES OF ORIGIN
safeguards. *See* SAFEGUARDS
sanitary and phytosanitary measures, 171
services provisions. *See* SERVICES
subsidies, export, on agricultural goods,
  155
tariff elimination, 86
taxation measures, exceptions for, 274
technical barriers to trade, 171
telecommunications. *See*
  TELECOMMUNICATIONS
temporary entry. *See* TEMPORARY
  ENTRY
textiles and apparel goods. *See* TEXTILE
  AND APPAREL GOODS
trade in goods. *See* TRADE IN GOODS

CIFTA
  accession, no provision respecting, 282
  antidumping and countervailing duties.
    See ANTIDUMPING AND
    COUNTERVAILING DUTIES
  balance of payments, exception, 265
  cultural industries, 270
  competition law, 260
  cultural industries, exemption of, 270
  customs procedures. *See* CUSTOMS
    PROCEDURES
  dispute resolution. *See* DISPUTE
    RESOLUTION
  duties, repair and alteration, re-entry
    after, 99
  effective, 38
  environmental issues. *See*
    ENVIRONMENTAL ISSUES
  free trade area, creates, 30, 39
  generally, 38
  import and export restrictions.
    See TRADE IN GOODS, import
    and export restrictions
  intellectual property, 171
  institutional structures. *See*
    INSTITUTIONAL STRUCTURES
  monopolies and state enterprises.
    See MONOPOLIES AND
    STATE ENTERPRISES
  national security, exception for, 262
  sanitary and phytosanitary measures, 171
  rules of origin. *See* RULES OF ORIGIN
  taxation measures, exceptions for, 274
  tariff elimination, 86
  technical barriers to trade, 171

COMPETITION LAW
generally, 259
international trade and, 7
CCFTA provisions, 260
CIFTA provisions, 260
NAFTA provisions, 260

COPYRIGHT. *See* INTELLECTUAL PROPERTY

COUNTERVAILING DUTY.
  See ANTIDUMPING AND COUNTERVAILING DUTIES

COUNTRY OF ORIGIN DETERMINATIONS.
  See RULES OF ORIGIN

CUFTA
antecedent of NAFTA, 31
Auto Pact, and, 95
entry into, 3
incorporation of provisions into NAFTA
  agricultural goods. *See* AGRICULTURAL GOODS, NAFTA provisions
  alcoholic beverages. *See* ALCOHOLIC BEVERAGES, CUFTA provisions
  automotive goods
    Auto Pact remission orders, 95
    non-Auto Pact remission orders, 96
    used vehicles, 97
  cultural industries. *See* CULTURAL INDUSTRIES, CUFTA provisions
  duty waivers, 93 n. 52
  financial services, CUFTA concessions. *See* FINANCIAL SERVICES, NAFTA provisions

CULTURAL INDUSTRIES
Canadian cultural policies
  cable
    ownership, 267
    programming, 268
    Country Music Television, 271
  content requirements, 267
  film distribution, 268
  foreign ownership restrictions, 267
  other discriminatory practices, 267
  periodicals, 267, 268
  television, 267
  trade restrictions, 267

CCFTA, exemption of cultural industries from, 270
CIFTA, exemption of cultural industries from, 270
CUFTA provisions
  covered services, effect of non-inclusion, 271
  exceptions to Article 2005
    forced divestiture, 273
    print-in-Canada requirements, 273
    retransmission rights, 273
    tariff elimination, 273
  exemption under Article 2005, 271
  grandfathering, effect of, 271
  retaliation under Article 2005, 271
definition of, 269
generally, 266
NAFTA
  incorporation of entirety of CUFTA provisions, 270
  Mexico and the United States, 270
WTO and
  jurisprudence: Periodicals Case, 47, 68, 69, 267, 268, 269, 272
  WTO agreements, no special treatment, 268

CUSTOMS PROCEDURES. *See also* TARIFFS
advance rulings, NAFTA, CIFTA and CCFTA, 139
certification of origin
  General Preferential Tariff, 139
  Least Developed Developing Country, 139
  NAFTA, CIFTA, and CCFTA
    common form of certificate, 139
    importer must have in possession, 139
customs user fees, prohibition
  CCFTA, 99
  NAFTA, 99
maintain records, 139
procedural fairness, as objective, 139
review and appeal, 139
Uniform Regulations
  NAFTA Chapter Five, and standards approach to
Working Group, NAFTA and CCFTA
  consultations through, in dispute resolution, 291 n. 46
  establishment of, 139

CUSTOMS UNIONS AND FREE
	TRADE AREAS
customs unions, 28
free trade areas, 29
generally, 28

CUSTOMS USER FEES. *See* CUSTOMS
	PROCEDURES

DISPUTE RESOLUTION
CCFTA general procedures
	Commission, request for meeting of, 291
	consultations, 290
	implementation of recommendations, 293
	non-violation nullification and impairment, 289
	panels
		establishment of, 291
		proceedings, 292
	scope, 289
	suspension of benefits, 293
	temporary entry, limitation, 294
CIFTA general procedures
	Commission, request for meeting of, 291
	consultations, 290
	implementation of recommendations, 293
	non-violation nullification and impairment, 289
	panels
		establishment of, 291
		proceedings
	scope, 289
	suspension of benefits, 293
common themes, 282
Dispute Settlement Understanding
	appeals, 288
	compensation, 288
	consultations, 187
	generally, 16, 286
	Government Procurement Agreement, application to, 289
	implementation of recommendations, 288
	panel process, 287
	suspension of benefits, 288
exclusion of private interests, 295
GATT 1994
	application of provisions to other WTO agreements
		generally, 284
		TRIPS Agreement, 201
	Articles XXII and XXIII, 284
	nullification and impairment, 285
generally, 16
investor/state dispute arbitration, CCFTA and NAFTA
	arbitral tribunals, 301
	awards, 303
	conditions to submitting a claim
		consent, 300
		waiver of other proceedings, 300
	consolidation, 302
	entitlement to make claim
	exclusions, 297
	Inter-American Convention, 303
	involvement of other Parties, 301
	New York Convention, 303
	procedure
		choice of
			Additional Facility Rules, 299, 300
			ICSID Convention, 299, 300
			UNCITRAL Arbitration Rules, 300
		experts, appointment by tribunal, 302
		international law, 302
		interpretations by Commission, binding, 302
	provisions that can give rise to claims, 296
	standing to submit a claim, 298
NAFTA general procedures
	antidumping and countervailing duty matters. *See* ANTIDUMPING AND COUNTERVAILING DUTIES
	Commission, request for meeting of, 291
	consultations, 290
	implementation of recommendations, 293
	non-violation nullification and impairment, 289
	panels
		establishment of, 291
		proceedings
	scope, 289
	suspension of benefits
		financial services, limitation, 293
		generally, 293
	temporary entry, limitation, 294
	which procedures apply, 294

DUMPING. *See* ANTIDUMPING
	AND COUNTERVAILING DUTIES

DUTIES. *See also* TARIFFS
antidumping, *See* ANTIDUMPING AND
    COUNTERVAILING DUTIES
commercial samples and printed
    advertising materials
    CCFTA, 99
    NAFTA, 99
computer goods, creation of mini
    customs union under NAFTA, 99
countervailing. *See* ANTIDUMPING
    AND COUNTERVAILING
    DUTIES
relief from
    Canadian programs
        remission
            company specific, 94
            automotive goods. *See*
                AUTOMOTIVE GOODS
            textile and apparel goods.
                See TEXTILE AND
                APPAREL GOODS
        concessionary rates, 93
    drawback and deferral
        duty deferral
            described, 90
            foreign trade zones, United
                States, 91
            inward processing, Canada, 90
            maquiladoras, Mexico, 91
        duty drawback described, 90
        NAFTA provisions
            exceptions, 92
            restrictions and prohibitions
                described, 91
                rationale for, 91
    waivers
        based on performance
            requirements
            CCFTA prohibition, 99
            NAFTA prohibition, 93
        other
            CCFTA provision, 99
            NAFTA provision, 93
repair and alteration, re-entry of goods
    after
    CIFTA and CCFTA, provisions of, 99
    NAFTA, provisions of, 99
temporary admission of goods
    CCFTA, provisions of, 99
    NAFTA, provisions of, 99

EMPLOYMENT. *See* LABOUR ISSUES;
    TEMPORARY ENTRY

ENERGY GOODS
Canadian policy re oil industry, 106
gasoline, WTO jurisprudence respecting,
    68, 71
International Energy Program, 107
NAFTA provisions
    import and export restrictions, 107
    national security. *See* NATIONAL
        SECURITY

EMERGENCY ACTION.
    See SAFEGUARDS

ENVIRONMENTAL ISSUES
CCFTA text and
    clarification respecting GATT 1994
        exceptions, 74
    investment. *See* INVESTMENT,
        CCFTA provisions
    prevalence of certain environmental
        and conservation agreements
        over, 185
CIFTA text and
    clarification respecting GATT 1994
        exceptions, 74
Environmental Cooperation Agreement,
    4, 6, 185
GATT 1994
    exception in Article XX(b)
        application to environmental
            measures, 74
    exception in Article XX(g)
        application to exhaustible living
            natural resources, 74
generally, 184
international trading system, and, 6
NAFTA text and
    clarification respecting GATT 1994
        exceptions, 74
    investment. *See* INVESTMENT,
        NAFTA provisions
    prevalence of certain environmental
        and conservation agreements
        over, 185
    standards-related measures
        legitimate objective,
            environmental protection
            as, 182
        tautologous provision respecting,
            178
TBT Agreement
    legitimate objective, environmental
        protection as, 182

ESSENTIAL SECURITY INTERESTS.
     See NATIONAL SECURITY

EXPROPRIATION. See INVESTMENT,
     CCFTA obligations, NAFTA
     obligations

EXPORT TAXES. See TRADE IN
     GOODS, export taxes

FINANCIAL SERVICES
GATS provisions re
     Annexes on Financial Services, 252
     agreement on specific commitments,
          252
generally, 244
NAFTA provisions re
     CUFTA concessions, preservation of,
          249
     incorporation of certain NAFTA
          investment provisions, 249
     non-discrimination
          application to provinces and states,
               248
          national treatment
               cross-border trade in financial
                    services, 247
               equal competitive
                    opportunities, 248
               financial institutions
                    generally, 246
                    prospective rules, 246
          most-favoured-nation treatment,
               248
     reservations and specific
          commitments
          Annex VII
               Schedule A reservations, 251
               Schedule B reservations, 251
               Schedule C commitments, 251
          applicability of Annex I through
               Annex IV reservations, 250.
               See also RESERVATIONS:
               NAFTA AND CCFTA
     scope and coverage
          application to provinces and states,
               246, 248
          denial of benefits, 246
          financial institutions, 244
          financial services, 245
     specific commitments.
          See RESERVATIONS

FREE TRADE AREAS. See CUSTOMS
     UNIONS AND FREE TRADE
     AREAS

GATS
entry of persons. See TEMPORARY
     ENTRY
financial services. See FINANCIAL
     SERVICES
monopolies. See MONOPOLIES AND
     STATE ENTERPRISES
services. See SERVICES
state enterprises. See MONOPOLIES
     AND STATE ENTERPRISES
subsidies. See SUBSIDIES
telecommunications.
     See TELECOMMUNICATIONS
summarized, 26

GATT 1947
entry into force, 2
historical background, 1, 2
GATT 1994, and, 22
WTO Agreement, and, 4

GATT 1994
antidumping and countervailing duties.
     See ANTIDUMPING AND
     COUNTERVAILING DUTIES
balance of payments, 24, 264
cinematographic films, 24
contents
     GATT 1947, 22
     highlights summarized, 23
     other provisions, 23
country-of-origin marking, 140
dispute resolution, 24. See also DISPUTE
     RESOLUTION
environmental issues.
     See ENVIRONMENTAL ISSUES
export subsidies, prohibition of, 149
fees and formalities, 24
freedom of transit, 24
general exceptions, 24. See also TRADE
     IN GOODS, general exceptions
import and export restrictions.
     See TRADE IN GOODS, import
     and export restrictions
most-favoured-nation principle.
     See TRADE IN GOODS, most-
     favoured-nation principle
national security exception, 24, 261
national treatment. See TRADE IN
     GOODS, national treatment

procedural fairness, 24
safeguards, 164
state trading enterprises, 255
tariffs, bound under, 83
transparency, 24

GATT NEGOTIATING ROUNDS
Kennedy Round, 2
rounds summarized, 2 n. 1
Tokyo Round, 2
Uruguay Round
  agenda, 3
  conclusion, 4
  initiation of, 3

GENERAL AGREEMENT ON TRADE IN SERVICES. *See* GATS

GENERAL AGREEMENT ON TARIFFS AND TRADE. *See* GATT 1947

GENERAL AGREEMENT ON TARIFFS AND TRADE 1947. *See* GATT 1947

GENERAL AGREEMENT ON TARIFFS AND TRADE 1994. *See* GATT 1994

GENERAL PREFERENTIAL TARIFF (GPT), 80

GENERALIZED SYSTEM OF PREFERENCES (GSP), 30, 80

GOODS, TRADE IN. *See* TRADE IN GOODS

GOVERNMENT PROCUREMENT
agreements between Canada and other countries, summarized, 203
common themes, 203
generally, 202
Government Procurement Agreement
  bid challenge procedures, 213
  dispute settlement under. *See* DISPUTE RESOLUTION, Dispute Settlement Understanding
  exceptions, 213
  non-discrimination, 210
  offsets, prohibited, 212
  plurilateral agreement, as, 27, 204
  rules of origin, 210
  scope and coverage
    exclusions, 208
    specified construction services, 207
    specified goods, 206
    specified government departments and enterprises
      federal (central) government entities, 204
      other enterprises, 205
      provincial and state government entities, 205
    specified monetary thresholds, above
      levels, 208
      valuation of contracts, 209
    specified services, 206
  technical specifications, 211
  tendering practices, 211
  transparency, 212
NAFTA provisions
  bid challenge procedures, 213
  denial of benefits, 209
  dispute settlement under. *See* DISPUTE RESOLUTION, Dispute Settlement Understanding
  exceptions, 213
  non-discrimination, 210
  offsets, prohibited, 212
  privatization, and, 214
  rules of origin, 210
  scope and coverage
    exclusions, 208
    specified construction services, 207
    specified goods, 206
    specified government departments and enterprises
      federal (central) government entities, 204
      other enterprises, 205
      provincial and state government entities, 205
    specified monetary thresholds, above
      levels, 208
      valuation of contracts, 209
    specified services, 206
  technical specifications, 211
  tendering practices, 211
  transparency, 212
Tokyo Round Code, 202

HARMONIZED SYSTEM. *See* TARIFFS, tariff classification

IMPORT AND EXPORT RESTRICTIONS. *See* TRADE IN GOODS, import and export restrictions

INDUSTRIAL DESIGNS. *See* INTELLECTUAL PROPERTY

INFORMATION, DISCLOSURE OF exceptions respecting, 276

INSTITUTIONAL STRUCTURES
CCFTA
 committees and working groups, 281
 Free Trade Commission, 281
 Secretariat, 281
CIFTA
 committees and working groups, 282
 Canada–Israel Trade Commission, 282
 Secretariat, 281
NAFTA
 committees and working groups, 282
 Free Trade Commission, 281
 Secretariat, 281
World Trade Organization
 decisions of, 279
 establishment of, 2, 277
 significance of, 12
 structure of
  councils, 278
  committees, 278
  director general, 279
  secretariat, 279

INTELLECTUAL PROPERTY
Berne Convention described, 189
dispute resolution. *See* DISPUTE RESOLUTION
Geneva Convention described, 189
Integrated Circuits Treaty described, 190
generally, 186
intellectual property rights defined, 187
international trading system, and, 5
NAFTA provisions re
 control of anti-competitive practices, 192
 copyright, 192
 encrypted program-carrying satellite signals, 198
 enforcement of rights
  border enforcement, 201
  civil and administrative procedures, 200
  criminal procedures, 200
  interim relief, 200
 geographic indications, 195
 industrial designs
  generally, 195
  limited exceptions, 199
 international conventions, giving effect to, 188
 nationals, extension of protection to, 190
 national treatment, 191
 patents
  generally, 195
  limited exceptions, 199
 scope and coverage, 187
 semiconductor integrated circuits, layout designs of, 197
 sound recordings, 193
 technical assistance
 trademarks
  generally, 194
  limited exceptions, 199
 trade secrets, 197
 transitional provisions, 201
Paris Convention, 188
reciprocity
Rome Convention, 189
trade context of
TRIPS Agreement
 control of anti-competitive practices, 192
 copyright, 192
 enforcement of rights
  border enforcement, 201
  civil and administrative procedures, 200
  criminal procedures, 200
  interim relief, 200
 exception, public health and nutrition, 198
 geographic indications, 195
 industrial designs
  generally, 195
  limited exceptions, 199
 international conventions, comply with, 188
 most-favoured-nation treatment, 192
 nationals, extension of protection to, 190
 national treatment, 191
 patents
  generally, 195
  limited exceptions, 199
 scope and coverage, 187

328 INTERNATIONAL TRADE LAW

semiconductor integrated circuits,
  layout designs of, 197
sound recordings, 193
trademarks
  generally, 194
  limited exceptions, 199
undisclosed information, 197
UPOV Conventions, 190
World Intellectual Property
  Organization, 5

INTERNATIONAL TRADING SYSTEM
basis
  exceptions, 15
  generally, 7
  international standards, use of, 14
  non-discrimination, 13
  norms, creation of, 14
  procedural fairness, 15
  reduction of barriers, 13
  reservations, 15
  transparency, 14
managed trade, 11
policy instruments subject to discipline
  performance requirements, 10
  qualitative restrictions, 10
  quantitative restrictions, 8
  right of establishment, 10
  special trade remedies, 9
  subsidies, 9
  tariffs, 8
  voluntary export restraints, 9
rules based system, 11
trade barriers, difficulty in dismantling, 8

INTERPRETATION ISSUES
guides to interpretation
  generally, 40
  public international law, 43
  Vienna Convention 41
  WTO panel and Appellate Body
    Reports, 41
inconsistencies, resolving
  between agreements, which prevails,
    48
  within an agreement, 46
international agreements and subregional
  (provincial) governments, 50
textual analysis
  incorporation by reference, 45
  preamble, 44
  principle of effectiveness, 44
  scope and coverage provisions, 44
  tautologous provisions, 44

INVESTMENT
CCFTA provisions
  exceptions to
    government procurement, 225
    subsidies and grants, 225
  environmental matters, 225
  expropriation and compensation, 223
  minimum standard of treatment, 220
  national treatment
    generally, 219
    rule for provinces, 219
  most-favoured-nation treatment, 219
  non-conforming measures.
    See RESERVATIONS:
      NAFTA AND CCFTA
  performance requirements, 220
  reservations re. See RESERVATIONS:
    NAFTA AND CCFTA
  scope and coverage
    generally, 216
    financial institutions excluded, 218
    provinces, 219
  senior managers/boards of directors, 223
  special formalities, 223
  transfers, NAFTA and CCFTA, 223
international trading system, and, 5
Multilateral Agreement on Investment,
  negotiations, 216
NAFTA provisions
  exceptions to
    government procurement, 225
    subsidies and grants, 225
  environmental matters, 225
  expropriation and compensation, 223
  minimum standard of treatment, 220
  national treatment
    generally, 219
    provinces and states, 219
  most-favoured-nation treatment,
    NAFTA and CCFTA, 219
  non-conforming measures.
    See RESERVATIONS:
      NAFTA AND CCFTA
  performance requirements
  reservations re. See RESERVATIONS:
    NAFTA AND CCFTA
  scope and coverage
    generally, 216
    financial institutions excluded, 218
    provinces and states, applies to, 219
  senior managers/boards of directors,
    223
  special formalities, 223
  transfers, 223

Index   329

TRIMs Agreement
   summarized, 25
   trade-related investment measures, 222

LABOUR ISSUES
international trading system, and, 6,
Labour Cooperation Agreement, 4, 6, 185

MARKING OF GOODS. See RULES OF ORIGIN, non-preferential rules of origin

MARKING RULES. See RULES OF ORIGIN, non-preferential rules of origin, NAFTA provisions

MONOPOLIES AND STATE ENTERPRISES
exclusive service providers
   requirements of GATS, 256
generally, 254
monopolies
   requirements
      GATS, 256
      NAFTA, CIFTA, and CCFTA, 257
   right to designate, NAFTA, CIFTA, and CCFTA, 257
state enterprises
   requirements, NAFTA, CIFTA, and CCFTA, 259
   right to designate, NAFTA, CIFTA, and CCFTA, 259
state trading enterprises
   provisions of GATT 1994, 256

MOST-FAVOURED-NATION PRINCIPLE
basis for international trading system, as, 13
description of principle, 13

NAFTA
accession to, 282
agricultural goods. See AGRICULTURAL GOODS
alcoholic beverages. See ALCOHOLIC BEVERAGES
automotive goods. See AUTOMOTIVE GOODS
amendment to, 282
antidumping and countervailing duties. See ANTIDUMPING AND COUNTERVAILING DUTIES
background to, 31
balance of payments, exception, 265
competition law, 260
cultural industries. See CULTURAL INDUSTRIES
customs procedures. See CUSTOMS PROCEDURES
dispute resolution. See also DISPUTE RESOLUTION
   investor-state procedures summarized, 37
   state to state procedures summarized, 37
duties, effect on programs providing relief from. See DUTIES, relief from
entry into force, 31
environmental issues. See ENVIRONMENTAL ISSUES
export taxes prohibited, 104
financial services. See FINANCIAL SERVICES
free trade area, creates, 30, 33
GATT 1994, as extension of, 33
government procurement. See GOVERNMENT PROCUREMENT
import and export restrictions. See TRADE IN GOODS, import and export restrictions
institutional structures. See INSTITUTIONAL STRUCTURES
intellectual property. See INTELLECTUAL PROPERTY
investment. See also INVESTMENT
   summarized, 36
monopolies and state enterprises. See MONOPOLIES AND STATE ENTERPRISES.
national security, exception for, 262
parallel obligations, 35
reservations. See RESERVATIONS
rules of origin. See RULES OF ORIGIN
safeguards. See SAFEGUARDS
sanitary and phytosanitary measures. See TECHNICAL STANDARDS
services provisions. See also SERVICES
   summarized, 36
structure, 32
tariff elimination, 85
taxation measures, exceptions for, 274
technical barriers to trade. See TECHNICAL STANDARDS
telecommunications. See TELECOMMUNICATIONS
temporary entry. See TEMPORARY ENTRY

textiles and apparel goods. *See* TEXTILE AND APPAREL GOODS
trade in goods. *See also* TRADE IN GOODS
provisions summarized, 33

NATIONAL SECURITY
exceptions for
  CCFTA, 262
  CIFTA, 262
  GATS, 261
  GATT 1994, 261
  GOVERNMENT PROCUREMENT AGREEMENT, 213
  NAFTA
    energy goods, 262 n. 1
    general exception, 262
    government procurement, 213
    TRIPS Agreement, 262
    self-judging nature of, 262

NATIONAL TREATMENT
basis for international trading system, as, 13
description of principle, 13

NON-DISCRIMINATION.
basis for international trading system, as, 13

NORTH AMERICAN FREE TRADE AGREEMENT. *See* NAFTA

ORIGIN OF GOODS. *See* RULES OF ORIGIN

PATENTS. *See* INTELLECTUAL PROPERTY, NAFTA provisions

RESERVATIONS: NAFTA AND CCFTA
existing non-conforming measures, reservations respecting
  defined, 229
  federal (national) level
    Annex I reservations: NAFTA and CCFTA
      general description, 230
      Schedule of Canada (NAFTA and CCFTA)
        Investment Canada Act, 230
        other federal measures, 231
      Schedule of Chile (CCFTA), 232
      Schedule of Mexico (NAFTA), 231
      Schedule of the United States, 232
    articles affected by, 229
    Mexican Annex III reservations (NAFTA), 233
  provincial, state and local levels, 234
financial services. *See* FINANCIAL SERVICES, NAFTA provisions
generally, 15
MFN treatment, reservations respecting, 235
sectoral reservations under NAFTA and CCFTA Annex II
  articles affected, 234
  described, 234
  government debt instruments, 235
  legal services, 235
  minorities, 235
  ocean front land, ownership of, 235
  social services, 234
  telecommunications
    exclusion of enhanced and value-added services
    reservations, 235, 242
  transportation services, 235

RULES OF ORIGIN
generally, 124
GATT 1947, approach under, 125
government procurement. *See* GOVERNMENT PROCUREMENT
non-preferential and preferential rules of origin distinguished
  complication under NAFTA, 125
  generally, 124
non-preferential rules of origin
  country-of-origin marking, Canadian requirements, 144
  GATT 1994, rules respecting country-of-origin marking, 140
  generally, 124
  NAFTA provisions
    country of origin
      goods of a Party
        antidumping and countervailing duty matters, panel review, 158
        import and export restrictions, and, 102
        national treatment, and, 62
      marking, 143
      NAFTA tariff preference purposes, 144
      qualifying goods. *See* AGRICULTURAL GOODS

Marking Rules
    change to, U.S. position, 142
    generally, 142
    hierarchy of rules, 142
    override provision for NAFTA originating goods, 143
    textile and apparel goods, U.S. rules, 142
    trilaterally-agreed norms, absence of, 142
Rules of Origin Agreement
    disciplines during transition to harmonization, 141
    harmonization of non-preferential rules of origin, 141
    objective, 141
preferential rules of origin
    accumulation, NAFTA and CCFTA, 137
    autonomous trade regimes, Canada, 138
    basic terminology, 127
    Chilean accession to NAFTA, effect on CCFTA rules, 138
    change in tariff classification
        generally, 130
        when cannot occur, 131
        tariff shift, same as, 130
    CIFTA rules, United States and, 137
    de minimis rule, 132
    establishing goods are originating. *See also* CUSTOMS PROCEDURES
        generally under NAFTA, CIFTA, and CCFTA, 128
    free trade area, and, 127
    fungible goods and materials, 137
    generally, 124
    preferential tariff treatment, basis for determining eligibility for, 127
    Rules of Origin Agreement, general criteria, 138
    specific rules of origin, NAFTA, CIFTA, and CCFTA, 129
    Uniform Regulations, NAFTA and CCFTA, 126
    value-content requirement, NAFTA and CCFTA
        averaging, 137
        net cost, 134
        net cost method, 133
        transaction value, 134
        transaction value method, 133
        Valuation Agreement, use of, 134
        value of non-originating materials
            automotive goods under NAFTA, 136
            generally, NAFTA and CCFTA, 135
    wholly originating goods, 129

SAFEGUARDS
generally, 164
CCFTA
    bilateral actions
        other than textile and apparel goods, 166
        textile and apparel goods
            quantitative restrictions, 169
            tariff actions, 166
    global actions, 166
    procedural requirements, 169
CIFTA, 169
GATT 1994, provisions relating to, 164
NAFTA
    bilateral actions
        other than textile and apparel goods, 166
        textile and apparel goods
            quantitative restrictions, 169
            tariff actions, 166
    global actions, 166
    procedural requirements, 169
Safeguards Agreement
    defines "serious injury" and "threat of serious injury," 165
    Softwood Lumber Agreement, consistency with, 121
    summarized, 26
    orderly marketing arrangements, prohibits, 165
    time limits, sets, 165
    voluntary export restraints, prohibits, 165
special trade remedy, as, 10

SANITARY AND PHYTOSANITARY MEASURES. *See* TECHNICAL STANDARDS

SERVICES
CCFTA obligations re
    exceptions
        government procurement, 228
        subsidies, 228
    licensing/certification requirements, 228
    citizenship/residency requirements, 228

generally, 228
most-favoured-nation principle, 227
professional services, 227
non-conforming measures.
See RESERVATIONS
non-discrimination
local presence, 228
MFN treatment, 227
national treatment, 227
quantitative restrictions, 228
reservations re. See RESERVATIONS
scope and coverage
application to provinces and states, 227
cross-border provision of, 226
services covered, 226
telecommunications. See TELECOMMUNICATIONS
financial services. See FINANCIAL SERVICES
GATS obligations re
air transport services, Annex on, 240
exceptions
balance of payments. See BALANCE OF PAYMENTS
general, 239
national security. See NATIONAL SECURITY
financial services. See FINANCIAL SERVICES
maritime transport services, Annex on, 241
MFN obligation, 237
scope and coverage, 236
service supplier, 236
specific commitments, 238
trade in services, 236
transparency requirement, 237
international trading system, and, 4
NAFTA obligations re
financial services. See FINANCIAL SERVICES
government procurement. See also GOVERNMENT PROCUREMENT
exception, 228
licensing/certification requirements, 228
citizenship/residency requirements, 228
generally, 228
most-favoured-nation principle, 227
professional services, 227

non-conforming measures.
See RESERVATIONS
non-discrimination
local presence, 228
MFN treatment, 227
national treatment, 227
quantitative restrictions, 228
reservations re. See RESERVATIONS
scope and coverage
application to provinces and states, 227
denial of benefits, 227
cross-border provision of, 226
services covered, 226
subsidies, exception for, 228
telecommunications. See TELECOMMUNICATIONS

STANDARDS. See TECHNICAL STANDARDS

STATE ENTERPRISES.
See MONOPOLIES AND STATE ENTERPRISES

SUBSIDIES
export subsidies
agricultural goods, and,
See AGRICULTURAL GOODS, Agriculture Agreement.
See also AGRICULTURAL GOODS, CCFTA provisions; AGRICULTURAL GOODS, NAFTA provisions
GATT 1994, prohibition of, 149
GATS, provisions respecting, 238
Subsidies Agreement
actionable and non-actionable subsidies, 151
countervailing duties, and.
See ANTIDUMPING AND COUNTERVAILING DUTIES
prohibited subsidies, 150
specific subsidy, 150
subsidy defined, 150

TARIFFS. See also DUTIES
ad valorem, 76
bound tariffs under GATT 1994, 83
customs laws, Canadian
Customs Act, 79
Customs Tariff, 78
elimination of
CCFTA, 86

Index   333

CIFTA, 86
generally, 13
NAFTA, 85
rules of origin, link to in free trade
    areas, 30, 85, 126
policy instrument, as, 8, 75
reduction of
    generally, 13
    resulting from Uruguay Round, 84
tariff classification
    Harmonized System
        generally, 76
        tariff classification, use in, 77
tariff rate quotas
    agricultural goods and tariffication.
        See AGRICULTURAL GOODS
    generally, 76
    textile and apparel goods and tariff
        preference levels. See TEXTILE
        AND APPAREL GOODS
tariff treatment, Canadian customs laws
    Australia, goods of, 81
    British Preferential Tariff, 81
    Chile Tariff, 82
    General Preferential Tariff, 80
    Israel Tariff, 82
    Least Developed Developing Country
        Tariff, 80
    MFN Tariff, 80
    NAFTA Tariffs
        Mexico Tariff, 82
        Mexico–United States Tariff, 82
        United States tariff, 82
    New Zealand, goods of, 81
transparency of, 76
valuation
    ad valorem tariffs, and, 87
    Valuation Agreement
        other methods of calculating
            customs value, 88
        summarized, 25, 76
        transaction value as customs value, 87

TAXATION MEASURES
generally, 273
CCFTA, exceptions for, 274
CIFTA, exceptions for, 274
NAFTA, exceptions for, 274

TECHNICAL STANDARDS
common themes, 174
sanitary and phytosanitary measures
    CCFTA, 171
    CIFTA, 171

definition, 172
NAFTA, provisions of
    based largely on draft SPS
        Agreement, 35
    exceptions, 184
    level of protection, 179
    no obstacles to trade, 181
    non-discrimination, 180
    procedural fairness, conformity
        assessment, 182
    provincial and state laws,
        application to, 176
    right to adopt, 177
    risk assessment, 178
    transparency, 183
    use of international standards, 178
SPS Agreement, provisions of
    exceptions, 184
    level of protection, 178
    no obstacles to trade, 181
    non-discrimination, 180
    procedural fairness, conformity
        assessment, 182
    provincial and state laws,
        application to, 176
    right to adopt, 177
    risk assessment, 178
    summarized, 25
    transparency, 183
    use of international standards, 178
technical barriers to trade
    CCFTA, 171
    CIFTA, 171
    definitions
        conformity assessment procedure,
            174
        standard, 174
        standards-related measure, 173
        technical regulation, 174
    NAFTA, provisions of
        based largely on draft TBT
            Agreement, 35
        exceptions, 184
        level of protection, 179
        no obstacles to trade, 181
        non-discrimination, 180
        procedural fairness, conformity
            assessment, 182
        provincial and state laws,
            application to, 176
        right to adopt, 177
        risk assessment, 178
        transparency, 183
        use of international standards, 178

TBT Agreement, provisions of
   exceptions, 184
   level of protection, 178
   no obstacles to trade, 181
   non-discrimination, 180
   procedural fairness, conformity
      assessment, 182
   provincial and state laws,
      application to, 176
   right to adopt, 177
   risk assessment, 178
   summarized, 25
   transparency, 183
   use of international standards, 178

TELECOMMUNICATIONS
basic services described, 242
CCFTA provisions re
   access to basic services, 242
   non-discrimination requirements,
      NAFTA and CCFTA, 242
   reservations, 242
enhanced or value-added services
   described, 242
GATS provisions re
   agreement improving market access,
      243
   Annex on, 243
NAFTA provisions re
   access to basic services, 242
   non-discrimination requirements,
      NAFTA and CCFTA, 242
   reservations, 242

TEMPORARY ADMISSION
business persons. *See* TEMPORARY
   ENTRY
goods
   temporary admission of. *See* DUTIES
   re-entered after repair or alteration.
      See DUTIES

TEMPORARY ENTRY
ancillary to services and investment
   provisions, 5, 252
CCFTA provisions re
   business person defined, 253
   temporary entry to business persons,
      253
GATS Annex on Movement of Natural
   Persons Providing Services, 252
generally, 252
NAFTA provisions re
   business person defined, 253

dispute resolution, limitation. *See*
   DISPUTE RESOLUTION,
   NAFTA procedures
temporary entry to business persons,
   253

TEXTILE AND APPAREL GOODS
bilateral actions, NAFTA and CCFTA
   absence of procedural standards, 169
   quantitative restrictions, 169
   tariff actions, 168
country of origin of
   NAFTA preferential tariff purposes, 144
   substituted U.S. rules, 143
duty relief, Canada
   textile duty remission programs, 97
   Textile Reference Guidelines, 98
import-export restrictions
   bilateral restraint agreements, 115
   Import Control List, 121
   Long Term Arrangement, 115
   managed trade, as example of, 11
   Multifibre Arrangement, 115
   NAFTA provisions, 117
   Short Term Arrangement, 115
tariff preference levels
   CCFTA provisions, 119
   defined, 117
   NAFTA provisions, 117
Textile Agreement
   integration into GATT, 116
   no new restrictions, 116
   summarized, 24
   transitional safeguard rules, 117
Textile Monitoring Body, 116, 278

TRADE IN GOODS
agricultural goods. *See* AGRICULTURAL
   GOODS
alcoholic beverages. *See* ALCOHOLIC
   BEVERAGES
antidumping and countervailing duties.
   See ANTIDUMPING AND
   COUNTERVAILING DUTIES
automotive goods. *See* AUTOMOTIVE
   GOODS
customs procedures. *See* CUSTOMS
   PROCEDURES
emergency action. *See* SAFEGUARDS
energy goods. *See* ENERGY GOODS
export taxes, prohibition of
   CCFTA, 104
   CIFTA, 104
   NAFTA, 104

Index 335

general exceptions
  CCFTA
    incorporation of Article XX of
      GATT 1994, 73
    modifications of Articles XX(b)
      and XX(g), 74
  CIFTA
    incorporation of Article XX of
      GATT 1994, 73
    modifications of Articles XX(b)
      and XX(g), 74
  GATT 1994
    Article XX
      interpretation, 66
      scope of, 73
      text of, 66
  NAFTA
    incorporation of Article XX of
      GATT 1994, 73
    modifications of Articles XX(b)
      and XX(g), 74
  use of, 74
government procurement
  exception for in Article III:8 of GATT
    1994, 60
  of goods. *See* GOVERNMENT
    PROCUREMENT
import and export restrictions
  Canadian law on
    export controls
      general, 120
      softwood lumber, 120
    import controls
      Import Control List, 121
      other, 123
      prohibited goods, 122
  CCFTA provisions
    exceptions, 103
    export restrictions, disciplines
      GATT 1994 exceptions, linkage
        to, 104
      normal channels of supply
        pricing, 106
      proportionality, 104
    goods from non-Parties, 103
    incorporation of Article XI of
      GATT 1994, 102
    incorporation into under CCFTA,
      CIFTA, and NAFTA, 102
    minimum import and export
      prices, 102
  CIFTA provisions
    exceptions, 103
    goods from non-Parties, 103

  incorporation of Article XI of
    GATT 1994, 102
  incorporation into under CCFTA,
    CIFTA, and NAFTA, 102
  minimum import and export
    prices, 102
  GATT 1994 provisions
    Article XI, general prohibition and
      exceptions, 101
  NAFTA provisions
    exceptions, 103
    export restrictions, disciplines
      GATT 1994 exceptions, linkage
        to, 104
      normal channels of supply
        pricing, 106
      proportionality, 104
    goods from non-NAFTA countries,
      102
    incorporation of Article XI
    incorporation into under CCFTA,
      CIFTA and NAFTA, 102
    minimum import and export
      prices, 102
most-favoured-nation principle
  GATT 1994
    advantage, broad definition of, 53
    Article I, 52
  sectoral arrangements and, 53
  significance for government policy, 53
national treatment
  CCFTA
    incorporation of Article III of
      GATT 1994, 62
    requirement for provinces, 62
  CIFTA
    incorporation of Article III of
      GATT 1994, 62
    requirement for provinces, 62
  GATT 1994
    Article III, generally, 54
    Article III:1 (No Protection to
      Domestic Production), 55
    Article III:2 (Internal Taxes and
      Charges), 55
    Article III:4 (No Less Favourable
      Treatment), 59
    Article III:8 (Exceptions), 60
    directly competitive or
      substitutable products, 57
    like products, 55
  NAFTA
    incorporation of Article III of
      GATT 1994, 61

requirement for provinces and
    states, 61
significance for government policy, 63
rules of origin. *See* RULES OF ORIGIN
technical standards. *See* TECHNICAL
    STANDARDS
tariffs. *See* TARIFFS. *See also* DUTY
textile and apparel goods. *See* TEXTILE
    AND APPAREL GOODS

TRADEMARKS. *See* INTELLECTUAL
    PROPERTY, NAFTA provisions

TRANSPORTATION
reservations re. *See* RESERVATIONS

URUGUAY ROUND. *See* GATT
    NEGOTIATING ROUNDS

WORLD TRADE ORGANIZATION. *See*
    INSTITUTIONAL STRUCTURES

WTO AGREEMENT
accession, 280
amendments, 279
Annex 1A, Multilateral Agreements on
    Trade in Goods
  General Agreement on Tariffs and
      Trade. *See* GATT 1994
  Agreement on Agriculture. *See*
      AGRICULTURAL GOODS,
      Agriculture Agreement
  Agreement on the Application of
      Sanitary and Phytosanitary
      Measures. *See* TECHNICAL
      STANDARDS, SPS Agreement
  Agreement on Textiles and Clothing.
      See TEXTILE AND APPAREL
      GOODS, Textile Agreement
  Agreement on Technical Barriers to
      Trade. *See* TECHNICAL
      STANDARDS, TBT Agreement
  Agreement on Trade-Related
      Investment Measures.
      See INVESTMENT, TRIMs
      Agreement
  Agreement on Implementation of
      Article VI of the General
      Agreement on Tariffs and Trade
      1994. *See* ANTIDUMPING
      AND COUNTERVAILING
      DUTIES, Antidumping
      Agreement
  Agreement on Implementation of
      Article VII of the General
      Agreement on Tariffs and Trade
      1994. *See* TARIFFS, Valuation
      Agreement
  Agreement on Preshipment
      Inspection, 25
  Agreement on Rules of Origin. *See*
      RULES OF ORIGIN, Rules of
      Origin Agreement
  Agreement on Import Licensing
      Procedures, 26
  Agreement on Subsidies and
      Countervailing Measures.
      See ANTIDUMPING AND
      COUNTERVAILING DUTIES,
      Subsidies Agreement; and
      under SUBSIDIES, Subsidies
      Agreement
  Agreement on Safeguards. *See*
      SAFEGUARDS, Safeguards
      Agreement
Annex 1B, General Agreement on Trade
    in Services. *See* GATS
Annex 1C, Agreement on Trade-Related
    Aspects of Intellectual Property
    Rights. *See* INTELLECTUAL
    PROPERTY, TRIPS Agreement
Annex 2, Understanding on Rules and
    Procedures Governing the
    Settlement of Disputes.
    See DISPUTE RESOLUTION,
    Dispute Settlement Understanding
Annex 3, Trade Policy Review
    Mechanism, 27
Annex 4, Plurilateral Agreements
  Agreement on Government
      Procurement.
      See GOVERNMENT
      PROCUREMENT, Government
      Procurement Agreement
dispute resolution under. *See* DISPUTE
    RESOLUTION
Multilateral Trade Agreements
  bind all members, 22
Plurilateral Trade Agreements
  bind only members that accept them,
      22
structure, 278
umbrella agreement, as, 21

ABOUT THE AUTHOR

Jon R. Johnson is a partner in the international law firm Goodman, Phillips & Vineberg and a member of the Bar of the Province of Ontario. He holds an LL.M. in Business Law from Osgoode Hall Law School. Mr. Johnson served as a legal adviser in Canada's Trade Negotiation Office for the *Canada–U.S. Free Trade Agreement* and also advised Canada's Office of Trilateral Trade Negotiations on the negotiation of the *North American Free Trade Agreement*. He is the author of numerous publications including *The North American Free Trade Agreement: A Comprehensive Guide* (1994).